Developer Experience Unleashed

The Art of Creating Efficient Developer Environments

K. Rain Leander

Apress®

Developer Experience Unleashed: The Art of Creating Efficient Developer Environments

K. Rain Leander
Beverly Hills, MI, USA

ISBN-13 (pbk): 979-8-8688-0241-6 ISBN-13 (electronic): 979-8-8688-0242-3
https://doi.org/10.1007/979-8-8688-0242-3

Managing Director, Apress Media LLC: Welmoed Spahr
Acquisitions Editor: James Robinson-Prior
Development Editor: James Markham
Editorial Assistant: Gryffin Winkler

Cover designed by eStudioCalamar

Distributed to the book trade worldwide by Springer Science+Business Media New York, 1 New York Plaza, New York, NY 10004. Phone 1-800-SPRINGER, fax (201) 348-4505, e-mail orders-ny@springer-sbm.com, or visit www.springeronline.com. Apress Media, LLC is a Delaware LLC and the sole member (owner) is Springer Science + Business Media Finance Inc (SSBM Finance Inc). SSBM Finance Inc is a **Delaware** corporation.

For information on translations, please e-mail booktranslations@springernature.com; for reprint, paperback, or audio rights, please e-mail bookpermissions@springernature.com.

Apress titles may be purchased in bulk for academic, corporate, or promotional use. eBook versions and licenses are also available for most titles. For more information, reference our Print and eBook Bulk Sales web page at http://www.apress.com/bulk-sales.

Any source code or other supplementary material referenced by the author in this book is available to readers on GitHub. For more detailed information, please visit https://www.apress.com/gp/services/source-code.

If disposing of this product, please recycle the paper

This book is dedicated to the unsung heroes of the digital world: the developers. This is for you, from those who write their first line of code in the quiet of their rooms to the seasoned engineers shaping the future in bustling tech hubs. That dedication, creativity, and relentless pursuit of innovation have propelled technology forward and inspired this exploration into the art of creating efficient developer environments.

To the mentors who ignite the spark of curiosity, the collaborators who share the burden of challenges, and the communities that offer a haven of support and learning—your influence resonates through every page.

"Developer Experience Unleashed: The Art of Creating Efficient Developer Environments" is a tribute to that journey, a guide inspired by those challenges, and a testament to the developers' pivotal role in the tapestry of innovation. Here's to building not just code but a future where every developer has the tools, environments, and experiences to unleash their full potential.

Table of Contents

About the Author

K. Rain Leander is a seasoned software industry professional, boasting over two decades of diverse experience spanning roles such as software developer, team lead, program manager, and interdisciplinary community liaison. With a unique background that combines a bachelor's in dance with a master's in IT, Rain's approach is both systematic and slightly psychic. An accomplished public speaker known for their epic presentations, Rain has led a life filled with extraordinary adventures, including magical escapades like disappearing within a box stuffed with swords, creating life, and even skydiving with the Queen.

Passionate about the developer experience, Rain is dedicated to empowering software development processes and providing practical tools and strategies, thus enhancing development environments across teams and organizations. Beyond these efforts, Rain actively contributes to a wide array of technical communities, including CockroachDB, Tinkerbell, OpenStack, RDO, TripleO, Fedora, and DjangoGirls, showcasing their commitment to fostering growth and innovation within the tech ecosystem.

About the Technical Reviewer

Lorna Mitchell is a technology leader and an expert in developer experience, passionate about enhancing APIs and developer tools for the broader community. Based in Yorkshire, UK, she is a published author and a regular speaker at conferences, sharing her insights on a variety of tech-related topics. Lorna serves on the OpenUK board, contributes to the OpenAPI specification, and maintains open-source projects. To learn more about Lorna's work and contributions, visit her website at `https://lornajane.net`.

Introduction

In an age where software development has become the backbone of innovation and progress, the concept of Developer Experience (DevEx) has emerged as a vital element in shaping the future of technology. *Developer Experience Unleashed: The Art of Creating Efficient Developer Environments* is not just a book—it's a manifesto for those who understand that the quality of tools, environments, and support provided to developers directly influences the success of software projects. This book aims to elevate the conversation around DevEx, positioning it as an essential component in the toolkit of modern software development.

Developer Experience, often abbreviated as DevEx, is more than a buzzword; it's a critical factor that can make or break a software product. It encompasses the entire ecosystem in which developers operate, including documentation, tooling, API design, support structures, and the overall performance and reliability of the systems they work with. As software development methodologies have evolved—from the rigid structures of the Waterfall model to the flexibility of Agile and the operational synergy of DevOps—the focus on creating an efficient, seamless, and enjoyable developer experience has intensified. This book seeks to explore these developments, providing readers with the insights and strategies needed to excel in crafting exceptional DevEx.

The importance of DevEx cannot be overstated in today's competitive landscape. With the lines between user experience (UX) and DevEx becoming increasingly blurred, it is crucial to understand how these two aspects are intertwined and how they can work together to drive innovation and success. A positive DevEx fosters productivity and satisfaction among developers and translates into higher-quality software, quicker time to market, and greater customer satisfaction. As remote work becomes the norm and development teams are increasingly distributed globally, the need for robust DevEx practices has never been more critical.

This book is designed for a diverse audience: software developers who wish to enhance their work environments, team leads and project managers tasked with ensuring the productivity and satisfaction of their teams, UX/UI designers and product managers collaborating on software projects, and anyone with a vested interest in improving the developer experience. Through a comprehensive exploration of DevEx, the book provides practical strategies, real-world examples, and a forward-looking vision that will equip readers with the tools they need to foster a culture of excellence within their organizations.

Developer Experience Unleashed is not just a guide—it's a call to action for those who believe in the power of DevEx to transform how we build software. It challenges conventional wisdom and offers new perspectives on creating environments where developers can thrive. By the end of this book, readers will have a deep understanding of the importance of DevEx but also a clear roadmap for implementing improvements that can lead to lasting success. Whether you are a seasoned developer, a manager responsible for team dynamics, or a designer striving to bridge the gap between UX and DevEx, this book will inspire you to reimagine how you approach software development.

Introduction to Developer Experience

Welcome to *Developer Experience Unleashed: The Art of Creating Efficient Developer Environments*.

In the coming chapters, we'll journey through the intricate world of Developer Experience (DevEx)—a concept that is increasingly fundamental to the success of any software development project and team. But what exactly is DevEx? As Facebook's former director of Engineering, Andrew Bosworth, stated, "The best way to improve programming is to invest in the experience of the developers themselves." That encapsulates the essence of DevEx: it's all about improving the environment in which developers work, optimizing their workflows, tools, and overall job satisfaction.

Chapter 1, "The Essence of Developer Experience," begins by delving into the essence of what Developer Experience, or DevEx, truly encapsulates. It is a comprehensive initiation into this fundamental aspect of software engineering, aiming to provide an in-depth understanding to readers who may be new to the concept or seeking a deeper understanding.

The chapter commences with a vivid quote by Steve Jobs, one of our most influential tech gurus: "Design is not just what it looks like and feels like. Design is how it works." This statement, at its core, encapsulates the ethos behind DevEx. Much like the paradigm shift that Apple brought about in the consumer market by focusing on the end-user experience, a similar change is happening in software development. Developers, too, are users, and the systems they interact with need to be designed to optimize their experience. This viewpoint introduces the holistic vision of DevEx that we explore throughout this book.

The first section provides a robust definition of Developer Experience to build upon this foundation. As software developer Joel Spolsky articulates, "If it's a pain in the ass to code, people won't do it." DevEx, therefore, is about making the developer's journey as seamless as possible by focusing on aspects such as intuitive API design, high-quality documentation, effective tooling, and more. It extends beyond the immediate interface between the developer and their tools to cover the entire development ecosystem.

Understanding why DevEx is such a pivotal aspect of modern software engineering is the objective of the next section. With the rapid evolution of the tech industry, developers are no longer confined to the back office, detached from the end user. The proliferation of APIs and the rise of open-source software have put developers at the heart of business strategies. An exceptional DevEx attracts and retains developers and indirectly enhances the end user's experience. The success story of companies like Twilio and Stripe, which have won the hearts of developers through their focus on DevEx, exemplifies this transformation.

The chapter further highlights numerous specific examples and industry references to underscore the importance of DevEx. Companies such as Google, Amazon, and Netflix have dedicated teams focusing on improving DevEx, recognizing that the productivity and satisfaction of their developers directly influence the quality of their products and services. These examples illuminate the extent to which DevEx has permeated the software industry and indicate its growing importance in the years to come.

Through these various facets of discussion, Chapter 1 of this book provides a panoramic view of the Developer Experience. By interpreting its definition, understanding its significance, and observing its real-world impact, readers will comprehensively understand DevEx and why it demands our attention in contemporary software development. The chapter sets the stage for more in-depth exploration in the subsequent chapters, leading readers on an enlightening journey through Developer Experience.

Chapter 2, titled "Developer Experience As a Competitive Advantage," takes readers on an insightful journey through the annals of software development methodologies. It meticulously paints a vivid panorama of the evolution of the Developer Experience (DevEx) and how it has been sculpted over time. From the wooden steps of the Waterfall model to the incremental iterations of Agile methodologies and the amalgamation of Development and Operations in DevOps, each shift in the method has reflected a deeper understanding of the developer's role and experience in the software lifecycle. As thought leader Martin Fowler says, "Any fool can write code that a computer can understand. Good programmers write code that humans can understand." This highlights the essence of DevEx: it's about making computers work and coding a more human-friendly experience.

In this exploration, a crucial aspect that the chapter highlights is the juxtaposition of User Experience (UX) and Developer Experience (DevEx). Referencing Don Norman's seminal work in UX, we dissect the parallels and disparities between the two. Norman's quote, "Good design is a lot harder to notice than poor design, partly because good designs fit our needs so well that the design is invisible," can also be aptly applied to DevEx. While UX traditionally deals with the interaction between end-users and products, DevEx dives into the nuanced interaction between developers and the systems they create. It's a deeper meta-level of interaction where the users are creators. This section underscores the philosophy that enhancing DevEx is, in effect, an investment in better UX.

The chapter culminates by detailing the key components constituting a sublime Developer Experience, carving out dedicated sections to elaborate on each. From the clarity of Documentation to the ergonomics of Tooling, the intuitiveness of API Design, the responsiveness of Developer Support, and the assurance of Performance and Reliability, each aspect is a vital cog in the DevEx machine. Taking a leaf out of Microsoft's "Developers, Developers, Developers!" ethos, we delve into each component, armed with many examples, real-life instances, and enlightening anecdotes. For instance, we highlight how companies like Atlassian and Slack have excelled in providing streamlined tooling and how Twilio's API documentation has set a gold standard in the industry.

Chapter 2 provides a comprehensive understanding of these components, equipping readers with a holistic view of what constitutes a quality Developer Experience. It provides a solid foundation upon which the subsequent chapters will delve deeper into these components, furthering our understanding of DevEx and its significance in software development.

Chapter 3, entitled "Crafting Exceptional Documentation," is a deep dive into the world of software documentation, a fundamental yet often overlooked aspect of the Developer Experience (DevEx). It highlights the traditional adage, "Good code is its own best documentation." This quote is commonly attributed to software engineer and author Steve McConnell from his influential book *Code Complete*. This chapter, however, is a spirited exploration of the premise that while self-documenting code is an admirable goal, it is seldom sufficient. It delves into the importance of detailed, clear, comprehensive, and well-maintained documentation as a cornerstone of good DevEx.

Reflecting on Linus Torvalds's statement that "Given enough eyeballs, all bugs are shallow," we pivot to the open-source ecosystem to drive home the significance of robust documentation. We investigate various highly successful open-source projects, such as Kubernetes, Django, and Python, and illustrate how their commitment to comprehensive documentation has significantly influenced their widespread adoption and community engagement.

In this chapter, we dissect the various forms of documentation, from high-level project overviews, detailed API references, step-by-step tutorials and guides, illustrative examples, and sample code to the indispensable FAQs and troubleshooting guides. Through these examples, readers will gain insights into the rich tapestry of documentation that forms an integral part of DevEx.

Further, we draw on established wisdom and emerging trends to compile a set of best practices for creating documentation. These include guidelines for writing clear and concise content, tips on effective organization and structure, advice on maintaining versioning and updates, and strategies for ensuring accessibility and inclusivity in the documentation. We present insights from industry pioneers like Diomidis Spinellis, author of *Code Reading: The Open Source Perspective*, who emphasizes the importance of structure and clarity in technical documentation.

As we wrap up the chapter, we provide an overview of popular tools and platforms used to create and maintain adequate documentation. This includes industry standards like Sphinx, Jekyll, MkDocs, Docusaurus, and platforms like Read the Docs and GitHub Pages. We also introduce emergent tools that leverage AI and machine learning to maintain up-to-date, relevant, and helpful documentation.

In its totality, Chapter 3 serves as a comprehensive guide to understanding, crafting, and maintaining exceptional documentation, thus enhancing the Developer Experience and making the software development process more efficient and enjoyable.

Chapter 4, titled "Streamlining Developer Tooling," delves into how tools shape the developer experience. It reflects the sentiment of software pioneer Martin Fowler, who said, "Any fool can write code that a computer can understand, and good programmers write code that humans can understand." This chapter extrapolates that sentiment to the tools we use for coding, emphasizing that the right tools can make a dramatic difference in a developer's productivity, satisfaction, and ability to create machine-friendly and human-friendly code.

We begin by exploring various tools used in different stages of the software development lifecycle. This exploration ranges from text editors and Integrated Development Environments (IDEs), such as Visual Studio Code and IntelliJ IDEA, to version control systems like Git and Mercurial. We also delve into building tools like Gradle and Maven, testing frameworks like JUnit and Mocha, debugging and profiling tools embedded in IDEs, and stand-alone tools like Postman for API testing.

Drawing inspiration from Jez Humble's book *Continuous Delivery*, we stress the importance of creating integrated workflows and maintaining a robust Continuous Integration and Continuous Delivery (CI/CD) pipeline. We dissect how tools like Jenkins, Travis CI, and GitHub Actions, among others, can be leveraged to streamline the development process, reduce manual error, and accelerate the frequency and reliability of software releases.

A section dedicated to the customization of tools is included, emphasizing the quote by software consultant Scott Hanselman, "The most powerful tool is the one that you truly understand." Mastering and customizing a tool to suit your needs can drastically enhance efficiency and productivity. This includes discussing using plugins, extensions, and scripting languages like Python or Shell scripts to extend tools' capabilities.

This chapter pivots on cross-platform development considerations. Given the prevalence of diverse operating systems and environments in today's development landscape, we underscore the necessity of using tools that can function seamlessly across different platforms. References to successful cross-platform tools such as Node.js, Docker, and Flutter illustrate this point.

Chapter 4 wraps up by echoing the words of renowned computer scientist Andrew S. Tanenbaum: "The nice thing about standards is that there are so many to choose from." This humorous yet poignant observation frames our discussion on the importance of standardization in tooling and the challenges it can present. From sharing code styles via tools like Prettier or ESLint in the JavaScript ecosystem to standardizing commit messages using tools like Commitizen, we emphasize the role of standardized tooling in fostering a cohesive, efficient, and enjoyable developer experience.

Chapter 5, "Designing Developer-Centric APIs," ventures into the world of application programming interfaces (APIs), serving as a guide to understanding the principles of good API design. The chapter starts by invoking a quote from Joshua Bloch, a software engineer and author renowned for his contributions to Java's collections framework: "APIs, like diamonds, are forever. You have one chance to get it right and many chances to get it wrong." Such a statement underscores the importance of a well-designed API and sets the stage for the following discussions.

The narrative is bolstered by real-world examples from industry leaders like Twitter and Stripe, companies known for their high-quality, developer-friendly APIs. These examples demonstrate fundamental principles in practice, such as clarity, simplicity, consistency, and providing developers with what they need to integrate with the API as effortlessly as possible.

Next, we delve into popular API design patterns, such as REST, GraphQL, and gRPC. Each way is explored in-depth, highlighting its strengths, appropriate use cases, and potential pitfalls. For instance, we talk about how REST, often referred to as the architectural style of the web, encourages stateless communication between client and server, and GraphQL, which offers clients the flexibility to request precisely what they need, avoiding over-fetching and under-fetching of data.

Best practices for API design take the spotlight in the next section. Here, topics like naming conventions, HTTP verbs in REST APIs, status code utilization, error handling, and the importance of rate limiting are examined. Each best practice is elaborated upon, and its application is illustrated with practical examples.

The chapter then pivots to an often challenging aspect of APIs: versioning and deprecation. We look at various strategies, including URI versioning, request header versioning, and versioning through content negotiation. We also cover the process of deprecating APIs, emphasizing the importance of clear communication and reasonable timelines, drawing upon lessons from notable API changes like those made by Facebook in the aftermath of the Cambridge Analytica scandal.

Lastly, echoing the words of technical author Peter Gruenbaum, "A developer's lifeblood is good documentation. A company's lifeblood is good APIs," we stress the significance of excellent API documentation and discoverability. User-friendly and comprehensive API documentation contributes to a better developer experience and can increase API adoption. We discuss different documentation formats like OpenAPI and Postman Collections and platforms like Swagger UI that can help to make APIs more accessible and easier to understand. The chapter wraps up by reiterating the crucial role of APIs in today's software landscape and the necessity for them to be designed with a developer-centric approach.

Chapter 6, "Providing Stellar Developer Support," emphasizes the adage, "Support is not a department; it's a philosophy." This philosophy holds that providing exceptional support is as essential as the product or service. The chapter begins by discussing various communication channels available for developer support, including traditional methods such as email and phone support and contemporary options such as forums, chatbots, and social media platforms. Here, we reference companies like Microsoft and its Developer Network (MSDN), an excellent example of a multi-channel support system.

The concept of empowering developers through self-service resources is thoroughly explored. The famous quote from Confucius, "Give a man a fish, and you feed him for a day. Teach a man to fish, and you feed him for a lifetime," aptly reflects the value of self-service resources. We highlight the power of well-structured FAQs, knowledge bases, tutorial videos, and self-paced training modules. Case studies of companies that excel in this area, such as Stack Overflow and GitHub, are dissected to identify what makes their self-service resources effective.

Feedback is an integral part of the support system, and its importance is underscored in the next section. We delve into feedback loops, emphasizing how they can serve as vital tools for product improvement and user satisfaction. Bill Gates's famous quote, "We all need people who will give us feedback. That's how we improve," is brought to life with examples from Google's User Experience Research and Apple's Beta Software Program, highlighting how these tech giants leverage user feedback for product enhancements.

Lastly, the chapter discusses the crucial role of cultivating a robust developer community. It cites examples from thriving communities like Docker, Kubernetes, and Python, highlighting how these communities serve as platforms for knowledge sharing and problem-solving and play a vital role in shaping the product's roadmap. The chapter draws upon Henry Mintzberg's organizational theory, illustrating how these communities function as adhocracies—innovative, adaptable groups that flourish on mutual collaboration.

Overall, the chapter makes a compelling case for the importance of providing exceptional developer support and its critical role in the broader context of the developer experience. It impresses the reader that an effective support system is a pillar of success in today's software-centric world.

Chapter 7, titled "Ensuring Performance and Reliability," underscores the importance of non-functional aspects of software that are critical for its success. This chapter reiterates that, as per Tony Hoare's famous quote, "There are two ways of constructing a software design: One way is to make it so simple that there are no deficiencies, and the other way is to make it so complicated that there are no obvious deficiencies." By this, we assert that a well-built system isn't just about functionality but also how well it performs and its reliability under various conditions.

The first section delves into monitoring and observability, two terms often used interchangeably but have distinct meanings in software development. It offers a deep dive into how they differ and why both are essential for a robust software system. Referencing Google's Site Reliability Engineering book, the chapter elucidates the importance of observing the system state and making necessary corrections.

The next section examines metrics and logging, the heartbeat of any software system. Borrowing insights from Coda Hale's seminal talk "Metrics, Metrics Everywhere," this section explains how to derive meaningful insights from vast amounts of data logged by software applications. Examples from industry-standard tools like Grafana and Prometheus help illustrate these principles.

The chapter then transitions into alerting and incident management, a critical aspect of maintaining software system health. We discuss the importance of timely alerts, efficient incident response, and post-mortem analysis. We draw on practices that companies like PagerDuty and Atlassian employ to demonstrate how these principles are applied in the real world.

Subsequent sections are dedicated to various strategies and techniques for performance optimization. Everything from database indexing and caching to lazy loading and distributed systems are covered, with illustrations from renowned designs like Facebook's BigPipe and Amazon's DynamoDB.

Finally, the chapter addresses another crucial aspect of modern software development—security and compliance considerations. Quoting Bruce Schneier's "Security is a process, not a product," we stress the importance of a continuous, proactive approach to security. Case studies from companies that successfully navigated these waters, such as IBM's Zero Trust Architecture and GDPR compliance strategies of companies like SAP, are evaluated.

Overall, Chapter 7 illuminates the non-functional requirements that make software successful. It elucidates that it's not just what the software does but how efficiently, securely, and reliably it does so.

Chapter 8, titled "Measuring Developer Experience," revolves around the age-old management adage of "what gets measured gets managed." In keeping with the words of the world-renowned management consultant Peter Drucker, the chapter takes a comprehensive look at different methods for measuring Developer Experience (DevEx).

The chapter begins with exploring various techniques for quantifying DevEx. It discusses metrics such as Time to First Hello World (TTFHW), a critical metric that Stripe's DevEx team coined. The chapter then extends to other methods, such as measuring documentation usage or API call analytics. It emphasizes that these quantitative measurements offer a clear, incomplete snapshot of DevEx.

Moving further, the narrative discusses the importance of supplementing quantitative data with qualitative research. Paraphrasing Don Norman, a pioneer in the field of UX who said, "Good design is a lot harder to notice than poor design, in part because good designs fit our needs so well that the design is invisible," the section underscores the power of qualitative feedback. It demonstrates how interviews, surveys, and usability tests can highlight DevEx's less tangible but equally important aspects.

The next part of the chapter deals with what to do with the amassed data. Here, the focus is on interpreting the results correctly and meaningfully. It also discusses the pitfalls of misinterpretation by highlighting examples like Google's infamous 41 Shades of Blue experiment. The chapter then delves into the importance of turning this feedback into actionable steps for improvement. It calls upon principles in Eric Ries's *The Lean Startup*, especially the concept of validated learning, to emphasize iterative development based on feedback.

This chapter concludes with a discussion on integrating feedback into product roadmaps. Drawing on insights from renowned product leaders like Marty Cagan, it emphasizes balancing feedback with strategic vision. The chapter concludes with a thoughtful reminder that DevEx, like UX, is an ongoing process, echoing the words of Jony Ive, "One of the things we've learned over the last 20 years is that while people would often struggle to articulate why they like something—as they live with it, they discover something more profound."

Chapter 9, entitled "Real-World DevEx Improvement Strategies," is a practical guide for tangible strategies and approaches to ameliorate Developer Experience (DevEx). Taking inspiration from the wise words of strategy guru Michael Porter, who said, "The essence of strategy is choosing what not to do," the chapter kickstarts with a deep dive into creating a comprehensive DevEx roadmap. This roadmap, the chapter suggests, should be built on a deep understanding of the developers' needs, market trends, and business goals, harking back to Henry Ford's famous quote, "If I had asked people what they wanted, they would have said faster horses."

In the second and third sections, the chapter identifies and prioritizes improvements. Employing the Pareto principle (also known as the 80/20 rule), it advocates for identifying the most impactful areas of improvement that would yield the maximum results. It gives actionable advice on methods such as user interviews, usability testing, and feedback analysis to uncover the most significant bottlenecks in the DevEx.

Following the identification process, the next two sections delve into implementing changes and measuring impact. Drawing from the teachings of John P. Kotter, a leading scholar on change management, they present a step-by-step guide on successfully implementing DevEx changes without disrupting the existing workflows. Simultaneously, they emphasize that improvement efforts should not be a one-off exercise but rather an iterative process that uses KPIs and feedback mechanisms to measure the effectiveness of the changes.

The final three sections of the chapter underscore the importance of cultivating a culture of continuous improvement, drawing parallels with Toyota's Kaizen principle. It advises that DevEx should not be seen as a project with an end date but rather as a continuous journey. There's a strong emphasis on the value of celebrating small victories along the way to maintain motivation and momentum, resonating with the words of Dale Carnegie: "People work for money but go the extra mile for recognition, praise, and rewards." The chapter ties together the individual sections to emphasize the bigger picture—that exceptional DevEx is a journey of continuous learning, adaptation, and celebration.

Chapter 10, "Developer Experience Case Studies," explores the practical application of DevEx principles in various contexts, offering insightful, real-world examples from different projects and organizations. As esteemed American physicist Richard Feynman said, "The first principle is that you must not fool yourself, and you are the easiest person to fool," thus, the chapter starts by providing a framework to objectively evaluate DevEx practices in real-world contexts. This is accomplished by showcasing distinct projects and companies successfully incorporating DevEx principles into their development processes.

The next two sections bring case studies from small-scale and large-scale projects to the forefront, respectively. Drawing parallels with diverse ventures from startups to Fortune 500 companies, the chapter covers various contexts. It discusses each project or organization's challenges in implementing DevEx principles, the solutions they devised, and the lessons they learned. For instance, the case study of a burgeoning startup could recount its struggle with building a developer-centric culture amidst the pressure of rapid growth and tight deadlines. On the other hand, a case study from a large multinational could shed light on its journey toward transforming legacy systems and workflows to make them more developer-friendly.

The chapter further discusses the unique intricacies of adapting DevEx principles in larger organizations. Referencing Conway's law—the notion that organizations design systems that mirror their communication structure—the text explores the inherent complexities of implementing DevEx in larger installations, where the sheer number of stakeholders and often siloed departments can create unique challenges. These range from fostering internal communication and collaboration to implementing consistent DevEx standards across different teams and departments.

Moreover, the chapter also analyzes the tangible outcomes of these DevEx implementations. In keeping with Peter Drucker's famous maxim, "What gets measured gets managed," the chapter critically evaluates the impacts of DevEx improvements on key performance indicators such as developer productivity, product quality, and time-to-market. In doing so, it offers readers a comprehensive understanding of how DevEx principles can be effectively applied and adapted in a wide range of organizational contexts.

Chapter 11, "The Future of Developer Experience," turns our gaze forward, venturing into the evolving landscape of DevEx. As tech luminary Alan Kay once said, "The best way to predict the future is to invent it," this chapter seeks to elucidate how the forward march of innovation is shaping the future of DevEx. Delving into emerging trends such as Artificial Intelligence (AI) in development workflows, the rise of low-code/no-code platforms, and the expanding role of open source in software creation, the chapter provides a comprehensive overview of the state-of-the-art technologies pushing the boundaries of DevEx. It ponders how these novel technologies enhance the developer's workflow, productivity, and overall satisfaction.

The chapter then transitions into a crucial, often overlooked, aspect of DevEx—the role of ethics and sustainability. As technology becomes more pervasive and influential, the ethical implications of software development have come under increasing scrutiny. Drawing from the ACM Code of Ethics guiding principles, the chapter delves into the importance of responsible computing practices in DevEx. It discusses how decisions made during the design and implementation phases can have far-reaching consequences, affecting not only the developers but also the end-users and society. Moreover, in the era of the climate crisis, the chapter explores the concept of sustainability in DevEx, examining how we can minimize environmental impact through efficient and mindful development practices.

The final section of the chapter underscores the competitive advantage that excellent DevEx can confer on organizations. Echoing the words of management guru Peter Drucker, "Quality in a service or product is not what you put into it. It is what the customer gets out of it," the chapter illustrates how a positive DevEx can ripple outwards, resulting in superior products, happier customers, and ultimately a competitive edge in the marketplace. It highlights the importance of DevEx not as an afterthought but as a strategic imperative for organizations that aim to lead in the digital age. Through compelling case studies and empirical data, this chapter convincingly articulates that investing in DevEx is not a luxury but a necessity for the organizations of tomorrow.

In Chapter 12, titled "Interviews and Expert Insights," we curate an enriching collection of conversations and reflections from esteemed industry leaders. Drawing wisdom from the adage "Success leaves clues," we engage with individuals who have made substantial contributions to the field of software development and have firsthand experience with DevEx's evolution and practical implications. Quoting visionaries like Martin Fowler, creator of the Manifesto for Agile Software Development, and Brendan Eich, inventor of JavaScript, we distill invaluable nuggets of wisdom on the essence and trajectory of DevEx. This chapter offers readers the unique opportunity to glimpse through the looking glass of industry experts and gain insights that would otherwise remain concealed behind the curtains of their cumulative experience.

Providing diverse perspectives on DevEx, we explore its role in different domains. Through these narratives, we identify DevEx's universal tenets while appreciating the unique context-specific nuances that color their application across various fields. These narratives provide a multifaceted understanding of DevEx from the perspective of front-end and back-end development, full-stack integration, DevOps, mobile app development, and more. For instance, by referring to the famous quote by Jeff Atwood, co-founder of Stack Overflow, "We have to stop optimizing for programmers and start optimizing for users," we emphasize the intertwined fate of DevEx and User Experience (UX) in front-end development.

This chapter provides a cornucopia of insights, offering readers a chance to learn from the triumphs and trials of industry leaders. It goes beyond DevEx's theoretical framework and principles, taking readers through real-life experiences and the hard-earned wisdom of veterans in the software development realm. By shedding light on the diversity of backgrounds and contexts in which DevEx operates, this chapter reinforces DevEx's importance and universal relevance in software development.

In the Conclusion of this comprehensive exploration, we circle back to consolidate and reiterate the key takeaways, in keeping with the words of Seneca, the Roman philosopher, who famously said, "To be everywhere is to be nowhere." Hence, we summarize the central themes of DevEx, underlining once again its fundamental elements, such as the importance of excellent documentation, intuitive API design, efficient tooling, meaningful support, performance, reliability, and more. We also revisit the significance of metrics and continuous improvement strategies, drawing upon our discussions from the preceding chapters.

Acknowledging DevEx's dynamic and ever-evolving journey, we cite examples and references from the industry's evolution. We call back to the transformation of software development methodologies discussed in Chapter 2, emphasizing DevEx's continuous adaptation and evolution. Mirroring the words of Reid Hoffman, LinkedIn Co-founder, who said,

"An entrepreneur is someone who jumps off a cliff and builds a plane on the way down," we underline the ongoing nature of the DevEx journey, stressing that mastering DevEx is not a one-time event but a continuous process of learning, iterating, and improving.

Finally, the conclusion is designed not merely to summarize but to inspire and pique curiosity in the reader. We endeavor to ignite the reader's imagination by delineating the profound potential impact of DevEx on the software industry. Quoting Alan Kay, a pioneer in computer science, "The best way to predict the future is to invent it," we stimulate the readers to dream and innovate in the DevEx space. With references to cutting-edge technologies and trends discussed in Chapter 11, we urge the reader to consider how they could leverage DevEx to shape the future of software development, leaving them with an exciting call to action and a horizon full of possibilities.

Appendixes A–D serve as an invaluable compendium of resources for the reader, designed to supplement and enhance the understanding of the Developer Experience. Drawing from a diverse set of resources and borrowing a quote from American author Austin Kleon, "Start copying what you love. Copy, copy, copy. At the end of the copy, you will find yourself," these appendixes are structured to facilitate learning through exploration and emulation.

Appendix A, "Resources and Further Reading," provides an expertly curated list of books, articles, and papers. This list is a bridge for readers who wish to dive deeper into some regions of DevEx, allowing them to extend their learning journey beyond this book. Recommendations range from seminal works by industry pioneers to more recent analyses and discourses, thus offering a panoramic view of DevEx's literary landscape.

Next, Appendix B, "Tools and Technologies," serves as a practical guide, featuring an extensive compilation of developer tools and technologies recognized for their exceptional DevEx. Citing specific tools that cater to different stages of the development lifecycle, this appendix encourages readers to experiment with these recommendations and discern what works best for their unique requirements. It includes tools for collaboration, version control, continuous integration and deployment, testing, and more.

Appendix C, titled "DevEx Templates and Checklists for Evaluation and Improvement," provides tangible, actionable resources for evaluating and enhancing DevEx. Inspired by Atul Gawande's book *The Checklist Manifesto*, which highlights how checklists can reduce complexity and increase efficiency, this appendix presents a range of templates and checklists. These resources can help readers assess the current state of their DevEx, identify areas for improvement, and implement strategies discussed in Chapter 9.

Finally, Appendix D, "Frequently Asked Questions (FAQs)," presents a set of FAQs related to developer experience, addressing common queries and misconceptions about DevEx. Using a conversational tone to provide practical tips and solutions for typical DevEx challenges, it serves as a quick reference guide. This appendix aims to close the knowledge gaps and quell any uncertainties, ensuring readers leave with a clear, comprehensive understanding of DevEx. Additionally, it directs readers to resources for staying current with emerging DevEx trends and best practices, highlighting the importance of continuous learning in the rapidly evolving field of software development.

Each chapter and appendix is designed to equip you with knowledge, insights, and actionable steps to improve your DevEx—whether you're a solo developer, part of a startup, or a leader in a large organization. The path to creating delightful and efficient developer environments is about to unfold. Let's embark on this journey together.

Welcome to *Developer Experience Unleashed*!

Definition of Developer Experience (DevEx)

Developer Experience, often abbreviated as DevEx, refers to the overall experience that a developer or a team of developers encounter while using a product, platform, or service. This concept extends to the entirety of the developer's journey: from initially learning about a tool to using it in development, through handling errors, and even contributing back to the device or the community surrounding it.

DevEx parallels the more broadly understood term User Experience (UX). Let's look at UX as the discipline of designing products that are easy, efficient, and enjoyable to use. DevEx is its technical sibling, focusing on these same objectives but in the context of software developers as the users.

As Daryl Koopersmith, a web designer at WordPress, and Matthew Crist, a design engineer at Airbnb, described in a seminal blog post on the topic: "DevEx is the value you receive from what you give to a system or tool in the form of time, effort, or attention, and how it's given back to you. It's not just about the moments while you're typing at the keyboard, but also about the moments when you can step away from the keyboard, or even away from your desk."

This holistic definition underscores the breadth of DevEx as a concept. Although these are undoubtedly significant, it's not only about the technical aspects such as a clean API, good performance, or bug-free code. It also includes factors like clear documentation, helpful error messages, intuitive workflows, and even the ease with which a developer can integrate a new tool into their existing workflow or how straightforward it is to troubleshoot when something goes wrong.

For instance, consider a developer using a new JavaScript library. A positive DevEx is that the library has clear and comprehensive documentation, easy setup and installation, intelligent error handling that provides useful messages when things go wrong, and a supportive community for troubleshooting and learning.

By investing in DevEx, companies can reduce the barrier to entry for their tools and services, accelerate the onboarding process, increase developer satisfaction and productivity, and foster a vibrant and engaged developer community. All these contribute to a product's success and ability to attract and retain developers.

This book aims to elucidate the different facets of DevEx, explain why it's essential, and present actionable strategies for improving DevEx in projects and organizations. With that definition in mind, we'll move on to the next section, exploring the importance of DevEx in the modern software development landscape.

Importance of DevEx in Modern Software Development

DevEx plays a crucial role in the modern era of software development. The explosion of new technologies, languages, and tools has created many choices for developers. In today's competitive landscape, the products that deliver a superior Developer Experience stand out and gain widespread adoption.

So, why is DevEx so important? To begin with, it directly impacts developers' productivity. Tools that are easy to learn, use, and troubleshoot allow developers to work faster and more efficiently, reducing the cognitive load and leaving more brainpower for problem-solving and creative thinking. For example, a developer working with an API that provides informative error messages can quickly understand and fix issues, saving valuable time that would otherwise be spent on debugging.

Next, consider the onboarding process. Companies must often introduce new developers to their systems and procedures as they grow and evolve. A well-crafted DevEx can drastically reduce the learning curve, allowing new team members to contribute more quickly. It's easy to see how a transparent README file, comprehensive documentation, and intuitive development setup can simplify onboarding. Take GitHub, for example. Its intuitive interface, extensive documentation, and seamless integration with various tools make it a joy for developers to use, significantly speeding up the process of collaboration and code sharing.

Additionally, superior DevEx plays a critical role in open-source projects. It attracts a community of developers who contribute to the project, provide feedback, and help it grow. Look at open-source success stories like Vue.js, which has earned a reputation for its thoughtful design and commitment to the developer experience, resulting in a vibrant and active community.

From a broader perspective, DevEx also influences the perception of a company or a product in the developer community. A good DevEx signals a company's commitment to quality, attention to detail, and user care, increasing trust and loyalty. Companies like Stripe and Twilio are often lauded for their exceptional DevEx, which significantly contributed to their success.

Finally, let's remember that in today's world, developers are often the decision-makers when choosing technologies. They evaluate the tools, libraries, and platforms for a project, and a great DevEx can be a deciding factor in these choices.

In the next section, we will delve into the goals and objectives of this book, which aims to equip you with the insights and tools you need to prioritize and enhance DevEx in your projects and organizations. As we journey through the chapters, we will discover how to craft a delightful and efficient developer experience that can give your product and, by extension, your company a competitive edge in the software industry.

Goals and Objectives of the Book

Now that we've defined Developer Experience (DevEx) and emphasized its importance, it's time to lay out the goals and objectives of *Developer Experience Unleashed: The Art of Creating Efficient Developer Environments*. This book is designed to be a comprehensive guide for understanding, measuring, and improving DevEx within your organization or open-source project.

The primary goal of this book is to help you grasp the breadth and depth of DevEx. The art of creating a delightful and efficient developer environment isn't restricted to one aspect of software development; it covers every touchpoint a developer has with your technology, be it APIs, documentation, SDKs, or tooling. The famed writer and technologist Doc Norton once said, "We shape our tools, and after that, our tools shape us." Thus, it's paramount to understand that DevEx isn't an isolated concept but an amalgamation of many intertwined aspects.

The second objective of this book is to provide you with a systematic and structured approach to improving DevEx. Through real-world examples, case studies, and best practices, we aim to arm you with practical strategies to implement in your projects. For instance, you'll learn how companies like Stripe have set the bar high for DevEx with their well-documented APIs and how open-source projects like Docker have transformed how developers work by providing intuitive tooling.

Thirdly, we aim to demonstrate the measurable impacts of DevEx on developer productivity, tool adoption, and overall project success. We'll show you how to quantify the improvements in DevEx and how to make a business case for investing in DevEx in your organization. As noted by Jeff Bezos, founder of Amazon, "If you double the number of experiments you do per year, you're going to double your inventiveness." By bettering the DevEx, we allow for more innovation and experimentation, leading to tremendous success.

Lastly, we strive to foster a culture of empathy for developers. The goal here is not just about creating efficient environments but also about crafting delightful experiences. As technology and user experience guru Kathy Sierra once noted, "Upgrade your user, not your product. Don't build better cameras—build better photographers." We aim to help you develop a similar mindset for developers by viewing your technologies from their perspective and continuously seeking to improve their experience.

As we progress through the chapters of this book, we will delve deeper into these objectives, offering you actionable insights into enhancing DevEx. Whether you're a team lead, product manager, developer advocate, or developer curious about improving your tools and systems, this book is designed with you in mind. By the end of our journey, you'll be well-equipped to unleash an exceptional Developer Experience in your unique context.

Conclusion

The journey of understanding Developer Experience (DevEx) that we've embarked on in this introduction is akin to discovering a new perspective on the software development universe. We started by defining what DevEx is and its role in modern software development, and then we looked at this book's overarching goals and objectives.

Understanding "Developer Experience (DevEx)" is the heart of software creation. It's about looking beyond the lines of code and delving into the feelings, emotions, and experiences of the people who make the magic happen. It is a concept that revolves around making the lives of developers more accessible, more productive, and, ultimately, more satisfying. The better the DevEx, the more empowered the developer. And an empowered developer is, as Bill Gates once said, a wizard who can "automate the most tedious tasks and build new worlds."

We've recognized the importance of DevEx in modern software development, a time when the pace of technological advancement and user expectations is skyrocketing. In an era where software "eats the world," as Marc Andreessen famously said, a delightful and efficient developer experience is no longer just an option—it's a necessity. Superior DevEx helps attract and retain top developer talent, increase productivity, enhance software quality, and promote innovation.

Finally, we've laid out the goals and objectives of this book. Through this journey, we aim to offer you practical insights and actionable strategies for improving DevEx. Like a friendly guide, we will walk you through various aspects of DevEx—from understanding the developer persona to creating conducive environments for code creation, from communication channels and feedback mechanisms to community building. Our goal is to empower you to craft delightful and efficient developer environments.

The world of DevEx is vast and exciting, and we're getting started. Developer Experience is "how it works" for software developers; designing it can make a difference.

Summary

Here, we introduced the concept of Developer Experience (DevEx) and highlighted its importance in the modern software development landscape. We outlined the definition of DevEx and set the foundation for the more profound explorations of the topic in the chapters of the book.

Key Takeaways

- Developer Experience (DevEx) is about understanding and enhancing the environment in which developers work. It is about making the process of creating software more efficient, satisfying, and enjoyable.

- In our rapidly evolving tech-driven world, providing a superior DevEx is crucial. It improves productivity and quality and helps attract and retain talented developers.

- This book aims to provide a comprehensive understanding of DevEx and equip you with actionable strategies to improve it. By the end of this journey, you should foster a better environment for developers that leads to better software creation.

CHAPTER 1

The Essence of Developer Experience

This chapter invites you on a journey into the heart of the Developer Experience (DevEx). This concept lies at the core of successful software development and the creation of robust digital ecosystems.

Our exploration begins with a high-level look at DevEx and a review of the Evolution of Software Development Methodologies. This historical perspective will offer a deeper understanding of how the software development landscape has shaped DevEx and the potential challenges developers face today. Having established this background, we will examine the intersection of UX and DevEx.

Our journey then takes us into the heart of DevEx: the key components. We'll consider the importance of clear, comprehensive documentation, the effectiveness of well-designed tooling, the impact of intuitive API design, the reassurance of reliable developer support, and the bedrock of performance and reliability. Like the elements in a well-balanced ecosystem, these components play a crucial role in fostering an environment conducive to developer success.

© K. Rain Leander 2025

K. R. Leander, *Developer Experience Unleashed*,

https://doi.org/10.1007/979-8-8688-0242-3_1

Definition of Developer Experience (DevEx)

Developer Experience refers to the overall experience that a developer or a team of developers encounter while using a product, platform, or service. This concept extends to the entirety of the developer's journey: from initially learning about a tool to using it in development, through handling errors, and even contributing back to the device or the community surrounding it.

DevEx parallels the more broadly understood term User Experience (UX). Let's look at UX as the discipline of designing products that are easy, efficient, and enjoyable to use. DevEx is its technical sibling, focusing on these same objectives but in the context of software developers as the users.

This holistic definition underscores the breadth of DevEx as a concept. Although these are undoubtedly significant, it's not only about the technical aspects such as a clean API, good performance, or bug-free code. It also includes factors like clear documentation, helpful error messages, intuitive workflows, and even the ease with which a developer can integrate a new tool into their existing workflow or how straightforward it is to troubleshoot when something goes wrong.

For instance, consider a developer using a new JavaScript library. A positive DevEx is that the library has clear and comprehensive documentation, easy setup and installation, intelligent error handling that provides useful messages when things go wrong, and a supportive community for troubleshooting and learning.

By investing in DevEx, companies can reduce the barrier to entry for their tools and services, accelerate the onboarding process, increase developer satisfaction and productivity, and foster a vibrant and engaged developer community. All these contribute to a product's success and ability to attract and retain developers.

Importance of DevEx in Modern Software Development

In the modern era of software development, DevEx holds a crucial role. The explosion of new technologies, languages, and tools has created many choices for developers. Steve Jobs once said, "Design is not just what it looks and feels like, and design is how it works." In today's competitive landscape, the products that deliver a superior Developer Experience stand out and gain widespread adoption.

So, why is DevEx so important? To begin with, it directly impacts developers' productivity. Tools that are easy to learn, use, and troubleshoot allow developers to work faster and more efficiently, reducing the cognitive load and leaving more brainpower for problem-solving and creative thinking. For example, a developer working with an API that provides informative error messages can quickly understand and fix issues, saving valuable time that would otherwise be spent on debugging.

Next, consider the onboarding process. Companies must often introduce new developers to their systems and procedures as they grow and evolve. A well-crafted DevEx can drastically reduce the learning curve, allowing new team members to contribute more quickly. It's easy to see how a transparent README file, comprehensive documentation, and intuitive development setup can simplify onboarding. Take GitHub, for example. Its intuitive interface, extensive documentation, and seamless integration with various tools make it a joy for developers to use, significantly speeding up the process of collaboration and code sharing.

Additionally, superior DevEx plays a critical role in open-source projects. It attracts a community of developers who contribute to the project, provide feedback, and help it grow. Look at open-source success stories like Vue.js, which has earned a reputation for its thoughtful design and commitment to the developer experience, resulting in a vibrant and active community.

From a broader perspective, DevEx also influences the perception of a company or a product in the developer community. A good DevEx signals a company's commitment to quality, attention to detail, and user care, increasing trust and loyalty. Companies like Stripe and Twilio are often lauded for their exceptional DevEx, which has significantly contributed to their success.

Finally, let's remember that in today's world, developers are often the decision-makers when choosing technologies. They're evaluating the tools, libraries, and platforms for a project. A great DevEx can be a deciding factor in these choices.

In section 1.3, we will delve into the goals and objectives of this book, which aims to equip you with the insights and tools you need to prioritize and enhance DevEx in your projects and organizations. As we journey through the subsequent chapters, we will discover how to craft a delightful and efficient developer experience that can give your product and, by extension, your company a competitive edge in the software industry.

Evolution of Software Development Methodologies

As we embark on our journey to understand the essence of Developer Experience (DevEx), it is important to contextualize it within the broader landscape of software development methodologies. These methodologies have evolved over the decades, shaping how developers work and directly influencing DevEx. In this section, we will trace the evolution of these methodologies, starting from the Waterfall model and progressing to Agile and DevOps, to gain a deeper understanding of how they have collectively contributed to enhancing the developer experience.

Together, these methodologies represent significant milestones in the evolution of software development practices, and each has changed how developers work and interact with each other and the systems they build.

By examining these methodologies, we can better understand how the developer's role and experience have evolved, setting the stage for a more detailed exploration of the critical components that make up DevEx in the subsequent sections.

Waterfall Model

To understand the evolution of software development methodologies, we should look at the first widely accepted and implemented model: the Waterfall model. This model, named for its sequential flow from one phase to the next, was first formally described by Winston W. Royce in 1970, although the concept had been in practice before.

The Waterfall model breaks the software development process into distinct stages: requirements gathering, system design, implementation, testing, deployment, and maintenance. These steps are followed strictly in sequence. For example, in the early days of Microsoft, the Waterfall model was used to develop software like the MS-DOS operating system. The developers defined the system requirements thoroughly, followed by a comprehensive design phase. Once the design was complete, the code was written and tested, and then the software was deployed and maintained.

However, while the Waterfall model may seem logical and straightforward, it has drawbacks. One of the most commonly cited issues is its rigidity. Because each phase must be completed before moving to the next, it takes time to accommodate changes or new requirements later in the development process. Furthermore, users often only see a work-product version late in the development cycle, making it challenging to provide meaningful feedback or confirm that the software meets their needs.

Despite these limitations, the Waterfall model laid the groundwork for all subsequent software development methodologies. It introduced the notion of systematic, step-by-step progress through distinct stages, which remains at the heart of software development even as more flexible and iterative methods have emerged. As we journey through the evolution of these methodologies, we'll see how the principles of DevEx have been shaped and influenced by the strengths and weaknesses of each approach. The lessons learned from the Waterfall model have played a crucial role in understanding what makes a great developer experience.

Agile Methodologies

Agile methodologies emerged in response to the limitations of the Waterfall model, especially its inflexibility in the face of changing requirements and the users' late involvement in the development cycle.

The seeds of Agile were sown in the mid-1990s, and the philosophy truly blossomed in 2001 with the creation of the Agile Manifesto. It laid out four core values:

1. Individuals and interactions over processes and tools

2. Working software over comprehensive documentation

3. Customer collaboration over contract negotiation

4. Responding to change over following a plan

The Agile Manifesto represents a radical shift in mindset. It is a flexible, iterative approach to software development emphasizing collaboration and customer involvement. Agile is not one methodology but an umbrella term encompassing various methods like Scrum, Extreme Programming (XP), and Kanban, each with its particular practices but all sharing the core Agile values.

One of the most widely used Agile methodologies, Scrum, provides a prime example of Agile principles in action. Scrum divides development into time-boxed sprints, usually lasting two to four weeks. At the end of each sprint, the aim is to deliver a potentially shippable product increment, facilitating early and ongoing user feedback.

Take Spotify, for instance. The music streaming giant famously adopts an Agile approach with its squads, tribes, and guilds structure. It promotes autonomy, enabling developers to make decisions quickly and adapt to changes while focusing on delivering a high-quality user experience. This practice showcases how Agile methodologies, focusing on people, interaction, and swift response to change, can create an environment conducive to a positive developer experience.

Agile has challenges. It requires high collaboration and communication, often necessitating co-located teams. Without careful management, frequent changes can lead to scope creep. Moreover, Agile's bias for action over documentation may leave some teams needing more documentation.

Despite these potential pitfalls, Agile methodologies' impact on the software development world has been revolutionary. By prioritizing individuals, collaboration, and responsiveness, Agile has helped shift the focus toward improving the developer experience. As we continue our exploration of software development methodologies, we'll see how the Agile philosophy has influenced and paved the way for the emergence of DevOps.

DevOps

As we journey along the timeline of software development methodologies, our next stop is DevOps, a process that emerged in the mid-2010s as a natural evolution of Agile principles. DevOps represents a confluence of two critical parts of the software life cycle: development (Dev) and operations (Ops). This fusion, captured in the term "DevOps," symbolizes a profound shift towards unifying software development and software operation.

DevOps was conceived out of the need for greater efficiency, better quality, and faster delivery. Agile practices had already broken down some of the silos in software development, but a gap remained between development and operations teams, resulting in bottlenecks and inefficiencies. DevOps, therefore, emerged as a way to bridge this divide.

The essence of DevOps lies in the words of John Willis, one of its early advocates: "DevOps is a cultural and professional movement." At its heart, DevOps is about fostering a culture of collaboration, shared responsibility, and learning. It encourages automation, monitoring, and rapid response to change, which often leads to practices such as continuous integration, continuous delivery, and infrastructure as code.

One compelling example of DevOps in action is Netflix, which has embraced DevOps to maintain its industry-leading position. Netflix employs a "You build it, you run it" principle, which makes developers responsible for the entire lifecycle of their service, from development to deployment and maintenance. They use various automated tools to manage deployment, testing, and monitoring, allowing them to deploy hundreds or thousands of times daily. This developer ownership over the entire lifecycle improves the developer experience and aligns with the DevOps philosophy of shared responsibility and rapid iteration.

However, similar to Agile, DevOps has its challenges. Successful DevOps implementation requires a significant shift in mindset, which can be a cultural hurdle in some organizations. Additionally, it necessitates a high degree of automation, which can be a technical challenge. The risk of burnout is also higher as the boundaries between different roles blur.

Regardless, the positive impact of DevOps on developer experience cannot be understated. By encouraging collaboration, continuous learning, and ownership, DevOps can significantly enhance the developer experience. Moreover, DevOps practices such as automation, continuous integration, and infrastructure as code directly contribute to creating an efficient and enjoyable environment for developers, which is the essence of great DevEx.

This concludes our journey through the evolution of software development methodologies. As we proceed, we'll see how these principles permeate other aspects of DevEx, such as documentation, tooling, API design, and more.

The Intersection of UX and DevEx

DevEx does not exist in a vacuum; it intersects with and is influenced by the larger field of user experience (UX). Understanding this intersection is crucial for appreciating the broader context in which DevEx operates and recognizing its significance for the final product.

User experience, as defined by the International Organization for Standardization, encompasses "all aspects of the end-user interaction with the company, its services, and its products." While UX typically refers to an end user's experience, such as a person using a software application or a website, DevEx specifically targets developers as the users. Developers might interact with APIs, libraries, SDKs, or other tools as part of their work. In this context, developers are also users; hence, their experience matters.

This perspective of developers as users broadens the scope of what we traditionally consider UX. The principles that guide good UX design— ease of use, accessibility, performance, and more—apply just as much to DevEx. Like UX, DevEx seeks to eliminate pain points, streamline workflows, and create positive interactions with the product or service.

One area where the intersection of UX and DevEx becomes apparent is in the design and use of APIs. APIs are a vital touchpoint for developers and are a crucial component of many software systems. For instance, Twitter's API is used by developers worldwide to create applications that interact with the platform. To improve the DevEx, Twitter, like many companies, puts substantial effort into its API design, documentation, and support. They aim to make their APIs easy to use, understand, and integrate into other systems. In doing so, they directly apply UX principles to improve the developer experience.

Another common intersection point is in the development tools. For instance, the rise of integrated development environments (IDEs) like JetBrains' IntelliJ IDEA or Microsoft's Visual Studio Code has significantly improved DevEx. These tools are designed with the developer in mind, providing features like auto-completion, syntax highlighting, debugging tools, and more. Here again, the principles of UX are applied to make the developer's life easier.

However, while there is an overlap between DevEx and UX, it's essential to note that the developers' needs are unique. Developers often deal with complex problems and require profound control and customization that may be less common in traditional UX design. Therefore, while DevEx can learn from UX, it also needs its unique approach.

In conclusion, understanding the intersection of UX and DevEx is pivotal to creating software that delights end-users and empowers developers. Applying UX principles to developer-facing interfaces and recognizing the developer's unique needs can significantly enhance the quality of the developer experience. In the following sections, we will delve into DevEx's critical components, each representing an opportunity to apply these principles and enhance the developer's interaction with the product.

Key Components of DevEx

Having traversed the historical path of software development methodologies and explored the confluence of User Experience (UX) and Developer Experience (DevEx), we have now come to the heart of our journey: the key components of DevEx.

Imagine that you're about to construct a building. You've studied the history of architecture and considered how to create an experience that is in sync with the needs and desires of those who will occupy the building. Now, it's time to get your hands on the bricks and mortar, the physical materials that will bring your vision to life. That's what this section is all about.

Five critical pillars of DevEx will guide our exploration:

- Documentation

- Tooling

- API Design

- Developer Support

- Performance and Reliability

These pillars, akin to the fundamental principles of architecture, play a critical role in establishing an environment where developers can do their best work. These key components give form to DevEx, embodying its principles in concrete ways that directly affect a developer's daily work.

Documentation

Documentation is a pillar of developer experience. It is likened to a roadmap for developers, guiding them in navigating and using the software effectively. This is the resource developers first turn to when trying to understand a new API, library, or development tool or encountering an issue or error. Hence, well-structured, clear, and comprehensive documentation is vital to a positive developer experience.

The cornerstone of adequate documentation is clarity. The information must be presented in a way that is easy to understand and follow. As Albert Einstein once said, "If you can't explain it simply, you don't understand it well enough." This is especially true for documentation. The onus is on the writer, who must turn complex technical details into digestible information that the developer can quickly absorb and apply. Using plain language, providing examples, and avoiding unnecessary jargon is essential to ensure clarity.

One shining example of good documentation is Stripe's API documentation. It is interactive, concise, and includes working code snippets in multiple programming languages. It allows developers to understand and experiment with the API directly in the browser, offering a smooth onboarding experience.

Completeness is another crucial aspect of documentation. It should cover all aspects of the software, including its features, the details of its API endpoints (if any), everyday use cases, and known issues or limitations. It should also guide the developer in handling errors and troubleshooting common problems. This comprehensive approach allows developers to self-serve and reduces the need for additional support.

However, more than having an exhaustive set of documentation is required. It needs to be well-organized and searchable so that developers can find the information they need quickly. A good search function is often the key to making considerable documentation sets usable. Twilio is one company that does this well, with a robust search feature and a well-organized content hierarchy in their documentation.

Furthermore, documentation should be collaborative, continuously updated, and maintained as the software evolves. This requires a culture of documentation within the team, where updating the docs is an integral part of the development process.

Tooling

In the context of developer experience, tooling refers to the software and applications developers use to create, test, debug, and deploy their code. These tools are like the compass, map, and Swiss Army knife in a developer's exploration of the digital landscape; they are essential instruments that can make the journey more productive and enjoyable.

The selection of tools used in a development environment significantly influences the developer's experience. This spans text editors, Integrated Development Environments (IDEs), version control systems, build tools, test frameworks, and deployment tools. These should ideally be intuitive to use, easy to configure, and robust enough to handle the complexity of the projects they're used for.

A shining example is the IntelliJ IDEA by JetBrains, an IDE praised for its intelligent code completion, on-the-fly error detection, and quick-fix suggestions. The tool has consistently improved the developers' experience by automating tasks, allowing them to concentrate on more complex and creative coding parts.

However, tooling continues beyond the level of individual developers. At the team and organizational level, we see the importance of tools that facilitate collaboration and version control, such as GitHub, which allows teams to work together on projects without stepping on each other's toes. Similarly, continuous integration and continuous delivery (CI/CD) tools like Jenkins automate the processes of testing and deploying software, making it more efficient and less error-prone.

Additionally, "dogfooding," which refers to a company using its product, is an excellent strategy for improving tooling. It allows teams to experience their tools from a user's perspective, encouraging empathy and understanding of the user's needs. Slack is a well-known example of a company that practices dogfooding. They use their communication platform for all their internal communication, helping them continually identify areas for improvement.

However, while tooling plays a vital role in DevEx, it's crucial to remember that more tools don't sometimes make DevEx better. Introducing new tools must be considered carefully to avoid overwhelming developers and increasing the complexity of the development environment. The goal should be to create a coherent and streamlined toolchain that supports the developer's workflow without causing unnecessary disruptions.

API Design

The Application Programming Interface (API) is a vital tool in software development. It's the conduit between different software components or other software systems. Whether we're talking about web APIs, libraries, frameworks, or even operating systems, API design is instrumental in defining the developer experience (DevEx).

A well-designed API is more than just a technical interface—it's a user interface for developers. As Josh Bloch, the lead architect behind the Java Collections Framework, has said, "APIs should be easy to use and hard to misuse." This statement encapsulates the essence of good API design.

APIs should be designed with a developer-first mindset. They should be intuitive, predictable, and concise. They should adopt conventions and patterns familiar to the developers who will use them, whether those conventions come from the programming language the API is written in or from widely adopted best practices in the field. Developers should be able to anticipate an API's behavior by looking at its interface.

A brilliant example of API design is the Stripe API, often touted as the gold standard in the industry. Stripe has built their API with a focus on simplicity and consistency, and it uses meaningful and straightforward naming conventions, which make it intuitive to understand. The API's surface across different endpoints reduces the cognitive load on developers, enabling them to predict the API's behavior accurately. Stripe has also invested heavily in thorough, clear, and user-friendly API documentation, enhancing its usability.

Error handling is another crucial aspect of API design that directly impacts DevEx. Good APIs provide informative, clear, and actionable error messages, which help developers diagnose and fix issues quickly. For instance, Twilio's API design includes detailed error messages and links to documentation about each error, aiding developers in troubleshooting.

Versioning is yet another essential aspect of API design. Changes and updates to APIs are inevitable, but they should not disrupt the existing users of the API. Semantic versioning, where changes in the version number indicate the level of changes in the API, has become an industry standard, allowing developers to anticipate the nature and impact of updates.

API design is an art where empathy for the developer-user guides the process. When designed with this empathy, APIs provide a delightful developer experience and drive the adoption and success of the software they support. API design is a core aspect of DevEx that warrants keen attention and thoughtful design.

Developer Support

Developer support is a critical aspect of DevEx that is sometimes undervalued, yet it profoundly influences the developer's journey with a tool or platform. Essentially, it creates an environment where developers can swiftly overcome roadblocks, learn effectively, and, most importantly, feel valued.

Offering timely and relevant assistance is essential for a positive developer experience. This can be achieved through multiple channels, such as forums, chat groups, email support, and social media. Stack Overflow, a renowned online platform where developers can ask questions and find solutions, is a great example. It has effectively transformed the landscape of developer support, offering a community-driven approach to problem-solving.

However, more than merely answering questions is required, and the support quality matters significantly. A great piece of advice comes from Jeff Atwood, the co-founder of Stack Overflow: "The cardinal sin of community, in my eyes, is to treat newcomers poorly because they aren't acclimated to the strange (to them) customs and practices of your community." Empathetic and courteous responses solve problems, build trust, and foster a sense of community.

Moreover, support shouldn't be viewed as a reactionary measure to problems. Proactive support, in the form of comprehensive and user-friendly documentation, FAQ sections, tutorial videos, and regular webinars or workshops, empowers developers to overcome obstacles independently.

Examples of solid developer support are prevalent among the top tech companies. For instance, Shopify has a dedicated "Shopify Help Center," where developers can find detailed guides and tutorials about their APIs and SDKs. Similarly, Twilio's "Docs" provides quickstart guides, API reference documentation, and sample codes to ease the developer's journey.

Innovative support methods like GitHub's "Learning Lab" are also emerging. In this method, developers learn new skills by working through fun, real-world scenarios shared directly in their GitHub repository. It's an interactive and engaging way of learning new tools and concepts.

Support also extends to offline environments. Many organizations hold developer conferences, meetups, and hackathons, which serve as platforms for developers to learn, network, and share their experiences. Google's I/O and Apple's WWDC are iconic examples of such events.

Developer support is more than just about addressing problems as they appear. It's about creating an ecosystem where developers feel empowered to learn, explore, and innovate. It's about treating developers not as mere users but as members of a community that grows together.

Performance and Reliability

While we've been discussing several essential aspects of the developer experience, none can exist in a vacuum. A tool or platform's performance and reliability are the underpinning bedrock upon which all other elements of DevEx must stand. They're the invisible heroes of a developer's journey, mainly going unnoticed until something goes wrong.

Performance refers to the speed and efficiency of a tool, platform, or system and how well it fulfills its intended functions. For developers, this could mean the execution speed of a piece of code, the response time of an API, or the efficiency of a code editor or Integrated Development Environment (IDE). As Donald Knuth famously said, "Premature optimization is the root of all evil." Still, performance optimization at the right time can be a source of immense satisfaction and productivity for developers.

On the other hand, reliability refers to the consistency with which a system performs its intended function without failure. It's about how often a service experiences downtime, how frequently bugs occur, or how predictable and consistent an API's behavior is. Essentially, it's about trust. When developers invest their time and resources into a tool or platform, they expect it to work consistently and dependably.

Take, for example, the popular programming language Python. Its performance and reliability have played a significant role in its widespread adoption. Python scripts execute quickly, libraries and frameworks like NumPy and Django provide efficient functionality, and the language itself is dependable with a very predictable syntax and behavior. Similarly, GitHub's responsible version control system and near-constant uptime have made it the go-to platform for collaborative software development.

Another example can be seen with cloud service providers like AWS, Google Cloud, and Microsoft Azure. These platforms promise—and deliver—a high level of uptime reliability, which is often contractually guaranteed in Service Level Agreements (SLAs). They've also heavily invested in performance, offering services that can handle high-volume network traffic and computational tasks. This has earned them the trust of millions of developers and organizations worldwide.

However, the path to high performance and reliability can be challenging. Major outages, like the one GitHub experienced in 2018 or the AWS outage in 2020, serve as reminders that achieving a high level of performance and reliability requires continual effort, investment, and improvement.

In the grand scheme of DevEx, performance and reliability form the structure's foundation. Without them, all the excellent documentation, empathetic support, and powerful tooling are like a beautiful house built on sand. They complete the developer experience, ensuring that developers can work with confidence and peace of mind, knowing their tools and platforms won't disappoint them.

It's crucial to remember that the essence of DevEx lies not just in the individual components we discussed but, more importantly, in how they come together to form a cohesive, satisfying, and empowering developer experience.

Summary

This chapter provides an in-depth exploration of the concept of Developer Experience. We trace the historical evolution of software development methodologies and examine their impacts on DevEx. We highlight the symbiotic relationship between UX and DevEx and dive into the critical components of a solid and effective Developer Experience.

Key Takeaways

- The evolution of software development methodologies, from the Waterfall Model to Agile and DevOps, has influenced the dynamics of Developer Experience, shifting from a linear, siloed perspective towards a more collaborative, iterative, and integrated approach.

- The Developer Experience (DevEx) and User Experience (UX) are deeply interconnected. Improving DevEx often leads to an enhanced UX, creating a continuous cycle of innovation and refinement.

- Clear and comprehensive Documentation acts as a roadmap, guiding developers through their journey, minimizing confusion, and accelerating progress.

- Effective Tooling, like a well-equipped toolbox, empowers developers, enhancing productivity and job satisfaction.

- Intuitive API Design is vital for fostering seamless interaction between various software components and services, making developers' work more accessible and efficient.

- Reliable Developer Support acts as a safety net, offering assistance and reassurance when challenges arise and enhancing DevEx.

- Systems performance and Reliability are foundational to DevEx, providing the bedrock on which all other components rest.

Let's carry these insights as we continue our journey through the rest of the book, further enhancing our understanding of crafting a delightful and efficient Developer Experience.

CHAPTER 2

Developer Experience As a Competitive Advantage

In this chapter, we are set to embark on an insightful journey into the world of Developer Experience (DevEx), delving into its multifaceted role that extends far beyond the confines of immediate workspaces. We'll explore how DevEx, a concept pivotal in today's technology-driven world, plays a significant role in sculpting not just the day-to-day environment in which developers work but also how it fundamentally influences the broader aspects of a company's success. We will examine its impact on a company's market position, its ability to innovate and adapt, and how it shapes the overall organizational health and growth. This exploration is not just about understanding what makes a great DevEx but also about its ripple effects across various company dimensions—from employee satisfaction and productivity to customer experience and brand reputation. By delving deep into DevEx, we aim to uncover how it is a critical pillar that can uplift or undermine a company's standing in the fiercely competitive tech market.

We start by looking at the vital importance of DevEx in attracting and retaining top developer talent. In a field where skilled developers are a hot commodity, having an exceptional DevEx can set a company apart, making

© K. Rain Leander 2025
K. R. Leander, *Developer Experience Unleashed*,
https://doi.org/10.1007/979-8-8688-0242-3_2

it a magnet for talent. We'll explore real-life case studies from renowned
tech companies that have leveraged their development environments
and culture as major attractions in their hiring strategies. Additionally,
we discuss how an enhanced DevEx plays a crucial role in reducing staff
turnover and fostering a loyal and stable workforce.

Next, we focus on how a meticulously developed DevEx can improve
productivity and ignite team innovation. This chapter delves into
the various tools, practices, and cultural factors that create a thriving
development environment. You'll see through examples from industry
front-runners how investing in DevEx isn't just beneficial but essential. It
leads to streamlined workflows, enhanced creativity, and faster product
development cycles, all contributing to a company's growth and relevance
in the market.

Then, we'll explore an often-overlooked aspect of DevEx: its impact
on brand perception and loyalty. Here, you'll learn how a positive DevEx
reaches beyond just the development team and influences the broader
tech community's view of a company. This section sheds light on how
developers can become ambassadors for their company, fostering a
positive market image. It also touches on how incorporating ethical
practices, community involvement, and sustainability into the DevEx
framework can bolster a company's reputation and customer loyalty.

Throughout this chapter, our focus extends beyond mere tools and
technologies to include the culture, values, and practices that collectively
define DevEx. We aim to thoroughly understand how cutting-edge
companies use DevEx as a strategic tool in a competitive landscape by
weaving together real-life examples with insightful strategies. We strive
to equip you with the knowledge and tools to transform DevEx into a
significant competitive edge for your company.

Attracting and Retaining Talent

This section illuminates how DevEx transcends mere technological capabilities and delves into a more human-centric approach. It's about creating and fostering environments where developers excel in technical tasks and feel genuinely valued and motivated.

In the competitive landscape of technology, attracting top talent is as much about the technologies and tools at their disposal as it is about the culture and environment they work in. This section explores how a positive and enriching DevEx can be a crucial differentiator for organizations looking to attract the best in the field. It's not just about offering cutting-edge technologies; it's about creating a workplace where developers feel supported, engaged, and part of a meaningful journey.

Moreover, retaining talent in the fast-paced and ever-evolving tech world goes beyond financial incentives. It encompasses providing a work environment where developers can grow, innovate, and feel a sense of accomplishment and satisfaction. This involves understanding their needs, aspirations, and challenges and building a DevEx that responds effectively to these aspects.

This section delves into the strategies and best practices that make DevEx a cornerstone for attracting and retaining talented developers. It acknowledges the importance of marrying technical excellence with a people-first approach, emphasizing that the best developer environments cater to their talent's professional and personal growth. This nuanced understanding of DevEx is pivotal for organizations looking to thrive in the competitive tech landscape by harnessing the full potential of their development teams.

Attracting Talent: The Role of a Positive DevEx

In the fiercely competitive tech industry, attracting top-tier talent is a multifaceted challenge where the role of a positive Developer Experience (DevEx) is paramount. Prospective employees in this dynamic field look beyond lucrative paychecks; they search for work environments that offer opportunities for growth, innovation, and a strong sense of belonging. This is where a well-considered approach to DevEx becomes a critical factor in drawing talented professionals.

A prime example of a positive DevEx's impact in attracting talent is evident in the approach adopted by companies like Google. Their DevEx strategy strongly emphasizes creativity, freedom, and a culture of open communication. This approach has consistently made Google a magnet for attracting talent. By providing developers with cutting-edge tools and fostering a work environment that actively encourages innovation, Google caters to modern developers' desires and aspirations. This approach goes far beyond the basics of job satisfaction, touching on more profound aspects of what makes a work environment engaging and fulfilling.

Moreover, this focus on fostering a positive DevEx makes a profound statement about a company's values. It demonstrates a commitment to not just the professional but also the personal development of their employees. This resonates with like-minded individuals who are skilled and seek a workplace where their values and aspirations align with the company's. By prioritizing the needs and aspirations of developers in their DevEx approach, companies can attract talent that is not just technically proficient but also deeply invested in the ethos and culture of the organization.

The role of a positive DevEx in attracting talent in the tech industry cannot be overstated. It's an approach that recognizes the multifaceted needs of modern developers, offering them an environment where they can thrive, innovate, and feel a genuine sense of connection. This chapter section delves into how nurturing a positive DevEx is essential for companies looking to attract and retain the best talent, ultimately shaping a work culture that is innovative, inclusive, and aligned with the evolving expectations of today's tech professionals.

Retaining Talent: Beyond the Initial Attraction

Retaining talent requires more than initial attractions. It demands a sustained commitment to a positive DevEx. Netflix's culture, for example, is built around the idea of "Freedom and Responsibility." They empower their developers with the freedom to take on challenges and the responsibility to deliver without micromanagement. This level of trust and empowerment is critical to their high retention rates.

The role of continuous learning and development cannot be overstated. Companies like Amazon invest heavily in training and upskilling their workforce, recognizing that the growth of their employees directly contributes to the company's growth. By providing opportunities for professional development, these organizations ensure that their teams are up-to-date with the latest technologies and feel valued and invested in.

Creating a Community and Culture

Creating a community and culture within a workplace is pivotal to fostering a positive Developer Experience (DevEx) that extends beyond mere workstations and project assignments. Here, the focus is on how cultivating a sense of belonging and inclusivity is instrumental in enhancing employee satisfaction and retention.

An exemplary case of this approach is Salesforce, a company renowned for its inclusive and supportive culture. Salesforce strongly emphasizes equality, trust, and the well-being of its employees, integrating these values into every aspect of its operations. Their approach to DevEx is not just about providing the right tools or engaging work; it's about fostering a community where each individual feels heard, valued, and a part of something larger than themselves. This sense of community is crucial in creating an environment where developers can thrive professionally and personally.

At Salesforce, the focus on community and culture manifests in various ways, from policies and programs promoting equality and diversity to initiatives prioritizing employee well-being. This comprehensive approach to DevEx acknowledges that employees' satisfaction and retention are deeply intertwined with how they perceive their place within the company. Job satisfaction is significantly enhanced when developers feel part of a supportive and inclusive community. It's a strategy that goes beyond mere job satisfaction, influencing deeper aspects of employee engagement and loyalty.

Creating a community and culture within an organization is integral to a positive DevEx. Companies like Salesforce demonstrate how strongly emphasizing community, equality, trust, and well-being can lead to a more satisfied and committed workforce. This chapter section highlights the importance of these cultural elements in building a workplace where developers feel genuinely valued and connected, which, in turn, significantly contributes to their satisfaction and retention. The discussion here underscores the notion that a positive DevEx is not just about the technical environment but also about the human connections and the culture that envelop it.

The Impact of Remote Work

The rise of remote work has revolutionized the Developer Experience (DevEx), introducing new challenges and opportunities in how companies approach team engagement and cohesion. In an era where physical offices are no longer the default, companies are rethinking their DevEx strategies to adapt to the needs of a remote workforce. This adaptation is crucial to ensure that the physical distance does not lead to disconnection or disengagement among employees.

Slack and Zoom have become indispensable for daily communication and collaboration in the remote work environment. However, the challenge for companies goes beyond providing these technical tools. The key lies in fostering a sense of connection and belonging among remote employees. It's about crafting an environment where remote workers feel just as much a part of the team as those in the office. A notable example is GitHub, which has created an inclusive environment for its remote workforce. Their approach to remote DevEx transcends geographical barriers, ensuring full engagement and inclusion in the company's culture and operations.

A robust and thoughtfully designed DevEx is essential for attracting and retaining top talent in the tech industry, especially in remote work. Companies that prioritize the well-being, growth, and satisfaction of their developers are likely to see a significant enhancement in skills and productivity within their workforce. This investment in a positive DevEx cultivates a loyal, innovative, and highly effective team. Creating an effective DevEx for remote employees involves more than just the right tools; it requires nurturing a culture that supports and values each team member, regardless of location.

Boosting Productivity and Innovation

The concept of Developer Experience (DevEx) is pivotal in enhancing productivity and driving innovation within organizations. This vital aspect of software development goes beyond the mere technicality of coding; it encompasses the entire ecosystem in which developers work. A superior DevEx ensures that developers are equipped with the right tools and working in an environment that fosters creativity, encourages exploration, and supports continuous growth.

When developers are provided with a conducive working environment, it naturally leads to an increase in productivity. This doesn't just mean faster coding or more efficient workflows; it implies a deeper engagement with their work, leading to high-quality outputs and innovative solutions. A superior DevEx is characterized by streamlined tools and processes, which reduce unnecessary burdens on developers and free them up to focus on creative problem-solving. It's about creating an environment where the mundane aspects of the job are handled efficiently, allowing developers to channel their energies into what they do best: innovating and creating.

Moreover, innovation in the tech world is closely tied to developers' freedom and opportunities to explore new ideas. An environment that encourages exploration and experimentation is a breeding ground for innovation. When developers feel supported in taking risks and trying out new ideas, they are more likely to develop breakthroughs that can transform the industry. This culture, where experimentation is valued and failure is seen as a stepping stone to success, is essential in fostering innovation.

Additionally, the balance of autonomy and guidance plays a crucial role. Developers thrive in an environment where they can make decisions and take ownership of their projects. Yet, they also benefit from clear goals and guidance to ensure their efforts align with the company's objectives. This delicate balance allows developers to feel empowered and trusted, boosting their motivation and productivity.

Boosting productivity and innovation through an enhanced DevEx is a multi-dimensional approach. It involves providing the latest tools or technologies and creating a nurturing environment that values creativity, supports exploration, and invests in continuous learning. This approach is critical to building a thriving and innovative tech team capable of pushing the boundaries of technology and driving the organization toward new heights of success.

The Catalyst for Productivity: Streamlined Tools and Processes

Enhancing developer productivity is fundamentally linked to streamlining tools and processes, a crucial concept in software development. This approach focuses on how integrating efficient tools and methodologies can significantly boost developers' efficiency and creativity.

A quintessential example of streamlining in practice is the adoption of continuous integration and continuous deployment (CI/CD) pipelines in development workflows. Companies like Netflix and Amazon have leveraged these practices to automate the building, testing, and deployment processes. This automation minimizes manual intervention, substantially reducing the time required to launch new features and implement bug fixes. Such efficiency is not just about speed; it fundamentally changes the nature of the development cycle. By removing repetitive and time-consuming tasks, developers can redirect their focus toward more creative problem-solving and innovation.

Another key aspect of streamlining is the adoption of cloud-based development environments. Platforms like Microsoft Azure and Google Cloud have revolutionized how developers work by providing access to powerful computing resources and scalable infrastructure on demand. This cloud-based approach offers incredible flexibility, allowing developers to test new ideas and scale applications efficiently, free from physical hardware limitations. The cloud environment enables a level of agility and experimentation vital in the fast-paced world of software development.

Using streamlined tools and processes, including CI/CD pipelines and cloud-based environments, catalyzes productivity in software development. These technologies and methodologies are more than just tools; they represent a shift in development approaches, focusing on efficiency, flexibility, and creative freedom. By embracing these streamlined approaches, companies can foster an environment where developers are empowered to innovate, experiment, and efficiently bring their ideas to fruition. This shift is integral to creating a developer experience that not only enhances productivity but also nurtures the creative potential of the development team.

Fostering Innovation: Encouraging Exploration and Experimentation

Innovation is the driving force behind technological advancement, and companies that foster a culture of exploration and experimentation often find themselves at the forefront of this progress. Encouraging developers to think outside the box and pursue creative projects can lead to groundbreaking solutions and products.

A notable example of this approach is Google's "20% time" policy. This innovative policy allows employees to dedicate one day a week to working on side projects that interest them outside of their regular job responsibilities. This freedom to explore has led to the creation of some of Google's most successful products, such as Gmail and AdSense. This policy not only fosters innovation but also enhances job satisfaction among developers. It gives them a sense of value and recognition for their creative contributions beyond their daily tasks.

Likewise, hackathons and innovation sprints have become popular in companies like Facebook and IBM. These events provide platforms for developers to collaborate intensively on new ideas, often leading to innovative solutions. Hackathons are more than just coding marathons; they allow team members to step out of their usual roles, think creatively, and collaborate in new ways. These events lead to the development of new products and solutions, significantly boosting team morale and enhancing collaboration skills.

The emphasis on fostering innovation through exploration and experimentation is crucial in today's fast-paced tech industry. It's about creating an environment where developers are encouraged to take risks, try new things, and push the boundaries of what's possible. This approach drives technological advancement and cultivates a vibrant, dynamic workplace where creativity is valued and nurtured.

Balancing Autonomy with Guidance

The balance between autonomy and guidance is a critical factor in enhancing the productivity and innovation of developers. In the tech industry, where creativity and efficiency are highly valued, this balance plays a significant role in how developers approach their work and contribute to their organization's success.

On the one hand, autonomy is a powerful motivator for developers. Being free to make decisions and take ownership of their projects leads to a more profound sense of engagement and motivation. This sense of ownership encourages developers to push boundaries, explore new ideas, and fully invest themselves in their work. Autonomy fosters an environment where creativity can flourish and innovative solutions emerge.

On the other hand, providing clear goals and guidance is equally essential. While freedom is vital, it needs to be channeled in a direction that aligns with the company's objectives. Clear guidance helps ensure that developers' efforts contribute effectively to the organization's broader goals. It provides a framework for developers to exercise their creativity and ensure their innovations are relevant and impactful.

A prime example of a company that has mastered this balance is Apple. Known for its groundbreaking and innovative products, Apple maintains a delicate equilibrium between giving its engineers the freedom to innovate and ensuring their innovations align with the company's goals. This approach has enabled Apple to consistently produce products that are not only technologically advanced but also closely aligned with the company's vision and market strategy.

Balancing autonomy with guidance empowers developers to be creative and take initiative while ensuring their creativity serves a purpose and contributes to the company's success. This balance is crucial for fostering an environment where developers can be productive and innovative, driving the company forward in its technological pursuits.

Learning and Growth Opportunities

Continuous learning is a critical cornerstone of productivity and innovation in the tech industry. When companies invest in the ongoing education and professional development of their developers, they enhance individual competencies and contribute to the organization's overall innovation capacity.

IBM, for example, showcases the profound impact of such investment. The company's commitment to employee training programs ensures its workforce remains at the forefront of the latest technological advancements and best practices. This dedication to continuous learning is about maintaining skill levels and fostering a perpetual growth and adaptability culture. As developers stay updated with emerging technologies and methodologies, they become more adept at driving innovation, keeping the company competitive and forward-thinking in a rapidly evolving industry.

Boosting productivity and innovation through an enhanced developer experience (DevEx) extends beyond equipping teams with the latest tools or cutting-edge technologies. It encompasses creating an environment that nurtures creativity, encourages exploration, and carefully balances autonomy with clear guidance. Investing in continuous learning and professional development is vital to this equation. By prioritizing these aspects, organizations can build a robust DevEx strategy that resonates deeply with developers, enhancing their skills, engagement, and satisfaction.

Building Brand Loyalty and Advocacy

Building brand loyalty and advocacy is essential to fostering a robust Developer Experience (DevEx). This goes beyond just enhancing immediate productivity; it plays a pivotal role in how developers perceive and interact with the brand. A well-crafted DevEx creates an environment where developers not only feel satisfied with their work but also become advocates for the brand and its products.

When developers have positive experiences with a company's tools, technologies, and culture, their loyalty to the brand naturally strengthens. This loyalty is born out of a sense of satisfaction and engagement with their work and the environment provided to them. In such scenarios, developers are more likely to speak positively about the company, recommend its products and services, and share their favorable experiences with others in the industry. This advocacy is invaluable as it comes from genuine appreciation and trust in the brand.

Moreover, valued and supported developers contribute to the company's goals and visions. They become more than just employees; they become brand champions, internally and externally. This sense of ownership and belonging leads to a more profound commitment to the company's success and fosters a community of passionate advocates about their work and the impact they create.

Investing in a positive DevEx is not just about optimizing the technical aspects of development; it's about nurturing a relationship between the developers and the brand. This relationship, built on trust, respect, and satisfaction, is critical to transforming developers into loyal advocates. Such advocacy enhances the company's reputation in the tech community and contributes significantly to its growth and success. This subsection delves into how a well-structured DevEx strategy can be instrumental in building a loyal community of developers who are not just employees but ardent supporters and ambassadors of the brand.

Creating Evangelists through Exceptional DevEx

Creating evangelists within a company often starts with providing developers with an exceptional Developer Experience (DevEx). When developers enjoy a seamless, efficient, and empowering work environment, they naturally become brand advocates. They share their positive experiences with peers, effectively becoming vocal champions for the company's products and services.

A prime example of this phenomenon can be seen in the cult following of Apple's development ecosystem. Apple has gained widespread acclaim for meticulously crafting its developer environment. They provide developers with sophisticated and user-friendly tools, comprehensive and easily accessible documentation, and robust community support. This level of care and attention to detail attracts developers and instills a sense of pride and satisfaction with the products they create using these tools.

This positive relationship between the developer and the company doesn't just end with personal satisfaction. It transcends into a form of advocacy where developers become keen to share their positive experiences with others. They become brand evangelists, often passionately endorsing their tools and technologies. This advocacy is incredibly valuable as it comes from genuine appreciation and trust in the brand's commitment to creating a supportive and efficient developer environment.

Apple's success in turning developers into brand advocates is a testament to the power of a well-crafted DevEx. By ensuring that every aspect of the developer's journey is thoughtfully designed and executed, Apple has created a loyal community of developers who are not just users of their tools but also active promoters of the Apple ecosystem.

Creating brand evangelists through exceptional DevEx is about delivering great products and building relationships with developers based on trust, satisfaction, and empowerment. This approach leads to a community of deeply connected advocates for the brand, furthering its reach and impact in the tech world. Companies that understand and implement this strategy effectively can create a robust network of supporters, driving innovation and brand loyalty.

Open-Source Projects: A Testament to Community Engagement

Open-source projects such as Linux and ReactJS are excellent examples of how community involvement in development can cultivate deep loyalty among developers. These projects operate on a model that encourages active contributions and feedback from diverse developers, making each contributor feel like an integral part of the product's evolution.

In the open-source world, the relationship between a developer and the project is not just transactional; it's collaborative and deeply engaging. Developers are not merely software users but contributors, problem-solvers, and innovators. In projects like Linux and ReactJS, every line of code, every bug fix, and every enhancement from the community contributes to the project's growth and success. This participatory nature of open-source projects provides developers with a unique opportunity to shape the software they use and rely on.

Such an inclusive approach to software development not only enhances the quality and innovation of the product but also fosters a strong sense of ownership and pride among the developers involved. They see the tangible results of their contributions and recognize their role in the project's success, which fosters a deeper connection to the work and the community around it.

This sense of belonging and investment leads to strong brand loyalty and advocacy among developers. They become champions of the open-source project, not just because they use it, but because they have had a hand in building it. This community-centric model is a powerful driver of loyalty, making open-source projects like Linux and ReactJS not just software products but vibrant ecosystems of collaboration, innovation, and shared success.

Feedback Loops and Developer-Centric Marketing

Incorporating and acting on developer feedback is critical in building loyalty and fostering a positive developer experience. This approach demonstrates to developers that their opinions and experiences are valued, significantly impacting their perception of and loyalty to a brand. Google's Issue Tracker for Android development is a prime example of how a company can effectively engage with its developer community. By providing a platform where developers can report issues and suggest improvements, Google is committed to continually enhancing its development tools and APIs. This responsiveness improves the overall quality of the development environment and fosters a positive image among developers, who feel heard and respected by the company.

In addition to leveraging direct feedback, developer-centric marketing strategies are equally influential in nurturing a solid relationship with the developer community. These strategies go beyond traditional marketing efforts, focusing instead on showcasing the company's commitment to and understanding developers' needs. Successful case studies, developer conferences, and hackathons are potent tools.

Microsoft's Build Conference is an exemplary instance of developer-centric marketing done right. This event serves as a platform to spotlight new technologies and tools and underscores Microsoft's focus on empowering developers. By showcasing the latest innovations, sharing insights, and providing networking opportunities, such events create a vibrant community atmosphere that resonates deeply with developers. They offer a space where developers can learn, share, and connect, further solidifying their bond with the company.

These strategies—actively responding to feedback and engaging in developer-centric marketing—are fundamental in creating a brand that developers trust and advocate for. It's a holistic approach that combines understanding and addressing developers' technical needs with fostering a sense of community and belonging. This blend of responsiveness and community engagement is critical to building a brand that is not only used by developers but also championed by them.

Ethical Practices and Sustainability in DevEx

In the contemporary world of technology, ethical practices, and sustainability are becoming increasingly important factors in Developer Experience (DevEx). Developers today are not only concerned with the technical aspects of their work but are also increasingly mindful of the ethical implications and sustainability of their practices. Companies that prioritize and embed values such as data security, privacy, inclusivity, and environmental sustainability into their development practices are finding a deeper resonance with the developer community.

When a company takes a strong and clear stance on issues like data security and privacy, it sends its developers a message of responsibility and trustworthiness. In an era where data breaches and privacy concerns are rampant, a commitment to safeguarding data integrity and user privacy can significantly elevate a developer's trust in a company. This trust is a critical component of loyalty, as developers are more likely to align themselves with organizations that share their ethical values and demonstrate a commitment to protecting user interests.

Inclusivity in the development process is another area that is garnering attention. Developers seek work environments where diversity is not only recognized but celebrated. Companies that foster inclusive work cultures and develop products that cater to a diverse user base demonstrate an understanding of the modern societal landscape. This commitment to inclusivity often results in higher job satisfaction and a sense of pride among developers, who feel aligned with the company's ethos.

Additionally, environmental sustainability in development practices is becoming a decisive factor for many developers. As awareness about climate change and ecological impacts grows, developers are increasingly looking to contribute to companies that are conscientious about their environmental footprint. Organizations that adopt sustainable practices, whether in energy usage, resource allocation, or waste reduction, appeal to environmentally conscious developers. This alignment of values can be decisive in attracting and retaining talent.

Integrating ethical practices and sustainability into DevEx is crucial in today's tech landscape. Companies that align their development practices with these values are more likely to foster loyalty and advocacy among their developers. These aspects of DevEx go beyond job satisfaction; they tap deeper values and principles, making developers proud to be associated with and advocate for their organizations.

The Ripple Effect of Positive DevEx

The impact of a positive Developer Experience (DevEx) extends far beyond individual developers' confines. When developers are satisfied and engaged, they naturally become advocates for the tools and environments they use, often sharing their positive experiences across various platforms. Forums, blogs, and social media become channels through which these developers express their satisfaction, influencing the decisions of their peers and broader circles. This organic form of advocacy, stemming from genuine user satisfaction, is invaluable to brands, often proving more effective and authentic than traditional marketing efforts.

Building brand loyalty and advocacy in DevEx is a multifaceted endeavor. It requires a holistic approach beyond providing superior tools and resources. Central to this is fostering an inclusive community where developers feel they belong and are valued. In such environments, developers are more likely to share their positive experiences and recommend the brand to others.

Responding to feedback is another critical aspect. When developers see that their input is valued and acted upon, it reinforces their loyalty to the brand. This responsiveness improves their tools and environment and deepens their connection to the company.

Engaging in developer-centric marketing also plays a significant role. By showcasing successful case studies, organizing developer conferences, and hosting hackathons, companies can demonstrate their commitment to and understanding of the developer community. These events and stories highlight the company's dedication to empowering developers, further cementing their loyalty and advocacy.

Moreover, upholding ethical standards in all aspects of DevEx is crucial. Today's Developers are increasingly aware of and concerned about data security, privacy, inclusivity, and environmental sustainability issues. Companies that prioritize these values in their development practices resonate more deeply with the developer community, fostering a sense of shared principles and goals.

Building brand loyalty and advocacy through DevEx is about creating a complete experience that resonates with developers on multiple levels. It's about crafting an environment that meets their technical needs, aligns with their values, and offers them a platform to grow and excel. Companies can leverage DevEx to build a loyal and vocal developer community by focusing on these aspects, creating a ripple effect that extends their reach and influence far beyond their immediate user base.

Summary

In this chapter, we've explored the vital role of Developer Experience (DevEx) in the tech industry. DevEx is a crucial strategy for companies aiming to thrive in a competitive environment. It's more than just a concept; it's a comprehensive approach to creating a nurturing work environment that drives business success and innovation.

We discussed how a strong DevEx is essential for attracting and retaining top talent in a market where skilled developers are in high demand. Companies can significantly reduce turnover and cultivate a loyal workforce by providing an engaging and supportive development environment.

The chapter also highlighted how DevEx boosts productivity and innovation by combining the right tools, practices, and cultural elements. This leads to improved workflows, creative problem-solving, and faster product development.

Furthermore, we looked at how DevEx extends its influence beyond the immediate development team, impacting the company's overall brand perception and loyalty in the tech community. DevEx encompasses the physical tools and technologies and an organization's culture, values, and ethical practices.

DevEx emerges as a strategic asset in today's business landscape, offering a blueprint for companies to transform into brands known for excellence, innovation, and ethical values.

Key Takeaways

- DevEx is instrumental in attracting and retaining top developer talent, which is crucial in the competitive tech industry and enriches the talent pool.

- A positive DevEx contributes to a stable and loyal workforce by effectively reducing turnover rates.

- Investing in DevEx leads to more efficient workflows, fosters creativity, and speeds up product development cycles, thus enhancing productivity and innovation.

- The benefits of a strong DevEx extend beyond the immediate development team. They influence the company's overall brand perception and loyalty in the tech community, broadening its impact.

- DevEx involves nurturing a culture that values ethical practices, community engagement, and sustainability, underlining its cultural and moral significance.

- In the current market landscape, a robust DevEx is essential for any company looking to stand out, innovate, and grow, making it a strategic business asset.

- This chapter guides companies in leveraging DevEx to become a brand synonymous with excellence, innovation, and ethical values, acting as a blueprint for transformation.

CHAPTER 3

Crafting Exceptional Documentation

This chapter will delve into what makes the Developer Experience (DevEx) tick: well-crafted documentation. Think of this chapter as a compass guiding you through the intriguing landscape of creating, managing, and optimizing documentation to create a delightful and efficient developer environment.

Whether you're a seasoned veteran or a newcomer keen to learn, this chapter will prove enlightening as it traverses the what, why, and how of producing quality documentation.

So let's embark on this journey together as we unveil the profound impact of thoughtfully crafted documentation on the Developer Experience. Whether you're an experienced developer, a technical writer, or a product manager, this chapter has invaluable insights for you. Let's turn the page and discover the art of crafting fun and efficient developer environments through exceptional documentation.

The Importance of Documentation

The Importance of Documentation in enhancing Developer Experience (DevEx) cannot be overstated. Imagine buying a new gadget, only to find that the instruction manual is indecipherable or non-existent. You may be

© K. Rain Leander 2025
K. R. Leander, *Developer Experience Unleashed,*
https://doi.org/10.1007/979-8-8688-0242-3_3

frustrated and may even abandon your new purchase altogether. The same principle applies in software development: comprehensive, accessible, and precise documentation is the instruction manual that empowers developers to make the most of your software product.

At its core, documentation serves as a bridge between software creators and users. It captures and communicates the why, what, and how of your product: why certain design decisions were made, what the software is capable of, and how to use it effectively. In this way, documentation helps facilitate a shared understanding, reducing the cognitive load for developers and enabling them to focus on innovation rather than deciphering the software's nuances.

As software products have become increasingly complex, the role of documentation in guiding, educating, and supporting developers has become paramount. A 2017 GitHub survey highlighted this fact, with 93% of respondents stating that incomplete or outdated documentation is a pervasive problem in open-source projects. This underlines the critical role of documentation in teaching developers how to use a new software product.

High-quality documentation can also have a significant impact on developer productivity. An often-cited study by the University of Cambridge found that software developers spend about 50% of their time on avoidable rework that could be eliminated with better information sharing—such as through improved documentation. Hence, good documentation is not a mere add-on but a core contributor to your development team's efficiency.

Furthermore, robust documentation also fosters a sense of community among users. It serves as a platform for knowledge sharing, collaboration, and problem-solving, enhancing the overall value of your software product. For example, the Python community's emphasis on comprehensive documentation has been credited with the language's popularity and widespread adoption.

Lastly, documentation plays a significant role in ensuring inclusivity. It allows developers with different backgrounds, experience levels, and preferred learning styles to learn at their own pace, fostering a more diverse and inclusive developer community.

In summary, documentation is a critical aspect of DevEx. It helps educate new users, supports efficient development, facilitates collaboration, and promotes inclusivity. As we proceed further into this chapter, we'll delve deeper into different types of documentation and their unique roles in enhancing DevEx, followed by best practices in crafting exceptional documentation and the tools and platforms that can aid in this process. Remember, like the blueprint of a complex building, good documentation lays the foundation for developers to explore, understand, and build upon your software product.

Types of Documentation

It's crucial to recognize that documentation isn't monolithic and comprises related resources, helping developers understand, use, and troubleshoot your software. A robust documentation ecosystem consists of the following:

API References

Tutorials and Guides

Examples and Sample Code

FAQs and Troubleshooting Guides

Each serves a distinct but complementary role, providing developers with a holistic understanding of your product.

These four types of documentation weave together to create a robust developer knowledge base. By catering to different learning styles and use cases, they ensure that all developers—whether they prefer learning through reading, doing, or troubleshooting—find the support they need to work effectively with your software.

As we explore these types of documentation, remember the analogy of a well-stocked toolbox. A good toolbox is more than just a single tool. It's valued for its diversity of instruments; similarly, exceptional documentation features a range of resources, like the API Reference.

API Reference

As we delve deeper into the heart of the various forms of documentation that shape DevEx, the first category we encounter is API References. Picture an API Reference as a detailed blueprint of a complex machine. It shows every component, how they fit together, and what each part does. It's an integral part of any developer's toolkit, acting as a comprehensive directory of the functionalities provided by an API, its endpoints, data formats, and more.

API References are the hard facts of the software world. They are designed to be comprehensive, accurate, and precise, detailing every possible function, method, class, endpoint, or data model a developer could interact with. The API Reference should provide an overview of the capabilities and the details of each request or response. A practical API Reference should clearly define each endpoint, including HTTP methods (e.g., GET, POST, PUT, DELETE), URL paths, query parameters, request and response payloads, status codes, and authentication requirements.

One of the best practices in creating an API Reference is to utilize OpenAPI specifications. OpenAPI is a standard format that allows developers to define and document RESTful APIs. Using OpenAPI, you can automatically generate a structured and consistent API Reference that includes machine-readable documentation, code examples, and even interactive tools for testing API calls directly from the documentation. The OpenAPI definition serves as documentation and a contract, ensuring the API is implemented as described.

To better understand API References, consider Stripe's API Reference. As of 2023, Stripe is renowned for offering one of the best examples of clear, comprehensive API documentation. The online reference provides a detailed list of all the API's endpoints, data models, and error formats. Each endpoint is described with HTTP methods (like GET or POST), a URL path, and a short description. Furthermore, potential request parameters and example responses are given, complete with explanations of each field, to assist developers in understanding how to make effective API calls.

What makes Stripe's API Reference exemplary is not just its comprehensiveness but also its interactive nature. Developers can make "test" API calls directly within the documentation, receiving example responses. This offers an immediate understanding of how the API behaves in real-world scenarios, bridging the gap between theory and practice. Stripe also includes detailed descriptions and use case scenarios to illustrate when and why each endpoint might be used, significantly enhancing the developer's understanding.

Including examples and detailed descriptions is crucial in API References. Examples provide concrete usage patterns that help developers quickly grasp how to interact with the API. At the same time, descriptions offer the necessary context to understand the purpose and behavior of each endpoint. These examples should cover typical and edge-case scenarios, demonstrating the API's flexibility and robustness.

However, even the best API Reference can't stand alone. While it's the "what" and "how" of an API, it doesn't necessarily explain the "why." That's where other forms of documentation, such as tutorials and guides, step in to give context, demonstrate use cases, and guide developers on a more narrative journey through the software. Tutorials can show how to integrate the API into a project from start to finish, while guides can address more complex scenarios or common workflows.

Nevertheless, a solid, detailed, and accessible API Reference is the bedrock upon which great Developer Experience is built. By leveraging tools like OpenAPI, providing interactive elements, and ensuring thorough explanations and examples, an API Reference can transform into an invaluable resource that significantly enhances the developer's journey.

In our next section, we will explore these complementary forms of documentation, starting with tutorials and guides, the narrative companions to the factual API Reference. But as we move forward, remember API References' critical role in the overall documentation landscape. They are the compass by which developers navigate the vast landscape of APIs, offering direction and clarity amidst complexity.

Tutorials and Guides

If API References are the blueprints of your developer toolkit, consider tutorials and guides as hands-on instruction manuals. They provide the context and the "why" that complements the "what" of API References. While API References meticulously list the functions and endpoints, tutorials and guides showcase how these components come together to solve real-world problems.

Tutorials and guides offer a narrative, a step-by-step walkthrough of a given task or problem. They are the mentor accompanying developers on their journey, always ready to provide practical guidance. The aim is to help developers understand not just the individual components of an API but how these components interconnect to form a cohesive whole.

However, it's essential to strike the right balance in the scope of your tutorials and guides. Providing too much information can overwhelm developers, turning a learning experience into a tedious one. Conversely, offering content that is too basic may fail to engage more advanced users, leaving them without the depth they need to solve complex problems. Tailoring your tutorials to the appropriate audience is crucial, ensuring they are comprehensive enough to be helpful but concise enough to be digestible.

Let's take a concrete example to visualize this better. Twilio, a cloud communication platform, offers an extensive list of tutorials alongside their API Reference. One of their tutorials, "Send an SMS in 5 Minutes," guides developers through sending an SMS using the Twilio API.

The tutorial doesn't just list the steps; it breaks down the process in an engaging, understandable way. Developers are not only given code snippets but also explanations of what each line of code is doing. It presents the larger picture, enabling the developer to comprehend the underlying concept and how the pieces fit together.

Similarly, Docker, the open-source platform, has guides that help developers learn their tools. One such principle is "Get Started with Docker," which walks users through setting up Docker, running a simple hello-world container, and building and deploying a sample application.

By the end of the tutorial or guide, developers should have a functional piece of code and a deeper understanding of the API's capabilities. The knowledge gained isn't just theoretical but immediately applicable.

However, the utility of a tutorial or guide is directly proportional to its quality. A well-structured tutorial with clear instructions, proper explanations, and meaningful examples will foster learning, whereas a poorly constructed one may lead to confusion and frustration. In addition, carefully consider the amount and complexity of information presented. The right balance ensures the tutorial is accessible to its intended audience without sacrificing the depth needed for thorough understanding.

In the following sections, we will explore different types of documentation, such as examples and sample code, FAQs, and troubleshooting guides, which supplement the foundation laid by API References and the contextual understanding offered by tutorials and guides. In the interconnected ecosystem of DevEx, each type of documentation plays a crucial role, contributing to the richness of the developer experience.

Examples and Sample Code

The proverb, "A picture is worth a thousand words," captures the essence of the role examples and sample code play in software documentation. Examples and sample code help developers visualize the concepts, understand them, and learn how to use your product practically.

What API References and Tutorials do at a theoretical level, examples and sample code accomplish in practice. They bridge the gap between understanding and implementation, turning abstract concepts into concrete code developers can run, modify, and learn from.

Sample code helps developers see what a correct implementation looks like. Consider the Stripe API, for instance. Stripe, a company that provides APIs for online payment processing, has a section in its documentation dedicated to code samples.

Their sample code for creating a payment intent reads:

```
`  `

$ curl https://api.stripe.com/v1/payment_intents \
    -u sk_test_4eC39HqLyjWDarjtT1zdp7dc: \
    -d amount=2000 \
    -d currency=usd \
    -d "automatic_payment_methods[enabled]"=true
`  `
```

This code demonstrates to developers how to implement a payment intent using Stripe's API. It also subtly communicates the expected formatting and style, encouraging good coding practices by picking meaningful example values and parameter combinations.

On the other hand, examples often take the form of case studies or everyday use cases that developers might encounter. They can also be more elaborate versions of sample code, showing how various API calls and endpoints can be combined to solve complex problems.

For instance, GitHub's documentation includes guides that take developers through common workflows, such as managing branches in your repository or syncing changes from the original repository if you're working on a fork. These examples are crucial in helping developers understand the API's potential applications and how to use it effectively in their context.

However, a few key points to remember while developing examples and sample code:

> **Accuracy**: The code should run without errors. Outdated or incorrect code samples can improve developer experience and satisfaction. To ensure accuracy, consider having another developer review the code and test it in a fresh environment. This extra step helps catch potential issues that might not be apparent during initial development.

> **Completeness**: Include all necessary information to run the code. Do not assume knowledge on the developer's part. If the sample requires some environment setup or context, provide that information.

> **Simplicity**: Keep the code samples as straightforward as possible. The purpose is to educate, not to confuse.

Examples and sample codes are invaluable assets in your documentation. They illuminate the path for developers, providing tangible illustrations of the theoretical concepts described in your API references and tutorials. In the following sections, we'll explore FAQs and troubleshooting guides, which serve as the emergency toolkit when developers encounter obstacles or issues.

FAQs and Troubleshooting Guides

Just as a ship is equipped with lifeboats for emergencies, your documentation should also contain safeguards for when developers face issues. Frequently Asked Questions (FAQs) and Troubleshooting Guides serve this purpose, offering immediate answers and solutions to common questions or problems that may arise while using your software.

While FAQs have been a traditional approach to addressing common queries, they are waning in current practice. Ideally, the questions they address would be covered more effectively by well-structured documentation that integrates answers into the natural flow of content. However, the concept of support deflection, central to FAQs, remains vital.

FAQs are designed to handle recurring questions that users typically ask. They provide a quick and accessible way for developers to find answers to their questions without diving deep into the documentation. For example, Microsoft's FAQ for their Azure DevOps service contains questions such as "How is Azure DevOps different from Azure DevOps Server?" providing concise and informative answers to alleviate confusion and support user understanding.

The goal of a FAQ is to save users time and reduce the load on your support team. Addressing common questions upfront minimizes the number of support tickets, freeing your team to focus on more complex and unique issues.

On the other hand, Troubleshooting Guides act as the first line of defense when developers encounter issues or roadblocks. They offer structured and detailed solutions to known problems, working as a diagnostic tool for developers to resolve issues independently.

Let's take the example of Docker. Docker, a popular tool for creating, deploying, and running applications using containers, has a comprehensive troubleshooting guide in their documentation. It includes sections like "Troubleshoot common Docker problems" and "Diagnose and get support for Docker Desktop issues." These guides offer step-by-step instructions to diagnose and resolve common issues, saving the developer time and frustration.

When writing FAQs and Troubleshooting Guides, consider the following best practices:

Be Proactive: Regularly update these sections based on the issues and questions developers encounter most frequently. However, strive to incorporate these answers directly into the main documentation to reduce reliance on a standalone FAQ section. User feedback, support ticket analysis, and community discussions can be valuable sources of insight.

Be Clear and Concise: Write answers and solutions in simple language. The goal is to help the developer resolve the issue quickly, not to display technical prowess.

Use a Logical Structure: Organize FAQs and Troubleshooting guides logically and efficiently, but prioritize embedding this structure into the core documentation. Group related questions and categorize troubleshooting topics to make finding relevant content more manageable.

FAQs and Troubleshooting Guides are crucial components of DevEx. They enable developers to find quick answers to their questions and resolve issues efficiently, reducing frustration and increasing productivity. Even as the format of FAQs evolves, anticipating and addressing common problems upfront remains critical to delivering a positive developer experience.

Documentation Best Practices

Crafting exceptional documentation isn't a singular act but a combination of practices focused on clarity, organization, continuous updates, and a commitment to accessibility and inclusivity. It's about viewing your documentation not as an afterthought but as an integral part of the developer experience. Remember, your documentation is often the first point of contact for users, which plays a vital role in shaping their journey with your product. So, craft it with care.

These best practices are about maintaining a high-quality standard and creating a delightful developer experience. As we delve into the following sub-sections, think of them as pieces of a puzzle fitting together to complete the picture of adequate documentation.

Writing Clear and Concise Content

An essential principle in creating exceptional documentation is writing clear and concise content. This means that Python's official documentation provides the information developers need without extraneous details or unnecessary complexity, which can lead to confusion or misunderstanding. The goal is to create documentation that speaks directly to developers, enabling them to quickly grasp concepts, procedures, and requirements.

One could argue that writing clear and concise content is more of an art than a science, but several best practices can guide you in this endeavor:

> **Simplicity Is Key**: Keep sentences short and straightforward. Use plain language that your audience can easily understand. Avoid jargon unless it's necessary and has been previously defined. A survey conducted by GitHub in 2017 revealed that technical jargon was one of the main barriers developers faced when trying to understand documentation.

Be Specific: Use concrete examples and specific details to illustrate abstract concepts. As the saying goes, "Show, don't tell." For instance, rather than just explaining how a particular function in your API works, provide a brief code snippet that demonstrates the process in action. This tangible demonstration can help solidify understanding.

Prioritize Clarity over Cleverness: There are better places to showcase your mastery of metaphor or intricate writing style than Documentation. You aim to help the developer understand your software rather than impressing them with your linguistic prowess. Be mindful of this when writing.

Use Active Voice: Writing in the active voice is more direct and easier to understand. For example, "The function calculates the sum" (active voice) is more precise than "The sum is calculated by the function" (passive voice).

Consistency Is Crucial: Consistency in terminology, format, and style creates a sense of familiarity and predictability, which can significantly enhance the readability of your documentation.

Iterate and Refine: Writing clear and concise documentation is an ongoing process. Always be open to feedback from your user community, and don't be afraid to iterate and refine your content. Remember, your documentation is a living document.

A practical example of clear and concise writing in documentation can be found in the ReactJS docs. They have excelled in presenting complex ideas in a simple, easy-to-understand manner. In particular, their explanation of "Components and Props" stands out. They begin with a straightforward definition, followed by a concrete example, making it easy for developers of all levels to understand.

Writing clear and concise content is an ongoing commitment to your developers' understanding and success. It fosters an environment that respects their time and cognitive load, ultimately contributing to a superior Developer Experience. It is not just about having something to say; it's about saying it in a way the developer can readily absorb and apply.

Organization and Structure

Just as crucial as the content itself, the organization and structure of your documentation play a pivotal role in its effectiveness and usability. When we discuss organization and structure, we're talking about how information is logically grouped, sequenced, and presented to make it easy for users to find, understand, and use.

There are several fundamental principles and best practices to consider when organizing and structuring your documentation:

> **Logical Structure**: Information should be structured to make sense to the users. This often means organizing information from the general to the specific or from the most commonly used features to the least used ones. An effective logical structure helps users build a mental model of how your software or technology works.

Consistency: Layout consistency helps users quickly recognize and interpret information. This includes consistent use of headings, subheadings, lists, diagrams, and code snippets. The Java documentation, for example, maintains a consistent layout across all their API documentation pages, which makes it easy for developers to locate the information they need.

Easy Navigation: Users should be able to navigate your documentation easily. This can be achieved through a well-structured table of contents, breadcrumbs, clear headings and subheadings, a robust search feature, and effective hyperlinks.

Task-oriented Structure: Where possible, structure your documentation around tasks that users want to accomplish. This involves providing step-by-step instructions, use cases, and examples geared toward helping users achieve their goals.

Scannability: People often scan web content rather than reading it word by word. Use visual cues like headers, bullet points, tables, and bold or italic text to highlight important information and make your content easy to scan.

Segmentation: Divide your content into manageable chunks or sections. Smaller segments are easier to understand and remember, allowing users to quickly find and focus on the specific information they need.

One standout example of well-structured and organized documentation is the Stripe API documentation. It is segmented into clear sections (e.g., "Core Resources," "Payment Methods," etc), offers quick links to various parts of the documentation, and provides a right-hand navigation panel for easy browsing of the current page's contents. Its task-oriented approach with clear instructions and consistent layout makes it user-friendly and highly efficient.

Good organization and structure in the documentation are more than just aesthetic considerations. They significantly contribute to the content's ease of use and understandability, improving the developer's overall experience. Your documentation should be designed with a deep understanding of your user's needs and a sincere desire to make their journey as smooth as possible.

Versioning and Updates

As software evolves, so must its documentation. Keeping your documentation up-to-date and in sync with software versions is crucial to delivering an exceptional developer experience. Outdated documentation can be frustrating, wasting time and effort and resulting in incorrect software usage.

Versioning: Whenever a new version of your software is released, ensure your documentation accurately reflects these changes. This may include updating API references, changing screenshots, amending code samples, and altering guides to reflect new or revised features. Versioning your documentation ensures that users of different versions of your software can find relevant information.

Consider providing version-specific documentation, where users can select the software version they use, and the documentation adjusts accordingly. A great example of this can be seen in the Python documentation. Python allows users to switch between the documentation for different versions effortlessly, helping users of all Python versions find accurate, relevant information.

Updates: Regularly review and update your documentation to ensure its accuracy. This includes changes that result from software updates but also clarifications, additional examples, typo corrections, or improvements in the explanations. This ensures that your users always have access to the most current, correct, and comprehensive information.

To provide smooth updates, consider maintaining a documentation changelog. This records all significant changes made to the documentation, such as adding new sections, significant revisions, or corrections. This provides transparency and lets users see what has changed, just as they might in a software changelog.

Deprecations: When particular features or aspects of your software are deprecated, your documentation should reflect this. It's best to indicate that the quality is deprecated and suggest alternatives. This guides users toward the proper usage of your software, reducing frustration.

Remember that versioning and updates aren't just about changing the content; they're about clearly communicating those changes to your users. They must know when information has changed, why, and how those changes impact their interaction with your software.

The heart of versioning and updating practices is your commitment to your users' success. It underscores your promise that you won't leave your users behind while your software evolves. Instead, you'll give them the tools and knowledge they need to evolve with you.

Accessibility and Inclusivity

True to the spirit of developer experience, documentation should be accessible and inclusive. This is the difference between creating a product that merely serves your users and one that respects and values them. When discussing accessibility and inclusivity, we're referring to a broad spectrum of considerations, including language, ability, and diversity.

Accessibility: Documentation should be accessible to all, including those with disabilities. This can be achieved through careful design decisions and adherence to web accessibility standards. Use readable fonts, ensure a high contrast between text and background colors, and use alt-text for images. Ensure your documentation is navigable via keyboard alone, catering to users who can't use a mouse. Consider using semantic HTML to support assistive technologies, such as screen readers.

The Web Content Accessibility Guidelines (WCAG) is an excellent resource for learning more about creating accessible web content. Implementing these guidelines is not just good practice; it's a legal requirement in many places.

Inclusivity: Inclusivity goes beyond just accessibility. It's about ensuring your documentation is friendly, welcoming, and usable by a diverse audience. Avoid jargon and write in plain language, making your content understandable to users of different proficiency levels. Be mindful of cultural differences and avoid examples that could be offensive or exclusive.

Remember that not all your users are native English speakers. While writing technical documentation in English is standard, offering translations can make your product accessible to a broader audience.

Gender-neutral Language: The tech industry has traditionally been male-dominated, and our language often reflects this. However, the industry is changing, and our language should change, too. Use gender-neutral language in your documentation. Instead of "he" or "she," use "they" or simply refer to the user. This simple shift makes your content more inclusive.

As Caitlin Geier, an expert in UX design and digital accessibility, noted in a 2022 interview, "When you're inclusive in your language and design, you're communicating to your users that you see them, you respect them, and you value them. Inclusion isn't just about being nice—it's about demonstrating your values and fostering trust."

When you focus on accessibility and inclusivity, you improve your documentation and build a more welcoming and supportive tech community. And that, in itself, is a step toward better developer experiences.

Tools and Platforms for Creating and Maintaining Documentation

The first step is understanding how to craft exceptional documentation clearly, but that knowledge must be supplemented with the right tools and platforms. In this era of digital technology, the list of such tools is extensive and continually growing. Let's explore some popular options that have proven beneficial in creating and maintaining high-quality, user-friendly documentation.

From text editors to documentation-specific tools, there are many options available. Among them, tools like Microsoft Word and Google Docs are simple to use and widely adopted, allowing for collaborative editing and essential document organization. However, tools like Markdown editors, LaTeX, or AsciiDoc might be more suitable for more technical documentation. These allow for syntax highlighting, inline code snippets, and other features useful for technical writing.

Markdown, in particular, has gained significant popularity in recent years. GitHub, the world's most prominent host of source code, uses Markdown as its primary language for documentation. As the developer and writer Sean C Davis says, "Markdown is so simple. It's beautiful. And its simplicity is its greatest benefit."

For larger projects or teams, dedicated documentation platforms can provide robust solutions. These include tools like Read the Docs, Sphinx, and Jekyll, which provide potent features such as version control, automatic generation of a table of contents, and easy integration with version control systems like Git. Furthermore, these tools often support exporting your documentation in formats like HTML, PDF, or even ePub, making it accessible for different user preferences.

Tools for API documentation deserve special mention. OpenAPI, formerly known as swagger, is an open standard for describing HTTP APIs. It allows you to create a detailed API specification, and tools like SwaggerUI and Redoc can turn this specification into interactive documentation. These tools help build clear and consistent documentation and offer features like client SDK generation and API discoverability.

Additionally, OpenAPI supports the "docs as code" concept, where documentation is part of the codebase, enabling version control, collaboration, and integration into CI/CD pipelines. This approach aligns with modern software development practices, ensuring your documentation is always in sync with the latest code changes. Postman, another popular tool, allows for the easy sharing of API collections and provides a platform for creating and viewing API documentation.

Another crucial part of maintaining documentation is managing and tracking changes and updates. Version control systems, like Git, are incredibly beneficial for this. Using Git, you can track every change made in your documentation, see who made the changes, and even revert to previous versions if necessary. Coupling this with platforms like GitHub or Bitbucket allows collaboration and public contribution, further enhancing the documentation process.

Various tools can help ensure that your documentation adheres to best practices regarding accessibility and inclusivity. Accessibility checking tools like the WAVE Web Accessibility Tool or aXe can help identify areas of your documentation that might be difficult for users with disabilities to access.

Lastly, remember that getting feedback on your documentation is critical for continuous improvement. Tools like UserVoice or Disqus can be integrated into your documentation to allow users to provide comments and suggestions.

The tools you choose can significantly impact the quality and efficiency of your documentation process. While the tools and platforms mentioned here are among the most popular and widely used, remember that the best tool depends on your specific needs and context. As writer and developer Erik Dietrich wisely advised, "Choose your tools with your needs and context in mind, not someone else's."

Key Takeaways

- Documentation is the heart of Developer Experience (DevEx) and is a crucial tool for knowledge transfer, discovery, and collaborative enhancement of the codebase.

- Various types of documentation, such as API references, tutorials, examples, FAQs, and troubleshooting guides, serve distinct roles and form a holistic documentation ecosystem.

- Clear and concise content, logical organization and structure, careful versioning and updates, and ensuring accessibility and inclusivity are integral best practices in crafting exceptional documentation.

- Documentation is not a static entity but a dynamic aspect of your project that requires consistent updates and improvements.

- Various tools and platforms are available to assist in creating and maintaining documentation, and the right tool depends on your specific needs and context.

- High-quality documentation considers the needs of a diverse range of developers, making it inclusive and accessible.

Streamlining Developer Tooling

As we embark on the journey through Chapter 4, "Streamlining Developer Tooling," we will immerse ourselves in the universe of tools that a developer wields. Much like a craftsman choosing their tools, a developer must select the suitable instruments to carry out their work efficiently. These tools are not merely a means to an end but a crucial component of the developer experience, influencing productivity, collaboration, and overall quality of work. To quote Antoine de Saint-Exupéry, "Perfection is achieved, not when there is nothing more to add, but when there is nothing left to take away." In this vein, we aim to find the perfect set of tools, streamlined and tailored to each project's unique requirements.

Selecting the Right Tools for Your Project

If you think of software development as an intricate dance, our tools could be likened to the dance floor and the music guiding our steps. The right choice of tools can make a significant difference in our performance, making our movements fluid and graceful, while the wrong selection can make us stumble and falter.

© K. Rain Leander 2025
K. R. Leander, *Developer Experience Unleashed*,
https://doi.org/10.1007/979-8-8688-0242-3_4

Selecting the right tools for your project is more than picking the most popular or sophisticated tools. It's about understanding your project's unique requirements and rhythms, your team's capabilities and preferences, and the task. In the following sections, we'll look at these tools, helping you understand their features, benefits, and suitable use cases. So, let's get ready to dance!

Text Editors and IDEs

Choosing the right text editor or Integrated Development Environment (IDE) is crucial in establishing an efficient development workflow. These tools are the bread and butter of a developer's daily tasks, where they spend significant time coding, debugging, and testing. As our friend and prolific programmer Jon Skeet once said, "Choose your tools wisely, and you'll enjoy the coding journey as much as the destination."

The decision between a text editor and an IDE depends mainly on the nature and complexity of your project, the language you're coding in, and your personal preference as a developer. Text editors such as Sublime Text, Atom, or Visual Studio Code are lightweight and fast, making them ideal for more straightforward projects or when you need to write and edit code quickly. They're also highly customizable, with many plugins and extensions available to tailor the tool to your needs.

For example, in Sublime Text, you can use packages like "Package Control" to add syntax highlighting for various languages or install code snippets that streamline repetitive tasks by inserting frequently used code structures with minimal effort.

IDEs, on the other hand, are comprehensive software suites that provide a slew of features like code completion, advanced debugging, and integrated testing right out of the box. Tools like IntelliJ IDEA, Eclipse, or Microsoft's Visual Studio offer a more integrated experience and can significantly increase productivity, particularly for larger and more complex projects. But remember that this feature increase often comes at the cost of resource usage, which can be a trade-off depending on your system capabilities.

For instance, in Microsoft's Visual Studio, features like IntelliSense provide real-time code suggestions that help you write code faster with fewer errors. The integrated debugger lets you step through your code line by line, making identifying and fixing issues easier. Additionally, the refactoring tools let you restructure your code safely and efficiently across large projects.

Take, for example, Visual Studio Code (VS Code). Launched in April 2015, it has rapidly gained popularity among developers. One of its strengths is its versatility, made possible by an extensive library of extensions that lets you customize your workspace to support numerous languages and frameworks. This adaptability, coupled with its inbuilt features like Git integration, IntelliSense for code autocompletion, and a built-in terminal, make it a favored choice for many developers.

On the other hand, for Java developers working on complex applications, IntelliJ IDEA offers deep insights into your code, with advanced refactoring tools, comprehensive database tools, and intelligent code completion that makes writing and maintaining code enjoyable.

Remember, there's no one-size-fits-all solution. The best tool for you will depend on your unique project requirements and personal preferences. So, don't hesitate to try different tools and find the one that makes your coding journey as smooth and enjoyable as possible. Remember the wisdom of Abraham Lincoln, who said, "Give me six hours to chop down a tree, and I will spend the first four sharpening the axe." Your text editor or IDE is your axe in software development—take the time to select and sharpen it.

Version Control Systems

Among the essential tools in a developer's toolkit, version control systems (VCS) rank near the top. They serve as the time machine of your coding world, allowing you to track changes, revert to previous versions, and collaborate efficiently with others. As Linus Torvalds, creator of Git and the Linux kernel, humorously remarked about early file transfer practices, "Only wimps use tape backup: real men just upload their important stuff on FTP, and let the world mirror it." While the quote reflects an older era of technology, it underscores the importance of robust methods for safeguarding and sharing your work–principles at the heart of modern version control systems.

Version control systems come in two primary flavors: centralized version control systems (CVCS), such as Subversion (SVN), and distributed version control systems (DVCS), like Git. CVCS has a single, central repository of the code. On the other hand, in DVCS, every developer's working copy of the code is also a repository that can contain the complete history of all changes.

Git, first released in April 2005, has become the de facto standard for version control, particularly for open-source projects. Git's distributed nature allows for seamless collaboration among team members, enabling each developer to work independently on their local copy of the project. Changes are then merged into a shared main repository. Notably, Git's distributed nature doesn't imply a lack of centralized organization. Platforms like GitHub, GitLab, and Bitbucket provide a central hub for team collaboration, code review, issue tracking, and continuous integration services, enhancing Git's functionality.

Subversion, or SVN, while older and less popular than Git, still holds its own in specific contexts. SVN's simpler model can be more intuitive for beginners, and its handling of binary files and directories is sometimes considered superior to Git. However, it lacks the distributed aspect of Git, which can slow down workflows and limit offline productivity.

When choosing a version control system for your project, you'll need to consider factors such as the size and distribution of your team, the nature of your project, and your specific requirements for functionality. For many teams, particularly those working on open-source projects, Git's features, speed, and widespread adoption make it an obvious choice. However, it's essential to make an informed decision based on the specific needs of your project and team.

As you navigate your journey in development, remember that a robust version control system is not just a luxury—it's a necessity. It safeguards your code, enhances collaboration, and, when used effectively, can significantly improve your development workflow and your overall Developer Experience.

Build Tools and Automation

"The best part of programming is the time saved on the other side of it," said computer scientist Alfred Aho. Indeed, the power of programming comes to life when we can automate repetitive tasks, and in software development, build tools are at the heart of this automation.

Build tools and automation are crucial in improving the Developer Experience (DevEx) by streamlining the development process. They're responsible for automating tasks such as compiling code, running tests, packaging binaries, managing dependencies, and deploying your application. By relieving developers of these manual tasks, building tools frees up time for more creative and problem-solving aspects of development.

Selecting the right build tool often depends on the programming language you're using and the complexity of your project. For instance, Maven and Gradle are popular choices in the Java ecosystem. Initially released in 2004, Maven introduced a standard build lifecycle and a declarative approach to project configuration. Gradle, which arrived in 2009, expanded upon these features with a powerful and expressive domain-specific language based on Groovy, providing the flexibility to model complex builds.

In JavaScript development, Node.js brought many build tools and task runners. Grunt, first released in 2011, was one of the pioneers, providing a scriptable way to automate tasks like minification, compilation, unit testing, and linting. Gulp, introduced in 2013, took this a step further with a code-over-configuration approach and a streaming build pipeline based on Node.js streams. The introduction of Webpack in 2013 brought sophisticated bundling and dependency management capabilities, making it particularly well-suited for large, complex JavaScript applications.

Another critical aspect of build automation is Continuous Integration/Continuous Deployment (CI/CD). Tools like Jenkins, Travis CI, and CircleCI allow you to automate the integration of changes from different developers and the application deployment, often several times a day. This approach enables teams to catch and fix integration issues early, leading to more stable software and faster development cycles.

Selecting the right build tool and automation strategy can profoundly impact your team's productivity and happiness. Consider factors such as the complexity of your project, the size of your team, your deployment strategy, and the tool's community and ecosystem when making your decision. The goal should be to streamline and simplify as much of the process as possible, allowing developers to focus on what they do best: creating fantastic software.

Testing Frameworks and Tools

There's an adage in software development: "If it's not tested, it's broken." Indeed, testing is a non-negotiable aspect of creating reliable and maintainable software. This section will explore the importance of the proper testing frameworks and tools. These are integral components of the developer toolset that contribute significantly to an efficient and delightful Developer Experience (DevEx).

In any software project, testing serves as the safety net. By systematically checking that each part of the system works as expected, you can catch and fix bugs before they reach the end users. Testing tools help automate this process, and selecting the right ones is often specific to the programming language, development methodology, and testing you plan to carry out.

Test-driven development (TDD) is one of the core methodologies in modern software development. In TDD, you write tests before writing the code, ensuring that each new feature or function is designed to pass the test. This approach leads to cleaner, more reliable code, making refactoring safer and more accessible. TDD typically involves three steps: writing a failing test, writing code to make the test pass, and then refactoring the code while ensuring the test still passes. TDD is most effective when integrated into the development process, with unit tests being run automatically as part of the continuous integration pipeline.

Unit testing, for example, examines the most minor testable parts of your software to ensure they function correctly in isolation. Kent Beck, the creator of Extreme Programming, introduced JUnit, a pioneering unit testing framework for Java, in 1998. JUnit's design influenced many other testing frameworks across different programming languages. Python's unittest, C#'s NUnit and JavaScript's Jest are some examples, each built with the unique features and idioms of their respective languages in mind.

Beyond TDD, additional testing methodologies like Behavior-Driven Development (BDD) focus on the system's behavior from the user's standpoint. Alongside unit tests, end-to-end (E2E) and integration tests help ensure your components work correctly. Tools like Selenium, first released in 2004, have been instrumental in automating browser interactions for E2E tests. Cypress, launched in 2014, offers a more modern, streamlined approach to E2E testing in the JavaScript ecosystem.

BDD takes a different perspective, focusing on the system's behavior from the user's standpoint. Cucumber, released in 2008, is a popular tool in this space. Describing tests in plain language encourages collaboration between developers, QA, and non-technical stakeholders.

71

Performance testing tools like Apache JMeter, LoadRunner, or Gatling ensure your system can handle the expected load and respond quickly. For security testing, tools like OWASP ZAP and Nessus help you identify vulnerabilities in your software.

Remember, no single testing tool or framework will cover all your needs. You'll likely need a combination of them tailored to your specific context. When selecting testing tools, consider their learning curve, how well they integrate with your existing development tools, the robustness of their community, and their ability to grow with your evolving needs.

With the proper testing frameworks and tools in place, developers can confidently make changes, safe in the knowledge that they'll be alerted if they unintentionally break anything—a critical component of a positive Developer Experience. As Robert C. Martin rightly put it, "The act of designing software is one of making many small decisions, and any of them could be a disaster. This is why we need tests."

Debugging and Profiling Tools

Regardless of how diligently we write and test our code, there will always be a time when something doesn't work as expected. This is where debugging tools come into play. As Brian W. Kernighan, a prominent software engineer, once said, "Debugging is twice as hard as writing the code in the first place." Selecting the right debugging and profiling tools can make this complex process significantly more accessible and enhance the developer experience.

Debugging tools allow developers to inspect their running code line by line, observing variables' values and the program flow. These tools' availability and feature sets vary by language and platform, but the fundamental concepts are widely applicable.

IDEs often come with built-in debugging tools. For example, IntelliJ IDEA for Java and PyCharm for Python feature robust debuggers that integrate directly into the development workflow. Visual Studio, a popular

IDE for .NET developers, features a highly sophisticated debugger with advanced features like conditional breakpoints and "Edit and Continue" capability, which allows developers to change code while debugging and continue execution.

Stand-alone debugging tools are available for developers who prefer text editors or command-line interfaces. GDB (GNU Debugger) has been a mainstay for C and C++ developers since its introduction in 1986. Node.js developers often turn to Chrome DevTools or the Node.js debugger, offering comprehensive debugging features.

While debugging tools help us understand why our code doesn't work correctly, profiling tools help us understand why it doesn't work efficiently. Profilers monitor the execution of a program, recording statistics like memory usage and execution time. This information allows developers to identify performance bottlenecks and optimize their code accordingly.

Python's built-in "cProfile" module is an excellent example of a profiler. In the .NET ecosystem, JetBrains' dotTrace and dotMemory offer in-depth profiling for performance and memory usage. Java developers often turn to tools like VisualVM and YourKit.

It's important to mention that profiling should not be an afterthought but a regular part of your development cycle. As a renowned computer scientist, Donald Knuth, stated, "We should forget about small efficiencies, say about 97% of the time: premature optimization is the root of all evil. Yet we should not pass up our opportunities in that critical 3%."

Choosing the right debugging and profiling tools for your project leads to more stable and efficient software, enabling developers to understand their code better. The ability to peek under the hood of your running application, scrutinize every detail, and enhance its performance is crucial for creating delightful and efficient developer environments.

Integrating Tools and Workflows

As a master blacksmith skillfully selects, integrates, and applies his tools to shape a piece of metal, developers must also adeptly select and integrate tools within their workflows to shape a piece of software. This section focuses on the vital practices of integrating tools and streamlining workflows, explicitly diving into Continuous Integration and Continuous Delivery (CI/CD), code review processes, and automated testing and deployment.

The importance of integrating tools and establishing robust workflows cannot be overstated. GitHub co-founder Tom Preston-Werner pointed out in a 2011 interview, "If your company has a development workflow that is thought out and easy to understand, it's going to make developers' lives easier."

Throughout this section, you'll encounter the principles and practices that can significantly affect your software development journey's efficiency, effectiveness, and enjoyment. After all, tools are only as good as the craftspeople using them and the processes they're integrated into. So, let's forge ahead and explore these critical aspects of software development.

Continuous Integration and Continuous Delivery (CI/CD)

In the symphony of software development, the smooth flow of code from a developer's machine to the production environment is paramount. You may ask, "How can we ensure that our code integrates seamlessly with others and is always in a releasable state?" This is where the principles of Continuous Integration (CI) and Continuous Delivery (CD) come into play. Consider them as conductors of our orchestral performance, ensuring that all sections (code) are in harmony and ready for the final performance (production).

Continuous Integration (CI) is a practice that encourages developers to integrate their code into a shared repository frequently, preferably several times a day. Each integration is then automatically built and tested to catch any integration issues or bugs as early as possible. One of the champions of this practice is Martin Fowler, who noted in 2006, "Continuous Integration doesn't get rid of bugs, but it does make them dramatically easier to find and remove."

Many CI tools are available to help implement this practice, including Jenkins, Travis CI, and CircleCI. Let's take Jenkins as an example. Developed in 2011, Jenkins is an open-source automation server enabling developers to build, test, and deploy their applications. Jenkins can be configured to pull code from a version control system, build the code, run tests, and then send feedback to developers.

Continuous Delivery (CD), on the other hand, ensures that the codebase is always in a deployable state, even in the face of multiple developers making changes simultaneously. It extends CI by deploying all code changes to testing and/or production environments after the build stage. As Jez Humble, one of the key advocates of CD, wrote in 2010, "Thus, Continuous Delivery aims to make it practical to work in small, rapid steps and that this is as applicable in operations as it is in development."

Continuous delivery tools automate manual deployment's tedious, error-prone steps, making it faster and more robust. Tools like Spinnaker, Harness, and GoCD help you with automated canary analysis, deployment pipelines, and rollbacks if anything goes wrong. For example, Spinnaker, developed at Netflix and released in 2015, supports multiple cloud platforms and provides high control and visibility into your deployment process.

CI and CD work harmoniously to minimize risks, catch issues early, and make the release process more robust. However, adopting CI/CD is not just about tools; it's a culture change. It's about fostering a culture of shared responsibility, where developers are not just coding but also contributing to testing, integration, and deployment. Executing well leads to more frequent, reliable releases and higher-quality software. It's a melody that, once you hear it, you'll not want your development team to dance to any other tune.

Code Review Processes

Code reviews, also known as peer reviews, are the safety net of your software development process. As Steve McConnell mentioned in his 2004 book *Code Complete*, "Peer reviews catch 60% of the defects." This collaborative process of meticulously dissecting a colleague's code allows bugs, performance issues, and style inconsistencies to be detected and corrected before they make their way into production.

A code review process involves multiple parties: the author of the code and one or more reviewers. While it's common to assume that code reviewers should be managers or senior developers, involving the entire team, including junior developers, can be incredibly beneficial. New developers often ask insightful questions that might be overlooked by more experienced team members, leading to better knowledge exchange and overall code quality. This process not only assures the quality of the code but also encourages knowledge sharing and fosters a collaborative team culture. As stated by Bill Gates in a 1975 memo to Microsoft developers, "One thing we've found at Microsoft is that a few key people can have a tremendous impact because the review mechanism is so effective."

There are several ways to perform code reviews. Some teams prefer meeting in person (or virtually) and going through the code changes together. Others find using code review tools that allow asynchronous reviews more efficient. These tools often integrate directly with your version control systems, making commenting on specific lines or blocks of code easy.

GitHub, launched in 2008, is one such tool that has revolutionized the code review process with Pull Requests (PRs). A Pull Request is a proposal of changes that developers can discuss, review, and even make further changes until the code is deemed ready for merging into the main codebase. Other tools, such as Bitbucket and GitLab, also offer similar features, and specialized tools like Crucible (from Atlassian) provide a more focused environment for in-depth code reviews.

Additionally, code review tools often support automation. For example, you can automate the initial review process using tools like SonarQube and CodeClimate, which can scan code for potential issues—such as security vulnerabilities, code duplication, and complexity—and provide feedback alongside human reviews. This automation allows human reviewers to focus on more complex aspects like code logic, architecture, and design, making the review process more efficient and effective.

When setting up a code review process, it's essential to establish guidelines to keep reviews constructive and respectful. An excellent example of such guidelines is Google's Engineering Practices documentation, which advises reviewers to critique the code, not the coder, and authors to accept criticism graciously and not take it personally.

A structured code review process is vital to improving code quality and collaboration. The right tools can support and streamline the process. However, the value of code reviews lies in the human element— the respectful exchange of ideas and mutual learning. By involving the entire team in this process, you improve the code and foster a culture of continuous learning and collaboration.

Automated Testing and Deployment

Automated testing and deployment, often called "Continuous Testing" and "Continuous Deployment," are crucial components of a modern, efficient development environment. They expedite the development process and minimize the chance of errors during these stages. Microsoft's CEO, Satya Nadella, once said in a 2018 interview, "The way you push agility is by taking friction out of the process."

Let's first delve into automated testing. Simply put, it's the practice of writing code to test your code. The idea is to validate your software's functionality, performance, and security without the time-consuming manual labor. These automated tests range from unit tests (which test individual functions or methods) to integration tests (which test how different parts of the application interact) and end-to-end tests (which test the entire flow of an application from a user's perspective).

Automated testing tools, such as JUnit for Java, PyTest for Python, or Mocha for JavaScript, make creating, running, and maintaining these tests easy. Moreover, coverage tools like Istanbul or Cobertura help ensure that your tests adequately exercise your code. In "Test-Driven Development: By Example" (2002), Kent Beck emphasizes the importance of such testing methodologies, stating, "If you don't write tests for your code, then you don't care if it works."

Now, let's move on to automated deployment. This is shipping your tested code to the production environment without manual intervention. With this approach, you can rapidly react to market changes and continuously deliver value to your users. Tools like Jenkins, CircleCI, and GitHub Actions enable you to set up pipelines for automated build, test, and deployment stages.

These tools listen for specific triggers (like code merges or push events) and execute predefined tasks. So, when a developer merges their feature branch into the main branch, the tool automatically runs tests, builds the software, and, if everything checks out, deploys it to the production environment. Timothy Fitz popularized the concept of continuous deployment in a 2009 blog post, stating, "The biggest benefit of continuous deployment is the reduction of risk in your release process."

However, automated testing and deployment are not without challenges. They require upfront effort to set up and maintain, and improperly configured automation can lead to disastrous consequences. However, the benefits of speed, accuracy, and developer productivity make this investment worthwhile. As you adopt these practices, remember that automation is a tool, not a solution in and of itself. It is part of a more significant philosophy of iterative improvement and developer responsibility that drives the DevOps culture.

Customizing and Extending Tools

This section delves into customizing and extending developer tools to suit your unique workflows and project needs better. After all, one size doesn't fit all, especially in software development. Here, we explore how you can mold and shape your tools with plugins, extensions, and scripting to enhance productivity, improve the developer experience, and promote a more efficient and smooth development process.

Overall, the power of customization and extension of developer tools through plugins, extensions, and scripting cannot be overstated. These practices ensure that your tools align with your workflow, promote productivity, and reduce tedious, manual work, ultimately crafting a delightful and efficient developer environment.

Plugins and Extensions

Moving into this section, our focus shifts to customization, a critical feature that elevates our selected tools from functional to transformative. Specifically, we delve into plugins and extensions, incredibly powerful add-ons that can significantly amplify the capabilities of your developer tools, adapting them to your specific needs and supercharging your productivity.

Remember that your tools should be as unique and tailored as the project you're working on, so don't hesitate to shape them to your vision. In the words of Alan Kay, the computer scientist who pioneered object-oriented programming, "The best way to predict the future is to invent it."

Plugins are add-on software components that provide specific functionality to an existing software application, allowing you to extend its default capabilities. For instance, consider the Visual Studio Code text editor. On its own, it's a powerful tool for writing code. However, the Python plugin morphs into an IDE specifically equipped for Python development, providing syntax highlighting, code suggestions, debugging features, and more.

Extensions, similarly, enhance the functionality of web browsers and some software applications, allowing developers to customize their workspace and automate everyday tasks. For example, Google Chrome has thousands of extensions on its Web Store, each designed to add functionality to the browser, ranging from ad blockers and password managers to web development tools.

When choosing plugins or extensions, ensure they align with your project needs, have a good reputation within the community, and are well-maintained. Consider the example of the Prettier extension for Visual Studio Code. Introduced in 2017, it rapidly gained popularity because it enforces a consistent coding style across teams, a feature cherished in collaborative development projects. Its active maintenance and constant updates have solidified its position as an indispensable extension for many developers.

Remember, plugins and extensions are about adding new features and improving the developer experience. Choose those that make your coding journey smoother and more enjoyable because, as Perl creator Larry Wall said, "Developers should have fun. The joy of coding is the joy of creative effort."

Continuing from our exploration of plugins and extensions, diving deeper into identifying, integrating, and effectively using these tools to enhance productivity is essential.

Identifying Effective Plugins and Extensions

The first step is identifying plugins and extensions that align with your project needs. Consider your day-to-day tasks, the languages you use, the design principles you adhere to, and the collaborative practices of your team.

For instance, if you're a web developer, extensions like "React Developer Tools" or "Redux DevTools" in Chrome could be instrumental in debugging your applications. If you are working in a team using Git, the "GitLens" extension in Visual Studio Code can provide valuable insights into code authorship and changes right in your editor.

Online forums, software communities, and expert blogs can be valuable resources for discovering plugins and extensions recommended by other developers in your field.

Evaluating Quality and Fit

More is needed for a plugin or extension to provide an exciting feature; it must also be reliable, well-maintained, and a good fit for your project. Consider the community's reviews and feedback about the tool. Is it widely used? What do other developers say about it? Is it actively maintained and updated?

Look at the number of downloads and the rating of the plugin or extension as a starting point. However, newer, less popular plugins might still offer valuable functionalities. Always consider the fit for your project and your workflow over popularity.

For example, a plugin like "ESLint" for JavaScript linting might have a smaller user base than "Prettier" but offers highly customizable linting rules. If such customization aligns with your project's requirements, "ESLint"is a better fit for you.

Leveraging Plugins and Extensions

Once you've identified and evaluated a plugin or extension, the next step is to integrate it into your workspace and start leveraging its capabilities. Take the time to learn the features and explore the documentation. Plugins and extensions offer many functionalities, some of which may take time to be apparent.

For instance, the "Debugger for Chrome" extension in Visual Studio Code provides an integrated debugging experience for JavaScript. Initially, you might use it to examine variables through your code. However, as you dig deeper, you'll discover its powerful features, like "conditional breakpoints" or "logpoints," which can significantly boost your debugging efficiency.

Remember that plugins and extensions are about molding your tools to fit your needs. Don't hesitate to explore, experiment, and even swap out plugins as your requirements evolve.

I hope you're beginning to see the transformative power of plugins and extensions. By choosing and utilizing these tools wisely, you can create a development environment that's not only highly productive but also a joy to work in. As you navigate through this world of infinite customization, remember the wise words of computer science pioneer Grace Hopper, "The most dangerous phrase in the language is, 'We've always done it this way.'" Embrace change, stay adaptable, and keep inventing your future.

Scripting and Automation

On our journey to streamline developer tooling, we will focus on a theme vital to increasing efficiency and productivity: scripting and automation. As Marc Andreessen, co-founder of Netscape and a pioneer of the modern Internet, famously said, "Software is eating the world." Nowhere is this truer than in the world of scripting and automation, where software can do tedious, time-consuming tasks on our behalf, freeing us to focus on higher-level problems.

Scripting, at its core, involves writing short, simple programs that automate tasks within a larger software environment. These scripts can be written in many languages, with Python, Bash, and JavaScript being some of the most popular. Think of scripts as our small coding assistants, handling tasks like running tests, building your software, setting up environments, or checking code for stylistic consistency.

A striking example of the power of scripting is the use of "build scripts" in software projects. These scripts can be written in languages like Bash or Python or by using build automation tools like Make, Gradle, or npm scripts, automating the compiling of source code into executable code, running tests, and generating documentation. Automating these tasks ensures that they are done the same way every time, reducing errors and allowing developers to focus on the tasks that truly require their expertise.

Automation, the sibling of scripting, takes this concept and expands it across the entire software development lifecycle. It involves creating systems that can operate and make decisions independently, significantly reducing the amount of manual work involved in the software development process. From automated testing frameworks that ensure your code is bug-free to deployment automation tools that make releasing new software versions a breeze, automation is a game-changer for developer productivity.

Consider, for instance, the rise of automated testing frameworks like Selenium, introduced in 2004. Selenium revolutionized the field of software testing by providing a tool for automating browser actions, effectively simulating user interactions with web applications. It demonstrated that not only could tedious tasks be automated but complex ones as well.

Automation doesn't just stop at testing; it also extends to deployment. For example, Jenkins, introduced in 2011, is a widely adopted tool for automating the entire process of deploying applications, from integrating changes and running tests to deploying the software in various environments. Jenkins integrates well in CI/CD pipelines. Still, newer tools like GitHub Actions, introduced in 2019, and GitLab CI/CD offer more modern, cloud-native solutions that tie directly into your version control system. These tools simplify the automation process by allowing developers to define workflows that automatically trigger builds, tests, and deployments every time changes are made to the codebase.

Scripting and automation also play a vital role in the "shift left" strategy–finding and addressing issues earlier in the software development lifecycle. Automating and integrating tests into the CI/CD pipeline, issues can be caught as soon as code is committed, significantly reducing the time and cost associated with fixing bugs later in the development process. For example, using Git hooks, developers can run scripts that automatically check code style, run unit tests, or even deploy the code to a staging environment every time they push changes to a repository. This immediate feedback look is critical in shifting testing and quality assurance tasks earlier in the development cycle.

While automation can drastically improve efficiency, striking a balance is essential. Over-automation can lead to complex, hard-to-understand systems that obscure more than they aid. Striking the right balance is crucial, and the best automation strategies often come from a deep understanding of the development workflow and its pain points.

As you consider your development processes, look for tasks that are repetitive, time-consuming, or prone to human error. Those are prime candidates for automation. Start small, iterate, and learn as you go. Remember Bill Gates's words: "The first rule of any technology used in a business is that automation applied to an efficient operation will magnify efficiency."

The world of scripting and automation is vast and continuously evolving. Harnessing its power can lead to unprecedented increases in productivity and job satisfaction. By embracing the principles and practices of automation, you're not just improving your developer tooling—you're redefining what's possible.

Cross-Platform Development Considerations

Before diving into platform and architecture choices, staying aligned with our focus on developer tools and workflows is essential. The tools you choose for cross-platform development are as critical as the frameworks or architectures you select for your application. As we enter the realm of cross-platform development considerations, it is essential to remember Steve Jobs' words, "Design is not just what it looks like and feels like. Design is how it works." This quote encapsulates the importance of thoughtful consideration in crafting applications that perform well across different platforms and offer a consistent and user-friendly experience.

When thinking about cross-platform development, consider how your developer tools can streamline the process of writing, testing, and deploying code across multiple environments. Integrated development environments (IDEs) like Visual Studio or JetBrains Rider, for example, offer built-in support for cross-platform frameworks like Xamarin, Flutter, or React Native, enabling you to build and test your application across different platforms from a single codebase. Tools like Docker can also help you create consistent development environments that mimic production across various operating systems, reducing the "it works on my machine" problem.

In our increasingly interconnected world, applications are expected to run smoothly on various devices and operating systems, each with specifications, screen sizes, and user interaction models. Developers are tasked with the challenging but rewarding task of creating apps that can thrive in this diverse environment. Therefore, choosing development tools and frameworks should cater to your target platforms and enhance productivity by simplifying, managing, and deploying cross-platform code.

So, how do we navigate this complex landscape? Start by ensuring that your development environment is set up to support the specific needs of cross-platform development, including emulators, testing frameworks, and version control systems that accommodate multiple platforms.

By integrating these tools into your workflow, you create a robust development process that supports the complexities of cross-platform application development while focusing on efficiency and quality.

Understanding Cross-Platform Development

Cross-platform development involves building software applications that run on multiple computing platforms, such as Windows, macOS, Linux, iOS, Android, and web browsers. This approach can result in significant time and resource savings, as you're essentially crafting a singular codebase that can be deployed across various platforms instead of writing separate codebases for each one.

Cross-platform development originated from the desire to reach a broader audience without reinventing the wheel for each platform. Tim Berners-Lee, the inventor of the World Wide Web, once said, "The power of the Web is in its universality." This statement resonates deeply with the essence of cross-platform development. By adopting this approach, developers can ensure their software is accessible to a more extensive user base, regardless of their device or operating system.

Understanding cross-platform development involves recognizing the commonalities and differences between platforms. Commonalities allow us to write a shared codebase, while platform-specific code must address the differences. For example, while a specific user interface element might be shared across Android and iOS, how it behaves or is displayed might differ. We must handle these differences appropriately to provide a seamless and intuitive user experience.

While the process sounds daunting, the benefits can be substantial. According to a survey by Statista in 2020, the global population of smartphone users was 3.5 billion, with Android and iOS being the leading operating systems. By leveraging cross-platform development, we can reach this diverse and enormous user base with a single codebase, significantly increasing efficiency and lowering development costs.

Moreover, cross-platform development allows for easier maintenance and faster updates. Instead of updating several codebases, you have a singular one to manage, meaning bug fixes, enhancements, and new features can be rolled out more swiftly, improving the overall user experience and developer efficiency.

However, as powerful as cross-platform development can be, it has unique challenges. As we explore this topic further in the subsequent sections, we'll delve into the tools that support cross-platform development, the key considerations you should bear in mind, and what the future might hold for this fascinating field of software development.

Tools for Cross-Platform Development

In the digital landscape, many tools have emerged that support cross-platform development. These tools empower developers to create applications for different platforms with a single codebase, ultimately streamlining the development process and increasing efficiency. In this section, we'll discuss a few of these significant tools, their origins, and their impact on modern cross-platform development.

First and foremost, let's take a look at React Native, introduced by Facebook in 2015. React Native is a JavaScript framework that enables you to build mobile applications using the same code for both Android and iOS. Tom Occhino, the engineering manager for React at Facebook, in his opening keynote at Facebook's React.js conference in 2015, quoted, "With React Native, you can develop at a fraction of the time it takes today with the same quality, performance, and feel of traditional native applications." This revolutionary statement set the stage for what React Native would become—an efficient way for developers to build performance-optimized applications with a native feel. The framework achieves this by translating your JavaScript code into native code for each platform.

This paradigm shift was monumental because it allowed developers to utilize their JavaScript knowledge to build mobile applications, effectively bridging the gap between web and mobile development. Moreover, Facebook's application serves as a testament to the capabilities of React Native, showing that large-scale, performance-critical applications can be built with this framework.

On the desktop front, Electron, introduced by GitHub in 2013, has gained popularity. Electron allows for developing desktop applications using web technologies (JavaScript, HTML, and CSS). Electron has democratized desktop application development by enabling web developers to utilize their existing skills to build desktop applications.

One of the best examples of Electron's success is Visual Studio Code (VS Code). Microsoft launched VS Code in 2015 as an Electron app. By offering a highly extensible, feature-rich, yet lightweight editor, VS Code quickly garnered much attention and has become one of the most popular development environments. Similarly, applications like Slack and Discord have also been built using Electron, demonstrating its efficacy in creating high-quality, cross-platform desktop applications.

Another tool worth mentioning is Xamarin. Launched in 2011, Xamarin is a Microsoft-owned framework for building Android and iOS applications using .NET and C#. Unlike React Native, which uses JavaScript, Xamarin leverages .NET, making it an excellent choice for developers already invested in the Microsoft ecosystem.

Each of these tools—React Native, Electron, Xamarin, and many others—offers unique capabilities and features for cross-platform development. When selecting the right tool for your project, you'll want to consider factors like the required performance, your team's expertise, the community and support around the tool, and the nature of the application you're building.

Keep in mind that these tools are not a one-size-fits-all solution. Each platform has user interface guidelines and expectations, and each tool has strengths and weaknesses. Understanding these nuances will help you decide which tools to use for cross-platform development projects.

As we continue our exploration of cross-platform development, in the next section, we'll delve into the key considerations and challenges you should be aware of as you embark on your cross-platform development journey.

Considerations in Cross-Platform Development

Cross-platform development, with all its promise of code reusability and wider user reach, comes with unique considerations. To successfully employ cross-platform strategies and tools, navigating the challenges and quirks accompanying them is essential.

Design and User Interface (UI) Considerations

A significant consideration in cross-platform development is the design and UI. Platforms have different design languages, UI elements, and user interaction patterns. For example, the Material Design language of Android is distinctly different from the Human Interface Guidelines of iOS. Even within these design languages, various versions of the platforms introduce changes that might affect the look and feel of the application.

Furthermore, certain UI elements may behave differently across all platforms, creating a jarring user experience if not appropriately handled. For example, the tabbed navigation at the bottom of the screen, a typical design in iOS apps, may need to be put in the right place in an Android environment where navigation drawers are more common.

Performance Considerations

Performance can be a concern with cross-platform development, particularly for resource-intensive applications. While cross-platform frameworks have improved dramatically in performance, they may not always match the speed and responsiveness of a native app, especially for complex tasks. Developers should consider these potential performance discrepancies and test their applications on different platforms and devices to ensure satisfactory performance.

Access to Platform-Specific Features

Certain features or capabilities might be unique to a specific platform. For instance, Apple's FaceID biometric system is specific to certain iOS devices. These platform-specific features must be more readily available or require additional work to implement in a cross-platform setting. Developers must consider these platform-specific limitations when planning the app's features and functionality.

Maintenance and Update Cycles

While "write once, run anywhere" is appealing, it's important to remember that different platforms have different update cycles, bug fixes, and deprecations. Ensuring that your cross-platform app remains compatible with these updates can present maintenance challenges.

Moreover, cross-platform development frameworks have update cycles, which may introduce new features or deprecate existing ones. Developers should consider the cost of maintaining their codebase in light of these updates.

Developer Experience

The choice of a cross-platform tool can significantly impact the developer experience. Aspects like documentation quality, community support, ease of debugging, and integration with existing toolchains can influence developer productivity and satisfaction.

Choosing a tool like React Native, with a large community and extensive online resources, might provide a better experience than a less popular tool with limited support.

While cross-platform development has advantages, the considerations are multifaceted and require thoughtful attention. As a developer, you must balance maintaining a consistent user experience across platforms and adhering to platform-specific guidelines and expectations.

By understanding these considerations and incorporating them into your decision-making, you're not just crossing platforms but bridging gaps. You're ensuring that the experience of using your app feels just as natural, efficient, and delightful, whether it's being used on a PC in New York, a smartphone in Tokyo, or a tablet in Paris. And that, my friend, is truly the art of creating delightful and efficient developer environments.

The Future of Cross-Platform Development

As we peer into the future of cross-platform development, there's a palpable sense of excitement, for we stand on the precipice of immense technological advancements. The rise of web technologies and ever-increasing hardware performance paints a promising picture for the future.

One emerging technology that has generated significant buzz in recent years is WebAssembly, which was introduced in 2015. WebAssembly—or wasm for short—is a binary instruction format for a stack-based virtual machine. This might sound a bit technical, but at a high level, it means that WebAssembly is a new way of running code in your web browser that's fast, efficient, and secure.

The magic of WebAssembly is its ability to run high-performance applications across multiple platforms right in the browser. It's like the cross-platform promise but taken to the next level because it's not just about operating systems anymore—it's about the web as a platform in and of itself.

In a blog post introducing WebAssembly, Mozilla wrote, "WebAssembly is designed to be a low-level virtual machine that runs code at near-native speed by taking advantage of common hardware capabilities available on a wide range of platforms." This means WebAssembly has the potential to open up new avenues for powerful applications that were previously out of reach for cross-platform development.

Another exciting direction in the future of cross-platform development is the evolution and refinement of the existing tools we discussed earlier, like React Native and Electron. The communities behind these tools are continually pushing the boundaries of what's possible, optimizing performance, expanding the APIs available, and enhancing developer ergonomics.

Let's take React Native as an example. The team behind React Native announced a significant re-architecture of the framework in 2018, codenamed Fabric. Fabric aims to improve the performance of React Native applications, make the framework more flexible, and improve the developer experience. With updates like these, React Native and similar tools continue to evolve, ensuring they remain relevant and robust options for cross-platform development.

Furthermore, new technologies are on the horizon that could disrupt the cross-platform development space. For instance, Google's Flutter framework for building natively compiled mobile, web, and desktop applications from a single codebase is gaining significant attention. Launched in 2017, Flutter promises high-quality native experiences and is worth watching as it matures.

The future of cross-platform development is bright and full of potential. With emerging technologies like WebAssembly, the continuous evolution of existing tools, and the advent of new frameworks, developers will have a rich set of options for crafting delightful and efficient cross-platform applications.

It's an exciting time to be a developer, indeed. As we navigate this journey together, remember that the end goal is not just about choosing the right tools or adhering to best practices—crafting truly delightful experiences for the end user, regardless of the platform they use. With this user-centric mindset, you'll be well-equipped to make the most of the opportunities that cross-platform development presents today and in the future.

While cross-platform development presents unique challenges and considerations, it offers a powerful way to reach a broader audience without maintaining multiple codebases. As we delve into this intricate topic, remember the importance of "designing how it works," you'll be well on your way to crafting truly delightful and efficient cross-platform applications.

Key Takeaways

- Selecting the right tools for a project is paramount to the overall success and efficiency of the development process.

- Integrated Development Environments (IDEs), version control systems, build tools, and testing frameworks are fundamental tools in a developer's toolkit.

- The importance of robust debugging and profiling tools cannot be overstated.

- Continuous Integration and Continuous Delivery (CI/CD), code review processes, automated testing, and deployment are powerful techniques for enhancing productivity and reducing errors.

- Customizing and extending tools through plugins, extensions, and scripting can significantly improve their utility and efficacy.

- Cross-platform development considerations are essential in today's diverse technological environment, and developing with these in mind increases the reach and relevance of our software.

As we close this chapter, let us carry these insights forward. After all, tooling is not merely about efficiency or productivity; it's also about crafting a developer experience that is truly delightful and fulfilling.

CHAPTER 5

Designing Developer-Centric APIs

In this chapter, we navigate the world of API design with a clear focus on the developer experience. As you'll discover, an API is more than a mere interface between software components. It's a journey of communication, a bridge that connects your organization's services to the ecosystem of developers who rely on them to build special applications.

We will first unravel the core principles that underpin effective API design. Following this foundation, we'll venture into the simple, practical patterns and practices that bring these principles to life. We'll then shed light on different API versioning and deprecation techniques and discuss their implications.

What good is a well-designed API if its users need help understanding its use? We address this through a comprehensive discussion on API documentation and discovery. By the end of this chapter, you'll have a well-rounded understanding of designing developer-centric APIs, offering developers a delightful and efficient environment.

Our goal is not to create an exhaustive list of rules but to guide you in shaping your approach, which is sensitive to your context, informed by best practices, and directed toward building APIs that developers love to use.

© K. Rain Leander 2025
K. R. Leander, *Developer Experience Unleashed*,
https://doi.org/10.1007/979-8-8688-0242-3_5

API Design Principles

Welcome to the fascinating and crucial world of API design principles. The intricate network of applications and services we interact with daily relies heavily on the cooperation facilitated by APIs, and as we've been discussing throughout this book, crafting an effective API is an art akin to architecture or sculpting. It's about shaping an environment that makes developers' lives easier, their work more efficient, and their outcomes more reliable. This section delves into five vital principles that, like pillars, uphold this architectural marvel: Consistency, Flexibility, Affordance, Efficiency, and Security.

By understanding and applying these five principles, we build functional and delightful APIs with which to work. An excellent developer-centric API isn't merely a tool; it's a companion that developers can rely on as they craft their digital masterpieces. Now, let's embark on this journey, pillar by pillar, to unveil the art of crafting such APIs.

Consistency

As we delve into the foundational principles of API design, we begin with an essential attribute at the heart of any well-crafted API—consistency. API design consistency is critical in ensuring a seamless developer experience. If an API behaves consistently, developers can make educated guesses about how other parts of the API will function, even without referring to the documentation. This accelerates their understanding and facilitates rapid, practical usage of the API. To quote the renowned computer scientist and software engineer Martin Fowler: "Any fool can write code that a computer can understand. Good programmers write code that humans can understand."

Consistency in API design spans several dimensions, including naming conventions, request and response structures, error handling, and more. Let's examine each in more detail.

Naming Conventions: Consistent naming conventions across all API endpoints make the API intuitive and easy to use. This includes using clear, descriptive names for endpoints and consistent verb-noun usage. For example, a RESTful API should consistently use the HTTP verbs (GET, POST, PUT, DELETE) across its endpoints—GET for retrieval, POST for creation, PUT for updating, and DELETE for removal.

Beyond verbs, it's crucial to maintain consistency in naming paths and parameters. Paths should be clear and hierarchical and reflect the structure of the resources they represent. For example, if your API manages users and their posts, a consistent path might look like "/users/{userId}/posts/{postId}." This makes the API predictable and aids in its discoverability and usability.

Parameters in name and location (e.g., query parameters, path parameters) should follow a consistent pattern throughout the API. For example, if you use "userId" as a path parameter in one endpoint, use the same parameter name across all endpoints referencing a user ID. Similarly, decide early on whether to place specific parameters in the query string or the path and stick to that decision consistently. This minimizes confusion and ensures developers can easily navigate and understand the API.

Request and Response Structures: The way an API accepts requests and returns responses should be consistent across all endpoints. For instance, if an API endpoint uses JSON in the request body, all endpoints should follow the same pattern. This consistency is essential for request types that usually have body data, such as PUT or PATCH. Ensuring these methods consistently accept JSON in the request body makes the API more predictable and easier to work with. Similarly, the structure of the API's responses should be consistent—whether it's the way data is nested or how metadata is included.

Error Handling: Consistency in error handling is crucial for diagnosing and rectifying issues. Error responses should have a consistent structure and provide meaningful messages. Furthermore, HTTP status codes (or equivalent mechanisms in non-RESTful APIs) should be compatible and adhere to established conventions. For instance, 404 for not found resources, 401 for unauthorized access, 500 for server errors, etc.

To ensure a standardized approach to error handling, consider adopting an existing standard such as RFC 9457, which provides guidelines on structuring error responses in APIs. Adopting such a standard helps ensure that error mistakes are consistent and follow widely recognized practices, making them easier for developers to understand and troubleshoot.

Pagination and Sorting: If your API provides a way to paginate or sort results, these mechanisms should be consistent across all endpoints. Consider also implementing standard practices for handling related data, such as links or nested data structures, following conventions like Hypertext Application Language (HAL). This approach not only standardizes pagination and sorting but also enhances the API's ability to represent relationships between resources in a consistent and discoverable manner.

A great example of consistent API design is the Stripe API. Introduced in 2011, Stripe set a new standard for API consistency and has been a model of good API design. From consistent use of HTTP verbs and unified error handling to predictable resource URIs, Stripe has provided developers with a highly compatible API that's easy to understand and use.

As you design your APIs, strive for consistency. Consistency facilitates developer learning, fosters confidence, and speeds up integration. It's about establishing and sticking to rules, even when exceptions seem appealing. But remember, abnormalities in API design can lead to exceptional difficulties in usage. As with any authority, there might be valid exceptions, but they should be thought through carefully and justified clearly.

In the following sections, we'll explore other principles that go hand-in-hand with consistency to create easy-to-use, robust, secure, and efficient APIs. As you read, remember that these principles are interconnected and often work best when considered as a whole rather than individually. After all, the goal is to create a pleasant developer experience that feels like a well-orchestrated symphony rather than a collection of disjointed notes.

Flexibility

As we continue our journey through API design principles, let's explore the concept of flexibility. In the world of APIs, flexibility isn't just a buzzword—it's a crucial principle that has substantial implications for the adaptability and longevity of your API.

Flexibility in an API is its ability to accommodate a wide range of use cases, meet various client needs, and evolve gracefully as those needs change over time. As Tim Berners-Lee, the inventor of the World Wide Web, aptly put it, "The goal of the Web is to serve humanity, and we build it now so that those who come to it later will be able to create things that we cannot imagine."

Here are some key aspects to consider when designing a flexible API:

> **Multiple Data Formats**: Offering numerous data formats, such as XML and JSON, can help accommodate clients' needs and preferences. Though JSON has become the de facto standard for most web APIs, some use cases might still benefit from XML or other formats.

> **Parameterization**: Allowing clients to specify what data they need via parameters increases an API's flexibility. This can include filtering, sorting, or defining the fields they want to receive in the response.

Versioning: APIs evolve. Ensuring your API can support multiple versions will help it adapt to changes while not breaking existing client integrations. Versioning is commonly implemented through URLs or request headers, which are widely accepted practices. While it's possible to include versioning in the request body, this approach is generally not recommended as it can lead to confusion and is less straightforward for clients to implement. Sticking to URL-based or header-based versioning ensures a more consistent and reliable method for managing API versions.

Extensibility: Designing your API with extensibility allows new features or data to be added without breaking existing functionality. For example, you can achieve this by supporting optional fields or allowing the aliasing of parameters, which lets the API grow and evolve while maintaining backward compatibility. Additionally, adopting flexible data structures, such as those that can handle unexpected fields without errors, helps ensure that your API can accommodate future changes seamlessly.

One notable example of flexibility in API design is the GraphQL specification, introduced by Facebook in 2015. GraphQL's design lets clients specify precisely what data they need, reducing over-fetching and under-fetching problems inherent in many RESTful APIs. For instance, a client application displaying a user's profile might only request the user's name and profile picture rather than fetching all user-related data, thereby improving efficiency. Additionally, GraphQL allows for more complex queries where a client can request related data across multiple resources in a single request. This makes it highly adaptable for applications needing specific, tailored data, such as an e-commerce site that needs to display a product with its associated reviews, prices, and availability in a single API call.

Another example is the Twitter API. Early versions of the Twitter API provided a one-size-fits-all solution, which led to a lot of wasted data transfer for applications that only needed specific parts of the data. For instance, an app that simply wanted to display a user's tweet count had to fetch the entire user object, including unnecessary data like profile images and follower lists. Twitter introduced API versioning and a more flexible data access model as it evolved, significantly improving the developer experience. Now, developers can request only the specific data they need, such as the tweet count or recent tweets, reducing bandwidth usage and improving application performance.

However, it's important to remember that flexibility is not about building an API that does everything imaginable. It's about creating an API that provides just enough flexibility to meet various use cases without making it overly complex. Flexibility should be carefully balanced with simplicity to avoid the "paradox of choice," where too many options can lead to decision paralysis for the developer.

As we explore the other principles in API design, remember that these principles are not independent silos. They're interconnected. A truly developer-centric API marries consistency with flexibility, finds harmony between efficiency and affordance, and ensures security at every step. When done right, these principles can converge to create an API that is a joy to use and powers endless possibilities for the developers interacting with it.

Affordance

As we delve deeper into the principles of API design, let's explore "affordance," a concept that carries significant weight in creating intuitive and developer-friendly APIs.

The term "affordance" originated in perceptual psychology and was popularized in the context of design by Donald Norman in his book, *The Design of Everyday Things.* In simple terms, an affordance is a quality of an object or an environment that allows an individual to act. In the context of APIs, affordance pertains to the capability of the API to suggest its functionalities and how to interact with it.

An API with strong affordance makes its functionalities self-evident and intuitive to understand. Developers can perceive its structure, capabilities, and the actions they can perform with it, reducing the cognitive load and making it easier for them to build upon it. Here are some key ways to enhance the affordance of your API:

> **Descriptive Endpoints**: API endpoints should intuitively describe the resources they represent and the actions they can perform. RESTful APIs are prime examples, relying on standard HTTP methods like GET, POST, PUT, and DELETE. For instance, a "GET /users/{id}" endpoint immediately suggests that it fetches the user with the provided ID.
>
> **Hypermedia Controls**: Hypermedia controls (HATEOAS) can make your API's affordances explicit by providing information on what a client can do next directly within the responses. This is like the web, where we navigate through URLs embedded in the pages. For example, in an API that manages online orders, a response for an order might include links to related actions, such as

"cancel," "update," or "track shipment." Suppose a
client requests the details of an order. In that case,
the response might include the order details and
a link to cancel the order if it's still in progress or
a link to track it if it has been shipped. This allows
clients to discover available actions dynamically and
reduces the need for hard-coded logic in the client
application.

Consistent Error Responses: Providing meaningful
error messages with appropriate HTTP status codes
can guide developers on what went wrong and how
to fix it, thus enhancing your API's usability.

Well-structured Documentation: Good API
documentation shouldn't just list endpoints; it
should include examples, explain error responses,
and guide developers through typical workflows.
All modern APIs should publish an OpenAPI
description, which serves as both a machine-
readable definition of the API and a foundation for
generating human-readable documentation. Tools
like Swagger UI and Postman make it easy to provide
interactive documentation that lets developers
experiment with your API.

Consider GitHub's REST API as an excellent example of affordance in
practice. Each API endpoint in GitHub corresponds directly to a particular
functionality available on their web interface. Want to fetch a user's
repositories? The endpoint is "GET /users/{username}/repos." Want to
create a new warehouse? The endpoint is "POST /user/repos." It's intuitive
and maps clearly to a user's actions on the website.

However, remember that while affordance aims at making APIs more intuitive, it should not be an excuse for skipping comprehensive documentation. Even the most well-designed API can leave developers scratching their heads without clear, concise documentation.

Designing your API with affordance in mind is a crucial step toward making it developer-centric. It's all about empathy and understanding the developer's mindset. When developers can intuitively understand and interact with your API, you provide them with a tool and a satisfying and productive experience. As we progress toward discussing the principles of efficiency and security, remember that these principles work together, creating a harmonious balance that results in a joy-to-use API.

Efficiency

As we navigate the principles of API design, let's explore the concept of "efficiency." Efficiency in the context of API design is all about how swiftly and effectively your API can fulfill requests, providing the necessary data in a compact and easily understandable format.

Efficiency has two broad aspects in API design: processing efficiency and communication efficiency.

Processing Efficiency pertains to the speed and computational resources required for your API to handle requests. Efficient APIs ensure they utilize resources optimally and respond to requests as quickly as possible. It's not just about the speed of individual requests but also how well your API can handle multiple concurrent requests without significant performance degradation.

On the server side, processing efficiency can be achieved through several strategies, including effective caching, database indexing, asynchronous processing, and load balancing. For instance, Reddit's API uses a combination of these techniques to handle the vast number of requests it receives every day.

On the other hand, communication efficiency involves minimizing the amount of data transmitted over the network and optimizing the structure of that data to be easily consumed by the client. For example, a client may not always need every piece of data about a resource, so providing a way to specify exactly what they need can significantly improve communication efficiency.

The advent of GraphQL in 2015 brought this concept to the forefront. With GraphQL, the client specifies precisely what data it needs, which prevents over-fetching or under-fetching of data. This can significantly reduce the amount of data sent over the network, making the API more efficient, especially in mobile or low-bandwidth environments.

Efficiency should also be considered when designing the API's structure and conventions. Using standard HTTP methods and status codes in RESTful APIs, for example, contributes to efficiency as they are universally understood and easily interpreted by various HTTP clients. An API that adheres to established conventions is more accessible for developers to understand and more likely to interact efficiently with existing tools and libraries.

Remember, however, that efficiency does not exist in a vacuum. As you strive for a more efficient API, remember the other principles we've discussed: consistency, flexibility, and affordance. FOR INSTANCE, an API that returns responses quickly but is hard to understand could cause more headaches than it solves.

An efficient API is like a well-oiled machine—it does its job quickly, doesn't waste resources, and provides just what the user needs without any unnecessary baggage. And, it's a joy to use, helping to give the developers the excellent experience they deserve. With this understanding of efficiency, we're now equipped to delve into our final principle: security, a critical aspect of any API design.

Security

In our final exploration of the API design principles, we venture into a critical territory that holds the fort of trust and reliability—Security. Tim Berners-Lee, the father of the World Wide Web, stated, "The world of data is like an open book; in this world of open data, data security is the 'book cover' that keeps it intact." Protecting data transmitted through APIs, whether personal information or proprietary business data, is paramount.

In the context of API design, security involves measures taken to protect your API from threats like unauthorized access, data breaches, denial-of-service (DoS) attacks, and injection attacks.

One foundational aspect of API security is Authentication and Authorization. These processes verify who makes the request (authentication) and what they can access (authorization). APIs often use API keys, OAuth, or JSON Web Tokens (JWT) to ensure that only authorized clients can access them. For example, API keys are simple to implement and are often used for server-to-server communication or when access control is relatively straightforward. OAuth 2.0, on the other hand, is more suitable for scenarios where users need to grant third-party applications limited access to their resources without sharing credentials, such as in social media integrations. JWTs are typically used when you need stateless authentication, as they allow the server to authenticate requests without maintaining session state.

It's important to clarify that OAuth 2.0 is a standard rather than a protocol. While token-based, passwords are sometimes used within its framework, though the emphasis is on token exchanges rather than direct password sharing.

Data Encryption is another vital facet of API security. Ensuring data transmitted to and from your API is encrypted—unreadable to anyone without the correct decryption key—is crucial in maintaining data integrity and confidentiality. An example is the widespread adoption of SSL/TLS for securing data transmission. In addition to protecting data in motion, it's equally important to ensure data at rest is encrypted to safeguard against unauthorized access should the storage be compromised.

The emergence of OpenAPI Specification (OAS) has also contributed to enhancing the overall API experience, including security. By providing a clear, language-agnostic way to describe APIs, including their security schemes, OAS allows developers to generate accurate client code automatically. This ensures that security requirements are consistently implemented across different clients.

Rate Limiting is a practical measure for preventing DoS attacks, where an attacker overloads an API with many requests in a short time. Typically implemented in API gateways or middleware, rate limiting controls the number of requests a client can make within a specific time frame, helping to ensure fair usage and maintain service quality. Twitter's APIs, for instance, use rate limiting for this very reason.

Securing an API also involves safeguarding against injection attacks. Techniques like parameterized queries or prepared statements when interacting with a database can help protect against SQL injection attacks.

Security is not a one-time event but a constant process. It requires regular audits, updates, and a commitment to best practices. APIs are gatekeepers of valuable data, and any vulnerability can have consequences. Developers should feel confident about their data and users' data being safe.

As we explore API design patterns and best practices, let's keep consistency, flexibility, affordance, efficiency, and security principles at the forefront. They are the guardrails that keep our API design on track to creating a delightful developer experience.

API Design Patterns and Best Practices

As we move beyond API design principles, we delve into the world of API design patterns and best practices. We will journey through three popular and divergent API design paradigms that continue to shape how developers design and interact with APIs: RESTful APIs, GraphQL APIs, and gRPC APIs. Each of these paradigms carries unique characteristics and strengths that help them align with the principles we've discussed earlier.

Understanding these design patterns will give you an essential toolkit for designing your APIs. As we step into these API paradigms, consider the principles we discussed: consistency, flexibility, affordance, efficiency, and security. These principles will help guide you through the strengths and weaknesses of each design pattern and enable you to choose the best approach for your specific context.

RESTful APIs

REST, or REpresentational State Transfer, is a style of architecture for designing networked applications. The term was coined by Roy Fielding in his doctoral dissertation in 2000, and since then, it has become a general pattern for creating web APIs.

RESTful APIs, APIs that adhere to the principles of REST, have several key characteristics that align beautifully with our established design principles. Let's walk through them using examples from some of the most popular RESTful APIs today.

Resource Orientation

The cornerstone of a RESTful API is its focus on resources. Each resource is identifiable via a unique Uniform Resource Identifier (URI), typically a URL in the case of web APIs. For instance, the Twitter API has a resource URI for fetching a single user's details: "`https://api.twitter.com/2/users/{id}`." In this URI, "{id}" is replaced by the user's unique identifier. This consistent and intuitive structure makes the API easy to navigate.

Standard HTTP Methods

RESTful APIs leverage standard HTTP methods (or verbs) to denote actions on the resources, showcasing the principle of affordance. GET retrieves a resource, POST creates a resource, PUT updates a resource, and DELETE removes a resource. This pattern is widely used; for instance, the GitHub API uses these methods to manage repository resources.

Statelessness

Statelessness means that each API request must contain all the information necessary to process the request. The server does not store anything about the client's latest HTTP request. Each request from the client to the server must contain all the information needed to understand and respond to the request. This aligns with our principle of efficiency, as it simplifies the server design, makes the API calls independent, and allows responses to be cached, reducing processing and retrieval time.

Hypermedia As The Engine Of Application State (HATEOAS)

RESTful APIs often implement HATEOAS, a design principle that makes an API self-descriptive. Responses from the API include not only the requested data but also hyperlinks to related resources and valid actions. For instance, an API for a blogging platform might return a blog post along with links to the post's author and comments. This aligns with our principles of affordance and consistency, guiding the developer through the API.

Client-Server Architecture

The client-server architecture, an essential trait of REST, separates concerns between the server (data storage and processing) and client (user interface and user experience), aligning with our flexibility and efficiency principles.

Use of HTTP Status Codes

RESTful APIs take advantage of standardized HTTP status codes to indicate the success or failure of a request, such as 200 for victory, 404 for not found, and 500 for server errors. This practice improves consistency and helps developers understand and handle API responses effectively.

Let's take GitHub's API as a concrete example. Say you wish to fetch a specific repository. A GET request to "`https://api.github.com/repos/{owner}/{repo}`" will return detailed information about the storage, including its owner, creation date, last update date, number of forks, and so forth. A 200 status code indicates a successful operation, and the response includes links to related resources like branches and contributors.

RESTful APIs, with their resource-oriented design, use of standard HTTP methods, statelessness, implementation of HATEOAS, and use of HTTP status codes, offer a design pattern that is intuitive, flexible, and efficient. By adhering to widely accepted conventions, they reduce the cognitive load on developers, making it easier for them to integrate with the API successfully.

GraphQL APIs

As we continue exploring API design patterns, looking at a relatively newer but immensely influential design pattern, GraphQL APIs, is crucial. First released by Facebook in 2015, GraphQL is an open-source data query and manipulation language for APIs and a runtime for executing those queries with existing data.

GraphQL addresses many of the limitations of RESTful APIs, providing an enhanced developer experience and aligning closely with our API design principles. Let's explore its features in detail.

Single EndPoint and Query Flexibility

In contrast to REST, where you usually have multiple endpoints for different resources, GraphQL APIs typically expose a single endpoint. This endpoint responds to complex queries that express precisely what data the client wants. Clients dictate the shape and contents of the responses, thereby reducing over-fetching and under-fetching problems common in RESTful APIs. This aligns well with our principle of efficiency.

Consider a blogging platform with a GraphQL API. Instead of making multiple requests to fetch author information, blog posts, and comments, you can accomplish this in a single request by crafting a query that specifies these requirements.

However, this flexibility comes with trade-offs. The dynamic nature of queries can lead to more complex query construction and require additional tools for effective query management and optimization.

Moreover, at scale, the performance of GraphQL queries can become challenging to manage, especially with deeply nested data structures or large datasets. Developers must carefully design schemas and be mindful of the potential for increased server load.

Type System

GraphQL APIs are strongly typed. This means every piece of data and every field has a specific type, and all the interactions are checked against this type of system. The GraphQL-type system supports scalars, enums, custom scalars, and even interfaces and unions, providing a wide range of flexibility. This feature enhances consistency and ensures that the APIs are used correctly, as the type system helps to avoid incorrect operations.

Introspection

GraphQL's introspection system allows clients to query the schema for details about what queries, types, fields, and directives it supports. This powerful feature provides a way for tools to explore the schema, opening up possibilities for auto-generation of API documentation, dynamic type checking in clients, and more. This contributes to the principle of affordance, offering developers a way to discover how to interact with the API.

Real-time Data with Subscriptions

GraphQL offers subscriptions, providing a way to push data from the server to the clients in real time. Whenever the data underlying the subscription changes, the server tries the updated response to the client, offering an efficient way of handling real-time requirements. This is a feature that traditional REST APIs do not inherently support and aligns well with the principles of flexibility and efficiency.

Let's consider an example from GitHub's GraphQL API. Suppose you want to fetch a repository's name, description, the first three issues, and title. With GraphQL, you could formulate a single query to obtain all this data:

```
```
query {
    repository(owner:"octocat", name:"Hello-World") {
        issues(last:20, states:CLOSED) {
            edges {
                node {
                    title
                    url
                    labels(first:5) {
                        edges {
                            node {
                                name
                            }
                        }
                    }
                }
            }
        }
    }
}
```
```

This request would return precisely the data you requested in a single
round trip.

GraphQL APIs, with their single endpoint, flexible query language,
robust type system, introspection feature, and real-time data support,
provide a flexible, efficient, and consistent API design pattern. However,
it's essential to recognize the trade-offs, such as the need for additional
tooling and the potential for performance issues at scale, depending on the
complexity of the queries and data structures. By empowering developers
to request specific data they need, GraphQL APIs improve efficiency and
speed up development. It's no wonder that GraphQL has been quickly
adopted by many organizations and developers worldwide.

gRPC APIs

As we journey through API design patterns, our next stop is Google Remote Procedure Call (gRPC). While Remote Procedure Call (RPC) is a concept that predates REST, gRPC, released by Google in 2015, is a modern, high-performance, open-source framework designed to make communicating easier for applications. It's designed to handle the demanding nature of cloud computing and microservices. This communication framework has proven valuable, offering features that cater to our API design principles' efficiency, consistency, security, and flexibility.

Protobuf and Strong Typing

gRPC leverages Protocol Buffers (protobuf), a powerful binary serialization toolset and language developed by Google. With protobuf, you define the data structures and service interfaces in a strongly typed schema definition language (.proto files). This ensures consistency by providing a contract that the server and client follow. It aligns with the principle of character, enabling seamless interaction between the client and server and reducing the possibility of misunderstanding or miscommunication.

Multiple Language Support

gRPC has extensive language support, providing libraries for the most widely used programming languages. This language diversity offers excellent flexibility for developers to implement the client or server side of the gRPC API in a language they're most comfortable with.

Efficiency and Performance

The combination of HTTP/2 and protobuf makes gRPC very efficient on the wire and fast in terms of serialization and deserialization. HTTP/2, the network protocol gRPC uses, supports multiplexed requests over a single TCP connection, significantly increasing the overall efficiency and speed of network calls. gRPC is designed to handle heavy-load scenarios and provide low-latency communication, making it an optimal choice for microservices architecture and aligning it with the principle of efficiency.

Streaming and Real-time Communication

Unlike REST and GraphQL, gRPC naturally supports streaming data in both directions. This allows the server to send multiple chunks of data as a response or the client to send various pieces of data as a part of a single request, or even "bi-directional streaming," where both sides send a sequence of messages to the other. This makes gRPC a perfect fit for real-time data processing systems and any use case that requires live updates, thereby aligning it with the principles of flexibility and efficiency.

Security and Extensibility

Like other modern API styles, gRPC supports essential security features such as SSL/TLS for secure communication and token-based authentication. Moreover, while gRPC interceptors enable developers to plug in custom logic like authentication, logging, and monitoring into the request-response lifecycle, it's important to note that similar middleware or extension mechanisms are also available for REST and GraphQL APIs. These tools allow developers to maintain security and manage cross-cutting concerns across API implementations.

Consider a scenario where you're using gRPC to build a microservices architecture for an e-commerce platform. You could define a "ProductService" with a "GetProduct" method in the .proto file like so:

```
```
syntax = "proto3";
package dev.techdozo.product.api;
message GetProductRequest {
    string productId = 1;
}
message Get ProductResponse {
    string name = 1;
    string description = 2;
    double price = 3;
}
```
```

```
service ProductService {
    rpc getProduct(GetProductRequest) returns
    (GetProductResponse);
}
```

gRPC then generates client and server code from this protobuf definition, which you can use to implement your service and invoke it from the client side.

gRPC is a robust, efficient, and versatile communication protocol. With its strong type checking, high performance, support for streaming data, and security features, gRPC offers a compelling choice for API design, especially for large-scale, high-performance applications and microservices architectures.

API Versioning and Deprecation Strategies

After understanding the core design principles and the patterns behind successful APIs, we're ready to tackle a particularly tricky and crucial part of the API landscape: versioning and deprecation strategies. The delicate balance of maintaining a vibrant and evolving API while minimizing disruption to the clients who depend on it is one of the most challenging aspects of API design.

An API is more than a simple contract between a server and a client—it's a bridge that connects your organization's services and the developers who use them to build beautiful applications. As your services grow and mature, your APIs need to change to accommodate new features or improved ways of accessing data. However, change can be disruptive, and if not managed correctly, it can turn an API from a bridge into a barrier.

The journey through API versioning and deprecation is often overlooked until it's too late. But remember, an API is a bridge, not a barrier. With thoughtful versioning and deprecation strategies, we can ensure the bridge is always open, providing a delightful and efficient developer experience.

API Versioning

APIs are like living organisms. They grow, they evolve, and with time, certain parts of them may need to be changed or replaced. In the context of APIs, this phenomenon often manifests as changes in data structures, request parameters, and the behavior of endpoints. While usually aimed at improving the API, this evolution can also disrupt the existing ecosystem of clients and consumers. This is where API versioning comes in as a strategy for managing change while minimizing disruption.

Versioning is defining and maintaining multiple "versions" of your API that exist concurrently. It's like taking snapshots of your API at different stages of its lifecycle, allowing developers to choose which "snapshot" they interact with. The goal is simple: to ensure that when changes are introduced, existing clients can continue to use the API as they're accustomed to, while new clients can utilize the improved functionality.

But how exactly does one go about implementing API versioning? Several strategies have been adopted across the industry, each with unique benefits and trade-offs.

Firstly, we have URI versioning, where the version number is included directly in the URL of the API endpoint. For example, "`https://api.example.com/v1/users`" points to version 1 of the user's resource. The simplicity and explicitness of this approach are its main strengths. Anyone who looks at the URL will immediately know the version they're interacting with. However, this method has a notable drawback: it goes against the principle of URL stability, which states that a specific URL should always point to the same resource. URI versioning is beneficial when the API is used by multiple independent clients, where clarity and immediate understanding of the version being accessed are critical.

Next, we have media-type versioning, where the version number is embedded within the HTTP header. In this case, the version isn't part of the URL but is included in the HTTP request's "Accept" or "Content-Type" header. This method has the benefit of preserving URL stability, but the versioning could be more precise at first glance. This approach is often favored when you need to maintain a clean and stable URL structure, especially in APIs heavily used by third-party developers or where the URL structure is a vital part of the user experience. GitHub provides a practical example of this strategy, maintaining the duplicate base URLs while allowing developers to specify the version they wish to interact with via the headers.

Lastly, there's the approach of parameter versioning. Here, the version number is passed as a query parameter in the URL, such as "`https://api.example.com/users?version=1.`" This method allows for URL stability and offers a certain level of explicitness, but it can lead to confusion if not documented and communicated correctly. Parameter versioning might be suitable for APIs where backward compatibility is less of a concern or clients are expected to be familiar with the API's structure and versioning strategy.

When deciding on a versioning strategy, consider factors such as who controls the clients using your API and the technical expertise of those users. For instance, if you control both the API and the clients, you might opt for a versioning strategy that minimizes disruption but requires more careful handling, like media-type versioning. On the other hand, if developers of varying skill levels publicly consume your API, URI versioning might be the best choice for its simplicity and transparency.

While discussing these strategies, it's important to remember that each has its place and purpose. The choice between URI versioning, media type versioning, or parameter versioning doesn't have a universal "right" or "wrong." Instead, it's about understanding the needs of your API, its users, and your organization.

Versioning can sometimes be a necessary evil, a complex challenge one must navigate. But viewed from another angle, it is a testament to the ever-evolving, living nature of APIs—a necessary consequence of innovation and improvement. Like all parts of an API's design, versioning should be approached with the user in mind to make their experience as smooth and delightful as possible.

API Deprecation

Having traversed the terrain of API versioning, we now arrive at the next waypoint: API deprecation. Much like versioning, deprecation is an unavoidable part of the lifecycle of an API. It arises when an API, or a feature within an API, is marked for future removal and is discouraged from further use. While it might seem like a predominantly technical concern, deprecation is as much about communication as technology.

Understanding deprecation begins with acknowledging that your API is an evolving entity. As it grows and changes, some aspects will inevitably become obsolete or be replaced by more efficient, secure, or robust alternatives. While these changes are generally for the better, they pose a challenge: how do you ensure that your users—developers—are aware of, prepared for, and able to adapt to these changes?

This is where a well-executed deprecation strategy comes into play. It focuses on three main elements: clear communication, comprehensive documentation, and assistance in transitioning.

Firstly, clear and early communication is critical. Developers do not appreciate abrupt API changes, and you wouldn't enjoy a surprise party thrown at your workplace. When you decide to deprecate a feature or a version of your API, notify your users as soon as feasible. The method of communication might vary from email newsletters, in-product notifications, developer forums, or all of the above—the goal is to ensure that your users are informed well in advance.

In 2015, LinkedIn provided an excellent example of this. They announced the deprecation of their API v1 and the transition to v2 with a 60-day notice. This gave their users ample time to adapt their applications to the upcoming changes.

Secondly, equip your users with the necessary knowledge to adapt to the changes. Detailed documentation is crucial here, outlining the differences, why they are being made, and how they will affect the API's functionality. This ensures that your users are aware of the change and understand it.

Finally, offer guidance for the transition. Don't just tell your users what will change; show them how to adapt. Provide code samples, migration guides, and other resources that ease the transition. This is not just about minimizing disruption—it's about showing your users that you care about their experience.

Another vital tool to consider in your deprecation strategy is sunset headers. These headers are included in API responses and notify the users of the date after which a particular API or feature will no longer be supported. This can constantly remind your users about the upcoming deprecation and encourage them to migrate to the updated version or part.

As we delve deeper into these strategies, remember there's no one-size-fits-all strategy. The choice between different versioning and deprecation strategies heavily depends on your API, its user base, and your team's capacity to support these strategies. However, the underlying principle remains the same: fostering a smooth transition for your users with as much transparency, support, and empathy as possible. Because at the end of the day, the goal of a developer-centric API is not just about creating powerful and flexible tools but about making them a joy to use.

API Documentation and Discovery

After immersing ourselves in the seas of API design principles, investigating the nuances of various API patterns, and dissecting the complex subjects of versioning and deprecation strategies, we now find ourselves at the shores of documentation and discovery. While they may seem mundane next to the technical depths of our prior explorations, both of these subjects are critical when designing developer-centric APIs.

In essence, API documentation and discovery bridge your API and its users. This bridge serves not only to connect but also to guide and enlighten, significantly influencing the developer's experience and their perception of your product. In this section, we'll delve into the three primary subsections, each pivotal in its own right: API documentation, documentation formats, and API discovery.

As we move forward, remember that adequate API documentation and discovery strategies are about empathy and communication. By providing straightforward, user-friendly, and accessible resources, you demonstrate respect for your API's users. This respect forms the basis of designing APIs that are not only powerful and flexible but also a joy for developers to use. Let's set foot on this exciting journey to unravel the secrets of API documentation and discovery.

API Documentation

API documentation serves as the bridge connecting your API to its users. It's like a compass that guides developers through your API's landscape, steering them in the right direction while providing valuable hints and signposts. Let's take a deeper dive into the core aspects of API documentation.

Understanding the Importance of API Documentation

API documentation is often the first contact developers have with your API. Therefore, its quality significantly affects developers' perception of your product. According to the Postman State of API Survey, well-structured and clear documentation is consistently cited as one of the critical factors in a positive API experience. Poorly written, incomplete, or outdated documentation can deter developers, no matter how good the API is.

Essential Elements of API Documentation

To be effective, your API documentation should provide clear, concise, and complete information about how to use your API. It should also include an overview that helps developers quickly assess whether your API meets their needs. Here are some aspects your documentation should cover:

> **Overview**: Provide a high-level summary of your API, including its purpose, key features, and how it fits within the larger ecosystem. This lets developers quickly determine if your API suits their use case.

> **Authentication:** This is how developers gain access to your API. Whether using API keys, OAuth, or another method, your documentation should clearly explain how to authenticate requests and obtain an API key if required.

> **Endpoints**: An API is nothing without its endpoints. Your documentation should list all available endpoints, describe what they do, and provide examples of how to use them.

Data Structures: Your documentation should detail the request and response formats your API uses, including any data structures, forms, and conventions developers need to know.

Error Handling: Everyone makes mistakes, even developers. Your API will inevitably return error messages at times. Ensure your documentation explains what those errors mean and how to resolve them.

Rate Limiting: If your API imposes any rate limits, document them. Developers need to know these limits to design their applications appropriately.

Case Study: Stripe's API Documentation

Stripe, the online payment processing platform, is a shining example of excellent API documentation. Stripe's API documentation stands out due to its user-friendliness, comprehensive nature, and the inclusion of practical elements that cater directly to the needs of developers.

Here are some notable features of Stripe's API documentation:

Code Samples: Stripe includes code samples for each API endpoint in various languages. This is incredibly useful for developers because they can copy, modify, and use these samples directly in their applications.

Clear Explanations: Stripe's API documentation clearly explains each endpoint and parameter. They don't just tell you what to do; they also explain why you should do it, fostering a deeper understanding of their API.

Interactive Elements: One of the standout features of Stripe's documentation is its interactive elements. Developers can make API calls within the documentation, giving them a hands-on experience that enhances their understanding and comfort with Stripe's API.

By learning from Stripe's approach to API documentation, we can understand that excellent API documentation is about more than just listing endpoints and data structures. It's about empathy and communication, meeting developers where they are, and helping them achieve their goals. The quality of your API documentation can be a crucial differentiator for your product and a token of respect for your API's users. This is an essential part of designing APIs that are not only powerful and flexible but also a joy for developers to use.

And with that, we've wrapped up our deep dive into API documentation, the compass that guides developers through your API's landscape. Next, we'll explore the various formats API documentation can take, which is another crucial aspect of providing a top-notch developer experience.

API Descriptions and Documentation Formats

API descriptions and documentation formats are crucial to presenting your API to developers. While related, they serve different purposes. API descriptions define your API's structure, endpoints, and data formats in a machine-readable format, which can then be used to generate human-readable documentation. Understanding both concepts is essential for creating exceptional API documentation.

Let's journey through some of the most commonly used formats for API descriptions and how they relate to generating documentation.

OpenAPI (Previously Known As Swagger)

OpenAPI is arguably the most popular format for API descriptions. It is a specification for machine-readable interface files for describing, producing, consuming, and visualizing RESTful web services. Formerly known as Swagger, it was renamed OpenAPI when it donated to the OpenAPI Initiative (OAI) in 2016.

OpenAPI allows you to describe your API's structure, endpoints, and request/response formats in a machine-readable format. This description can then be used with documentation generators like Swagger UI to create interactive, human-readable documentation automatically. The OpenAPI specification can be written in YAML or JSON, offering flexibility depending on your preference or needs.

Companies like SendGrid and Twilio use the OpenAPI specification for their API documentation. This enables them to offer interactive documentation where developers can try out API calls directly within the documentation.

RAML (RESTful API Modeling Language)

RAML, or RESTful API Modeling Language, is another popular choice for documenting APIs. It is a YAML-based language that succinctly describes RESTful APIs with the help of code reuse, consistency, pattern recognition, and performance optimization.

RAML excels in its simplicity and readability, with support for code reuse that can make maintaining complex API documentation more manageable. While RAML serves as an API description format, developers will also need a documentation generator to create user-facing documentation from these descriptions. It also supports the inclusion of documentation alongside API definitions.

API Blueprint

API Blueprint is a powerful high-level API description language for web APIs. Written in Markdown, API Blueprint is designed with simplicity and clarity, making it a good choice if you're looking for a more human-readable format.

While API Blueprint might not be as widely used as OpenAPI or RAML, it offers a unique combination of readability and expressiveness. Companies like Apiary use API Blueprint to create API documentation that is both understandable and easy to navigate. However, as with other description formats, you'll need a tool to convert the API Blueprint description into comprehensive, developer-friendly documentation.

Choosing the Right Format

The choice of API description format depends on your specific needs and constraints. Consider factors such as the complexity of your API, your team's familiarity with the structure, the tools available for generating and displaying documentation, and the needs of your API's consumers.

Ultimately, it's not so much about the specific format as it is about ensuring your API documentation is clear, comprehensive, and developer-friendly. As the adage goes, "The best documentation is the one that gets read."

Remember, the description format is just a vehicle for delivering information about your API. Regardless of your chosen design, the goal should always be to provide documentation that helps developers understand and effectively use your API. And with this, we have covered the landscape of API documentation formats, each with unique strengths and considerations.

API Discovery

Let's focus now on API discovery, which sometimes feels like searching for a hidden treasure in a dense forest. But it doesn't have to be. If effectively managed, API discovery can be a seamless process that allows developers to find your API, comprehend its purpose, and understand how to integrate it into their projects.

The Importance of API Discovery

Think of API discovery as a marketing channel for your API. This is the process by which developers stumble upon, learn about, and eventually decide to use your API. Whether operating in a B2B or B2C context, a well-executed discovery process can widen your API's reach, increase its user base, and enhance its overall perception of the developer community.

The Twitter API serves as a compelling example. Over the years, the Twitter API has gained popularity due to its broad exposure and the company's efforts to simplify its discovery. Developers can easily find it through search engines, API directories, and social media, making it a cornerstone of countless third-party applications.

Search Engine Optimization (SEO)

Search Engine Optimization (SEO) plays a significant role in API discovery, and developers often turn to search engines to find APIs that meet their needs. Therefore, ensuring your API documentation and related content are SEO-friendly can increase the visibility of your API.

When crafting your API's online content, consider incorporating keywords developers might use when searching for APIs. Also, consider structuring your content for readability, both for humans and search engines, using practices such as using relevant meta tags and creating descriptive URL paths.

API Directories

Listing your API on public API directories can also boost its discoverability. These directories act as "Yellow Pages" for APIs, where developers can browse various APIs by category or search for specific functionality. Examples of such guides include RapidAPI, Public APIs, and API List.

Developer Portals

A well-designed developer portal can significantly enhance API discovery. It serves as a central hub for all information related to your API and provides easy access to documentation, SDKs, tutorials, and community discussions.

For instance, Twilio's developer portal effectively showcases the capabilities of its various APIs. It offers interactive tutorials, demos, and easily accessible documentation. These elements make it easier for developers to understand and use the APIs and make the discovery process more engaging.

Community Engagement

Engaging with the developer community through forums, webinars, blog posts, and social media can also improve API discoverability. This can be a platform to showcase your API's features, share updates, and address user queries.

Effective API discovery is not a matter of chance but a carefully orchestrated process that combines multiple strategies. It is about making your API easy to find, comprehend, and use, showing respect for your API's users, and ultimately, crafting APIs that are not just powerful and flexible but a joy for developers to use.

API Governance: Implanting, Enforcing, and Maintaining Design Principles

As we conclude our exploration of API design principles and practices, it's crucial to address a vital aspect that ensures these principles are not just theoretical but are actively implemented and maintained throughout the lifecycle of your API: API Governance.

API governance refers to the framework and processes that guide APIs' design, development, and maintenance to ensure they adhere to established principles and best practices. Effective governance helps maintain consistency, security, and quality across all organizational APIs, contributing significantly to a positive Developer Experience (DevEx).

Implanting API Governance

The first step in API governance is implanting the design principles across the API development process. This can be achieved through

Design Standards and Guidelines: Establishing a comprehensive set of standards and guidelines that all API developers within the organization must follow. These should cover naming conventions, versioning strategies, error handling, and security protocols. Having clear, documented standards ensure that every API built aligns with the overall design philosophy of the organization.

Training and Onboarding: New developers should be introduced to these standards as part of their onboarding process. Regular training sessions help reinforce these principles and keep the team updated on any changes or new best practices.

Enforcing API Governance

Once the design principles are implanted, the next challenge is to enforce them consistently across all APIs. Some strategies include

> **Automated Tools and Linters:** Use tools that automatically check API code against the established guidelines. Linters and code analysis tools can enforce naming conventions, detect security vulnerabilities, and ensure compliance with versioning strategies.

> **Code Reviews:** Regular code reviews are an essential part of enforcing governance. All API-related code should be reviewed by peers or senior developers well-versed in the organization's design principles. Involving the entire team in these reviews, not just senior members, encourages knowledge sharing and ensures everyone is aligned with the API governance practices.

> **Approval Processes:** Implementing a formal approval process for API changes or new API releases can ensure that all new developments meet the required standards before they go live.

Maintaining API Governance

Finally, API governance is not a one-time task; it requires ongoing effort to maintain the integrity of your API ecosystem:

> **Version Control and Documentation:** Keep thorough documentation of all versions and changes to the API. This helps track the API's evolution and ensures that all modifications adhere to the governance standards.

> **Regular Audits and Feedback Loops:** Conduct regular audits of your APIs to ensure they continue to meet governance standards. Additionally, feedback loops should be established with API consumers to identify areas where the API may need improvements or updates to stay aligned with best practices.

> **Continuous Improvement:** API governance should evolve with the API landscape. As new tools, techniques, and standards emerge, be prepared to adapt your governance framework to incorporate these innovations, ensuring your APIs remain cutting-edge and developer-friendly.

By implementing a robust API governance framework, organizations can ensure that their APIs consistently deliver a high-quality developer experience, maintain security, and adapt smoothly to changes. This governance not only enforces the principles we've discussed but also embeds them into the fabric of the API lifecycle, ensuring they endure over time.

Key Takeaways

- API design should prioritize developer experience, focusing on consistency, flexibility, affordance, efficiency, and security.

- RESTful, GraphQL, and gRPC APIs each offer unique strengths and trade-offs. Choosing the right one depends on your specific use case and requirements.

- API versioning and deprecation are crucial parts of managing change in APIs. Clear communication and effective strategies can minimize disruption to developers.

- Comprehensive, accessible, and intuitive documentation is vital to a developer-friendly API. Making the API easy to discover enhances the developer experience.

- Security is a non-negotiable aspect of API design and should be considered from the inception of the API design process.

- Implementing a robust API governance framework is essential for maintaining the integrity, consistency, and quality of your APIs. It ensures that design principles are not only established but also enforced and adapted over time, ultimately enhancing the developer experience.

As we move forward, let's keep this learning in mind, applying and adapting it as we continue to improve our craft of creating delightful and efficient developer environments.

CHAPTER 6

Providing Stellar Developer Support

Welcome to Chapter 6, where we delve into what makes a delightful and efficient developer environment—providing stellar developer support. This essential component in the developer experience encourages developers to use and stick with your tools, builds trust, and fosters a collaborative community around your platform or product. This chapter will demystify the various aspects of providing top-notch developer support.

We'll examine the multifaceted world of communication channels and see how providing developers with the right resources can empower them to solve issues independently, enhance their experience, and free up your support resources. We'll also review how to learn from your developers to continually refine and enhance your product, platform, or service and see how to create a vibrant ecosystem around your product or platform.

In his book *The Cathedral and the Bazaar*, Eric S. Raymond famously said, "Given enough eyeballs, all bugs are shallow." This sentiment speaks volumes about the power of community in software development. Consider, for example, how Linus Torvalds' call to the development community in 1991 to contribute to his new operating system, Linux, created one of the world's largest and most active developer communities.

By the end of this chapter, you will have a comprehensive understanding of how to provide stellar developer support. Let's get started on this journey. The developers are waiting.

© K. Rain Leander 2025
K. R. Leander, *Developer Experience Unleashed*,
https://doi.org/10.1007/979-8-8688-0242-3_6

Communication Channels

As we navigate through the intricate ecosystem of developer support, one crucial component that stands out is the myriad of communication channels available for providing support. These channels, ranging from traditional email and support tickets to interactive platforms such as social media and instant messaging, form the arteries of developer support, each with unique strengths and use cases. This section will explore these avenues, shedding light on their benefits and challenges and how best to harness their potential to provide stellar developer support.

Understanding these channels, their strengths, limitations, and optimal use cases is fundamental to providing exceptional developer support. By the end of this section, you'll be equipped with a comprehensive understanding of these diverse communication channels, empowering you to craft a holistic, multichannel developer support strategy that caters to developers' unique needs and preferences.

Email and Support Tickets

While newer, more interactive communication channels have emerged, email and support tickets remain essential for structured and trackable communication. This subsection explores these channels' roles, benefits, and best practices in providing stellar developer support.

As a communication channel, email has been widely used since the 1990s and continues to be a mainstay in developer support. Despite its asynchronous nature, email's versatility and accessibility make it a reliable tool for handling more complex, low-urgency issues. It allows the support team and the developer to have a well-documented conversation that can be revisited.

For instance, MailChimp, a leading email marketing platform, has long utilized email support to provide comprehensive help to its users, including developers. Their dedicated team responds to queries, typically within 24–48 hours, ensuring that users get the help they need without delay.

Support tickets, however, provide a more structured and traceable method of managing support requests. Developers can raise tickets detailing their issues or queries, and the support team can track, manage, and resolve these tickets systematically.

Zendesk, a customer service software company, is a good example. It utilizes a robust ticketing system that allows developers to raise tickets with specific details like the type of issue, urgency, and attached files, aiding the support team in providing effective and timely help.

When employing email and support tickets, the key is to ensure timely, accurate, and empathetic responses. An automated acknowledgment of receipt, followed by a substantive response within a reasonable time, enhances the developer's experience.

Maintaining transparency about the process and the estimated resolution time can also help manage expectations and build trust. For instance, GitHub, a platform widely used by developers, provides users with detailed information about how their support requests will be handled and what they can expect during the process.

One important consideration is the staffing needed for these channels. Depending on the volume of inquiries, you may need a dedicated support team to efficiently handle email and ticket responses. Additionally, ensure that team members are well-trained to communicate clearly and empathetically, especially since these channels often deal with more complex issues.

A common pitfall to avoid with these channels is using overly technical language. While developers are typically tech-savvy, the communication language should be clear, concise, and jargon-free. Remember, the goal is to help the developer understand and resolve their issue, not to showcase technical prowess.

In conclusion, even in an age dominated by instant messaging and social media, email and support tickets are crucial for developer support. With timely responses, transparency, and clear communication, these channels can significantly enhance the developer experience and form the backbone of a solid developer support strategy.

Forums and Community Platforms

Forums and community platforms serve as foundational pillars in the ecosystem of developer support. They provide a space for developers to ask questions, share experiences, learn from each other, and contribute to the collective knowledge base of the developer community. This subsection delves into the power of these platforms and the best practices for creating and managing them effectively.

Forums have been the go-to resource for developers for decades, and their utility continues to be relevant even in the current era of instantaneous communication. Platforms like Stack Overflow, GitHub Discussions, or even Google Groups offer developers an asynchronous mode of communication where they can post their queries and wait for responses from the community.

For example, Stack Overflow, launched in 2008, has become the go-to resource for developers worldwide. It has a user base of millions who come together to help each other solve coding issues. Stack Overflow's strict guidelines and reputation points system help maintain a high standard of questions and answers, which enhances the value developers derive from the platform.

On the other hand, community platforms are more about creating an engaging and inclusive space for developers. They can be either product-focused, such as the Developer Community of JetBrains, or technology-focused, such as the Reactiflux Discord Community for React Developers.

Community platforms are not just about solving problems but also about learning, sharing ideas, and networking. They often organize events like hackathons or webinars, which allow developers to learn new things, showcase their skills, and connect with their peers.

Creating a successful forum or community platform involves much planning and effort. First, it's crucial to establish clear guidelines about the nature of discussions allowed, the code of conduct, and the general etiquette to be followed. Effective moderation is essential in maintaining the community's health, keeping discussions constructive, and preventing the spread of misinformation or inappropriate content.

To manage a forum or community platform well, you need to appoint experienced moderators knowledgeable about the subject matter and can enforce the guidelines fairly. Regular engagement from the community managers and moderators is also necessary to keep the platform vibrant and relevant.

An essential aspect of running a forum or community platform is acknowledging and appreciating the contributions of community members. Gamification techniques such as badges, reputation points, or highlighting the "Top Contributors" can be used to motivate and appreciate community members for their contributions.

Staffing and resource considerations are also critical. Depending on the size of the community, you may need full-time community managers and moderators. The success of these platforms often hinges on consistent engagement and the ability to foster a positive, supportive atmosphere.

Remember, a thriving community is one where members feel heard, respected, and appreciated. So, fostering an environment of mutual respect and learning is essential. When managed well, a forum or community platform can become an invaluable resource for developers and a key driver of a positive developer experience.

In conclusion, while forums and community platforms offer tremendous potential in providing stellar developer support, they demand a thoughtful and empathetic approach to community building and management. A successful forum or community is about resolving queries, fostering a sense of belonging, and cultivating an environment of shared learning and growth.

Social Media and Instant Messaging

In an era where communication has become instantaneous and ubiquitously available, it's no surprise that social media and instant messaging platforms have become integral to developer support. This subsection explores these tools as communication channels, providing a thorough understanding of their potential and the best practices for using them effectively.

Social media platforms, such as Twitter, LinkedIn, and Facebook, are not just tools for marketing or customer relations; they are also powerful platforms for providing developer support. For example, Twitter's real-time nature makes it an effective tool for developers to reach out for quick assistance or to report issues. An engaging presence on these platforms lets you stay in touch with your developers, understand their concerns, and promptly address them.

GitHub, for instance, effectively uses Twitter for support. They have a dedicated support account, @GitHubHelp, where they handle queries and help developers. This showcases their dedication to support and provides a quick way for developers to address their concerns.

On the other hand, instant messaging platforms such as Slack or Discord have become a hub for real-time collaboration and communication. These tools offer an interactive platform for developers to share code, discuss problems, and collaboratively find solutions. For example, the Apache Software Foundation has a Slack workspace dedicated to its various projects, where developers can interact with the project contributors and other community members.

However, as much as these platforms offer significant advantages, their use also comes with challenges. Social media can sometimes be noisy, and relevant communication can get lost amidst the volume of posts. Therefore, it is crucial to manage these channels diligently, respond to queries promptly, and acknowledge every piece of feedback to ensure developers feel heard. A dedicated team to monitor and respond to social media inquiries is often necessary to maintain support quality.

Instant messaging platforms, while interactive, can also become chaotic if not properly managed. To manage these spaces effectively, it's essential to structure them with clearly defined channels or groups based on topics or project components. This organization helps keep conversations focused and relevant, making it easier for developers to find the necessary information.

Another important aspect is the integration of these channels into your overall support system. Integrating social media and instant messaging platforms with your support ticketing system or CRM can help manage support requests more effectively, ensure none are lost, and allow better tracking and resolution. Tools like Zapier or Integromat can help automate these integrations.

Consider the staffing implications as well. Social media and instant messaging often require real-time or near-real-time responses, which can demand more resources than asynchronous channels like email. Depending on the scale of your operations, you may need dedicated social media managers and community moderators to handle these channels effectively.

Remember, the objective of using social media and instant messaging for developer support is not just to resolve issues but also to build relationships with your developers. A human, compassionate, and empathetic approach can go a long way in creating a supportive environment where developers feel valued and heard.

So, while social media and instant messaging platforms provide opportunities for instant, accessible, and human-centric developer support, they also demand thoughtful management and integration. Balancing their potential with their challenges is the key to leveraging these tools effectively for stellar developer support.

Empowering Developers with Self-Service Resources

As we transition from communication channels, we now focus on how we can empower developers to solve their problems independently. Self-service resources are instrumental in this empowerment, enabling developers to find solutions on their terms and timelines. This approach enhances their problem-solving skills and contributes to a sense of self-efficacy and satisfaction in their work.

This section will delve into three fundamental types of self-service resources that every organization should consider when designing developer support: knowledge bases, troubleshooting wizards, and interactive learning resources. All these resources have unique strengths and contribute significantly to empowering developers, creating a more efficient and delightful developer experience.

As we further dissect these elements in this section, we will dive into specifics and examples that underline their importance in developer support. Providing such resources not only lightens the load on your support team but also enhances the developer's experience and proficiency with your product, building their confidence and cementing their loyalty to your platform. As you read through the section, think about how these resources can be tailored to meet the unique needs of your developer community.

Knowledge Bases

When we speak of self-service resources in developer support, one of the first things that come to mind is a well-structured, comprehensive, and user-friendly knowledge base. A knowledge base is an information repository that provides developers with detailed guides, how-to articles, API documentation, FAQs, code samples, and more. It is like a library open round the clock, providing valuable resources and information right at the fingertips of developers.

A study by Forrester Research in 2021 revealed that 70% of customers prefer to use a company's website to get answers to their questions rather than use phone or email support. This statistic speaks volumes about maintaining a robust knowledge base as part of your developer support infrastructure.

A compelling example of a practical knowledge base is the AWS Documentation portal. AWS Documentation is highly developer-centric, offering comprehensive resources that include detailed guides, SDK documentation, tutorials, and best practices. The platform also integrates with interactive tools and real-world examples, making it an invaluable resource for developers working with AWS services. The highly accessible and interactive nature of this knowledge base makes it an exemplary resource for developer support.

However, building a thriving knowledge base is a challenging task. It involves consistently curating and updating content, ensuring the information is accurate, relevant, and aligned with the latest product updates and changes. It also involves architecting the information in an easily navigable and discoverable way. The goal is to empower developers to quickly find the information they need, reducing their dependency on direct support channels.

The search functionality is crucial to consider when building a knowledge base. Developers should be able to search for and find the information they need quickly. Google's developer documentation stands as a testament to this. Their documentation is armed with powerful search functionality, using natural language processing and AI to provide highly relevant search results, making the exploration process more efficient for developers.

A well-maintained and easily navigable knowledge base reduces the load on your support team and empowers developers to resolve issues independently, fostering a sense of competence and satisfaction. The investment requires time and effort, but the returns regarding improved developer experience and engagement are substantial.

In the subsequent sections, we will delve deeper into other self-service resources like troubleshooting wizards and interactive learning resources. We will build a comprehensive picture of how these tools collectively contribute to an empowered and self-sufficient developer community.

Troubleshooting Paths

In the realm of developer support, providing clear and efficient troubleshooting resources is essential for fostering a positive developer experience. One of the most effective ways to do this is by offering troubleshooting paths—structured, step-by-step guides designed specifically for technical audiences. These paths guide developers through common issues methodically, enabling them to diagnose and resolve problems independently.

Troubleshooting paths cater directly to the needs of developers by offering concise, actionable steps that align with how they prefer to work. Unlike generic support tools, these paths allow developers to maintain control over the troubleshooting process, quickly finding the necessary information without unnecessary interaction or delays.

For instance, Google's Cloud Documentation includes comprehensive troubleshooting paths that cover a wide range of issues across their services. These paths are meticulously organized, often including diagnostic steps, relevant API documentation, and code snippets that help developers pinpoint and fix problems efficiently.

Microsoft's Azure DevOps offers another strong example with extensive guides that address common issues in CI/CD pipelines. These guides provide step-by-step instructions and link directly to related tools and features within the Azure portal, helping developers quickly apply fixes within their workflow.

Stripe, a popular payment processing platform, provides interactive troubleshooting paths within its developer portal. These paths help developers diagnose issues related to payment processing, such as failed transactions or webhook configurations, and offer code examples, diagnostic tools, and best practice recommendations.

Creating effective troubleshooting paths involves a deep understanding of the common challenges developers face when using your platform or APIs. Regular updates are crucial to ensure these resources remain relevant and aligned with any changes in your product. Each step in the path should be clearly explained with links to related resources such as API references, best practice guides, or community forums, offering a holistic support experience.

The integration of troubleshooting paths into a broader developer portal or knowledge base further enhances their utility. This allows developers to seamlessly navigate between troubleshooting steps and other helpful resources, such as real-time monitoring tools in AWS CloudWatch or security best practices in Okta's developer documentation, without breaking their workflow.

Involving experienced developers in the creation and maintenance of these paths can ensure that they reflect real-world use cases and are genuinely useful. Additionally, incorporating feedback mechanisms can help continuously refine these paths based on user experiences, making them even more effective over time.

Troubleshooting paths and other technical resources are invaluable tools for empowering developers to solve issues independently. By focusing on clarity, relevance, and accessibility, these resources can significantly enhance the overall developer experience, ensuring that your platform is both user-centric and technically robust.

Interactive Learning Resources

Interactive learning resources form the third pillar of empowering developers with self-service tools, knowledge bases, and troubleshooting wizards. As the name suggests, these resources allow developers to learn by doing, creating a hands-on experience that can be significantly more effective than traditional passive learning methods.

A 2020 report from eLearning Industry found that learners who engaged with interactive content had a 50% higher retention rate than those who used traditional resources. The power of interactive learning lies in its capacity to actively engage users, which makes it a fantastic tool for developer support.

Interactive learning resources come in many shapes and sizes, from simple interactive documentation to comprehensive coding boot camps. Regarding the developer community, tools such as online coding playgrounds, interactive API explorers, and guided tutorials provide invaluable platforms for developers to explore and familiarize themselves with your services.

Stripe's API Explorer is an excellent example of an interactive learning resource. It enables developers to make API calls directly within the documentation, allowing them to see how the API works in real time. This hands-on approach empowers developers to understand the Stripe API better, reducing the need for support intervention and empowering developers to resolve their issues independently.

Codecademy, on the other hand, offers an entire platform dedicated to interactive learning. Developers can follow guided lessons on various programming languages, APIs, and coding concepts, with interactive coding challenges built into every lesson. It's an immersive learning environment that allows developers to understand the code by writing and executing it themselves.

Another successful instance of interactive learning resources can be found in Google's Codelabs. These guided tutorials provide a hands-on coding experience and cover many of Google's products and APIs. Each Codelab includes step-by-step instructions, a dedicated workspace, and access to all the necessary resources. This immersive experience enables developers to grasp complex concepts more effectively.

When creating interactive learning resources, focus on the common challenges and tasks developers will face when using your product. Design scenarios that reflect real-world situations and guide developers toward best practices. Constantly update your resources to reflect product changes and address new challenges developers may face.

The real value of interactive learning resources lies in their capacity to provide a hands-on experience that fosters deep comprehension and independent problem-solving abilities. By offering these resources, you're helping developers become proficient in using your product and giving them the tools they need to continue growing and learning, which builds a stronger sense of community and loyalty toward your platform. As we progress to the next section, we'll examine the essential role of gathering and incorporating feedback in enhancing the developer support experience.

Gathering and Incorporating Feedback

Building delightful and efficient developer environments is not just about creating resources and tools; it's a dialogue. It's about listening to what developers say and incorporating their feedback into your offerings. In this section, we discuss three primary ways of gathering and incorporating feedback: through bug reports and feature requests, surveys and interviews, and user testing and observation.

These channels provide a comprehensive understanding of the developer experience. They allow you to see where you are succeeding, falling short, and opportunities for improvement. Remember, feedback guides you toward creating a more delightful and efficient developer environment. Let's dig deeper into each of these feedback mechanisms.

Bug Reports and Feature Requests

Bug reports and feature requests are at the front of the conversation with developers. They are direct, no-nonsense feedback channels that give you an intimate understanding of the strengths and weaknesses of your product or service.

A bug report is a cry for help. It is a message from a developer who has encountered an obstacle, a glitch, or a bug. As they navigate your product or service, they find that something needs to be fixed. The strength of a well-maintained bug reporting system lies in its capability to turn these frustrating moments into opportunities for improvement.

Take, for instance, the legendary bug reporting system at Mozilla, Bugzilla, which was initiated on August 26, 1998. Over the years, Bugzilla has become a testament to Mozilla's commitment to developer support. Through thousands of bug reports, developers have highlighted performance issues, security vulnerabilities, UI inconsistencies, and more. Each report represented a chance to improve and enhance the user experience. The result? A continually evolving, robust, and reliable product that developers can trust.

To ensure that your bug reporting system is efficient, it's crucial to maintain a transparent, concise, and well-documented process. Make it easy for developers to describe the problem, provide details about the environment in which it occurred, and, if possible, provide steps to reproduce it. Remember, the more accessible for a developer to report a bug, the more likely they will do it.

On the other side of the coin are feature requests. Unlike bug reports, which focus on problems with existing functionalities, feature requests illuminate what's missing and what could be. They are sparks of insight that could ignite the next big idea.

In 2014, GitHub, the renowned software development platform, introduced a new feature called "Pull Request." This feature, as the GitHub team describes it, "proposed changes from one branch to another branch." This feature didn't just appear out of thin air. It resulted from numerous feature requests from developers who wanted a more streamlined way to propose changes to a project. GitHub listened, incorporated the feedback, and "Pull Request" was born. This feature quickly became one of GitHub's most popular, transforming developers' collaboration on open-source projects.

Creating a welcoming environment for feature requests is essential. Whether it's a dedicated section on your forum, a form on your website, or even a well-monitored email address, providing a platform where developers can share their ideas makes them feel heard and provides an invaluable source of innovation.

As you navigate bug reports and feature requests, remember to appreciate the time and effort developers put into submitting them. Treat these feedback channels with respect, respond promptly, and show gratitude. This will encourage more feedback and foster a community of valued and heard developers. After all, a supported developer is an empowered developer.

Surveys and Interviews

Surveys and interviews represent two critical methods of obtaining valuable feedback from developers. By exploring each in detail, we'll delve into their strengths, when to use them, and best practices for execution. Remember, the goal here is to understand the developer experience with your product or service, their challenges, successes, and suggestions for improvement.

Surveys are a widely utilized and incredibly versatile tool for gathering quantitative data. They allow you to reach a broad audience, quickly gather data and statistically analyze results. These traits make surveys ideal for understanding the overall sentiment, tracking metrics over time, and identifying trends within your developer base.

Take the annual Stack Overflow Developer Survey as an example. Since 2011, Stack Overflow has conducted a comprehensive survey to understand the developer community better. This survey, with responses from tens of thousands of developers, provides invaluable insights into developers' preferences, work habits, and attitudes. These insights inform Stack Overflow's strategy and prove valuable for anyone building products or services for developers.

However, as valuable as surveys are, they have challenges. Crafting practical survey questions is both an art and a science, demanding clarity, neutrality, and precision. Misleading or ambiguous questions can skew results and lead to misinterpretations.

Interviews, conversely, provide a more qualitative understanding of the developer experience. Interviews enable a deep dive into individual perspectives, motivations, and pain points, offering a detailed narrative and more profound context than surveys.

Let's consider the redesign of the documentation site by the React Native team in 2021. They interviewed developers at different skill levels to understand the pain points in the existing documentation. Based on the feedback, they improved the content and restructured the whole documentation site to make it more intuitive and easy to navigate. The interviews provided an opportunity to hear the developers' frustrations in their own words and observe their emotional reactions, which was a powerful motivator for the team.

Conducting interviews requires thoughtful planning and excellent communication skills. You need to be mindful not to lead the interviewee and encourage them to share their thoughts openly and honestly. The power of interviews lies in their ability to reveal the human story behind the data.

To wrap up, surveys and interviews are complementary tools in your feedback arsenal. Use surveys to collect data from a large group, track trends, and quantify sentiments. On the other hand, use interviews to dive deep into individual experiences, understand motivations, and hearing the narrative behind the numbers. As Harper Lee once said in *To Kill a Mockingbird*, "You never really understand a person until you consider things from his point of view...until you climb into his skin and walk around in it." This is the spirit we bring to our interviews and surveys. We are trying to see the world from the developers' point of view, to walk in their shoes, and thus provide the support they truly need.

User Testing and Observation

Having discussed bug reports, feature requests, surveys, and interviews, let's turn to an equally crucial and informative feedback method—user testing and observation. User testing, also known as usability testing, is a technique used in user-centered design to evaluate a product by testing it on users. Observation, meanwhile, is a technique where developers are watched using the product in their natural environment, allowing you to understand how your product fits into their workflow.

These two techniques allow us to see the product from the user's perspective and give us insights into how our product is used in real-world scenarios. This first-hand feedback is invaluable in shaping your product's future iterations and improving your developer support.

User Testing generally provides users with a series of tasks to perform using your product. While they do so, they're usually asked to think aloud, explaining their thoughts and decision-making processes. The primary objective is to identify usability problems, gather qualitative and quantitative data, and ultimately understand the user's satisfaction with the product.

Let's take the example of redesigning the GitHub Actions feature in 2022. GitHub decided to improve the usability of the feature based on developer feedback. They conducted user testing where developers were given tasks to create, manage, and debug workflows. GitHub's UX team observed the process, gathered feedback, and used the insights to enhance the feature's usability. The result was a more intuitive and powerful tool that developers loved.

On the other hand, observation needs to be more structured and often conducted in the developer's natural environment, such as their office or home workspace. It's like ethnography, where the aim is to see how the product is used in the context of the user's life, including the challenges they face and how they overcome them.

For instance, when Microsoft was developing Visual Studio Code, they spent significant time observing developers in their natural settings, trying to understand their workflows, frustrations, and joys. They watched how developers interacted with the editor, navigated the code, and used the terminal and other tools. These observations helped shape many of the unique features of Visual Studio Code, contributing to its widespread popularity.

In conclusion, user testing and observation are potent tools to gather and incorporate feedback, helping to build a product that truly meets the needs of your developers. As Steve Jobs famously said, "You've got to start with the customer experience and work back toward the technology—not the other way around." With these techniques, you put the developer at the center, ensuring your product is built with their needs and experiences in mind.

Building and Nurturing Developer Communities

Having taken an in-depth look at different communication channels, empowering developers with self-service resources, and gathering and incorporating feedback in the preceding sections, we now focus on a crucial aspect of providing stellar developer support—building and nurturing developer communities. A vibrant, thriving community can be a game-changer, a potent catalyst for creating an environment where developers feel valued, motivated, and engaged.

However, building and nurturing a developer community is a task accomplished over time. It's akin to planting a seed and nurturing it into a tree. It requires time, effort, and a significant amount of patience. It's an ongoing process that necessitates a well-thought-out strategy and commitment.

As we delve into building and nurturing developer communities, we will break down some of the critical steps involved in the process:

- Clear guidelines or a code of conduct are crucial to creating an environment that promotes respectful, constructive interactions.

- A thriving community learns together and grows together.

- Acknowledging and rewarding contributions is a crucial motivator.

- A community that provides its members with the necessary resources and support sets them up for success.

Open communication channels within the community are paramount. In the following subsections, we'll unpack each step, providing examples and further insights into how they contribute to creating and nurturing developer communities. Each community's journey will be unique, but these principles form a universal blueprint to guide community builders toward success.

Establish Clear Community Guidelines

Before a community can flourish, it must have a solid foundation, and one of the fundamental elements of this foundation is a clear set of community guidelines. These guidelines, or codes of conduct, foster a respectful, inclusive, and constructive environment.

Setting Expectations

Clear guidelines help set the expectations for behavior within the community. They should be visible, easy to understand, and cover critical aspects such as respect for diversity, inclusivity, and a zero-tolerance policy for harassment or discrimination. This will ensure that all members, regardless of their background or level of experience, feel safe and welcome in the community.

For example, the Python Software Foundation has a well-defined Code of Conduct that they describe as a "social contract" for the community. It clearly outlines expected and unacceptable behavior and the consequences of violating the code.

Open Communication and Respectful Discourse

The guidelines should also promote open communication and respectful discourse. Encourage members to share their opinions, ask questions, and help others. However, ensure that any conversation or discussion should be respectful and considerate.

The Rust programming language community does an exemplary job of this, with guidelines that actively encourage open discussion while emphasizing respectful communication and consideration for others' viewpoints.

Consequences for Non-adherence

More than just having guidelines is required. There should be clearly defined consequences for non-adherence. When members understand the ramifications of violating the guidelines, they are more likely to abide by them.

For instance, the Ubuntu community's Code of Conduct has a transparent dispute resolution process. It explains the steps that will be taken if someone is found to violate the code, ranging from a reprimand to a temporary ban or, in extreme cases, expulsion from the community.

Encourage Reporting

Create a secure and accessible way for community members to report guidelines violations. Ensure that these reports are treated confidentially and that appropriate action is taken promptly.

GitHub is an excellent example of this, with its guideline encouraging users to report abusive behavior and providing a specific email address for such reports. GitHub also assures its community that it will investigate all reports and decide on the appropriate action.

Regularly Update the Guidelines

As your community grows and evolves, so should your guidelines. Regularly revisit your community guidelines to ensure they continue to foster a safe and inclusive environment. Feedback from the community can be instrumental in making these updates.

Clear and concise community guidelines are more than just rules; they're a statement of your community's values. They set the tone for the community, guide interactions, and promote a productive but also respectful and inclusive environment. As Simon Phipps, former president of the Open Source Initiative, aptly stated, "Communities don't just happen; they are made." Community guidelines are the blueprint for making a community that thrives on mutual respect and collaborative spirit.

Create Opportunities for Collaboration and Learning

Fostering opportunities for collaboration and learning is critical in building and nurturing a developer community. Your community should be a platform for developers to connect and an environment where they can learn, grow, and work together.

Learning Opportunities

Your community should offer rich learning opportunities. This can be achieved by providing access to comprehensive documentation, interactive tutorials, webinars, workshops, or even podcast discussions on industry trends and best practices.

For example, the Python community runs an educational summit concurrently with its annual conference, PyCon. This summit allows educators from various backgrounds to share their experiences, techniques, and tools for teaching Python. This kind of initiative enhances learning within the community and strengthens the sense of camaraderie among its members.

Collaboration Opportunities

In addition to learning, your community should be a hub for collaboration. You can facilitate this through code-sharing platforms, pair programming sessions, or open-source projects. Encourage community members to work together on solving complex problems or building applications.

The Drupal community is renowned for its strong culture of collaboration. Developers regularly contribute to the open-source Drupal CMS, and these contributions are acknowledged and celebrated at DrupalCon, the community's main event.

Hackathons and Coding Competitions

Hackathons and coding competitions can effectively stimulate collaboration and learning in a fun and competitive environment. These events can foster innovation, allow developers to demonstrate their skills, and provide a platform to learn from each other.

As highlighted earlier, the Global Game Jam began in 2009 and is a shining example of such an event. Developers worldwide come together to create games over 48 hours. This event encourages collaborative problem-solving and creativity; most importantly, it's a lot of fun!

Mentorship Programs

Mentorship programs can be a valuable resource for community members. Pairing less experienced developers with seasoned professionals provides a platform for knowledge sharing and personal development. Mentors can provide guidance, feedback, and support, which can be instrumental in a developer's growth.

Google's Summer of Code is an exemplary model for this, where student developers are paired with mentors from participating open-source organizations. This gives the students real-world software development experience and benefits the open-source organizations with fresh contributions.

Shared Learning Platforms

Consider setting up platforms where members can share their learnings and insights. This could be in the form of blogs, forums, or webinars. Such platforms can serve as a treasure trove of knowledge and foster a culture of shared learning within the community.

Stack Overflow, for instance, is more than just a question-answer platform. It is a community where developers can learn, share knowledge, and grow their careers. It exemplifies how shared learning platforms can facilitate a robust learning ecosystem.

In summary, creating opportunities for collaboration and learning is essential to nurturing a developer community. You can build a vibrant, engaged, and resilient community by providing platforms for shared learning, encouraging collaboration through various initiatives, and recognizing these efforts. As Linus Torvalds, the creator of Linux, once said, "Given enough eyeballs, all bugs are shallow." The more developers collaborate and learn, the stronger your community will become.

Recognize and Reward Contributions

The most vibrant communities are built on recognition and reward. A community member who feels appreciated will likely feel a more substantial commitment, leading to higher engagement. In this regard, recognizing and rewarding contributions are essential strategies for nurturing a healthy developer community.

Theodore Roosevelt once said, "People don't care how much you know until they know how much you care." This applies beautifully to developer communities. Developers need to feel that their contributions are valued, whether they're making significant code contributions, answering questions on community forums, or submitting constructive bug reports. Recognizing these efforts helps foster a sense of belonging and appreciation.

Let's delve into how to recognize and reward contributions effectively:

Public Recognition

Public recognition can be a powerful motivator. A simple shout-out in a community newsletter or a "developer of the month" feature on your community platform can go a long way. For instance, Salesforce uses its "Trailblazer Community" to highlight individuals who have significantly contributed to the Salesforce ecosystem.

Profile Badges

Badges offer a fun and visible way to acknowledge contributions. Platforms like GitHub and Stack Overflow use badges to recognize accomplishments, such as submitting pull requests, answering questions, or reaching a particular milestone. Badges can be a gratifying element that drives engagement and contribution within the community.

Swag and Perks

Who doesn't love free stuff? Swag—T-shirts, stickers, mugs, and the like—can be a delightful way to acknowledge contributions. But don't stop at physical goods. You can also offer perks like discounted or free access to your services, exclusive access to new features, or tickets to industry events.

Microsoft's MVP (Most Valuable Professional) program, for instance, not only provides recognition but also offers a host of perks, including free software, direct channels to Microsoft product teams, and invitations to the MVP Global Summit.

Financial Rewards

In some cases, financial incentives can be appropriate. As mentioned earlier, Google's Summer of Code rewards student participants who successfully complete their projects with stipends. Bug bounty programs, where companies reward developers who find and report vulnerabilities in their software, also fall into this category.

Opportunities for Growth

Recognition can also come in the form of personal and professional growth opportunities. This might involve showcasing a developer's work on your platform, inviting them to speak at a community event, or even providing them with mentorship opportunities within the community.

Remember that recognition and rewards should be aligned with your community's values and goals. Always strive for authenticity and fairness. It's not about creating a competitive environment but about celebrating achievements and encouraging a culture of shared success. Recognizing and rewarding contributions can turn casual community members into loyal advocates, making it an essential strategy in building and nurturing a thriving developer community.

Provide Support and Resources

Support and resources serve as the backbone of any thriving developer community. Just as we can't construct a building without the necessary materials and tools, we can't expect a community to flourish without providing the resources and support that its members need.

Imagine that the developer community is a garden, and the developers are the plants within it. To ensure the plants grow and thrive, you must provide suitable soil, sunlight, and water. Similarly, to nurture a thriving developer community, you need to provide the right mix of resources and support that cater to the needs of the developers.

Let's delve deeper into what this means:

Documentation

High-quality, comprehensive, and up-to-date documentation is one of the most valuable resources you can offer your developer community. Microsoft's Azure Documentation, for example, is a paragon of excellent documentation. It provides developers with a wealth of resources, from quickstarts and tutorials to API references and best practices, all aimed at enabling them to make the most out of Azure's services.

Learning Materials

The developer's journey is a continual process of learning and growth. By providing tutorials, walkthroughs, coding challenges, and even e-learning courses, you can help community members acquire new skills and deepen their understanding of the technology. Take, for instance, the Learn section of the official Python website, which is teeming with resources for learners at all levels.

Troubleshooting Guides

Sometimes, developers may stumble upon bugs or face issues while working on their projects. In such instances, readily available troubleshooting guides can help them quickly resolve problems and return to work. A well-crafted troubleshooting guide, such as the ones provided in the Android Developer Documentation, can save developers hours of frustration.

Technical Support

No matter how comprehensive your resources are, there will be times when developers need personalized help. Providing technical support, whether through a dedicated support team, a help-desk system, or even community-based support, can go a long way in helping developers overcome obstacles. The availability of support reinforces the message that they're not alone in their journey, fostering a sense of safety and encouragement within the community.

Development Tools and SDKs

Offering tools that facilitate development can boost productivity and make the development process more enjoyable. Providing SDKs specific to your technology or platform, as Facebook does for its Graph API, can empower developers to build more effectively and efficiently.

Platforms for Collaboration

Provide platforms where developers can collaborate on projects, share their work, and learn from each other. GitHub, for instance, is not just a platform for version control; it's a place where developers can contribute to open-source projects, learn from the code of others, and collaborate on building software.

In the end, providing support and resources is about empowering developers in your community. As Ken Blanchard said, "None of us is as smart as all of us." By providing the proper support and resources, you're not just helping individual developers but fostering a culture of shared learning and collaboration that can take the entire community to greater heights.

Promote Open Communication

Open communication is the lifeblood of any thriving community, especially a developer community. A constructive flow of ideas, opinions, queries, and experiences is the fundamental force that enriches the community culture and drives collective growth.

Think of open communication as a two-way street. It's about community members expressing their thoughts and ideas and how the leadership or the organization responds. Developers in the community should feel that their voice matters, that their feedback is acknowledged, and that their concerns are addressed effectively and in a timely manner.

Take, for example, Microsoft's journey with open-source and its developer community. In the early 2000s, Microsoft had a complex relationship with the open-source community. Only when Satya Nadella took over as CEO in 2014 did the company take a 180-degree turn toward open-source. His "Microsoft ❤ Open Source" declaration was not just a statement; it was a commitment to open communication and cooperation with the developer community. This open approach has significantly contributed to Microsoft's strong relationship with developers worldwide.

Implementing open communication within a developer community can take different forms, such as:

Forums and Discussion Boards

These platforms allow community members to start discussions, ask questions, share ideas, and provide solutions. They create an open space for interaction and encourage a culture of mutual learning. For instance, Stack Overflow's lively Q&A forum is a valuable resource for developers worldwide to share and gain knowledge.

Regular Community Meetings or AMAs

Hosting regular meetings, virtual hangouts, or "Ask Me Anything" (AMA) sessions with community leaders or project maintainers can boost engagement and foster transparency. These sessions allow developers to get insights, share their thoughts, or seek clarifications directly from the leaders.

Feedback Mechanisms

A system to receive and respond to feedback is crucial for maintaining open communication. Whether it's about a new feature, a bug, or community conduct, developers should have a channel to share their feedback and see it acknowledged and actioned. GitHub, for instance, uses a feature called "Issues," where developers can report bugs, request features, or provide feedback about the platform.

Open Access to Roadmaps

Transparently sharing the project or community roadmap helps keep everyone on the same page about the direction and plans. This openness helps set clear expectations and enables community members to provide more contextual and valuable feedback.

Promoting open communication does more than just build transparency; it contributes to a sense of belonging and community purpose. It lets community members know that their voice counts, fostering a culture of respect, inclusivity, and collaboration. Bill Gates once said, "We all need people who will give us feedback. That's how we improve," this principle holds in cultivating a vibrant developer community.

Key Takeaways

- Different communication channels cater to diverse developer needs and preferences. A combination of formal and informal and synchronous and asynchronous methods work best.

- Empowering developers with self-service resources promotes independence and reduces the load on your support team.

- Feedback is a gold mine for improvement. Actively gather and incorporate it to enhance your developer support.

- Building a thriving developer community fosters a sense of belonging among developers, encourages collaboration, and enriches your platform with a myriad of ideas and solutions.

- Developer support is not a one-time activity but a continuous process that requires commitment, adaptation, and a deep understanding of your developer's needs and experiences.

CHAPTER 7

Ensuring Performance and Reliability

In this chapter, we'll cover the performance and reliability of software development. We've embarked on a quest to hone the art of creating delightful and efficient developer environments, and this chapter, "Ensuring Performance and Reliability," is a significant waypoint on our journey.

In software development, performance and reliability are the fundamental building blocks that determine the stability and speed of your application and the trust your users place in your solution. These factors are also crucial to the Developer Experience (DevEx), as developers need reliable, high-performance environments to work efficiently and effectively. "Fast is fine, but accuracy is everything," this quote by Wyatt Earp, an old west lawman, surprisingly, applies to our world of software development as well.

By the end of this chapter, we'll be better equipped with the knowledge, strategies, and techniques to enhance the performance and reliability of our applications and, thus, significantly improve the developer experience. So, without further ado, let's dive into this journey to create more performant, reliable, and secure software.

© K. Rain Leander 2025
K. R. Leander, *Developer Experience Unleashed*,
https://doi.org/10.1007/979-8-8688-0242-3_7

Monitoring and Observability

As we journey into the heart of Chapter 7, we focus on the crucial elements of ensuring performance and reliability in software development. The first stop on this leg of the journey is a foundational and vitally important area: Monitoring and Observability.

The twin towers of Monitoring and Observability are critical pillars in maintaining the robustness and reliability of our systems. They allow us to understand what's happening under the hood of our applications, inform us when something goes wrong, and guide us when navigating the often choppy waters of diagnosing and resolving issues. From a Developer Experience perspective, having robust monitoring and observability tools in place means that developers can quickly identify and address problems, reducing downtime and improving the efficiency of the development process.

Monitoring can be seen as the constant pulse check of our systems. It involves collecting data points or metrics about our software's operations, like CPU usage, memory consumption, request latency, or error rates. In the wise words of Brendan Gregg, a senior performance architect at Netflix, "The first step in performance analysis or debugging is to monitor our systems."

Observability, on the other hand, is a measure of how well we can infer the state of our system based on the information it generates. It goes beyond simple monitoring, allowing us to understand the "why" behind what's happening. As Charity Majors, CEO of Honeycomb and a strong proponent of observability, puts it, "Observability is about being able to ask any question about what's happening on the inside of the system just by observing the outside, without having to ship new code to answer new questions."

Metrics and Logging

Welcome to our exploration of Metrics and Logging, two fundamental building blocks of monitoring and observability in software development. In this section, we'll define these concepts, their importance, and how to use them to ensure software performance and reliability effectively.

Metrics, at their simplest, are numerical values representing specific aspects of a system at a time. They are like the vital signs of your application—the heart rate, blood pressure, and body temperature of your software. They can be anything from the number of active users and the response time of a request to the CPU usage of your system.

Metrics are not just numbers; they tell a story about your application. As tech author Martin Fowler said, "Effective delivery of complex software systems involves much more than just writing code." Metrics allow you to measure the efficiency of your code and infrastructure, helping you identify trends, patterns, and anomalies. They allow you to answer questions like, "How is the performance of my system changing over time?" "What was the system's load when an incident occurred?" "Which parts of my system are underperforming?"

Logging, on the other hand, provides a detailed record of events happening in an application. If metrics are the vital signs, logs are the medical history of your software. They provide the context that helps you understand why something happened. They answer questions like "Why did the system crash at this point?" "What series of events led to this error?"

Logs can be system-generated as server logs or custom logs written by developers to track the flow of the application. For instance, Google began embedding custom logs in its code as early as 1999. These logs helped them trace the behavior of their complex systems and were instrumental in debugging and improving their algorithms.

Effective logging is about more than just recording as much data as possible. It's about capturing relevant, valuable data while avoiding information overload. Brian Cantoni, a noted engineer, once advised, "Just as with logging, the key to effective application monitoring and debugging is to generate just enough data."

A powerful combination of metrics and logging provides a holistic picture of your system's performance and health. From a DevEx perspective, having clear and accessible metrics and logs enables developers to diagnose and resolve issues quickly, improving their overall workflow. Metrics help you understand "What's happening in your system, while logs explain the "why" behind it. They are most effective when used together, complementing each other.

In the end, metrics and logging are more than just tools; they are your allies in building reliable, efficient, and performant software. They are essential for creating a developer environment where issues are quickly identified and resolved, contributing to a more seamless and productive development process. As tech leader Charity Majors puts it, "The best tool for the job is the one that your team will use...and use well."

Stay with us as we explore this journey more through monitoring and observability, continuing next with alerting and incident management. And remember, the goal is to build software and craft delightful and efficient developer environments. Metrics and logging are your guides on this path.

Alerting and Incident Management

As we continue our journey through monitoring and observability, let's delve into the crucial aspects of Alerting and Incident Management. If Metrics and Logging provide your software's heart rate and medical history, Alerting and Incident Management is akin to the emergency response system—dispatching aid when the vital signs indicate a potential problem.

Alerting is notifying the responsible individuals or teams when certain predefined conditions in a system are met or exceeded. These conditions, often called "thresholds," may signify something abnormal requiring immediate attention. Effective alerting ensures that developers are promptly informed of issues, enabling them to take swift action and maintain system reliability, a vital aspect of a positive Developer Experience. As monitoring expert Greg Poirier explains, "Alerting is about detecting anomalous behavior. If it's not an actionable alert, it's not a good alert."

For example, let's say you have a web application, and you've set an alert threshold for server response times. If response times exceed this threshold, the alerting system will notify the appropriate personnel to investigate and address the issue. This way, potential problems can be addressed proactively before they escalate into full-blown incidents affecting the end-user experience.

Effective alerting is a delicate balance. Set thresholds too low, and your team may be swamped with false positives, causing alert fatigue. Set them too high, and you may miss significant events. Software engineer Cindy Sridharan said, "Alert fatigue is real and counterproductive...Every alert must be actionable."

On the other hand, Incident Management is about how your team responds when things go wrong. It involves identifying, analyzing, responding to, and learning from incidents. It's the process that ensures a systematic approach to dealing with the unforeseen, emphasizing communication, coordination, and resolution. A robust incident management process ensures developers can efficiently manage and learn from incidents, reducing stress and improving workflow.

Consider the lessons from the 2012 Amazon AWS outage, which brought down high-profile services like Netflix, Instagram, and Pinterest. The post-incident analysis led to significant changes in Amazon's incident management practices, from improving system redundancy to better stakeholder communication.

A well-defined incident management process minimizes downtime and maintains user trust. It's not just about firefighting; it's about learning from the fires to prevent or mitigate future ones. As John Allspaw, former CTO of Etsy, once said, "All incidents are opportunities in disguise. An opportunity to learn more about how your system behaves, and an opportunity to improve it."

Alerting and Incident Management are crucial components of Monitoring and Observability. They form the emergency response of your system, ensuring that your team is promptly alerted of potential issues and equipped to manage incidents effectively. For developers, these processes are crucial to maintaining a smooth and predictable workflow, contributing to a better Developer Experience. They enable you to keep the high performance and reliability that modern users expect, turning challenges into opportunities for learning and growth.

As we delve deeper into Ensuring Performance and Reliability, we'll examine strategies for Performance Optimization in the next section. Remember, our journey is not just about creating software but crafting delightful, efficient developer environments where performance and reliability are not afterthoughts but ingrained into the very fabric of our development culture.

Performance Optimization Techniques

Creating a functional application isn't the end of the journey in software development. It's a critical starting point, but performance often determines the distance between a functional and successful application. An application that performs optimally offers a great user experience and a delightful developer experience. This brings us to our focus in this section—Performance Optimization Techniques.

The proverb, "You can't improve what you don't measure," rings particularly true here. Before enhancing performance, we need to understand the current state of our application. How is it behaving? Where are its weak points? To answer these questions, we turn to two critical tools in our performance optimization toolbox: Profiling and Benchmarking.

Profiling is akin to a health check-up of your application. It involves recording detailed information about your software's operation, such as memory usage, CPU time, or function call frequency. This helps identify any bottlenecks or inefficiencies in the code. Benchmarking, on the other hand, is about comparing. By measuring the performance of your application against a standard or previous version, you gain insight into where and how improvements have been made or can be made.

Once we have measured and understood our software's performance, the next logical step is to optimize it. However, real-world conditions often involve high-load scenarios and extreme use cases. We introduce Load Testing and Stress Testing to ensure our application can handle these.

Load Testing evaluates the system's behavior, usually high traffic or data volume, under a specific load. At the same time, Stress Testing pushes the system to its absolute limits to identify the breaking point. These tests help us identify weaknesses and fortify our software against real-world extremes.

As with any journey, the road to optimal performance and reliability requires a good map. These tools and techniques are our maps, guiding us toward creating robust applications under all conditions. Performance optimization is critical for developers because it directly impacts their ability to build and maintain responsive and scalable applications, leading to a more productive and satisfying development experience. As we explore each topic in detail, you'll find ways to apply these techniques to your work, creating functional but also robust and efficient software.

Stay tuned as we dive into these fascinating and crucial aspects of performance optimization, enhancing the developer experience one step at a time. As always, we're not just exploring these ideas academically; we're learning how to make them a practical part of our everyday development work. Buckle up; it's going to be an exciting ride.

Profiling

Suppose monitoring and observability are akin to regular health check-ups. In that case, profiling can be considered a detailed medical test that dives deeper to identify bottlenecks and areas for improvement. Profiling is a potent tool to enhance the performance and efficiency of your software, enabling you to provide an unparalleled developer experience.

Profiling is measuring a program's space (memory) or time complexity, viewing statistics about program performance in various function areas, or selectively modifying how program code behaves to improve efficiency. Like a detective with a magnifying glass, profiling helps us scrutinize our code to find areas for improvement or bottlenecks that need fixing. When we talk about profiling, an apt quote by a pioneering computer scientist, Donald Knuth, comes to mind: "We should forget about small efficiencies, say about 97% of the time: premature optimization is the root of all evil." Profiling allows us to focus our optimization efforts where they matter, eliminating guesswork or intuition-based decision-making. This leads to more efficient coding practices and better-performing applications, enhancing the Developer Experience by reducing time spent on debugging and performance issues.

A profiling tool is Google's open-source tool, pprof. This tool visualizes performance profile data to allow you to navigate the call tree and focus on the hotspots where the program spends most of its time. For instance, in a complex web server application, pprof might reveal that most processing time is spent serializing JSON responses. With this knowledge, you can investigate JSON serialization libraries that offer better performance.

Benchmarking

Benchmarking, on the other hand, is running a computer program, a set of programs, or different operations to assess the relative performance of an object by running several standard tests and trials against it. It's like the standardized testing of the software world, where we measure our software's performance against a predefined set of standards or compare it with similar software.

To visualize the concept of benchmarking, consider Apache JMeter, a popular open-source tool designed to load test functional behavior and measure performance. Let's say you have an API endpoint and want to know how it performs under a heavy load of 1000 requests per second. JMeter can simulate these requests and provide detailed metrics about the average response time, error rate, throughput, and other relevant information.

For developers, profiling and benchmarking are essential tools that provide critical feedback on application performance. This feedback allows them to make informed decisions on where to focus their optimization efforts, ultimately leading to more reliable and high-performing applications, a cornerstone of a positive Developer Experience.

Profiling and benchmarking are essential optimization techniques that help us elevate our software's performance. Through thoughtful profiling, we can identify and target the critical parts of our codebase that require optimization. Similarly, benchmarking provides a clear picture of our application's performance under different loads and conditions, helping us fine-tune the system to meet or exceed our performance goals.

In the following subsection, we'll explore another vital aspect of performance optimization—Load Testing and Stress Testing. But before we move on, remember the words of Bill Gates: "We all need people who will give us feedback. That's how we improve." In the context of our software, the feedback comes from tools like profiling and benchmarking. Let's keep this conversation going as we delve deeper into this fascinating subject.

Load Testing and Stress Testing

Imagine a newly constructed bridge. It looks solid and capable of handling a substantial amount of traffic. But the question is, can it? The answer lies in testing it by allowing a particular traffic volume, gradually increasing it, and eventually pushing it to the extreme. That's precisely what we do with Load Testing and Stress Testing in software development, ensuring that our applications can handle the demands of real-world usage.

Load Testing is putting demand on a system and measuring its response. It helps identify the maximum operating capacity of an application, along with any bottlenecks, and determine which element is causing degradation. When we simulate a realistic usage scenario with a load test, we can see how the application behaves and identify potential problems before they impact the end users.

A classic example of a load testing tool is Gatling. It allows you to create complex scenarios simulating real-world usage of your application. For instance, you could simulate the behavior of 10,000 users logging into your application, browsing pages, and completing various tasks over an hour. Gatling would then provide detailed reports about the response times, error rates, and other performance metrics under this load.

On the other hand, Stress Testing goes a step further. It involves testing beyond standard operational capacity, often to a breaking point, to observe the results. Stress testing helps identify the upper limit of your system, its robustness, and the component causing system failure.

One of the widely recognized stress testing tools is Apache JMeter. You could use JMeter to simulate a million users trying to access your application simultaneously. You'd find out how your system behaves under this extreme condition, how much it can handle before it breaks down, and how it recovers once the load returns to normal.

Load and stress testing are critical for developers because they reveal their applications' limits and potential failure points. By understanding these limits, developers can optimize their code and infrastructure to handle real-world demands more effectively, leading to more stable and reliable applications. This proactive approach to testing contributes to a more positive and predictable Developer Experience.

These tests help us enhance our system's performance and improve its stability and reliability. They equip us with knowledge and insights to design better software architecture that can handle heavy loads and extreme conditions, enhancing the developer experience significantly. As Grady Booch, an eminent software engineer and designer of the IBM Rational Unified Process (RUP), once said, "The function of good software is to make the complex appear simple." By incorporating load and stress testing into the development process, we ensure that our applications remain robust and reliable, even under the most demanding conditions, leading to a smoother and more enjoyable experience for developers.

As we progress, we will delve into the strategies that help us ensure that our system performs well under normal and extreme conditions and recovers gracefully from potential failures. But for now, let's carry forward the understanding that to ensure the best performance and reliability, we must put our software under rigorous and extreme conditions, just like the bridge we mentioned at the beginning. Let's continue on this enlightening journey of improving the developer experience.

Resilience and Fault Tolerance

In creating delightful and efficient developer environments, we have reached a critical crossroads where we delve into the concepts of Resilience and Fault Tolerance. As an elastic band returns to its original shape after being stretched, resilient systems recover and adapt to failures and changes. These characteristics are essential to maintaining a stable and predictable Developer Experience, as developers rely on resilient systems to ensure unforeseen issues do not disrupt their work. While the performance and optimization techniques discussed earlier in this chapter ensure your systems run optimally, resilience and fault tolerance techniques are about designing systems that can withstand unexpected disruptions.

Drawing an analogy from the world of architecture, Japanese architect Shigeru Ban once said, "I don't believe architecture has to speak too much. It should remain silent and let nature in the guise of sunlight and wind." Translating this wisdom to the digital domain, our systems should be designed to handle failures silently, allowing the smooth flow of data and operations akin to sunlight and wind in a building.

In this journey through resilience and fault tolerance, we'll unravel how they contribute to crafting reliable and robust systems. These systems stand firm in the face of adversities and recover and adapt, providing a delightful experience to developers and end users alike.

Redundancy and Failover Strategies

You may recall the famous quote from Thomas J. Watson, the former CEO of IBM, who once said, "If you want to succeed, double your failure rate." This adage emphasizes the importance of resilience and fault tolerance in software development, two critical components for building reliable software. In our first subsection, we will explore Redundancy and Failover Strategies.

When you hear the term "redundancy," you might think of unnecessary or duplicate effort, but in our world, redundancy is a blessing. It's all about having backup systems or components that can seamlessly take over if the primary system fails. Let's look at an analogy to understand this better: think of a commercial airplane. It has multiple engines, not for the sole purpose of powering the flight but to ensure that even if one engine fails, the plane can safely land using its remaining engines.

The same principle applies to software systems. For instance, you might have multiple servers running the same application. If one server fails, the others pick up the slack, preventing any disruption to the service your users are enjoying.

However, redundancy is only helpful if there is a mechanism to switch to these backup systems when things go wrong. That's where Failover Strategies come in. Failover is the process by which operational functions are transferred to a redundant system during a failure. It's like an automatic switch that turns on the backup generator when the power goes out.

Implementing redundancy and failover strategies can vary in complexity based on the requirements of your application. The key is to make these transitions as seamless and quick as possible to ensure minimal impact on end users. These strategies are crucial for developers because they ensure that the systems they depend on remain available and reliable, even in the face of failures, reducing downtime and frustration.

Take, for instance, the global content delivery network Cloudflare. On July 17, 2020, they faced a significant router failure in Atlanta, which could have been catastrophic, affecting millions of websites worldwide. However, due to their robust failover strategies and network redundancy, they could quickly route the traffic through other network paths, ensuring uninterrupted service for most users. It was a shining example of redundancy and failover in action.

As we delve deeper into redundancy and failover strategies, we'll explore various techniques and best practices, such as load balancing, replication, and heartbeat checks. Software development aims to anticipate and prepare for failure, not merely react to it. The presence of redundancy and well-planned failover strategies is a testament to this mindset. As we often say in the software world, "Hope for the best, but always plan for the worst."

Chaos Engineering and Fault Injection

Nora Jones, a pioneer in Chaos Engineering, once aptly said, "Chaos Engineering is the discipline of experimenting on a system to build confidence in the system's capability to withstand turbulent conditions in production." So, let's step into the fascinating world of Chaos Engineering and Fault Injection and learn how they can help us improve the resilience of our systems.

Netflix popularized the concept of Chaos Engineering with their Simian Army, a collection of tools designed to test and enhance the resilience of their system by intentionally introducing failures. The most famous of these is probably the "Chaos Monkey," which randomly terminates virtual machine instances and containers to ensure that engineers implement their services to be resilient to instance failures.

Imagine you're developing a microservices-based system. Everything works perfectly in a controlled environment, with all services running smoothly. But what happens if one of these services suddenly goes down or starts behaving erratically? This is where Chaos Engineering comes in, simulating these kinds of failures to understand how the system reacts and to identify and fix weaknesses.

Complementing Chaos Engineering is the Fault Injection practice, which induces faults or errors in a system to evaluate its robustness. It's like a vaccine, injecting a weakened or dead pathogen into the body to stimulate an immune response, which helps the body recognize and combat the fundamental disease if encountered later.

Let's look at a concrete example. Consider the well-known incident of February 28, 2017, when Amazon's S3 web service in the Northern Virginia region experienced a high error rate for about four hours, causing significant disruption to services depending on S3. Postmortem analysis showed that a typo during a routine debugging operation caused more servers to be taken offline than intended. This incident highlighted the importance of fault tolerance and the value of Chaos Engineering and Fault Injection, which could have simulated such a failure in a controlled way, leading to better preparedness and prevention of the incident.

For developers, Chaos Engineering and Fault Injection offer valuable insights into how systems behave under stress and failure conditions. By proactively identifying and addressing potential weaknesses, developers can build more resilient applications, leading to a more stable and predictable Developer Experience.

Chaos Engineering and Fault Injection can be intimidating as it involves deliberately harming your system. However, it's essential to understand that these practices are conducted in a controlled and mindful way, not randomly. They are about breaking things on purpose so that we can learn how to build more resilient systems.

Embracing Chaos Engineering and Fault Injection can give us a unique edge in understanding our system better, enabling us to deliver more robust and resilient software that our users can depend on, even in turbulent conditions. For developers, these practices help ensure that the systems they build are resilient and can withstand real-world challenges, leading to a more reliable and satisfying development experience. As you progress through this journey, remember the words of Austrian poet Rainer Maria Rilke, "The only journey is the one within."

Security and Compliance Considerations

In the ongoing conversation about crafting reliable and performance-optimized systems, it's impossible to overlook one facet that ties in deeply with reliability and performance: Security and Compliance. We've often heard the saying, "A chain is only as strong as its weakest link." In our digital ecosystem, that weakest link could be an overlooked security vulnerability or a non-compliance issue, leading to catastrophic consequences.

In this section, we will traverse the often-complex landscape of Security and Compliance considerations, which, when embedded as a core part of our developer environments, can ensure the integrity and safety of our systems and adherence to various regulatory mandates and requirements. For developers, having robust security and compliance measures ensures they can build and maintain applications confidently, knowing they are protected against potential threats and legal issues.

Security Considerations revolve around three fundamental principles, known as the CIA triad: Confidentiality, Integrity, and Availability. Let's refer to the 2017 Equifax data breach incident as a grim reminder. The personal data of 143 million consumers was exposed due to a vulnerability in their web application framework. The breach had massive financial and reputational implications for Equifax, emphasizing prioritizing security considerations in software development.

As developers, we must incorporate secure coding practices, use vulnerability scanning tools, and follow other security best practices. These measures include but are not limited to maintaining least privilege access, securing sensitive data, and adopting secure design principles like Security by Design and Privacy by Design.

Moreover, secure interactions between different components are crucial in our connected world. Take, for example, the rise of API vulnerabilities in recent years. According to Salt Security's 2021 API Security Report, 91% of organizations suffered an API security incident in 2020. This underlines the importance of implementing secure interaction principles such as proper authentication, data validation, and encryption for APIs.

Compliance Considerations are the other side of the same coin, ensuring our systems align with defined regulatory standards and practices. These can range from industry-specific regulations like HIPAA for healthcare and PCI DSS for payment security to general regulations like GDPR for data protection. Being compliant doesn't just prevent costly penalties and legal issues but also builds trust with users.

For instance, in July 2019, British Airways was fined £183 million for infringements of the General Data Protection Regulation (GDPR) following a data breach in 2018. This is a clear example of how non-compliance can lead to hefty fines and significant damage to a brand's reputation.

To navigate the vast sea of compliance, developers must understand the specific regulations applicable to their domain, whether healthcare, finance, education, or any other field. Also, implementing tools and practices that automate compliance checks can be immensely helpful.

For developers, understanding and implementing security and compliance measures are critical for ensuring that the applications they build are functional but also secure and compliant with relevant regulations. This leads to a more confident and stress-free development experience, knowing that potential risks are proactively managed.

Security and Compliance Considerations are integral components in the endeavor of ensuring performance and reliability. They form the invisible shield that not only guards against external threats and legal implications but also forms the backbone of a trustful relationship with the users. By embedding security and compliance into the development process, developers can create applications that are not only high-performing but also secure and trustworthy, contributing to a more positive Developer Experience. The following section will conclude this chapter with key takeaways and a summary of shared insights.

Key Takeaways

- Monitoring and Observability, involving metrics, logging, alerting, and incident management, form the foundation of proactive software maintenance and improvement.

- Performance Optimization Techniques like profiling, benchmarking, load testing, and stress testing help us understand our software's behavior and ensure it can handle real-world demands.

- Resilience and Fault Tolerance, achieved through redundancy, failover strategies, chaos engineering, and fault injection, enable our software to withstand and recover from unexpected disruptions.

- Security and Compliance are non-negotiable aspects of software development, demanding continuous attention and adaptation to evolving threats and regulations.

- Ensuring performance and reliability is a continual, systemic process impacting all software development lifecycle aspects.

CHAPTER 8

Measuring Developer Experience

In any project or initiative, the importance of tracking progress and success cannot be overstated. This principle holds especially true regarding understanding and enhancing the Developer Experience (DevEx). The methods to measure DevEx may not always be straightforward, but as we embark on the journey of Chapter 8, we'll navigate these murky waters together. However, this chapter isn't just about observing what others have done; it's about equipping you with actionable steps you can implement in your projects to measure and improve DevEx effectively.

Just as a sailor uses stars for guidance, we have our constellations as Key Performance Indicators (KPIs) to guide our journey in understanding DevEx. KPIs are quantifiable measures used to evaluate the success of an organization, employee, etc., in meeting objectives for performance. To make these KPIs actionable, we will explore practical steps for implementing and measuring them in your context. Let's explore four fundamental KPIs that hold significant relevance in DevEx.

As we journey through these KPIs, remember that they are not stand-alone measures. Like the jigsaw puzzle pieces, each contributes a part of the whole picture. The magic happens when they work together, illuminating a delightful and efficient Developer Experience. Consider how each KPI can be tracked within your existing tools or processes. For

© K. Rain Leander 2025
K. R. Leander, *Developer Experience Unleashed*,
https://doi.org/10.1007/979-8-8688-0242-3_8

instance, adoption rates could be measured through analytics software already in use, or you might need to set up new surveys to gauge retention rates effectively. So, let's set sail and delve into these fascinating KPIs!

Adoption and Retention Rates

In measuring the Developer Experience (DevEx), adoption and retention rates are among the first Key Performance Indicators (KPIs) you might consider. They are instrumental in understanding how your tools, frameworks, or APIs are perceived and used over time. They offer insight into how successfully your offerings have been integrated into the daily workflows of developers and how much value these developers find in them. Let's explore each of these two intertwined KPIs in detail.

The adoption rate measures the proportion of developers who have started using your tools, frameworks, or APIs during a given period. Simply put, it reflects your success in persuading developers to try your offerings.

The formula for calculating the adoption rate is usually expressed as:

(Number of New Users/Total Potential User Base) * 100%

To implement this, identify your ecosystem's baseline number of potential users. Use analytics tools to track how many new users have interacted with your product over a specific period. This can often be pulled directly from user registration data or API key requests.

While the adoption rate provides valuable insight, it only paints half the picture. The retention rate fills in the other half, measuring the proportion of developers who continue using your tools, frameworks, or APIs over a more extended period. The retention rate reflects developers' long-term value in your offerings.

The formula for calculating the retention rate typically goes like this:

((Total Users at End of Period - New Users Acquired)/Total Users at Start of Period) * 100%

To apply this, ensure your analytics track users over time. Tools like cohort analysis in Google Analytics or similar platforms can help you see who continues to use your product versus who drops off.

A high retention rate indicates that developers find your offerings beneficial over the long term and continue to derive value from them. On the other hand, a low retention rate can serve as an early warning sign, suggesting that despite initial interest (reflected in the adoption rate), developers may be experiencing challenges or dissatisfaction that leads them to abandon your offerings. To address this, consider implementing feedback loops where users who churn are surveyed or interviewed to understand their reasons for leaving.

Both adoption and retention rates are essential KPIs that can offer a holistic view of how well your tools, frameworks, or APIs resonate with developers. However, while they can provide a high-level view of DevEx, they must offer specific insights into what works well or needs improvement. To gain deeper insights, segment these KPIs by different user demographics or product features to pinpoint particular areas of strength or concern. For these insights, we'll need to delve into more granular KPIs, like time to first successful task completion, error rates, bug reports, and direct feedback from developers—which we'll explore in the following subsections.

Time to First Successful Task Completion

As we delve deeper into the Key Performance Indicators (KPIs) used to measure the Developer Experience (DevEx), we encounter the concept of "Time to First Successful Task Completion." This KPI measures the time it takes for a new user to reach a significant milestone using your tool, framework, or API for the first time. It is a robust measure of your offerings' ease of use and initial usability.

A well-documented example of this KPI comes from Stripe, a company renowned for its focus on excellent DevEx. Stripe's goal was to minimize the time a developer took to make their first successful API call. They realized that reducing friction and smoothing the initial experience increased the likelihood of developers adopting their API in their projects.

To implement this KPI in your projects, start by defining what a "successful task" looks like for your product. This could be making an API call, setting up an environment, or completing a specific feature in your tool. Once defined, use analytics to track the time new users take to achieve this milestone.

Time to First Successful Task Completion is usually measured from the moment a developer first engages with your product—when they first visit your website, download your SDK, or initiate a free trial—until they reach a predefined "success" milestone. This milestone will differ depending on your product. For an API, it might be the first successful API call. For a software library, it could be the first successful library integration into a project. For a developer tool, it might be the first completed task using the device.

This KPI offers valuable insight into the learning curve associated with your product. If developers can succeed quickly, they're more likely to feel optimistic about the experience, continue exploring your product, and ultimately integrate it into their projects. However, if the path to the first successful task must be clarified, developers might abandon your product and turn to alternatives.

To optimize Time to First Successful Task Completion, you need to consider various factors. Clear, concise documentation is vital, as are easy-to-follow getting-started guides. Break down complex processes into smaller manageable steps and provide interactive tutorials or guided walkthroughs. This will help developers navigate the initial stages more smoothly. Sound API design principles, like consistency, simplicity, and intuitiveness, can also play a significant role. Additionally, providing code samples, software libraries, SDKs, or other resources to help developers get started can significantly reduce the time needed to complete the first successful task.

Another practical step is to gather feedback directly from new users about their onboarding experience. Use surveys or interviews to understand their difficulties and iterate on your documentation or onboarding processes accordingly. Measuring and improving this KPI can result in a more delightful and engaging initial developer experience, increasing adoption and retention rates. However, it's important to remember that the developer's journey continues. Ensuring a smooth initial incident is the first step toward building a long-lasting and productive relationship with your developers. Following this, it is essential to understand and improve other areas of the DevEx, such as error rates, bug reports, and developer satisfaction, which we will discuss in the subsequent sections.

Error Rates and Bug Reports

Tracking error rates and bug reports forms another essential part of measuring Developer Experience (DevEx). These metrics offer crucial insights into your software, tool, or API's stability, reliability, and overall quality.

The error rate is the percentage of operations that fail for some reason, and it can highlight several issues, such as poor API design, inadequate documentation, or underlying bugs in your system. If the error rate is high, it may indicate a frustrating experience for your developers, which might prompt them to abandon your product and seek alternatives. To implement this effectively, set up automated monitoring systems that log errors in real time. Regularly review these logs to identify patterns and prioritize fixes based on the frequency and severity of the mistakes.

Consider the case of Microsoft during the early development of the .NET framework. The team set a target of maintaining an error rate below

1% during the early adopter phase. Whenever the error rate exceeded this threshold, they diligently investigated and resolved the underlying issues to maintain developer satisfaction and trust. You can adopt a similar approach by establishing specific error rate thresholds for your project. Set alerts to notify your team whenever these thresholds are exceeded, enabling rapid response and issue resolution.

Bug reports are another vital source of feedback. When developers encounter an issue they believe is a bug, they might report it through various channels, such as support tickets, forums, or bug-tracking tools. The volume, severity, and nature of these bug reports can offer deep insights into the areas that need improvement. To manage bug reports effectively, integrate a bug-tracking tool that categorizes and prioritizes issues based on their impact. Encourage developers to provide detailed information, such as steps to reproduce the bug, to help your team diagnose and fix the problem more efficiently.

Take, for instance, the Linux kernel development. The community actively encourages its vast user base to report bugs, which they document on platforms like Bugzilla. This transparent and inclusive process has helped make the Linux kernel one of the most reliable pieces of software. You can emulate this transparency by creating an open bug tracker where developers can view reported issues and track the progress of fixes. This builds trust and allows the community to contribute to solutions or workarounds.

Monitoring error rates and bug reports can guide the allocation of your development resources. If a particular area consistently triggers errors or attracts numerous bug reports, you should prioritize refining that aspect of your product. Addressing the issues that matter most to your developers can dramatically enhance their experience and your product's overall quality. Implementing regular review meetings to discuss high-priority bugs and error trends can ensure that your team stays focused on the most critical improvements.

However, it's also essential to note that not all errors are equal. Some might be "expected" errors resulting from developers pushing the boundaries of your system or misusing the API. Distinguishing between these "expected" errors and those that indicate real problems can be tricky but is crucial for accurately interpreting these metrics. Develop a classification system for errors, distinguishing between minor and critical failures. This will help your team focus on resolving the most impactful problems first.

In addition to quantitatively measuring error rates and bug reports, it's equally important to consider the developers' qualitative feedback about these issues. Developers' comments and complaints about specific problems often provide more nuanced insights than raw numbers alone. Set up feedback loops where developers can provide context for the errors they encounter, offering insights that might not be immediately obvious from the data alone. Use this qualitative feedback to guide deeper investigations into recurring issues.

In the following sections, we will look into other vital KPIs and delve deeper into the quantitative and qualitative research methods you can use to measure DevEx. As you will see, a comprehensive understanding of DevEx requires a mix of different ways and perspectives.

Developer Satisfaction and Feedback

As we conclude our discussion on Key Performance Indicators (KPIs), we arrive at one of the most subjective yet highly influential metrics in gauging Developer Experience (DevEx)—Developer Satisfaction and Feedback.

Satisfaction measures how happy developers are with your product or service. It reflects their overall experience and can be influenced by factors such as the ease of use of your platform, the quality of your documentation, the promptness of your support, and even the friendliness of your community. To implement this, consider conducting regular surveys and utilizing tools like Net Promoter Score (NPS) to capture developers' overall satisfaction and sentiment. Track these metrics over time to identify trends and areas needing attention.

Consider JetBrains, creators of popular development tools like IntelliJ IDEA and PyCharm. JetBrains conducts an annual Developer Ecosystem Survey to collect feedback and gauge satisfaction among developers. Their 2023 survey received responses from over 30,000 developers worldwide, providing them invaluable insights about developer satisfaction across different languages, tools, and frameworks. You can adopt a similar approach by tailoring surveys to your developer audience and focusing on specific aspects of your tools that directly impact their experience.

Conversely, feedback is direct information from developers about what they like or dislike and what they wish to see improved or added to your product. It is an invaluable resource for improving your tools and services. To make feedback actionable, create channels for continuous input, such as feedback forms, community forums, or direct communication through support tickets. Regularly review and categorize this feedback to prioritize improvements.

The world's leading software development platform, GitHub, is a great example. They are known for their robust feedback system, where developers can directly raise issues, suggest improvements, or voice their concerns. This active engagement and open feedback channel has been instrumental in making GitHub a platform tailored to developers' needs. You can emulate this by ensuring that your feedback channels are easily accessible and that responses to developer concerns are timely and transparent, showing that their input directly influences your product roadmap.

However, getting truthful and valuable feedback can sometimes be a challenge. Like everyone, developers may be reluctant to provide negative feedback or simply be too busy to give any feedback. To overcome this, consider offering incentives for feedback, such as discounts, exclusive content, or recognition within the community. Demonstrate how previous feedback has led to tangible changes, reinforcing the value of their contributions. Encouraging a culture of open and constructive feedback, possibly through incentives or by demonstrating that past feedback has led to fundamental changes, can help overcome these hurdles.

While developer satisfaction and feedback are primarily qualitative measures, they can be quantified through various methods. Net Promoter Score (NPS), satisfaction surveys, or sentiment analysis of feedback and comments are some ways you can transform these subjective measures into objective data. Additionally, implement regular reviews of this data to identify actionable trends and measure the effectiveness of your improvements.

Remember that while satisfaction and feedback are critical, they are most effective with the other KPIs discussed in this chapter. Developer experience is multifaceted, and a single metric rarely provides the complete picture. To get a holistic view, integrate satisfaction and feedback data with metrics like error rates, adoption rates, and time-to-first success, ensuring that every aspect of the developer journey is optimized.

As we progress, we'll explore more quantitative and qualitative research methods in greater depth. These methods will help you collect the data you need to measure DevEx and equip you with the skills to analyze and interpret this data effectively. Armed with this knowledge, you will be better placed to iterate, improve, and validate your developer products and services, ultimately leading to a better developer experience. To implement these methods, identify the most critical touchpoints in your developer journey and gather data. Use this data to drive your next iteration of improvements, ensuring that your developer community feels heard and supported every step of the way.

Quantitative and Qualitative Research Methods

The previous section discussed the critical performance indicators instrumental in measuring developer experience (DevEx). However, the landscape of DevEx is vast, and KPIs, while crucial, only illuminate part of the picture. It's essential to employ quantitative and qualitative research methods to gain a complete understanding, each providing unique insights into the developer's interaction with your tools. We must delve deeper using quantitative and qualitative research methods to understand comprehensively. Remember, we're seeking to gather data and hear the heartbeat of the developer's interaction with our tools. This journey of profound discovery involves various methods like surveys, interviews, usability testing, observation, analytics, and usage data.

In this section, we'll dive into each research method in detail, exploring its strengths and weaknesses and how best to utilize them to enhance the developer experience. The goal is to provide actionable steps to implement these methods effectively within your projects. After all, to craft a delightful and efficient developer environment, we need to understand the developer's journey—their struggles, victories, needs, and wants. Let's explore how you can start using these methods right away.

Surveys and Questionnaires

Surveys and questionnaires, the research stalwarts, are our first port of call in the voyage through quantitative and qualitative research methods for understanding the Developer Experience (DevEx). Their popularity in the field is unsurprising, given their versatility and the breadth of insights they can provide.

First, let's distinguish between the two. Although the terms are often used interchangeably, there are subtle differences. Surveys usually entail collecting quantitative data from a large audience to generalize the results, while questionnaires tend to gather more detailed, qualitative data.

To start with surveys, consider using tools like Google Forms, SurveyMonkey, or Typeform, which offer templates and features specifically designed for gathering and analyzing quantitative data. Quantitative surveys are instrumental in gaining statistical insights about your developer population. For example, a survey asking developers about their preferred programming language, the frequency of use of your platform, or their satisfaction on a scale of 1 to 10 can provide valuable metrics. These metrics can then be benchmarked or compared against industry standards to measure your platform's performance.

On the other hand, questionnaires can delve deeper, probing the why behind the what. To craft effective questionnaires, consider the context and the specific insights you need—use open-ended questions to gather rich, narrative data. Open-ended questions can unearth rich, contextual information and unexpected insights about the developer's experience.

To illustrate, let's take the Visual Studio Code (VS Code) case. In December 2022, the VS Code team conducted a developer survey to understand user preferences and behavior. You can emulate this by starting with a small study targeted within your developer community to gather similar insights. The survey included a mix of closed and open-ended questions. Quantitative data like "90% of respondents used the integrated terminal daily" helped the team understand the platform's most popular features. At the same time, open-ended questions like "What would you like to improve in VS Code?" offered in-depth user perspectives, leading to the introduction of new features in subsequent versions.

Despite their utility, surveys and questionnaires have a caveat: they heavily depend on the respondents' honesty and self-awareness. Sometimes, there may be a discrepancy between what developers say they do (or prefer) and their actual behavior.

To mitigate this, ensure that your surveys are designed to minimize bias. Your survey or questionnaire design should be thoughtful. Be clear about the purpose, ensure anonymity if required, keep it concise, and use a balanced mix of closed and open-ended questions. Paying attention to the phrasing and ordering of questions is crucial to avoid biasing the responses. You can also pilot your survey with a small group first to catch any issues before rolling it out to a larger audience.

When designed and executed correctly, surveys and questionnaires can offer a treasure trove of insights into the Developer Experience. From understanding the popularity of specific features to uncovering pain points, they serve as a cornerstone in measuring and enhancing DevEx. Start small, refine your approach, and scale up your efforts as you gain confidence in your methods. As we proceed, we will discover how these methods synergize with other research techniques in this quest.

Interviews and Focus Groups

Building on the foundation set by surveys and questionnaires, let's shift our gaze toward more immersive research methods: interviews and focus groups. These methods lean heavily into the qualitative research spectrum, affording us a more profound and intimate understanding of the developer's experience. To make these methods actionable in your projects, consider setting clear objectives for what you want to learn from these interactions and prepare specific questions that align with those goals.

Interviews are typically one-on-one sessions, ideally between a user (developer) and a researcher or product manager. They provide in-depth insights into developers' needs, pain points, and motivations. The nature of the conversation is exploratory, and the dialogue can be adjusted dynamically based on the developer's responses. To implement this effectively, start by identifying key developers who represent different segments of your user base and schedule interviews focusing on uncovering specific issues or opportunities for improvement. The flexibility of this method often leads to revelations that cannot be gleaned from more rigid data collection methods.

For instance, in an interview, you might ask a developer to describe their first experience with your product or how they felt when encountering a particular challenge. Document these insights and look for patterns that could inform changes or enhancements to your product. Such discussions can offer invaluable context and depth, revealing why certain features are adored, or some elements of your platform cause frustration.

Consider the case of GitHub. In early 2022, GitHub held in-depth interviews with developers using its platform. They discovered that developers appreciated the ease of collaboration that GitHub provided, but many needed help with the complexity of managing large-scale projects on the forum. This feedback sparked initiatives to improve project management capabilities, resulting in features like project boards and improved pull request handling. Similarly, after conducting interviews, you can prioritize the most common pain points and directly incorporate this feedback into your product roadmap.

Then, we have focus groups, which are group interviews. Typically, a focus group involves 6–10 participants and is led by a skilled moderator. The group setting encourages interaction among participants, bringing diverse viewpoints into the discussion and often surfacing trends or shared experiences that might not come up in individual interviews. To facilitate this, ensure your focus group includes diverse participants and design the session to encourage open dialogue and interaction.

For example, suppose you've just launched a new IDE and want to understand its reception among the developer community. A focus group comprising developers from different backgrounds and expertise levels can provide a rich discussion about the IDE's features, ease of use, integration capabilities, and more. Use the insights from these discussions to make targeted improvements, such as refining user flows, enhancing feature discoverability, or simplifying complex functions.

Remember, though, that interviews and focus groups also have their challenges. They require skilled moderators to ensure conversations stay on track and everyone's voices are heard. The data collected is often extensive and subjective, requiring careful analysis to extract actionable insights. To manage this, consider using thematic analysis software to help categorize and interpret the qualitative data you collect. Lastly, these methods can be time-consuming and costly compared to other research methods.

However, their depth of insights and context often outweigh the drawbacks, making interviews and focus groups a fundamental part of the developer experience research toolkit. When planning your research, allocate sufficient time and resources to conduct thorough interviews and focus groups and follow up by implementing changes based on the feedback. They bring us face-to-face with the humans behind the statistics, reminding us that at the heart of every excellent developer tool or platform is a developer seeking efficiency, simplicity, and perhaps a little joy in their craft.

Usability Testing and Observation

Now that we've looked at surveys, interviews, and focus groups, it's time to step into usability testing and observation. These two methods allow us to see developers in their natural habitat, so to speak, interacting with our tools and services in real time.

Usability testing can be as simple or complex as you make it. At its most basic, it involves observing a developer while they use your tool or service, noting where they encounter difficulties, and identifying areas for improvement. These sessions can be structured with specific tasks for the developer to complete or be more exploratory, where the developer freely interacts with your service. To implement this on your project, you could start by defining key workflows you want to test, such as signing up for an account, integrating an API, or completing a specific task. Invite a small group of developers to participate and use screen recording tools to capture their interactions for later review.

For example, in June 2023, MongoDB ran a series of usability tests on its Compass GUI platform. Developers were asked to complete tasks, including setting up a database, executing simple queries, and using the aggregation pipeline builder. Observing developers struggling with the aggregation pipeline builder led MongoDB to redesign this feature, significantly enhancing its intuitiveness and user-friendliness. You can replicate this by iterating on problem areas developers encounter in your product. After identifying friction points in a usability test, make incremental improvements and run follow-up tests to measure the impact of those changes.

Observation, also known as field study or ethnography, typically involves observing developers' daily tasks in their environment. This method gives an excellent insight into developers' workflows, how they use different tools together, and how they problem-solve when encountering issues. To try this, consider contacting a small group of your regular users and asking if you can observe them for a few hours while they work. This can be done remotely by sharing screens or in-person observation, depending on your relationship with the developers. It helps you understand not only the usability of your product but also its fit within the larger ecosystem of tools and processes that developers use.

A great example of this approach is how IDE provider JetBrains conducts annual Developer Ecosystem surveys. However, they supplement these surveys with observation studies to better understand developers' workflows and how they switch contexts, use shortcuts, and handle multitasking within the IDE. These observations helped JetBrains design more streamlined and context-aware features, leading to a smoother, more seamless developer experience. Consider supplementing your surveys or interviews with field observations. For example, you might discover that a commonly used feature requires too many clicks, which you wouldn't have noticed without observing the workflow.

Usability testing and observation do have their challenges. They can be time-consuming and potentially intrusive, and the data collected can be subjective and complex to analyze. To manage the time investment, start small. Conduct usability tests on a few features or observe just a few developers before scaling up. Create a systematic process for analyzing the results, focusing on patterns and recurring issues rather than individual outliers.

But the benefits often outweigh the challenges. These methods give a rich, nuanced understanding of the developer's journey and can reveal surprising insights and opportunities for improvement. When starting with usability testing or observation, building empathy with developers is essential. What frustrates them? What delights them? This understanding will help you prioritize improvements that have the most significant impact on the overall developer experience.

In essence, usability testing and observation bring us closer to the developer, allowing us to empathize with their struggles and celebrate their triumphs. They provide invaluable context, helping us create tools and services that meet the functional requirements and delight the developer, making their work easier, faster, and more enjoyable. Start by identifying key pain points and using these methods to drive iterative improvements. Over time, these practices will help refine your developer tools to better align with your users' real-world needs.

Analytics and Usage Data

The final method we'll explore in this section is analytics and usage data. This technique is critical as it allows us to glean insights from complex data that can directly inform our understanding of developer behavior, experiences, and product development efforts. To implement this in your projects, identify the key questions you want to answer about your developers' interactions with your tools. For example, you might want to know which features are most popular, where users drop off, or how long it takes them to complete critical tasks.

Analytics is the discovery, interpretation, and communication of meaningful patterns in data. In the context of developer experience, we often look at how developers interact with our tools, how much time they spend on specific tasks, and what features they use most, among other things. Consider using tools like Google Analytics, Mixpanel, or Amplitude to collect this data. These platforms allow you to track user interactions and generate reports to help you understand user behavior. Implementing event tracking on key actions—such as button clicks, page views, or API calls—can give you detailed insights into how developers use your product.

A perfect example is Google's usage of analytics data in its Chrome DevTools. By analyzing the usage data, the Chrome team discovered that the "Network" tab was frequently used, leading them to invest in making it more intuitive and robust. This sort of decision-making was only possible with the insight provided by analytics.

Usage data goes hand-in-hand with analytics. It is the raw data about how and when developers use your product. Usage data can be incredibly detailed, providing a timestamped log of every user's action within your tool or service. This can include data on feature usage, session length, frequency of use, navigation paths, and more. To effectively collect this data, you might set up event tracking for every critical action within your application, such as "login," "project creation," "feature X usage," or "documentation access." This allows you to see how often and in what order developers use different parts of your product.

It's also essential to understand the concept of "segments." A segment is a subset of your user base, grouped by shared characteristics or behaviors. For instance, you might segment your users by experience level, version of the tool they use, or type of projects they typically work on. Analyzing these segments can help you tailor your product improvements to the specific needs of different user groups.

For example, consider GitHub's introduction of its "Actions" feature in 2019. By carefully observing usage data, they noted that the adoption of "Actions" was slower among specific developer segments. In response, GitHub expanded its educational resources and tutorial materials to focus on "Actions," which boosted its adoption rates. This demonstrates how understanding segments within your user base can lead to targeted improvements that drive engagement and satisfaction.

When used correctly, analytics and usage data can be potent tools. They can show you where developers get stuck, what features they love, which ones they ignore, and how they progress through your service. For example, you might discover that many users drop off after a particular step in your onboarding process, indicating a potential friction point that needs to be addressed. This information can guide your design decisions, help prioritize feature development, and enable you to create an even better experience for your developers.

However, it's important to note that while usage data and analytics can tell you much about what developers are doing, they can't always tell you why. To get to the root cause of user behavior, combine your quantitative data with qualitative methods like user interviews or surveys. This dual approach allows you to validate your hypotheses and understand the motivations behind certain behaviors. That's where qualitative research methods, like the ones we've covered earlier, come into play. They provide the why behind the what, giving you a fuller understanding of the developer experience. In essence, both quantitative and qualitative methods complement each other, providing a well-rounded knowledge of the developer experience.

In the next section, we'll delve into how to analyze and interpret these results, identifying trends and patterns, and how to prioritize improvements based on these findings. Remember, the key to making the most of analytics and usage data is collecting information and knowing how to use it to drive meaningful change in your product and overall developer experience. So, let's carry on with our journey of understanding and enhancing the developer experience.

Analyzing and Interpreting Results

Understanding how to analyze and interpret the data from your DevEx measurements is just as crucial as collecting it. With this step, you would be left with heaps of raw data but more understanding of what it all means. You need to figure out where to focus your improvements, how to validate them, or how to progress toward a better developer experience.

In this section, we explore the three main stages of analysis and interpretation—identifying trends and patterns, prioritizing improvements, and implementing iterative improvements and validations. By walking through these stages, we aim to provide you with a roadmap for translating your raw DevEx data into actionable insights. Additionally, we will discuss practical approaches to classifying and categorizing responses, especially from usability studies, to help you systematically group and analyze the data.

In each stage, we'll see that the key to effectively analyzing and interpreting results lies not in isolated actions but in the seamless integration of these stages into a continuous, cyclical process. By the end of this section, you should comprehensively understand how to analyze your DevEx data, interpret the findings, and take action that makes a tangible difference in your developers' experiences.

Identifying Trends and Patterns

Once you've gathered data through surveys, interviews, usability tests, observations, and analytics, the real challenge is to make sense of it all. After all, data in its raw form is like a puzzle with countless pieces; our job is to piece them together to unveil the picture within. Deciphering the data to identify trends and patterns is integral to understanding the developer experience and guiding your strategies for enhancing it.

To start, it's helpful to categorize responses into specific themes or "buckets." For example, if you are analyzing usability study results, you could classify feedback such as "ease of navigation," "error messages," "performance," or "documentation clarity." This allows you to group similar responses and identify recurring issues or positive aspects.

When spotting trends and patterns, you're looking for recurring themes or significant data points from your research. These could be common behaviors, repeated feedback, spikes in usage data, or specific issues where developers face friction. Recognizing these patterns allows you to gain insight into the collective developer experience and perceive broader themes that might not be evident from individual data points. For example, after categorizing feedback into buckets, many developers mention difficulty with the onboarding process, signaling a trend that needs attention.

For example, if you find through surveys and interviews that developers frequently cite difficulties with a particular feature of your API, that's a trend. If usability tests consistently show developers struggling to complete tasks in a specific section of your application, that's a pattern. Or if your analytics data shows a significant drop in usage after a particular update, that's a trend you can't ignore.

The company saw relatively low adoption rates in the early days of Facebook's Graph API. Upon analyzing their feedback and usage data, they found a recurring pattern: developers found the API complex and challenging to navigate. Identifying this trend led to a significant redesign of the API, making it more user-friendly and consequently driving up adoption rates.

Identifying trends and patterns is only sometimes straightforward, as they can often be hidden beneath the surface. It's like being a data detective; you're looking for clues and connections, piecing together evidence, and uncovering the story hidden within the data. As you categorize and analyze data, consider using spreadsheets or specialized software like NVivo or Dedoose, which can help tag and group qualitative feedback systematically. These tools can also assist in visualizing the frequency of specific themes, making it easier to spot trends.

It's essential to approach this process with an open mind. Be ready to question your assumptions, and don't hesitate to dive deep. When examining usage data, for example, go beyond the obvious metrics. Explore different angles and consider all possible factors. Maybe a drop in usage isn't due to an update but correlates with a new competitor entering the market or a seasonal trend that affects your user base.

Identifying trends and patterns is fundamental in analyzing and interpreting results. It's all about connecting the dots, painting a holistic picture of the developer experience, and leveraging this understanding to inform future improvements. It's less about seeking definitive answers and more about illuminating the path forward for a continuously better developer experience. By categorizing and systematically analyzing your data, you can turn observations into actionable insights, providing a clear direction for enhancements that resonate with your developer community.

Prioritizing Improvements

Once we've identified the trends and patterns within our data, our task moves into determining where to focus our efforts to improve the developer experience (DevEx). Remember, our resources—time, human capital, or financial investment—are often limited. As such, we must prioritize what improvements to implement first. To move beyond merely observing case studies, I'll include actionable steps and tools you can use to prioritize improvements effectively within your projects.

When prioritizing improvements, it's crucial to balance the needs of the developers, the impact of the change, and the resources required to implement the update. Here's where your detective skills come into play once more as you aim to understand and evaluate the trade-offs. Start by gathering your team to assess each potential improvement's impact and effort collaboratively. Use tools like Trello or Asana to organize and visualize these assessments, ensuring that every team member's perspective is considered.

The "impact versus effort" matrix is a robust approach to prioritizing improvements. With this matrix, you can visualize the potential benefit of an improvement (its impact) against the resources needed to implement it (the effort). Improvements that fall into the "high impact, low effort" quadrant are typically your low-hanging fruits—those you should tackle first. Conversely, those in the "low impact, high effort" quadrant may not be worth your immediate attention. To implement this in your project, you can create a simple matrix in a spreadsheet or use project management software that supports prioritization frameworks, like Jira or Monday.com. This allows you to drag and drop tasks into the appropriate quadrants, making the decision process more interactive and transparent.

Take, for instance, the situation at Microsoft in the mid-2000s. They were developing the .NET Framework, but the complexity and inconsistent documentation made the learning curve for developers quite steep. Their research found a high-impact, low-effort solution: improving their documentation and making it more consistent. This change required relatively minimal resources but had a significant positive effect on the developer experience, as it lowered the entry barrier and reduced the time taken by developers to become productive. Consider starting with improvements to documentation in your project, especially if it's frequently cited in feedback. Improving documentation is often a high-impact, low-effort task that can quickly enhance the developer experience.

However, the impact versus effort matrix is one of many factors in prioritizing improvements. Developer feedback can play a critical role in this process. If developers express intense frustration about a particular feature, even if addressing it requires substantial resources, you should consider prioritizing it. To effectively incorporate feedback, set up regular check-ins or surveys to gather insights on pain points. Tools like Typeform or Google Forms can help automate this process, ensuring you continuously collect valuable data from your developer community.

Take, for instance, GitHub's decision in 2016 to address long-standing complaints about their notification system, even though it required significant engineering resources. This move was driven by vital user feedback, with developers voicing their struggles with managing notifications across multiple repositories. Even though this fell into the "high impact, high effort" category, the potential to enhance DevEx significantly made it a worthwhile investment. In your projects, identify high-impact, high-effort tasks that could substantially improve the developer experience, and consider creating a dedicated task force or sprint focused on tackling these challenges.

Lastly, always keep in mind that prioritizing improvements is a dynamic process. As new data comes in or circumstances change, your priorities might shift. Regular reassessment is vital, making this not a one-off activity but a continuous process that keeps your developer environment in sync with your developer community's evolving needs and expectations. Consider setting quarterly reviews where your team revisits the prioritization matrix and adjusts priorities based on the latest data. This keeps your development aligned with current needs and ensures you remain responsive to new challenges.

In essence, prioritizing improvements is strategically navigating the path of DevEx enhancement. It involves making informed decisions that balance impact and resources, guided by a deep understanding of developer needs and experiences. Done right, it ensures that your every step is a stride toward a more delightful and efficient developer environment. By following these actionable steps, you can move beyond merely observing successful case studies to actively applying these principles in your projects, driving tangible improvements in your developer experience.

Iterative Improvement and Validation

Improving the developer experience (DevEx) is more than just a one-and-done exercise. It's a continuous, iterative process akin to the software development lifecycle. After prioritizing and implementing improvements, we must validate their effectiveness and make further adjustments. This validation step, often overlooked, is critical to ensuring the changes deliver the desired impact. To make this process actionable, consider using specific methods such as A/B testing, user surveys, or usability testing to gather concrete data on the effectiveness of your changes. This allows you to measure the impact in real-world scenarios and refine your approach based on actual feedback rather than assumptions.

The beauty of iterative improvement lies in its cyclical nature—plan, act, observe, and react. It acknowledges that our first solution may not be the perfect one. Or even if it was perfect, then needs and contexts change. As Ken Schwaber and Jeff Sutherland, the creators of Scrum, stated, "Welcome changing requirements, even late in development. Agile processes harness change for the customer's competitive advantage."

A stellar example of iterative improvement and validation comes from Google's work on its cloud platform. In 2014, Google Cloud Platform (GCP) was lagging behind Amazon Web Services (AWS) and Microsoft Azure regarding usability and developer experience. Google conducted extensive research using quantitative and qualitative methods to understand the problems developers faced with GCP.

Armed with this data, they made many changes, including better error messages, improved documentation, and more intuitive user interfaces. But they didn't stop there. To ensure the changes were effective, Google employed iterative usability testing and analytics to gather data on how developers interacted with the updated platform. This allowed them to make evidence-based decisions in each subsequent iteration. After implementing these changes, they returned to their developer community for feedback to validate whether these improvements were making a difference.

To their delight, the feedback was overwhelmingly positive. However, developers also pointed out areas where issues persisted. For example, they appreciated the improved error messages but found that some still needed more details for troubleshooting. In the next iteration, Google took this feedback onboard and worked to address these residual concerns.

They repeated this cycle—implement, validate, refine—several times, and it paid off. In a few short years, GCP saw significant growth in its adoption, with many developers citing its enhanced usability and DevEx as a critical reason for choosing it over its competitors.

This iterative improvement and validation process underscores the importance of maintaining a two-way communication channel with your developers. As noted throughout this chapter, developers are not just users of your platform, API, or tool but partners in its development. To facilitate this, consider setting up regular feedback loops, such as quarterly surveys or feedback sessions, to keep the communication ongoing and ensure you stay aligned with developers' needs. By incorporating their feedback into your improvement cycles, you ensure that the changes you're making are not just well-intentioned but genuinely helpful and impactful.

Iterative improvement and validation are the heartbeats of effective DevEx management. By adopting a structured approach to iteration—using measurable criteria, continuous feedback, and clear communication—you can build a process that identifies and resolves issues efficiently and effectively. It propels continuous enhancement, keeping your platform or tool relevant, user-friendly, and attuned to the needs of your developer community. And, as we'll discuss in the next section, this iterative process feeds into your product roadmaps, helping to chart the course for your future development efforts.

Incorporating Developer Feedback into Product Roadmaps

In our journey to measure and improve developer experience (DevEx), we have discussed various methods and key performance indicators (KPIs) to understand and measure DevEx effectively. We've delved into qualitative and quantitative research methods, from surveys and interviews to usability testing and usage data analysis. We've looked at identifying trends and patterns, prioritizing improvements, and validating those improvements iteratively.

These methods and techniques are vital in their own right, yet they become truly transformative when they feed into a crucial process: incorporating developer feedback into product roadmaps. This process, which forms the cornerstone of this section, is where the real magic happens. It's where developer feedback becomes actionable, where it starts to shape the future of your product, and where it has a tangible impact on the DevEx you provide.

The beauty of this process lies in its cyclical nature: feedback drives the roadmap, shapes the product, affects the developer experience, and generates more feedback. This feedback loop forms the core of any effective DevEx improvement strategy. It's essential to break down each step into specific, implementable actions to make this process actionable in your projects. This involves collecting feedback and creating a systematic approach for analyzing it, prioritizing based on clear criteria, and communicating changes transparently with your team and developers.

By exploring each of these steps in-depth, we will understand how to incorporate developer feedback into product roadmaps effectively and in a manner that ultimately enriches the developer experience. Let's begin this exciting journey!

Understanding Developer Feedback

Understanding developer feedback is a critical initial step when incorporating their insights into your product roadmap. This process isn't merely about collating feedback but involves a more profound analysis to comprehend the real issues developers face. It's about peeling back the layers of the feedback to discover its root cause and then leveraging this understanding to inform your product roadmap.

For example, after collecting feedback, categorize it into actionable segments, such as "usability issues," "feature requests," or "performance concerns." This categorization helps understand the broader areas that need attention and makes aligning feedback with strategic goals easier. Further, for actionable implementation, consider using methods like root cause analysis (RCA) or the Five Whys technique that dig deeper into feedback and uncover the underlying issues that need addressing.

Let's begin by addressing why understanding developer feedback is essential.

Why Understanding Developer Feedback Is Important

With a deep understanding of developer feedback, your roadmap can avoid becoming a superficial list of features rather than a strategic plan for enhancing the developer experience. When you comprehend the issues from the developer's perspective, you can design solutions that address the real problems and thus provide more meaningful improvements to the developer experience.

This understanding allows you to align development priorities with real-world developer needs, ensuring your product evolves in ways that resonate with its users. It also helps you anticipate potential pain points before they become widespread.

How to Understand Developer Feedback

To understand developer feedback, you must first ensure that you're asking the right questions. Open-ended questions that promote more profound responses are beneficial here. For instance, instead of asking, "Did you find this feature useful?" you could ask, "How did this feature enhance (or hinder) your development process?" This question encourages developers to express their feelings and experiences, providing richer feedback.

In addition, consider implementing regular feedback loops, such as quarterly surveys or beta testing groups, where developers can continuously provide insights. This regularity helps track how perceptions evolve and ensures that your roadmap stays relevant.

Once you've collected the feedback, analyze it. Look for common themes or issues raised by multiple developers. Identifying these patterns can give you a sense of the prevalent concerns or pain points. Use tools like mind mapping or affinity diagrams to group related feedback, which can help you visualize the connections between different issues and prioritize them effectively in your roadmap.

Moreover, ensures that feedback analysis is a collaborative effort. Involve cross-functional teams in the process to gain different perspectives on the issues at hand and ensure that the solutions you design are comprehensive and feasible from a technical and business standpoint.

Case Study: Facebook's Android App

To illustrate the importance of understanding developer feedback, consider Facebook's approach to improving its Android app in 2015. The company noticed they were receiving repeated feedback about the poor performance of their app across different Android devices. The developers were initially puzzled because they had tested the app on popular Android devices in the United States.

However, upon further examination of the feedback, they discovered that the problem differed from the app. Instead, it was the diversity of Android devices and operating systems worldwide. Many users in developing countries use older Android devices with less memory and slower processors. These devices were not being used for testing by Facebook's developers, leading to performance issues.

Upon understanding this feedback, Facebook initiated the "2G Tuesdays" program, where their developers were encouraged to use slower Internet speeds one day a week. This initiative helped the developers to empathize with users in developing countries and improve the app's performance across all Android devices. This case study highlights the importance of empathy in feedback analysis. To replicate this in your projects, consider setting up simulation environments or personas that reflect the diverse contexts in which your developers operate. This will help you better understand and address the challenges they face.

Understanding developer feedback requires active listening, thoughtful questioning, and comprehensive analysis. It demands that you go beyond the surface-level symptoms to identify the root causes that impact the developer experience. Use collaborative tools like Miro or Mural to facilitate workshops with your team, where you can brainstorm and map out the root causes of the issues identified in the feedback. This collaborative approach ensures that the entire team is aligned on addressing the problems. It's this understanding that forms the solid foundation for your product roadmap.

Prioritizing Based on Feedback

Once you've understood the developer feedback, the next step is to prioritize improvements based on this feedback. Prioritization is a critical component of the roadmap creation process, as it assists in focusing your resources on the most impactful improvements. To make this process actionable, start by categorizing the feedback into themes or areas of concern. This helps organize the input, making identifying high-impact regions that align with your strategic goals easier. This section will delve into how to prioritize effectively.

Why Prioritizing Based on Feedback Is Important

Prioritizing based on feedback ensures that you consider the voices and needs of your users—the developers. Rather than developing features that seem important to you, you are relying on direct input from those using your platform or tools daily. This approach ensures the features and improvements you focus on align with your user base's needs, thus enhancing their experience. Implementing this process could involve regularly scheduled feedback review sessions with your team, where you discuss the feedback and decide on priorities based on current goals and resource availability.

How to Prioritize Based on Feedback

One popular framework for prioritization is the RICE framework. RICE stands for Reach, Impact, Confidence, and Effort. Here's a breakdown of each component:

> **Reach:** This considers how many people will be affected by the improvement within a certain period. To implement this, usage data should be regarded as to estimate how many developers interact with the feature regularly.

> **Impact:** This estimates the effect of the improvement on an individual user. You can gauge impact by reviewing feedback for mentions of significant challenges or pain points associated with the feature.

Confidence: This represents your confidence in your estimates. You might have lower confidence if you need clarification, leading to a lower score. To enhance confidence, qualitative feedback with quantitative data, such as user behavior analytics, must be combined to validate assumptions.

Effort: This estimates the amount of work the improvement will take to implement. The effort is inversely related to the score—the more effort required, the lower the score. Break down the effort into smaller tasks to get a more accurate estimate, considering factors like the complexity of the codebase and the availability of resources.

Each component is scored, and a final score is computed to help rank the possible improvements. Higher scores indicate a higher priority. To apply this practically, use a spreadsheet or project management tool to input and calculate RICE scores for each proposed improvement, enabling easy comparison and decision-making.

Case Study: Slack's Prioritization Process

To illustrate how a company prioritizes based on feedback, let's examine Slack's approach. In its early stages, Slack faced an array of feature requests and bug reports from its rapidly growing user base. The development team was overwhelmed and needed to prioritize.

The team decided to use a variation of the RICE framework, focusing primarily on impact and effort. They evaluated the effect of each potential improvement on the user experience and balanced it against the development effort required. By focusing on high-impact, low-effort tasks, they were able to deliver improvements that greatly enhanced the user experience without exhausting their resources. To complement a similar approach, consider conducting a "quick wins" analysis alongside the RICE framework, where you specifically target improvements that are easy to implement but have a significant positive impact.

For example, one piece of recurring feedback was users' difficulty searching for old messages. Recognizing the impact of improving this feature (high) and understanding that the development effort was reasonable (medium), Slack prioritized enhancing the search functionality. This improvement was well-received by users and significantly improved the user experience.

Prioritizing based on feedback is a delicate balancing act between your users' needs and your development team's capabilities. To effectively manage this process, establish clear criteria for what constitutes high priority and communicate these criteria to your team. Regularly revisit and adjust these priorities as new feedback and data become available. By understanding the feedback, assessing the reach, impact, and effort of potential improvements, and considering your confidence in your estimates, you can create a prioritization framework that allows you to build a roadmap that genuinely reflects the needs of your developer community.

Designing the Roadmap

Having understood the developer feedback and prioritized the necessary improvements based on that feedback, the next step in our journey is to design the roadmap. This roadmap will be the guiding light for your development team, showing them where to focus their efforts to deliver the best possible developer experience. To help readers implement this, consider starting with a simple, flexible roadmap template that can be adjusted as you gather more feedback and data. This will make it easier to translate strategic goals into actionable steps.

Purpose of the Roadmap

The roadmap serves as a strategic document that communicates the direction of your product development. It's a high-level view of what's planned, when it's happening, and why it's essential. The roadmap aligns the product's direction with the company's strategic goals, guiding the team's day-to-day work. For practical implementation, begin by clearly defining the strategic objectives that your roadmap should support. Ensure your team communicates and understands these goals to align everyone's efforts.

Structure of a Roadmap

The structure of your roadmap can vary depending on your specific needs, but most product roadmaps include certain key elements:

> **Timeline:** This is often arranged by quarters but can also be structured around releases or other relevant milestones. To implement this, create a visual timeline using tools like Trello, Asana, or any roadmap software that suits your team's workflow.

> **Themes:** These represent the high-level goals or areas of focus for a given period. The theme might be "Improve API Stability" or "Enhance Developer Documentation." Start by brainstorming with your team to identify key themes that align with your strategic goals and then prioritize them based on the feedback and data you've collected.

Features: These are the specific items that will be worked on. They should be grouped under the relevant themes and placed on the timeline where they're expected to be worked on. When planning features, ensure each directly ties back to the themes and strategic goals. Use feedback from developers to guide the selection and prioritization of these features.

Status: This indicates whether a feature is planned, in progress, completed, or delayed. To make this actionable, regularly update the status of each feature and communicate changes to your team and stakeholders. Consider using color codes or labels to make the status of each item immediately apparent on your roadmap.

Case Study: GitHub's Public Roadmap

A real-world example of a well-crafted roadmap is the GitHub public roadmap. GitHub, a platform millions of developers use worldwide, launched its public roadmap in mid-2020 to provide more transparency to its user community. The roadmap is grouped by quarters and has color-coded labels to indicate the status of each feature. Each feature is linked to a discussion thread, where users can provide further feedback and track progress.

This approach allows GitHub to show its commitment to improving the developer experience based on user feedback. Users can see what features are being worked on, what's coming up, and how their feedback shapes the product. To apply a similar approach, consider creating a public or internal-facing version of your roadmap where stakeholders can track progress and contribute input. This fosters transparency and ongoing engagement.

Iterating on the Roadmap

Remember that a roadmap is not set in stone. It's a living document that should evolve based on new feedback, changing priorities, and unforeseen challenges. Regularly revisit your roadmap to ensure it still aligns with your strategic goals and the needs of your developer community. To make this practical, set regular intervals (e.g., monthly or quarterly) to review and adjust the roadmap. Encourage your team to be agile and open to changes that serve your developers' needs better.

Designing a roadmap based on developer feedback is an exercise in transparency, empathy, and strategic thinking. To implement this, start small by incorporating feedback into your next sprint or feature release and gradually expand the scope as you refine your process. By showcasing your commitment to improving the developer experience based on feedback, you build trust with your developer community, foster a sense of ownership, and pave the way for continued growth and success.

Communicating the Roadmap

With the roadmap designed, communication is the final step in incorporating developer feedback into product roadmaps. This is where you reveal the roadmap to your developer community, setting the stage for future developments. To make this actionable, consider setting up a structured communication plan that outlines who will communicate what, when, and through which channels. This plan ensures that everyone involved knows their role and helps maintain consistency in messaging.

Transparency

Transparency is the keyword when it comes to communicating your roadmap. This means being open about what you plan to do and why you've decided to do it. Transparency builds trust and fosters a sense of collaboration with your developer community. Their feedback also establishes your commitment to improving the developer experience. For practical implementation, transparency could involve sharing the decision-making process behind the roadmap. Explain why certain features were prioritized over others and how feedback influenced these decisions.

In practice, this might involve publishing your roadmap on your website or community forum and providing regular updates on progress. GitHub's aforementioned public roadmap is an excellent example of this. To start, you might create a simple webpage or a dedicated section in your existing developer portal where the roadmap is easily accessible. Include a section for FAQs to address common questions and concerns about the roadmap.

Clarity

Communicating your roadmap also requires clarity. Developers should understand what you're planning, why you're planning it, and when they can expect it. This means avoiding jargon and instead using clear, concise language. It also means presenting your roadmap in a visually understandable format, such as a timeline or a Kanban board. Choose a visual format that aligns with your team's workflow for implementation. Tools like Trello, Jira, or even Google Sheets can create a clear visual representation of your roadmap that is easy for developers to navigate.

Dialogue

Lastly, communication should be a two-way street. In other words, it should create opportunities for further dialogue with your developer community. For instance, you could encourage developers to comment on your roadmap, ask questions, or provide additional feedback. GitHub achieves this by linking each item on its roadmap to a discussion thread. To make this actionable, set up regular feedback sessions or forums where developers can discuss the roadmap in more detail. Use tools like Discord, community forums, or live webinars to facilitate these discussions.

Case Study: Python Enhancement Proposal (PEP) Process

The Python Enhancement Proposal (PEP) process is a noteworthy example of effective roadmap communication. The PEP process is Python's way of collecting community input on new features, changes, or improvements. Each proposal goes through stages of discussion, review, and approval or rejection, all publicly accessible. If you're implementing a similar process, consider creating a simple workflow where proposals can be submitted, discussed, and tracked. This can be done through a dedicated forum or an issue tracker with public visibility.

One famous PEP was PEP 572, which proposed the addition of the "walrus operator" (:=) for assignment expressions. Throughout the process, the community was invited to provide feedback, leading to extensive discussions. Despite the initial controversy, the proposal was accepted and implemented in Python 3.8, released in October 2019. The entire process was open and transparent, reflecting Python's philosophy of community involvement.

Iterative Communication

As your roadmap evolves, your communication strategy should evolve. Regularly reassess your communication strategy: Are developers engaged? Are they providing feedback? Do they understand your plans? Based on your findings, adjust your communication strategy. For practical implementation, establish regular check-ins or retrospectives with your team to assess the effectiveness of your communication. This could be part of your sprint reviews or a separate process dedicated to roadmap communication.

Effectively communicating your roadmap is vital for incorporating developer feedback into product roadmaps. By being transparent and clear and fostering dialogue, you can ensure that your roadmap truly reflects the needs and desires of your developer community. To implement these practices, start by incorporating one or two strategies into your next communication cycle. Over time, refine and expand your approach based on the feedback and results you observe.

Key Takeaways

- Key performance indicators (KPIs) like adoption and retention rates, time to first successful task completion, error rates, and developer feedback are crucial for assessing developer experience.

- Both quantitative (like analytics and usage data) and qualitative methods (like surveys and interviews) are necessary for a comprehensive understanding of DevEx.

- The analysis and interpretation of data is a meticulous process that helps identify trends, patterns, and areas for improvement.

- Iterative improvement and validation, guided by data analysis, are critical for refining the developer experience.

- Developer feedback is invaluable. Understanding, prioritizing, and incorporating this feedback into the product roadmap helps shape a product that truly serves its users.

- Communicating the roadmap effectively with developers is essential for maintaining transparency and fostering an ongoing, constructive dialogue with the developer community.

Remember, all these processes and measurements aim to create delightful, efficient developer environments that meet and exceed your developer community's expectations. By using the techniques outlined in this chapter, you can keep your finger on the pulse of your developers' needs and experiences, guiding your product's evolution toward better DevEx.

CHAPTER 9

Real-World DevEx Improvement Strategies

In our journey to enhance the developer experience (DevEx), we're now turning to one of the most vital tools at our disposal: a DevEx Improvement Roadmap. This strategic document outlines the steps to improve DevEx and helps us navigate the complex and multifaceted journey toward a better DevEx. Our roadmap will serve as a beacon, illuminating our path and guiding our decisions and actions.

So, let's start this journey together. Remember, the road to improvement isn't always straight or smooth, but with a well-planned roadmap, we can navigate any bumps along the way and keep moving toward our destination.

Identifying Areas for Improvement

As we embark on the journey to improve developer experience (DevEx), it's essential to identify the areas where enhancements are needed. This is the initial step in creating a DevEx improvement roadmap. They gather symptoms, conduct tests, analyze data, and identify areas of concern.

© K. Rain Leander 2025
K. R. Leander, *Developer Experience Unleashed*,
https://doi.org/10.1007/979-8-8688-0242-3_9

In the realm of DevEx, our symptoms are the data we gathered in the previous chapter—key performance indicators (KPIs), developer feedback, usage data, and the results from our surveys, interviews, and usability tests. These symptoms are our indicators, telling us where to focus our attention.

However, unlike a physician who may only deal with one patient at a time, we are likely dealing with various developers, each with unique needs, goals, and pain points. Therefore, identifying areas of improvement requires not just an understanding of data but also empathy and perspective-taking.

As you embark on this journey, remember the words of design pioneer Charles Eames: "Recognizing the need is the primary condition for design." In other words, to create an improvement that resonates with developers, you first need to recognize and understand their needs.

Look for trends, outliers, and patterns. Dive deep into the developer feedback and see if you can uncover common issues or challenges when using your product. Qualitative feedback often provides context and color to quantitative data.

For example, suppose your product analytics show developers frequently abandon a specific workflow midway. In that case, this workflow is a potential area of improvement. Your developers' feedback and the results from usability tests might reveal that the workflow could be more complex or counterintuitive, giving you a starting point for your improvement roadmap.

After identifying potential areas for improvement, it's helpful to categorize them. Some typical categories might include "Documentation," "Onboarding," "API Usability," "SDK Functionality," "Sample Code Quality," "Error Messages," and "Performance." Categorization helps us better organize and prioritize the identified areas, which we will discuss further in the next section, "Prioritizing Initiatives."

In conclusion, identifying areas of improvement is a meticulous, thoughtful process. It requires you to understand your developers' needs, interpret the data collected, and use that information to recognize areas in your developer experience that could benefit from improvements. This process lays a solid foundation for your DevEx improvement roadmap and will guide your improvement initiatives toward creating delightful and efficient developer environments.

Prioritizing Initiatives

Once we have identified the areas that need improvement in our developer experience (DevEx), the next step in building our DevEx improvement roadmap is to prioritize these initiatives. Like a seasoned chef preparing a multicourse meal, we must carefully determine which dish to qualify first based on the cooking time, complexity, and the order in which they will be served. In the same way, the art of prioritizing involves strategic planning, understanding dependencies, and defining the order of execution that would yield the highest impact.

Understanding that resources—whether time, budget, or human capacity—are often limited, prioritization helps us direct these resources effectively toward the areas that matter most. However, prioritizing initiatives is not just about figuring out what to do first; it's also about identifying what can wait or, in some cases, what not to do.

Start your prioritization process by revisiting your identified areas for improvement. Reflect on the impact each advance will have on the overall DevEx. Consider the potential return on investment (ROI) for each initiative. Remember, the highest priority should be those initiatives that align with your organization's strategic goals and have the most substantial potential to improve DevEx. For instance, if "Onboarding" was identified as a critical area of improvement and improving this process aligns with your strategic goal to increase adoption rates, this initiative might be high on your priority list.

Some changes require relatively low effort but result in significant improvement. These are generally good candidates for early implementation. Some require considerable effort but promise substantial benefits. Balancing short- and long-term goals is crucial.

A common framework to aid in this prioritization process is the Eisenhower Matrix, also known as the Urgent–Important Matrix. This matrix helps you decide on and prioritize tasks by urgency and importance, sorting out less urgent and essential tasks that you should either delegate or not do.

In the context of DevEx, "important" initiatives will significantly impact the developer experience. In contrast, "urgent" ones often need immediate attention because developers are experiencing significant challenges or blockers in these areas.

Remember the words of Johann Wolfgang von Goethe, "Things which matter most must never be at the mercy of things which matter least." This quote serves as a reminder that prioritizing initiatives is all about focusing on what matters most—creating a delightful and efficient developer experience.

In conclusion, prioritizing initiatives is critical to your DevEx improvement roadmap. It ensures that your efforts are directed effectively toward achieving the highest impact on DevEx. By thoughtfully prioritizing your ambitions, you provide your team with constant work on the most meaningful projects, leading to a more delightful and efficient developer environment.

Setting Goals and Milestones

Setting clearly defined goals and milestones is essential to creating your DevEx improvement roadmap. The famous author and management expert Peter Drucker once said, "What gets measured gets managed." With clear goals and milestones, it is easier to measure progress, and with measuring progress, managing the improvement process becomes a manageable task.

Goals are the broad, overarching outcomes you want to achieve, guiding your strategic direction. They are generally long-term and take substantial effort and time to reach. For your DevEx improvement, "Improve the onboarding experience to increase the retention rate of new developers by 20% in one year." Notice how this goal is specific, measurable, attainable, relevant, and time-bound.

In contrast, milestones are the tangible, smaller steps that lead toward your goal. They serve as markers along your journey, helping to break down a larger goal into manageable chunks. For instance, to achieve the above purpose, milestones could include "Design a new onboarding tutorial by Q3," "Test the tutorial with a small user group by Q4," and "Launch the new tutorial and measure its impact on the retention rate by Q2 of the next year."

Setting milestones makes your goals feel more achievable and provides progress. They offer opportunities to celebrate small victories, boosting the team's morale. Putting too many milestones or making them unreasonably hard to reach can have the opposite effect. Striking a balance is vital.

For each goal and milestone, define the metrics you will use to measure success. Remember, these should be meaningful metrics that genuinely reflect improvements in DevEx. In our onboarding example, the metrics could be the completion rate of the tutorial, time spent on each section, user feedback, and, eventually, the retention rate of new developers.

Once you've set your goals and milestones, communicate them clearly to all stakeholders. This includes your team and other teams who may be affected by or involved in your DevEx improvements. Transparency in your goals ensures that everyone understands what you're working toward and why.

Also, remember that your goals and milestones aren't set in stone. As you get developer feedback and learn more about what works and what doesn't, you should revisit and adjust your goals and milestones as needed. This is all part of the iterative process of improving DevEx.

Setting SMART goals and achievable milestones provides a clear roadmap for your DevEx improvement efforts. It helps you focus your efforts, measure progress, and celebrate achievements while continuously improving the developer experience.

Implementing Changes and Measuring Impact

Now that we've designed a roadmap for improving Developer Experience (DevEx), the logical next step is to bring that roadmap to life. This section delves into the active phase of the DevEx improvement process, the stage where we roll up our sleeves and get our hands dirty with real action.

Just as a skilled composer knows that a symphony's beauty lies in the harmony of its many individual parts, so does an effective DevEx strategy hinge on the interplay of feedback, measurement, iteration, and shared understanding. As we traverse this section, we'll see how these threads combine to create a tapestry of continuous DevEx improvement.

Establishing a Feedback Loop with Developers

It's important to note that a detailed guide on analyzing and collecting feedback is covered in depth in Chapter Eight, "Measuring Developer Experience."

Establishing a feedback loop with your developers ensures that your changes are grounded in the reality of their experience and yield the desired impact. Remember, developers are the primary users of your systems and tools; their voices must guide your improvement efforts.

Think of the feedback loop as a cyclical process: you make changes, gather feedback, analyze this feedback, make improvements based on what you've learned, and repeat. You can facilitate this loop through various methods, like surveys, forums, one-on-one interviews, and social media interactions. For instance, structured surveys can provide quantitative insights while open forums and one-on-one interviews offer qualitative feedback that captures the nuances of developer experiences.

Consider the story of GitHub, a platform widely loved by developers. Its success can be partly attributed to its dedication to an active feedback loop. GitHub utilizes an Issues feature where developers can report bugs, request features, or suggest improvements. These public issues foster an open dialogue between GitHub and its developer community. As Mark Otto, a designer at GitHub, said in 2015, "Every day, the team at GitHub is using GitHub. We're reminded of our customers' struggles, successes, and sentiment." This system collects feedback and encourages a community-driven approach to problem-solving.

However, collecting feedback is only the first step. The true value lies in how you process and act upon this feedback. To make a feedback loop effective, the input must be actioned. For instance, in 2021, Visual Studio Code, an editor created by Microsoft, made several significant updates based on user feedback, demonstrating how feedback can guide product improvements. Program Manager Sana Ajani stated, "We truly build VS Code together with our community, and your feedback is vital in helping us understand your needs and how we can improve." Such a proactive approach improves the tool and deepens the product's and its users' relationship.

Analyzing and incorporating feedback into your strategies is crucial, as is communicating back to the developers. This two-way communication strengthens the feedback loop and fosters trust and respect with your developer community. When developers see their feedback being heard and acted upon, it enhances their satisfaction and engagement, driving a better DevEx. Additionally, transparency in this process—where you explain what was done based on the feedback and why specific suggestions for improvement have not been implemented—can further build trust.

To establish a strong feedback loop, you should develop channels to collect feedback, have a system to analyze and act on this feedback, and communicate the changes back to your developers. Starting with simple tools like Google Forms for surveys or using GitHub Issues for direct feedback can be effective. As you grow, more sophisticated platforms like UserVoice or Pendo can help manage and analyze feedback at scale. Doing so ensures that your changes are impactful and relevant and strengthens your relationship with your developer community, ultimately improving their experience.

Tracking Progress and Iterating on Improvements

Tracking progress is pivotal to understanding if your implemented changes are moving in the desired direction. It would be like navigating an unfamiliar city without a map or GPS. To avoid this disorientation, it's essential to use the right metrics that align with your goals and continuously monitor them to understand your progress.

Defining clear, measurable, and meaningful Key Performance Indicators (KPIs) can make tracking more effective. For example, if one of your goals was to reduce the onboarding time for new developers, the time taken from a developer signing up to make their first successful API call could be a useful KPI.

Atlassian, the team behind popular tools like Jira and Confluence, is an excellent example of this approach. They use detailed analytics to track developer engagement metrics, including active users, frequency of use, length of sessions, and interaction with different features. As Atlassian's Head of Developer Experience highlighted, "By closely monitoring these metrics, we can make data-driven decisions that help improve our tools and ultimately enhance the developer experience."

However, simply tracking progress is not enough; it is a means to an end. The insights derived from monitoring must be used to iterate and improve your strategies. The iterative process helps you refine and optimize your initiatives, ensuring they yield the best results. It encourages a mindset of continual learning and adapting, which is essential in an ever-evolving field like software development.

Take Google's development of Chrome, for example. As of 2023, Chrome is in its 91st version. Each version represents an iteration, an improvement over the last. This constant progression is based on tracking their performance, gathering feedback, and making improvements, a process that Ben Goodger, the lead engineer for Chrome, summarized: "Rapid iteration, along with our open community, are fundamental in achieving a high-quality browser."

Tracking progress and iterating on improvements is dynamic and iterative. You can continuously improve your strategies and boost your DevEx by defining relevant KPIs, monitoring your progress, and making data-driven iterations. Remember, improvement isn't a destination; it's a continuous learning, adapting, and evolving journey.

Sharing Successes and Lessons Learned Within the Organization

"Success," as Vince Lombardi once said, "is not just about making it; it's about making it together." This couldn't be more accurate in the context of improving the developer experience. Sharing successes is not just a pat on the back for those involved, but it's also an opportunity to promote a culture of acknowledgment, boost team morale, and set an example for others to follow.

For instance, in 2020, the Dropbox engineering team launched an initiative to improve their developers' experience. After achieving significant improvements in critical areas, such as reducing build times and the number of failing builds, the team celebrated their success by sharing the results widely within the organization. This public acknowledgment not only boosted the morale of the engineering team but also fostered a sense of ownership and pride in their work.

However, not just the successes should be shared but also the learnings, including those derived from failures. As the adage goes, "Failure is not the opposite of success; it's part of success." Organizations should strive to build a culture where failure is viewed as an opportunity for learning and growth, not as a taboo or a source of blame.

In 2015, Etsy, an online marketplace for handmade and vintage items, introduced a system of "blameless postmortems." After any significant production incident, the team would analyze what went wrong, why, and how to prevent it. Most importantly, these findings were shared company-wide, not as a finger-pointing exercise, but as a learning opportunity.

Communication is at the core of both these practices—sharing successes and learnings. Whether through internal blog posts, team meetings, newsletters, or dedicated recognition platforms, the key is communicating consistently, openly, and transparently. As Kim Scott, author of *Radical Candor*, says, "Transparent communication is the basis of all good teamwork."

Let's normalize celebrating successes, big and small, and embrace failures as steps toward success. Let's share our stories—the highs, the lows, the in-betweens—because it's through sharing that we inspire, learn, and grow together. Improving developer experience is a team sport, not a solo sprint.

Cultivating a Culture of Continuous Improvement

This section presents how culture—a shared set of beliefs, values, and practices—plays a crucial role in the continuous improvement of DevEx. Think of it as the fertile soil from which fruitful DevEx improvement strategies can sprout, thrive, and blossom.

This section, therefore, is not only about the "what" or the "how" of improving DevEx but also about the "why" and "who." It's about tapping into team members' motivation, passion, and creativity. It's about fostering a conducive environment where every person feels empowered to learn, grow, and innovate.

As we delve into these three aspects, remember that cultivating a culture of continuous improvement is not a one-off effort but a long-term commitment. It's about persistently nurturing a positive, dynamic, and growth-oriented environment. After all, as business guru Peter Drucker aptly said, "Culture eats strategy for breakfast." The strategies and tools you employ for improving DevEx are most effective when supported by a culture that champions continuous improvement. Let's start this exciting journey.

Encouraging Experimentation and Innovation

The most engaging tales from the annals of technological innovation often start with a daring experiment or an audacious idea. Thomas Edison, one of the world's most prolific inventors, once remarked, "I have not failed. I've just found 10,000 ways that won't work."

Cultivating a culture that encourages experimentation is a significant task and even more complex in software development. It requires balancing stability and creating room for trial and error. We'll start by examining what it truly means to foster an experimental culture. What are the prerequisites? What are the potential roadblocks, and how can we navigate around them?

To illustrate these points, we'll look at historical and current examples, such as the tale of Google's "20% time" policy. This initiative allowed engineers to dedicate one day a week to an independent project of their choosing, which led to breakthrough innovations such as Gmail and AdSense. However, it also had unintended side effects and fell by the wayside. What can we learn from this and other such stories? What's the right balance between freedom and structure?

Following our exploration of experimentation, we will move on to its close cousin—innovation. While investigation is about exploring possibilities and taking risks, innovation is about applying those learnings to create real value. Here, we'll introduce various strategies to drive innovation, from fostering diversity of thought to nurturing an environment that values and promotes unique ideas. Steve Jobs is a critical figure in this discussion whose famous words resonate with us: "Innovation distinguishes between a leader and a follower."

Remember, experimentation and innovation are the lifeblood of technological progress, and fostering them within a DevEx framework can lead to more satisfied developers and a more efficient, productive, and enjoyable working environment. Throughout this subsection, we'll explore practical tips, industry-tested strategies, and real-world examples, providing a comprehensive guide to encouraging experimentation and innovation within your organization.

Fostering a Growth Mindset Among Team Members

Now let's delve into one of the essential components of cultivating a culture of continuous improvement: instilling a growth mindset. The concept, proposed by psychologist Carol Dweck in her book *Mindset: The New Psychology of Success*, suggests that we can grow our brain's capacity to learn and solve problems.

A growth mindset is invaluable in the Developer Experience (DevEx) context. It encourages team members to view challenges as opportunities, perceives effort as a path to mastery, and treats failures as sources of learning. Fostering such a mindset within your team can significantly enhance their problem-solving capabilities, resilience, and overall performance.

However, instilling a growth mindset is more than just a motivational speech or a poster on a wall. It's a cultural shift that requires a concerted and consistent effort from all levels of an organization. It starts with leadership demonstrating a commitment to learning and iterating. It involves creating safe spaces for team members to take risks, make mistakes, and learn from them without fear of criticism or punishment.

To illustrate the transformative power of a growth mindset, let's consider the example of Microsoft under the leadership of CEO Satya Nadella. Upon assuming his role in 2014, Nadella aimed to transform Microsoft's culture from a "know-it-all" to a "learn-it-all" one. This cultural shift played a crucial role in reviving Microsoft's innovation engine and propelling its market value. In Nadella's words, "We are moving from a group of people who know it all to a group of people who want to learn it all."

Further, we'll explore strategies and practices to nurture a growth mindset among your team members. These include providing constructive feedback, promoting continuous learning, celebrating effort and progress over outcomes, and more. Additionally, we'll highlight how these practices enhance your DevEx and contribute to employee engagement, job satisfaction, and team cohesion.

Making this mindset a cornerstone of your culture equips your team with the resilience, curiosity, and drive necessary to navigate the ever-evolving software development landscape. Remember, as Carol Dweck famously stated, "In a growth mindset, challenges are exciting rather than threatening. So rather than thinking, oh, I'm going to reveal my weaknesses, you say, wow, here's a chance to grow."

Celebrating Milestones and Recognizing Achievements

Celebrating milestones and recognizing achievements are not just acts of validation; they are vital practices that fuel the ongoing journey of improving Developer Experience (DevEx). These moments of recognition serve as the waypoints that keep your team motivated, aligned, and focused on the path ahead.

To celebrate milestones effectively, it's crucial to understand that these celebrations do more than just acknowledge hard work—they signal to the team what behaviors, practices, and outcomes are valued and encouraged within the organization. This dual purpose instills a sense of pride and accomplishment, fosters engagement, and promotes the replication of successful behaviors across the team.

A famous saying in the software industry goes, "What gets measured gets managed." However, when nurturing a culture of continuous improvement, we can extend this adage to "What gets celebrated gets replicated." Whether it's an innovative solution to a tricky problem, a successful deployment, or simply the consistent demonstration of the team's core values, it's essential to take the time to celebrate these victories and make them meaningful.

Formal Recognition plays a key role in this. Establishing systems such as "Developer of the Month" awards or recognizing outstanding contributions in company-wide meetings can provide powerful value. These moments formally acknowledge achievements, signaling to the entire organization the importance of these contributions. Moreover, by presenting these recognitions in public settings, such as all-hands meetings, you amplify their impact, turning individual successes into collective celebrations.

Informal Recognition is equally important. Small gestures, such as shout-outs in team chats or a personal note of appreciation, can make a big difference. These acts of recognition, though less formal, are often more immediate and can be tailored to resonate personally with the recipient. This kind of recognition helps maintain a culture of continuous appreciation, where achievements are acknowledged as they happen, fostering a more dynamic and responsive environment.

Regarding Team Celebrations, consider hosting events that align with the milestones your team reaches. For instance, after a major project launch a team lunch or a virtual celebration can provide a moment of collective joy and relief. Events like hackathons or innovation days celebrate past achievements and inspire future creativity and collaboration, reinforcing a forward-looking mindset.

To ensure these celebrations are inclusive and authentic, it's crucial to Recognize Diverse Contributions. Acknowledge the efforts of all team members, including those who contribute behind the scenes. This can involve recognizing roles that might not always be in the spotlight, such as those involved in quality assurance, documentation, or mentorship. Additionally, being Culturally Sensitive and understanding the diverse backgrounds of your team will ensure that celebrations are respectful and inclusive, making everyone feel valued.

Personalizing Recognition is another way to keep celebrations authentic. Tailoring your acknowledgment of the individual or team's contributions makes the recognition feel more genuine and meaningful. It's about moving beyond generic praise to highlight what made a difference in the project or organization.

Finally, fostering Employee Involvement in the recognition process can amplify its impact. Encouraging peer nominations for awards or recognition not only spreads the responsibility of acknowledgment but also strengthens the sense of community within the team. This collective approach ensures that recognition is broad-based and reflects the team's values.

Remember, the journey shapes us, not just the destination. Celebrating milestones and recognizing achievements is about cherishing this journey and fueling the drive to keep moving forward. In the words of novelist Paulo Coelho, "People are capable, at any time in their lives, of doing what they dream of." By celebrating your team's achievements, you're reaffirming their capabilities and fostering a culture of continuous improvement geared toward turning dreams into reality.

Key Takeaways

- DevEx improvement is a nautical journey that requires a well-defined roadmap with clear goals and milestones.

- Implementation of changes and measurement of their impact is integral to DevEx improvement. It's about making changes and ensuring they make the desired impact.

- Establishing a feedback loop with developers can lead to invaluable insights and fuel DevEx improvement.

- The spirit of continuous improvement is central to DevEx enhancement. It means fostering a culture that encourages experimentation and learning from failures.

- Cultivating a growth mindset can significantly impact DevEx's improvement. It empowers teams to view challenges as opportunities for growth rather than hurdles.

- Celebrating milestones and recognizing achievements reinforces motivation and a sense of shared accomplishment, fueling further progress.

Remember that improving DevEx is a continuous journey, not a destination. It requires a delicate balance of strategy, execution, and a culture that fosters growth, innovation, and constant improvement. Every step forward, regardless of its size, brings you closer to creating a delightful and efficient developer environment. Happy navigating!

CHAPTER 10

Developer Experience Case Studies

As we venture into the intricate world of technology and software development, understanding the nuances of Developer Experience (DevEx) becomes crucial. DevEx is more than a concept; it's a comprehensive approach that profoundly impacts the success and efficiency of software and technology projects. This chapter delves into various case studies that illustrate the vital role of DevEx in different technological environments, ranging from open-source projects and enterprise software to startups and emerging technologies.

Each case study serves as a microcosm, offering valuable insights into the challenges and strategies of integrating DevEx principles in diverse settings. We begin by exploring open-source projects, where community-centric development, transparency, and collaborative problem-solving are critical. Here, the examples of Linux and Apache Hadoop illuminate how managing the balance between community ethos and commercial interests, alongside fostering robust ecosystems, is essential to the success of such projects.

By examining these varied scenarios, we gain a deeper understanding of how DevEx principles are applied and their significant impact on the success and evolution of technology projects. The case studies highlight the successful implementation of these principles and present

© K. Rain Leander 2025
K. R. Leander, *Developer Experience Unleashed*,
https://doi.org/10.1007/979-8-8688-0242-3_10

the challenges faced and the lessons learned along the way. They serve as a guide, illustrating that a deep understanding and prioritization of developer experience can lead to more effective, efficient, and successful outcomes in the technology sector.

Open-Source Projects

Delving into open-source projects reveals a landscape rich with innovation, collaboration, and continuous learning. This exploration is particularly insightful when examining two of the most influential projects in this domain: Linux and Apache Hadoop. These projects stand as benchmarks in software development and offer a deeper understanding of the various aspects that shape the developer experience (DevEx).

The journey of Linux is a remarkable example of community-centric development. The open contribution model adopted by Linux allows developers worldwide to participate, thereby broadening the scope of innovation and problem-solving. It showcases the incredible potential of a vast and diverse community to drive innovation and efficiently solve complex problems. The open contribution model adopted by Linux epitomizes the democratization of software development. This model has broadened the scope of participation and enriched the solutions that Linux provides. Linux's transparent and inclusive governance, illustrated by its use of the Linux Foundation and its community-driven decision-making process, ensures that a wide range of contributors can influence the project's direction. This governance model harnesses diverse perspectives and skills, contributing to Linux's resilience and adaptability. Additionally, the consistent release and update cycle of Linux provides its stability and adaptability, enabling it to remain relevant and responsive in the face of new technological challenges.

Similarly, the story of Apache Hadoop underscores the importance of flexible and adaptable design in the success of open-source projects. Hadoop's modular structure, which includes components like HDFS for storage and MapReduce for processing, allows it to cater to various significant data use cases and has contributed to its relatively accessible barrier to entry compared to other big data tools. While Hadoop remains niche, its design has made it more approachable for organizations venturing into big data. Furthermore, Hadoop's foundation in academic research, particularly from Google's MapReduce and the Google File System papers, has fostered a culture of innovation within its community. Another critical aspect of Hadoop's success is the development of a robust ecosystem, including tools like Apache Hive and HBase, which are also part of the open-source initiative under the Apache Software Foundation. This ecosystem approach has significantly expanded Hadoop's capabilities, demonstrating how a holistic approach to software solutions can drive adoption and innovation.

Both Linux and Apache Hadoop illuminate open-source projects' dynamic and complex nature. They reveal how these projects navigate challenges such as governance scalability, balancing commercial interests with community needs, ensuring data security, and improving the user experience for non-technical users. These case studies offer more than just insights into software development; they are lessons in building communities, leadership, and the relentless pursuit of innovation.

In the upcoming sections, we will dive deeper into these aspects, uncovering the key factors contributing to the success of such projects and the obstacles that need to be overcome. This detailed exploration aims to provide valuable insights for those directly involved in open-source projects and anyone interested in the broader themes of technology, collaboration, and community-driven innovation.

Success Factors and Best Practices

In exploring the open-source landscape, the profound success of projects like Linux and Apache Hadoop offers a treasure trove of insights into what drives widespread influence and robust development ecosystems. These projects are not just software; they represent the culmination of effective practices and principles honed over time.

Linux and Hadoop serve as prime examples, illustrating how certain factors and methodologies can significantly impact the trajectory of open-source projects. However, it is essential to note that while these projects have achieved significant success, they have also faced challenges, particularly in welcoming beginners and fostering an inclusive environment. Their journeys provide an in-depth look at the elements contributing to a project's success. These elements include fostering a community-driven development approach, prioritizing transparency in decision-making, and maintaining a commitment to continuous innovation and improvement.

The success of these projects isn't just about the end product; it's about the process and the environment that nurtures their growth. Developers worldwide contribute code ideas and solutions in these environments, creating a dynamic and collaborative space. That said, it's crucial to acknowledge the mixed reputation of these communities, particularly in the case of Linux, which has historically been perceived as less welcoming to minorities and beginners. As a result, aspiring to create more inclusive and supportive environments is an essential takeaway from these examples, alongside their technical achievements.

In understanding these success stories, we gain valuable insights into best practices that can be applied to other open-source endeavors. These practices underscore the importance of building and maintaining a healthy community, staying adaptable in the face of new challenges, and ensuring that a project remains open and accessible to contributors of all levels. However, fostering a truly welcoming and inclusive environment requires ongoing effort and conscious moderation of community dynamics. The lessons learned from Linux and Hadoop are invaluable for anyone looking to create or contribute to open-source projects, offering guidance on navigating the complexities and opportunities of this exciting field.

Unpacking Linux's Success: Collaborative Development and Inclusive Governance

Linux stands out as an exemplary model in open-source software, largely thanks to its thriving and diverse community. The success of Linux can be attributed to its unique approach to development, which is deeply rooted in community participation. The open contribution model of Linux is its cornerstone, inviting developers from all corners of the globe to take part. This inclusive approach has cultivated a rich amalgamation of ideas, driving innovation and facilitating swift resolution of problems. The wisdom of Linus Torvalds, the founder of Linux, encapsulates the essence of this approach. He famously remarked that with enough people scrutinizing, all problems become trivial. This statement reflects the underlying philosophy of Linux, where collaborative development is seen as the key to overcoming challenges.

Another critical factor contributing to Linux's success is its approach to governance. The platform is governed transparently and inclusively, reflecting a democratic decision-making style. This governance model welcomes input from contributors of varying backgrounds and expertise, ensuring that a wide array of needs and viewpoints are considered in the project's trajectory. Such an approach has fostered an environment where decisions are made collectively, benefiting from the diverse perspectives of its global community.

Lastly, the stability and adaptability of Linux are noteworthy, characterized by its consistent release and update cycle. This strategy ensures that the platform remains resilient and up-to-date with emerging technologies and security threats. Such reliability and responsiveness have made Linux a trusted choice for millions of users worldwide. The platform's ability to evolve while maintaining stability is a testament to the effectiveness of its development and governance model. This balance between innovation and reliability is why Linux remains a leading choice in open-source software.

Apache Hadoop: Revolutionizing Big Data with Modular Design and Innovation

Apache Hadoop is a foundational platform in big data processing, known for its ability to store and process vast amounts of data across distributed computing environments. Its modular design is a crucial aspect contributing to its widespread adoption. This flexibility enables Hadoop to be customized to meet diverse data processing needs, making it an indispensable tool for large and small organizations. The ability to tailor Hadoop to specific requirements ensures that it remains relevant and practical across various scenarios, from simple data sorting tasks to complex analytical processes.

Another cornerstone of Hadoop's success is its strong foundation in academic research and innovation. Originally inspired by Google's MapReduce and the Google File System (GFS) research papers, Hadoop was developed to handle large-scale data processing on commodity hardware, making it accessible and scalable. The origins of Hadoop in research papers have provided a robust theoretical base and fostered a culture of continual learning and development within the Hadoop community. This emphasis on research and innovation has driven the platform forward, leading to ongoing enhancements and introducing new features. This environment of constant improvement keeps Hadoop at the forefront of data processing technology, continually expanding its capabilities and applications.

Furthermore, developing a robust ecosystem surrounding Hadoop has significantly amplified its functionality. This ecosystem includes tools like Apache Hive, which provides an SQL-like interface for querying large datasets stored in Hadoop, and Apache HBase. This scalable, distributed database supports structured data storage for large tables. Integrating projects like Apache Hive and HBase into the Hadoop ecosystem has transformed it from a mere tool into a comprehensive data processing solution. This ecosystem approach means that Hadoop is not just a stand-alone product but a part of a more extensive, interconnected suite of tools. Each ecosystem component complements and enhances the others, offering a more holistic and powerful approach to data processing. This symbiotic development has been instrumental in establishing Hadoop as a versatile and effective solution for a wide range of data-related challenges.

Cross-Project Insights

The stories of both Linux and Apache Hadoop offer profound insights into the role of open-source principles in propelling technological progress. They stand as beacons in the ever-changing software development landscape, highlighting the enduring significance of collaboration, innovation, and adaptability. These projects have survived and thrived amidst the rapid evolution of technology, primarily due to their commitment to these core values.

Linux and Hadoop serve as instructive case studies, offering many lessons for navigating the intricate world of open-source development. They demonstrate the importance of balancing the needs of a diverse range of stakeholders—a particularly pronounced challenge in open-source projects where contributors come from varied backgrounds and bring different perspectives. This diversity, while challenging, also fuels the innovative spirit that drives these projects forward.

Moreover, both projects exemplify the creation and maintenance of a continuous improvement and collaboration culture. This culture is vital for fostering an environment where new ideas are welcomed and integral to the project's progress. The success of Linux and Hadoop underscores the notion that open-source projects are more than just about writing code; they are about building communities where individuals work together toward a common goal, sharing knowledge, and learning from each other. This approach has proven to be a powerful engine for technological advancement, and the lessons learned from these projects are invaluable for anyone involved in or interested in the world of open-source software development.

Challenges and Lessons Learned

Exploring the world of open-source software through the lens of seminal projects like Linux and Apache Hadoop reveals a landscape filled with both challenges and invaluable lessons. These projects, while vastly successful now, faced numerous hurdles throughout their development. Their journeys offer rich insights and learning opportunities for those considering open-source ventures.

Linux, for instance, stands as a testament to the power and potential of open-source software, but its path wasn't without obstacles. One of the primary challenges faced by Linux was scalability in its governance model. As the project expanded and the number of contributions grew, it needed to evolve beyond the sole maintainer pattern, where a single individual (like Linus Torvalds) made all key decisions. The project transitioned to a more distributed governance model with maintainers overseeing different subsystems, allowing for greater scalability and sustainability. Balancing the need for a structured governance model while maintaining the ethos of open contribution was a delicate task. This evolution in governance models underlines the importance of adaptable structures in open-source projects, mainly as they grow and evolve.

Apache Hadoop's journey also sheds light on the unique challenges in open-source development. Initially rooted in academic research, Hadoop had to bridge the gap between theoretical foundations and practical, real-world applications. Hadoop accomplished this by focusing on practical, incremental improvements, such as the development of a modular architecture that allowed it to be customized for various use cases, and by fostering a community of contributors who could extend its capabilities with new tools like Apache Hive and Apache HBase. Developing a robust ecosystem around Hadoop was crucial to its success. This required integrating various projects and tools into the Hadoop ecosystem, transforming it from a single tool into a comprehensive data processing solution.

These case studies highlight that navigating the complex world of open-source development is as much about managing and adapting to change as it is about leveraging the strengths of collaborative development. They illustrate the importance of balancing diverse stakeholder needs, prioritizing transparent and inclusive governance, and fostering a culture of continuous improvement and innovation. The experiences of Linux and Hadoop teach that to grow effectively, projects must evolve their governance structures, bridge the gap between theory and practice, and build robust ecosystems that support ongoing innovation.

Linux and the Challenges of Scalability

The journey of Linux, particularly in its scalability and governance, offers valuable lessons in managing the complexities of open-source projects. As Linux grew, it encountered significant challenges in scaling its governance model to keep up with increasing contributions. This expansion necessitated a more structured approach to managing the quality and coherence of development efforts. Linux adopted a hierarchical governance model, where maintainers are responsible for different subsystems, reporting to senior maintainers who report to Linus Torvalds. This layered structure allows for efficient decision-making while ensuring that changes are thoroughly reviewed and integrated smoothly, which is crucial in managing a project with the vast scope and scale of Linux. The evolution of Linux's governance model is a testament to the importance of adaptable governance structures in open-source projects. This adaptability is particularly crucial as projects grow and face new challenges. The ability of Linux to balance the need for a structured governance model while maintaining its ethos of open contribution is a critical aspect of its success story. This balance was achieved by clearly defining roles within the community, encouraging open dialogue among contributors, and ensuring that the project remains accessible to new developers. This balance ensures that while the project scales up, it retains the core values that have driven its growth.

Another intricate aspect of Linux's evolution is balancing commercial and community interests. With the involvement of large corporations in Linux's development, unique challenges emerged. These included aligning the commercial goals of businesses with the open-source ethos and the community's expectations. Linux managed this balance by establishing clear guidelines on contribution standards and maintaining a neutral stance on the commercial use of the code, ensuring that no single entity could dominate the project's direction. Linux's experience in this arena highlights the complexity of managing diverse stakeholder expectations. It is a delicate act to maintain the integrity and original goals of the open-source project while accommodating the interests of commercial entities. Achieving this balance is essential for sustaining long-term growth and keeping the community engaged and invested in the project.

How Linux navigated these challenges provides insightful examples for other open-source projects grappling with similar issues. The hierarchical governance model and clear guidelines for commercial involvement help ensure that Linux continues to thrive without losing sight of its foundational principles. This balancing act is about managing contributions and aligning visions and expectations across diverse stakeholders, ensuring the project thrives without losing sight of its foundational principles.

Navigating Data Security and User Accessibility in Apache Hadoop

Apache Hadoop's path in open-source projects sheds light on crucial aspects like data security, privacy, and user experience, particularly for non-technical users. Handling data security and privacy has been a paramount concern for Hadoop, given its capability to process enormous volumes of data. The challenges in this area were safeguarding the data, maintaining user trust, and adhering to various regulatory standards. Hadoop implemented advanced encryption techniques and access control mechanisms, such as Kerberos authentication, to address these challenges and ensure that only authorized users could access sensitive data. Additionally, Hadoop's community continually worked on enhancing its security architecture to comply with evolving regulatory requirements, such as GDPR, ensuring that data handling met international standards. This aspect of Hadoop's journey underscores the importance of integrating robust security measures in data-centric open-source projects. Data security and privacy are not just technical necessities but also critical factors in building and maintaining the trust of users who rely on the platform for processing sensitive information.

Another significant challenge Hadoop has faced is making its complex system accessible to non-technical users. The inherent complexity of its operations made it initially daunting for users without a technical background. Hadoop addressed this by developing user-friendly tools such as Apache Hive and Pig, allowing users to interact with Hadoop using SQL-like queries instead of complex MapReduce programming. Additionally, the introduction of graphical user interfaces like Hue made data management tasks more intuitive, lowering the entry barrier for less technical users. Addressing this issue involved developing additional tools and interfaces to simplify user interactions with the system. This aspect of Hadoop's evolution highlights a crucial lesson in open-source development: the importance of user-centric design.

For open-source projects, especially those with technical complexities like Hadoop, it's essential to focus on user experience. This means ensuring that platforms are robust and approachable for a broader audience, including non-technical users. Focusing on user experience and ease of use is vital to expanding the user base and enhancing the project's overall impact.

Learning from Linux and Apache Hadoop

The experiences of Linux and Apache Hadoop in the open-source realm provide a wealth of knowledge, particularly in navigating the challenges such projects face and leveraging their strengths. These case studies are rich with insights applicable across various software development domains.

One key lesson from both projects is the need for adaptability in governance as they scale. Linux and Hadoop had to evolve their governance models to balance order and quality control and nurture innovation. This evolution is crucial in open-source projects as they grow, ensuring that while there is a structure for decision-making and quality assurance, the spirit of innovation and open contribution that characterizes open-source projects is preserved.

Another important aspect is the balance of stakeholder interests. Open-source projects often involve diverse stakeholders, from individual contributors to large corporations. Linux and Hadoop show that balancing these varied interests is essential for sustainable development. This balance aligns participating companies' commercial objectives with the open-source community's broader goals.

Furthermore, the importance of security and privacy in today's digital age cannot be overstated. As seen with Hadoop, prioritizing these aspects is critical in maintaining user trust, especially for projects handling large volumes of data. Ensuring robust security and privacy measures is not just a technical requirement but a fundamental aspect of maintaining and growing the user base of open-source projects.

User accessibility is another crucial area of focus. Both Linux and Hadoop had to find ways to make their systems accessible to non-technical users. This aspect involves simplifying the user experience to ensure that the project is usable by those with technical expertise and is approachable and understandable for a broader audience. Enhancing user accessibility can significantly widen an open-source project's appeal and usability.

In the following sections, we will explore how these insights from Linux and Hadoop apply in other contexts, such as enterprise software, startups, and emerging technologies. This exploration aims to enrich our understanding of the multifaceted nature of developer experience across various environments, providing a comprehensive view of how these lessons can be applied in different settings.

Enterprise and Commercial Software

Exploring enterprise and commercial software in developer experience (DevEx) highlights the need for scalability, flexibility, and seamless integration in large-scale systems. Platforms like Microsoft's Azure DevOps and Salesforce demonstrate how successful enterprise software must balance technical depth with usability and adaptability. Azure DevOps provides an end-to-end DevOps toolchain that supports diverse programming languages and cloud environments, while Salesforce prioritizes user experience in the evolving CRM market. Both platforms exemplify the importance of creating integrated solutions that meet large organizations' varied and dynamic needs.

A critical aspect of their success lies in fostering strong community engagement and continuous innovation. Azure DevOps and Salesforce have developed ecosystems beyond mere software solutions, offering extensive documentation, marketplace extensions, and platforms for community interaction. However, they also face the challenge of managing complexity and customization as they grow, requiring a balance between technical depth and accessibility.

Ultimately, the journeys of Azure DevOps and Salesforce illustrate how DevEx principles can be effectively adapted to suit large organizations. These platforms have created robust software and fostered ecosystems that encourage growth, innovation, and a seamless user experience in the complex landscape of enterprise software.

Adapting DevEx Principles for Large Organizations

The adaptation of Developer Experience (DevEx) principles in the context of large organizations is a nuanced and critical topic, especially for significant enterprise platforms like Microsoft Azure DevOps and Salesforce. These platforms demonstrate a profound understanding of how to tailor DevEx to suit large-scale organizations' unique, often complex, and dynamic environments.

Microsoft Azure DevOps is a compelling example of this adaptation. Azure DevOps stands out for its ability to cater to various development practices and environments in enterprise software, where the needs and challenges constantly evolve. This platform is designed to offer an end-to-end DevOps toolchain that is comprehensive and flexible enough to accommodate various programming languages and cloud environments. This versatility is critical in an enterprise setting where different teams and projects may have differing requirements.

Similarly, Salesforce has made significant strides in adapting DevEx principles to fit the ever-changing landscape of customer relationship management (CRM). Salesforce's approach prioritizes user experience, reflecting a deep understanding of the CRM market's needs. This focus on user experience is not just about interface design; it's about creating an intuitive, responsive, continually evolving ecosystem to meet user needs. Salesforce's ability to adapt to these needs and its commitment to innovation set a benchmark for how DevEx principles can be effectively applied in a large-scale, customer-centric environment.

Azure DevOps and Salesforce highlight the importance of an integrated solution in the enterprise context. These platforms are not just software solutions; they represent ecosystems facilitating community engagement, extensive documentation, and marketplace extensions. This approach to building an integrated solution goes beyond technical capabilities; it's about creating an environment that fosters growth, collaboration, and continuous learning.

The challenge for large organizations in adapting DevEx principles lies in balancing technical depth with accessibility. The goal is to create robust and feature-rich platforms for technical users while being accessible and intuitive for less technically inclined users. This balance is crucial for ensuring the platform can serve a broad range of users within the organization, from developers and IT professionals to marketing teams and business analysts.

Adapting DevEx principles for large organizations is about understanding and addressing these environments' unique challenges and needs. It involves creating scalable, flexible, and user-centric solutions, ensuring they can handle large-scale enterprises' diverse and evolving requirements.

Enhancing Software Development with Azure DevOps

Microsoft Azure DevOps epitomizes implementing Developer Experience (DevEx) principles in an enterprise environment, showcasing how a comprehensive suite of tools can revolutionize the software development lifecycle. The platform is a prime example of providing a seamless, end-to-end developer journey, a core aspect of DevEx. With tools like Azure Boards for project tracking and Azure Pipelines for continuous integration and continuous delivery (CI/CD), Azure DevOps offers a unified experience that significantly simplifies and streamlines the workflow for developers. This integration ensures that every stage of the development process is interconnected, reducing friction and enhancing efficiency.

Another notable feature of Azure DevOps is its focus on customization and extensibility. The platform stands out in its ability to be tailored to the unique needs of large organizations. This adaptability aligns with the DevEx principle of flexibility, which is particularly crucial in diverse enterprise environments where requirements can vary widely. Additionally, the extensibility of Azure DevOps, facilitated through its rich marketplace, allows for seamless integration with many other tools and services. This capability underscores the importance of interoperability in DevEx, ensuring the platform can function effectively within a broader ecosystem of technology solutions.

However, the comprehensive nature of Azure DevOps also presents its own set of challenges. For instance, the platform's breadth and depth can lead to a steep learning curve for new users. The complexity involved in integrating a wide array of tools can be daunting, particularly for larger organizations with diverse teams and projects. Organizations must invest in training and change management to fully leverage Azure DevOps's capabilities. This investment is critical to ensure teams can effectively navigate and utilize the platform to its fullest potential. Overcoming these challenges is crucial to harnessing the power of Azure DevOps to enhance the overall developer experience within large, complex enterprise environments.

Building a Thriving Ecosystem with Salesforce

Salesforce has emerged as a leader in Developer Experience (DevEx), particularly notable for its success in navigating the complexities of customer relationship management (CRM) systems. Salesforce's unwavering commitment to user-centric design is crucial to its success. Despite the inherent complexities of CRM systems, Salesforce has maintained an intuitive and engaging user experience. This focus on user-centricity is a critical aspect of DevEx, emphasizing the creation of frictionless experiences that cater to the needs of both developers and end-users. Salesforce's ability to simplify and streamline the CRM experience demonstrates how a platform can be powerful and user-friendly, a balance essential in enterprise software.

In addition to its user-centric design, Salesforce has excelled in building a thriving ecosystem. This ecosystem includes an expansive marketplace known as AppExchange, a comprehensive set of APIs, and a vibrant community platform called Trailhead. Salesforce's approach to fostering this ecosystem aligns with the DevEx principles of community engagement and collaborative development. The AppExchange marketplace offers a wide range of applications and solutions, enhancing the functionality and versatility of the Salesforce platform.

Meanwhile, the APIs facilitate integration and customization, allowing developers to tailor the platform to their needs. As a community hub, Trailhead is pivotal in empowering users and developers through education and fostering a sense of belonging and collaboration within the Salesforce ecosystem.

However, Salesforce faces unique challenges, particularly in balancing customization with standardization. While a strength, the platform's high degree of customizability can sometimes lead to complex implementations that are challenging to maintain and scale, especially in large organizations. This presents a recurring challenge for Salesforce, highlighting the importance of preserving a DevEx focus on maintainability and scalability.

Addressing this challenge involves finding the proper equilibrium where the platform can offer extensive customization options without compromising on ease of maintenance and the ability to scale efficiently. This balance is crucial in ensuring that Salesforce remains a practical and effective solution for organizations of all sizes, navigating the intricacies of CRM with agility and resilience.

Common Themes in Large Organizations

When examining the adaptation of Developer Experience (DevEx) principles in large organizations, common themes emerge, particularly in the cases of Azure DevOps and Salesforce. These themes highlight the nuances of implementing DevEx in complex, large-scale environments.

A central theme observed in both Azure DevOps and Salesforce is the necessity of embracing change and innovation. This principle is fundamental to DevEx, especially in the rapidly evolving technological landscape. Continual evolution and adaptation in their offerings ensure these platforms remain relevant and practical. To effectively embrace change, these organizations have adopted agile methodologies, which allow for iterative development and constant feedback loops. This approach ensures that new features and updates are rapidly tested and integrated, keeping the platform aligned with user needs and technological advancements. In the tech world, where new developments and shifts occur frequently, the ability to adapt and evolve is not just a strength but a necessity. This responsiveness to change ensures that platforms like Azure DevOps and Salesforce continue to meet the changing needs of developers and organizations.

Another critical aspect in large organizations is balancing the diverse needs of various stakeholders. In such environments, DevEx extends beyond just catering to developers. It encompasses a broader spectrum, including management, operations, and end-users. Azure DevOps and Salesforce have implemented robust feedback mechanisms that involve regular consultations with all stakeholders to achieve this balance. This ensures that the development teams can prioritize features and improvements that address the broad spectrum of needs within the organization. This multidimensional approach to DevEx is essential for the success of enterprise software. It involves understanding and addressing the needs of different groups within the organization, ensuring that the software delivers value to all its users. This balance is challenging but critical in ensuring that enterprise software solutions are practical and widely adopted within large organizations.

Scaling DevEx practices as organizations grow is another key takeaway. What works for a small team or a startup might not suit a large enterprise. Therefore, DevEx principles in large organizations must be adaptable and scalable. Azure DevOps and Salesforce have employed modular design strategies, allowing different teams to adopt and customize the platform based on their needs. This modularity is key to scaling DevEx across various departments within a large organization. As organizations expand, their software needs become more complex, and the DevEx strategies must evolve to accommodate these changes. This scalability ensures that the practices remain relevant and practical, even as the organization grows and its needs become more complex.

Adapting DevEx principles for large organizations is about striking a delicate balance between offering comprehensive, integrated solutions and maintaining ease of use and flexibility. Platforms like Microsoft Azure DevOps and Salesforce serve as exemplars, providing valuable insights into successful DevEx strategies in enterprise software. Their experiences offer invaluable lessons for any organization aiming to enhance its DevEx in a large-scale setting.

These lessons are crucial for understanding how to navigate the complexities of DevEx in large organizations, ensuring that software meets technical requirements and enriches the overall experience for all stakeholders involved.

Balancing Stakeholder Needs and Expectations

Balancing stakeholder needs and expectations in large-scale enterprise software is a multifaceted and crucial aspect of maintaining an optimal developer experience (DevEx). This balance is particularly evident in platforms like Microsoft Azure DevOps and Salesforce, where the challenge lies in aligning various stakeholders' diverse and sometimes conflicting requirements while simultaneously fostering a positive and efficient DevEx.

In platforms like Microsoft Azure DevOps, the balance involves ensuring that the platform remains flexible and powerful enough for developers while also being accessible and understandable for other stakeholders like project managers and business analysts. Azure DevOps achieves this by offering a suite of tools that cater to the entire software development lifecycle, thus addressing the needs of different stakeholders involved in a project. It provides powerful tools for code integration and deployment for developers while it offers project tracking and management features for project managers.

Similarly, Salesforce, known for its customer relationship management (CRM) capabilities, faces the challenge of balancing the needs of sales and marketing professionals, IT teams, and developers. Salesforce tackles this by offering a highly customizable platform tailored to the specific needs of different departments within an organization. At the same time, it ensures that these customizations are manageable and maintainable, keeping the user experience at the forefront.

The complexity in balancing stakeholder needs in these platforms arises from users' diversity and varying technical expertise and goals. For instance, developers seek efficiency, flexibility, and robust technical capabilities, while business stakeholders look for reliability, security, and ease of use. Achieving this balance is crucial for the sustainability and success of such platforms, as it ensures that they can effectively serve a wide range of users and use cases.

This section on balancing stakeholder needs and expectations provides a deep dive into how large-scale enterprise software platforms manage this critical aspect. By examining the approaches of Microsoft Azure DevOps and Salesforce, we gain insights into how these platforms maintain an optimal DevEx while catering to the diverse needs of their varied user base. This balance is not just about meeting technical requirements; it's about creating an environment where all stakeholders can thrive and contribute effectively to the platform's success.

Microsoft Azure DevOps: Balancing Technical and Business Objectives

In the complex enterprise technology landscape, Microsoft Azure DevOps emerges as a platform that balances technical and business objectives. It addresses the needs of a diverse user base, including developers, project managers, QA testers, and operations teams. This diverse user profile demands a careful balance between providing sophisticated tools for technical tasks and ensuring these tools are user-friendly for management and planning purposes. Azure DevOps meets this challenge by offering features like Azure Boards, which are designed for project management and are accessible to non-technical stakeholders, while at the same time providing Azure Repos, which offers powerful source control management tailored for developers. This dual approach ensures that technical and non-technical users find the platform beneficial for their needs.

Another critical aspect of Azure DevOps is its integration with diverse ecosystems. In large organizations, software only functions in collaboration. Recognizing this, Azure DevOps is designed to ensure compatibility and integration with various external tools and platforms. This feature addresses stakeholders' expectations, who often depend on multiple systems to work harmoniously. By providing this level of integration, Azure DevOps positions itself as a versatile and indispensable tool within an organization's broader technology ecosystem.

However, Azure DevOps faces challenges, particularly in balancing the depth of its technical features with the need for accessibility to less technical users. This challenge is significant, as the platform aims to remain accessible and user-friendly without diluting its powerful technical capabilities. This balancing act is a continuous process, critical to maintaining Azure DevOps as a platform that is both robust for developers and approachable for other stakeholders. Ensuring this balance is vital to harnessing the full potential of Azure DevOps to enhance the overall developer experience within complex enterprise environments.

Salesforce: Aligning User Experience with Business Goals

Salesforce's approach to Developer Experience (DevEx) is a study of balancing user-centric design with business goals, especially given its wide range of users across sales, marketing, customer service, and IT departments. The platform's intuitive design is central to its success, catering to its users' diverse roles and expertise levels. This design philosophy faces the challenge of creating a sophisticated environment for technical users while also ensuring ease of navigation for those less technologically inclined. Achieving this balance is crucial in making Salesforce an effective tool for all users, regardless of their technical proficiency.

One of the key features of Salesforce is its extensive customization capabilities, allowing organizations to tailor the platform to their specific business needs. While this flexibility is a significant strength, it can also introduce complexity, particularly during system upgrades or when integrating with other systems. Balancing the ability to customize with the need for a manageable and standardized environment is essential. This balance ensures that Salesforce remains a versatile tool for businesses, adaptable to their unique requirements, yet still maintains a level of standardization crucial for ease of management and consistent user experience.

Another aspect of Salesforce's approach is maintaining a consistent cycle of innovation. Regular updates and the introduction of new features are imperative to keep the platform at the forefront of technology, aligning with stakeholders' expectations for a continually evolving and innovative tool. However, this fast pace of innovation must be carefully managed against the need for platform stability and predictability. Changes in large organizations can significantly affect various departments and operations. The challenge for Salesforce lies in introducing new capabilities and enhancements while ensuring these changes do not disrupt its users' existing workflows and processes. Balancing innovation with stability is crucial in an environment where cutting-edge features and reliability are highly valued.

Salesforce's success in aligning user experience with business goals hinges on its ability to provide an intuitive and user-friendly platform that caters to a wide range of users, manages the delicate balance between customization and standardization, and maintains a consistent yet careful approach to innovation. These elements are essential in meeting the diverse needs of stakeholders and ensuring that Salesforce remains a leading tool in enterprise environments. The platform's ability to navigate these challenges exemplifies effective strategies for aligning DevEx with broader business objectives, making Salesforce a model for other enterprise software solutions striving to achieve similar goals.

Common Strategies in Balancing Stakeholder Expectations

In the context of Developer Experience (DevEx) for enterprise and commercial software, managing the balance of stakeholder expectations is a complex yet crucial aspect. This balance requires a multifaceted approach, exemplified by platforms like Microsoft Azure DevOps and Salesforce. They demonstrate effective strategies for navigating the diverse needs and expectations within large-scale software environments.

One common strategy employed by both platforms is the establishment of robust communication channels. Effective communication is vital to understanding and addressing the concerns of various stakeholders. Regular feedback loops, user forums, and engagement surveys are instrumental in this process. They provide platforms like Azure DevOps and Salesforce with critical user needs and experience insights. These channels allow stakeholders to voice their opinions and concerns, ensuring their feedback is heard and considered in the development process.

Flexibility and adaptability are another cornerstone in balancing stakeholder expectations. The needs of users in large organizations are diverse and constantly evolving. Technical adaptability is essential, but there are other considerations. Flexibility in policies, support, and training is equally important. This approach ensures that the platforms can accommodate various use cases and adapt to changing requirements, making them suitable for multiple organizational stakeholders.

Data-driven decision-making is also pivotal in aligning platform developments with user needs and business objectives. Azure DevOps and Salesforce can make informed decisions by leveraging analytics to understand how different stakeholders use the platform. This data-driven approach helps tailor features and functionalities to match users' usage patterns and preferences, enhancing the overall user experience.

Balancing stakeholder needs and expectations in DevEx involves a comprehensive understanding of the diversity of user needs, maintaining a high degree of flexibility, fostering effective communication, and employing data-driven strategies. The experiences of Microsoft Azure DevOps and Salesforce provide valuable insights into managing these complex stakeholder ecosystems. These insights are crucial for large-scale software platforms and any organization looking to improve its DevEx in a dynamic and multifaceted environment.

Startups and Emerging Technologies

In tech startups, innovation and adaptability are not just buzzwords but essential practices for survival and success. This section offers a deep dive into this fast-paced world. It comprehensively explores how modern startups have navigated the evolving landscape of technology and market demands.

The ability of startups to pivot and adapt in a dynamic market is crucial. Real-life examples like Slack and Raspberry Pi offer compelling narratives of this adaptability. Slack, an internal communication tool for a gaming startup, transformed into a globally recognized business communication platform. This strategic shift in focus, prompted by market demand and potential, is a testament to the power of pivoting in response to evolving market landscapes.

Similarly, initially envisioned as an educational tool to teach introductory computer science, Raspberry Pi morphed into a versatile computing device. This transformation was driven by the needs and creativity of its user community, showcasing how startups can successfully pivot by engaging with and listening to their users.

Rapid prototyping and developing minimum viable products (MVPs) are other vital startup strategies. The initial version of Slack, which was minimal but focused on core functionalities like instant messaging and file sharing, exemplifies the significance of launching a product that, while simple, allows for iterative development based on user feedback. Raspberry Pi's journey from its prototype to its latest models demonstrates the value of continuous improvement and responsiveness to community feedback.

In these case studies, the integration of Developer Experience (DevEx) principles emerges as a critical driver of success. The focus on DevEx leads to products that push technological boundaries and resonate deeply with user needs and market trends. This approach is crucial in creating solutions that are not only innovative but also user-friendly and market-relevant.

The insights from these startups are not merely success stories; they are lessons in agility, user-centric development, and the relentless pursuit of innovation. They guide emerging startups and technologists, illustrating that adaptability and a keen understanding of the developer experience are essential for making a lasting impact in the ever-changing world of technology.

Pivoting and Adapting to Change

In the dynamic and often unpredictable realm of startups and emerging technologies, the ability to pivot and adapt to change is not just advantageous but essential. This part of the book delves into how some companies, notably Slack and Raspberry Pi, have exemplified agility and flexibility, crucial attributes for modern tech ventures.

The story of Slack serves as a quintessential example of successful pivoting. Originally developed as an internal communication tool for the game "Glitch," Slack's transformation into a globally recognized business communication platform is a study in adaptability and strategic reorientation. The company's ability to identify and respond to market demands, shifting from a gaming-focused tool to a broadly applicable communication platform, showcases the importance of being agile and responsive to changing market landscapes. For instance, when the gaming venture didn't succeed, the team noticed how integral the internal communication tool had become to their workflow. This realization led to the decision to pivot fully to developing Slack as a stand-alone product. This transition wasn't just about altering the product but a fundamental shift in the company's focus and strategy, underpinned by a keen understanding of market needs and potential.

Raspberry Pi presents another fascinating case of adaptability. Originally aimed at promoting computer science education in schools, Raspberry Pi was designed to be an affordable and accessible learning tool. However, it quickly gained traction beyond the educational sector. It evolved into a versatile computing device embraced by a diverse user community for various applications, from home automation to industrial control systems. This transformation highlights how startups can pivot by engaging with and listening to their user base. For example, when hobbyists and developers began using Raspberry Pi for projects beyond its educational intent, the company expanded its product line to include more powerful models capable of handling various tasks. Raspberry

Pi's evolution was driven by the creativity and needs of its community, illustrating the importance of being receptive to user feedback and willing to expand the vision beyond the original intent. The company's journey demonstrates how flexibility and a deep connection with the user community can lead to unexpected and successful paths.

These stories underscore a fundamental truth in the tech startup world: success often depends on the ability to pivot and adapt to change. This requires technical agility and an open strategic mindset to reevaluate and adjust the company's direction in response to market feedback and technological advancements. The lessons from Slack and Raspberry Pi— such as recognizing when to pivot based on product usage and community engagement, and not being afraid to shift focus entirely—are invaluable for any tech venture operating in today's fast-paced and ever-changing technological landscape. They highlight the necessity of staying flexible, being user-centric, and maintaining an openness to change, which are crucial for navigating the challenging waters of technological evolution and market demands. These case studies are inspiring examples for startups and emerging tech companies, showing how adaptability and a keen understanding of the market and user needs are vital to thriving in the competitive world of technology.

Slack: Transforming Communication in the Business World

The story of Slack, a now-renowned business communication tool, began quite unexpectedly. It originated as an internal tool developed by the gaming company Tiny Speck for its game "Glitch." However, a pivotal moment occurred when "Glitch" was discontinued. The team behind it recognized the potential of their communication tool, which led to the birth of Slack as a stand-alone product. This transition marked a significant shift from a specific in-house utility to a broader business communication solution.

Slack's rise in the business world can be attributed to its ability to address a fundamental need for streamlined communication, particularly resonant in an era where remote work was rapidly growing. The platform quickly gained traction, filling a gap in the market for efficient and integrated communication tools. What set Slack apart was its commitment to user-centric design. The development team placed a high emphasis on incorporating user feedback into the evolution of the platform. This approach allowed Slack to continuously refine and enhance its functionality, ensuring it remained relevant and effective for its growing user base.

The evolution of Slack is a classic example of rapid development and iteration in response to real-world use and feedback. Slack rapidly evolved from a Minimum Viable Product (MVP), showcasing the importance of agility in product development. This evolution wasn't just about adding new features; it was a thoughtful process of understanding what users truly needed and how Slack could better serve those needs.

Over time, Slack expanded its feature set, including integration capabilities with other tools and enhanced security features. This expansion was not random but a calculated effort to make Slack a comprehensive tool that could cater to the diverse needs of businesses of all sizes. The continuous addition of new features and enhancements propelled Slack from a simple messaging tool to an indispensable platform for business communication.

Slack's journey from an internal tool for a gaming company to a globally recognized business communication platform is a testament to the power of adaptability, user-centric design, and agile development. It highlights how understanding and responding to market needs and a commitment to continuous improvement and evolution can transform a simple idea into an essential tool for businesses worldwide.

Raspberry Pi: Democratizing Computing

Raspberry Pi's journey is a compelling narrative of how an educational tool transcended its original purpose to democratize computing on a global scale. Initially conceived to teach introductory computer science in schools and developed countries, Raspberry Pi quickly outgrew its educational confines. Its utility expanded remarkably, finding resonance in classrooms and among hobbyists, programmers, and even in industrial applications. This broadening of its market is a testament to its versatility and the universal appeal of accessible computing.

Central to Raspberry Pi's evolution has been its community's role. This diverse group of users has employed the device innovatively, pushing its boundaries far beyond its initial educational intent. The Raspberry Pi Foundation has taken cues from this vibrant user base, making the evolution of the device significantly community-driven. Each new model of Raspberry Pi has built upon its predecessor, showcasing a commitment to iterative improvement. This approach highlights the importance of staying attuned to user needs and technological advancements, ensuring that each iteration brings relevant and valuable enhancements to its users.

A defining feature of Raspberry Pi is its affordability, which has made it a cornerstone in the world of cost-effective innovation and prototyping. Its low cost has opened doors to various applications, from personal projects to significant scientific research, making computing and programming accessible to a broader audience. This accessibility has catalyzed creativity, allowing individuals and organizations worldwide to experiment and innovate without the burden of high expenses. By lowering the barrier to entry in the computing field, Raspberry Pi has not only fostered a wave of innovation but also empowered a new generation of creators and thinkers.

The stories of Raspberry Pi and Slack, each in their domain, highlight critical lessons for startups and technology ventures. They underscore the necessity of agility in responding to market dynamics and user feedback. More importantly, they exemplify the significance of maintaining a user-centric approach in product development. These narratives illustrate that the ability to pivot, adapt, and iterate in the ever-changing technology landscape is just as vital as the initial product concept. Through their journeys, Raspberry Pi and Slack demonstrate how startups can navigate changes, engage with their user base, and continually evolve, ensuring they remain relevant and thriving in a rapidly changing technological environment.

Rapid Prototyping and Minimum Viable Products (MVPs)

In the dynamic and innovative world of startups and emerging technologies, the concepts of rapid prototyping and developing Minimum Viable Products (MVPs) are not just techniques; they are crucial strategies for survival and success. The approach to MVPs taken by companies like Slack and Raspberry Pi underscores their pivotal roles in shaping the trajectories of these organizations.

Rapid prototyping is an approach that allows developers to create a working model of a product or feature quickly. This method is beneficial in the startup environment, where time and resources are often limited, and the need to iterate quickly is crucial. On the other hand, the concept of an MVP revolves around developing a product with just enough features to satisfy early adopters and provide valuable feedback for future product development. This approach effectively validates business concepts and understands user needs without investing significant resources into full-scale product development.

Slack's journey exemplifies the power of an MVP approach. Starting as a simple internal tool within a gaming company, it initially focused on essential functionalities like messaging and file sharing. This minimal version effectively demonstrated the potential of a streamlined communication platform. The key to Slack's success was its iterative development process, characterized by responsiveness to user feedback and market demand. As Slack evolved from its MVP, it gradually incorporated features like third-party integrations and enhanced security, always driven by a clear understanding of user needs and market trends.

Raspberry Pi presents another instructive example of this approach. Initially developed as an educational tool, Raspberry Pi rapidly expanded its scope to cater to a wide range of users, from hobbyists to professionals. This expansion was driven mainly by its community, which innovatively used the device. The Raspberry Pi team embraced this feedback, leading to iterative releases of new models, each improving on the last. This commitment to continuous adaptation and improvement was crucial to Raspberry Pi's widespread adoption and success.

The stories of Slack and Raspberry Pi illuminate the strategic importance of rapid prototyping and MVPs in the startup and technology sectors. These approaches allow startups to test and refine their ideas quickly, adapting to real-time market and user feedback. By focusing on core functionalities and gradually building upon them, startups can navigate the uncertainties of the market and technological advancements more effectively. These case studies highlight the successful implementation of these strategies and guide other startups looking to navigate the challenging yet rewarding path of technology innovation.

Slack: Setting the Bar for MVP Development

Slack's journey in software development is a standout example of how to set the bar for MVP (Minimum Viable Product) development. It began as an internal tool within Tiny Speck, a gaming company, intended to streamline communication among its team members. The initial version of Slack focused on core functionalities like messaging and file sharing. Even in its nascent stage, Slack demonstrated the potential of a streamlined communication platform, fulfilling a basic yet crucial need in team collaboration.

As Slack transitioned from an MVP to a full-fledged product, its development process was heavily driven by user feedback and market demand. This feedback-driven iteration was crucial to its successful evolution. Slack's team meticulously analyzed user input, allowing them to refine and expand the platform's features thoughtfully. Over time, they introduced enhancements such as third-party integrations and improved security measures. These additions were not just random enhancements but were carefully chosen based on a clear understanding of user needs and emerging trends in the market.

A critical aspect of Slack's development was its emphasis on user experience. The development team dedicated substantial effort to creating a clean, intuitive user interface, which made it accessible and appealing to a broad range of users. This user-centric design was not a one-time effort but a continuous process. Slack has consistently introduced updates and improvements, ensuring the platform keeps pace with and often stays ahead of the competition in the rapidly evolving landscape of business communication tools.

Slack's approach to MVP development and subsequent evolution is a textbook example for startups and software developers. It illustrates the importance of starting with a focused set of core functionalities, actively engaging with user feedback, and iteratively expanding and refining the product. This strategy, coupled with a strong emphasis on user experience, has enabled Slack to become a leading platform in business communication.

Raspberry Pi: Prototyping for Accessibility and Versatility

The Raspberry Pi's journey from an educational prototype to a versatile computing platform epitomizes the power of accessibility and adaptability in technology. The Raspberry Pi was initially developed to make computing and programming more accessible to students, particularly in educational settings. This noble intent was the driving force behind its creation, aiming to demystify computing and spark interest in computer science among the younger generation.

However, the Raspberry Pi's journey didn't stop there. It rapidly evolved, extending its reach far beyond the classroom. The platform began to cater to a diverse spectrum of users, ranging from hobbyists and enthusiasts to professional developers and engineers. This broadening of its user base was not incidental but a testament to the Raspberry Pi's inherent versatility and adaptability.

Central to Raspberry Pi's development has been its deep engagement with its user community. This community-driven approach has significantly influenced the evolution of the Raspberry Pi, ensuring that each iteration of the device reflects its users' real-world needs and creativity. The community's input has been invaluable in shaping the Raspberry Pi, making it a product that resonates with and is helpful to various people with varying needs and skill levels.

The iterative release of new Raspberry Pi models showcases the team's commitment to continual improvement and adaptation. Each new version builds upon the last, incorporating new features and enhancements based on user feedback and technological advancements. This iterative process is a hallmark of Raspberry Pi's development strategy, emphasizing responsiveness to user needs and technological shifts.

A key aspect of Raspberry Pi's appeal lies in its affordability. The team's dedication to keeping the device cost-effective has played a crucial role in its widespread adoption and fostering a culture of innovation and experimentation. Its affordability has opened doors for many projects, ranging from essential educational tools to sophisticated industrial applications. This versatility and accessibility have cemented Raspberry Pi's status as a popular tool for various projects, enabling diverse groups to engage in computing and programming.

The narratives of both Slack and Raspberry Pi in the realm of MVP development are instructive and inspiring. They exemplify the power of starting with a core, functional product and then iteratively refining and expanding it based on real-world use and feedback. This approach has proven successful, particularly in the dynamic and ever-changing landscape of technology startups and emerging technologies. These case studies provide deep insights into the processes, challenges, and successes associated with rapid prototyping and MVP development, offering valuable lessons for those navigating the exciting and often unpredictable world of technology startups.

Key Takeaways

- Open-source Projects

- Importance of community-driven development and collaborative problem-solving.

- Challenges in balancing commercial and community interests.

- Need for transparent, scalable, evolving governance and building a robust ecosystem.

- Enterprise and Commercial Software

- Adapting DevEx principles to fit complex organizational structures.

- Integration of comprehensive toolchains for varied user needs.

- Continuous innovation and user-centric design are crucial.

- Startups and Emerging Technologies

- Significance of pivoting and adapting to market changes.

- The power of MVPs and iterative development in validating and refining business concepts.

- Community engagement as a driver for innovation and product evolution.

- Overall Impact of Developer Experience (DevEx)

- DevEx is a critical factor across diverse technological domains.

- Emphasis on understanding and prioritizing developer needs and experiences.

- DevEx drives innovation, user satisfaction, and technological advancement in various settings.

CHAPTER 11

The Future of Developer Experience

At the heart of this chapter is exploring how emerging trends and technologies are reshaping the landscape of DevEx. We're not just talking about the latest tools or programming languages but paradigm shifts redefining what it means to be a developer. This includes the rise of low-code and no-code platforms, which democratize development and open up new possibilities for people from non-technical backgrounds. Artificial Intelligence and Machine Learning are not just tools in the developer's arsenal but are becoming integral to the development process. The realms of Virtual and Augmented Reality are no longer just the stuff of science fiction but are now tangible tools that developers can use to create immersive experiences. Blockchain technology and decentralized applications are challenging traditional data storage and transaction notions.

A significant portion of this chapter is devoted to the role of ethics and sustainability in DevEx. In an era where data breaches make headlines and environmental concerns are escalating, how do these issues influence the developer experience? We delve into privacy and data security, not just as technical challenges but as ethical imperatives. Accessibility and inclusivity are examined not just as compliance checkboxes but as moral obligations and opportunities for innovation. The environmental impact and energy efficiency of development practices are scrutinized, encouraging developers and companies to consider the ecological footprint of their digital solutions.

This chapter doesn't just look at the future; it aims to inspire and guide developers and organizations to shape it. By understanding and embracing emerging trends and ethical considerations, developers and companies can adapt to the future and play a vital role in defining it. The key takeaways offer a concise recap of the chapter, ensuring readers leave with a clear understanding of the critical points and how they can apply them in their professional lives.

As you read through this chapter, think of it as a map to navigate the evolving landscape of technology and development. It's a journey through the possibilities and responsibilities of DevEx.

Emerging Trends and Technologies

This section is like a window into the future, offering a glimpse of the following exciting and dynamic technological changes:

- The Rise of Low-Code and No-Code Platforms

- Artificial Intelligence and Machine Learning in Development

- Virtual and Augmented Reality Development

- Blockchain and Decentralized Applications

These sections have a recurring theme: the importance of ethics, sustainability, and accessibility in technology. DevEx isn't just about functionality or efficiency; it's about our responsibility to create a digital world that is secure, inclusive, and sustainable.

By exploring these emerging trends, developers gain insights into the latest tools and technologies and develop a keen sense of responsibility toward ethical and sustainable development practices. As we look toward the future, the landscape of developer experience is ripe with promises of innovation, inclusivity, and a steadfast commitment to bettering society through technology.

Low-Code and No-Code Platforms

In the ever-evolving landscape of modern software development, a transformative wave is reshaping how we conceive and build applications: the advent of low-code and no-code platforms. These innovative platforms are not just altering the technical development process; they are revolutionizing the entire ethos of application creation. By enabling rapid application development and deployment with minimal hand-coding, they are breaking down the traditional barriers that have long defined the realm of software engineering.

Low-code and no-code platforms are distinguished by their user-friendly interfaces, often featuring drag-and-drop components and intuitive design elements. This approach significantly reduces the need for extensive hand-coding, making the development process more accessible to a broader audience. It's a shift that empowers professional developers and those who have never written a line of code, such as business analysts, project managers, and other professionals, to participate in application development actively. This democratization of development is not just about simplifying the process; it's about fostering an environment where the power to create and innovate is distributed more equally across different skill sets and backgrounds.

The advantages of these platforms extend beyond their accessibility. The reduced upfront investment in setup, training, and deployment makes them particularly attractive for small and medium-sized enterprises and individual entrepreneurs. This efficiency is not limited to financial savings;

it also encompasses the time and effort involved in bringing an application from concept to launch. This process can be lengthy and complex in traditional development, involving multiple coding, testing, and debugging stages. Low-code and no-code platforms streamline this process, enabling quicker prototyping and faster deployment of functional applications. This agility is crucial in today's fast-paced, constantly evolving digital landscape, where adapting and responding quickly to market demands or user feedback can be a significant competitive advantage.

As we delve into low-code and no-code platforms, we must recognize that they represent more than just a set of tools; they are part of a broader shift in the technological paradigm. These platforms are reshaping the software development landscape, making it more inclusive, efficient, and responsive to the needs of a diverse range of creators and users. They are redefining what it means to be a developer and opening up new possibilities for innovation and creativity in the digital world.

The Rise of Low-Code and No-Code Solutions

In software development, an exciting transformation is unfolding with the rise of low-code and no-code solutions. These platforms are reshaping the landscape of software creation, marking a significant shift from traditional coding to a more inclusive and accessible approach. Historically, the development of software applications was a domain reserved for those with extensive programming knowledge. However, low-code and no-code platforms are breaking down these barriers and democratizing the software creation process.

Now, a diverse array of individuals, including business analysts, project managers, and even those with no formal coding experience, can design, build, and deploy applications. This shift is monumental in how applications are created and who gets to create them. It signifies a move toward a more inclusive technological world where the power to build and innovate is spread across a broader spectrum of society.

Adopting these platforms isn't just a passing trend; it's a growing movement with significant market implications. A report by Gartner in July 2021 projected a 23% growth in the low-code development technologies market in the following year, highlighting the increasing demand and reliance on these platforms. This surge in growth reflects a broader trend in the tech industry: a shift toward more agile, efficient, and user-friendly development processes.

Low-code and no-code solutions are not just simplifying the development process; they are also accelerating it. By enabling rapid prototyping and faster deployment, these platforms are becoming a cornerstone in businesses' strategy to stay competitive and innovative. They offer a way to quickly adapt to market needs, experiment with new ideas, and deliver solutions without the traditional time and resource constraints of conventional coding. As we look at this growing trend, it's clear that low-code and no-code platforms are not just changing how we build software; they are redefining who can be a creator in the digital age.

Key Features and Advantages

The allure of low-code and no-code platforms is deeply rooted in their key features and advantages, which have been game-changers in software development. One of the most striking features of these platforms is their visual development interface, often characterized by intuitive drag-and-drop functionalities. This visual approach to building applications has opened the doors to a new demographic of creators. Individuals who may have been intimidated by lines of code can now engage in the development process thanks to this user-friendly interface. It's akin to assembling a puzzle; you can visually piece together the components of your application, making the development process more accessible and less daunting for non-technical users. This shift is not just about simplifying the process; it's about empowering more people to turn their ideas into reality, irrespective of their coding proficiency.

Beyond accessibility, low-code and no-code platforms shine in their ability to facilitate rapid prototyping. In today's fast-paced world, where market demands and user needs are constantly evolving, the ability to quickly develop and iterate on applications is invaluable. These platforms enable organizations to respond to changes swiftly, test new ideas, and refine their offerings based on real-time feedback, all without the extensive time investment typically associated with traditional software development. Moreover, the integration capabilities of these platforms must be balanced. Most offer seamless integration with existing databases and web services, simplifying the often complex task of data connectivity and automation. This integration streamlines processes, allowing for a smoother flow of information and more cohesive system operations.

Lastly, the cost-effectiveness of low-code and no-code solutions is a significant advantage. They significantly reduce the need for a large team of experienced developers, reducing development costs and time. This aspect particularly appeals to small and medium-sized enterprises, which may need more resources but still aspire to innovate and stay competitive. In essence, low-code and no-code platforms are not just tools; they are catalysts for a more inclusive, agile, and cost-effective approach to software development, reshaping the landscape in profound and empowering ways.

Case Studies and Examples

In the landscape of low-code and no-code platforms, real-world case studies and examples paint a vivid picture of their transformative potential. Let's consider some of these groundbreaking platforms and how they're being utilized to revolutionize various business operations.

Take Salesforce's Lightning Platform, for instance. It is a quintessential example of a low-code platform empowering businesses far and wide. With its intuitive design and powerful capabilities, the Lightning Platform allows companies to create customized applications tailored to enhance customer relationship management (CRM) strategies. This platform isn't just about building applications; it's about creating solutions that resonate with the unique needs of each business, enabling them to forge stronger connections with their customers. The beauty of Salesforce's offering lies in its ability to simplify complex processes, allowing companies to develop effective CRM apps and seamlessly integrate with their existing Salesforce environment. This integration helps streamline operations and provides a more unified view of the customer, enhancing the overall effectiveness of the CRM efforts.

Another noteworthy example is Microsoft PowerApps. This platform has quickly risen to prominence in the realm of low-code development. PowerApps offers a dynamic environment where users can rapidly build and deploy custom business applications regardless of their technical background. The strength of PowerApps lies in its flexibility and connectivity. It allows users to link their apps to various data sources using pre-built connectors or creating custom ones. This capability to seamlessly integrate with existing data systems makes PowerApps particularly powerful. Businesses can leverage this to develop apps that automate and streamline their internal processes and enable them to make data-driven decisions more efficiently. The agility offered by PowerApps in developing tailored solutions is a boon for businesses looking to adapt quickly to changing market demands or internal operational needs.

These case studies exemplify how low-code and no-code platforms are more than just tools for creating applications; they are enablers of innovation and efficiency. By simplifying the development process and offering robust integration capabilities, platforms like Salesforce's Lightning and Microsoft PowerApps are helping businesses redefine how they operate, making technology an ally in their journey toward growth and customer satisfaction. The impact of these platforms extends beyond the realm of IT departments, touching every facet of a business and empowering a more comprehensive range of professionals to contribute to the digital transformation journey.

Challenges and Concerns

Addressing some of the challenges and concerns of technological advancement in the evolving world of low-code and no-code platforms is essential. Understanding these aspects is crucial for anyone delving into this field, whether a seasoned developer or a newcomer to software creation.

A primary concern with low-code and no-code platforms centers around scalability and performance. As businesses grow and their needs evolve, there's an underlying question: can the applications built using these platforms scale effectively to keep pace with this growth? This concern isn't just about handling an increased number of users or data volume; it's about maintaining performance levels, ensuring the reliability of the applications, and preserving user experience. While these platforms offer a quick and easy way to build applications, their ability to adapt and perform under the pressure of scaling is a critical aspect that businesses must consider.

Another significant challenge is the limitation in customization. Low-code and no-code platforms are designed to be flexible and user-friendly, but this often comes at the cost of deep customization. They provide a range of features and functionalities that cover a broad spectrum of everyday business needs. However, these platforms may need to catch up regarding highly specialized or unique requirements. This limitation can be a hurdle for businesses with complex, niche processes that require more tailored solutions. It balances the ease and speed of development these platforms offer and the need for specialized, custom-built functionalities.

Security and compliance are also paramount concerns. In an era where data breaches and cyber threats are increasingly common, ensuring that applications built on these platforms adhere to stringent security standards is crucial. Moreover, different industries often have specific regulatory requirements. For instance, the healthcare and finance sectors have strict data privacy and security guidelines. Ensuring that applications built using low-code and no-code platforms comply with these regulations is vital for legal compliance; it's also essential for maintaining customer trust and safeguarding sensitive information.

These challenges highlight the importance of a thoughtful approach when adopting low-code and no-code platforms. While they offer numerous advantages in speed, ease of use, and accessibility, it's vital to consider these platforms' scalability, customization capabilities, and adherence to security and compliance standards. By understanding and navigating these concerns, businesses can make more informed decisions about integrating these platforms into their technology strategies, ensuring they reap the benefits while mitigating potential risks.

Future Outlook

The trajectory of low-code and no-code platforms is painting an exciting picture for the future of software development. These platforms are not just fleeting trends; they represent a fundamental shift toward more inclusive, efficient, and agile development practices. As we look ahead, the evolution of these platforms is set to redefine the boundaries of what's possible in software development, making the process more accessible and less intimidating for a broader range of people.

The essence of this shift lies in how these platforms make technology more approachable. They simplify the complex process of bringing ideas to life, enhancing the developer experience. We expect these platforms to become even more powerful and sophisticated, offering greater customization and robustness. This evolution will likely address limitations, such as scalability concerns and customization constraints, making these platforms suitable for a broader range of applications and use cases.

The rise of low-code and no-code platforms signifies much more than a new set of tools; it represents a paradigm shift in software development. These platforms are poised to become crucial players in a future where the ability to rapidly deploy applications, adapt with agility, and include a diverse range of creators in the development process is paramount. This trend aligns perfectly with the ethos of enhancing the developer experience—breaking down barriers, democratizing the creation process, and enabling a more diverse group of people to participate in the technological revolution.

As this trend evolves, its impact on the Developer Experience (DevEx) will be profound. Low-code and no-code platforms are set to play a crucial role in shaping the future landscape of DevEx, redefining what it means to be a creator in the digital age. They are not just about making development easier; they are about empowering a new generation of developers and innovators, opening up a world of possibilities for those who may have never ventured into software development. The future of these platforms is bright, and their role in driving innovation and inclusivity in software development is undeniable.

Artificial Intelligence and Machine Learning in Development

Integrating Artificial Intelligence (AI) and Machine Learning (ML) into software development marks a pivotal moment in the evolution of programming. This transformation goes far beyond the automation of mundane tasks; it reshapes the fabric of development methodologies, leading to a more intelligent, efficient, and user-centric approach. As we venture into this new era, it's essential to understand how these technologies are not just tools in a developer's arsenal but are becoming integral components that redefine the development process.

AI and ML are bringing sophistication to previously unattainable software development. These technologies can learn from data, identify patterns, and make decisions with minimal human intervention. This capability opens up possibilities for developers, from automating complex coding tasks to optimizing algorithms for better performance. The impact of AI and ML is multifaceted; they enhance the efficiency of the development process, reduce the likelihood of errors, and enable the creation of more advanced, personalized applications.

Moreover, AI and ML are transforming the role of developers. Rather than repetitive coding tasks, developers can focus more on software development's strategic, creative problem-solving aspects. AI and ML tools are becoming collaborators, aiding developers in exploring new ideas, testing hypotheses, and bringing agility and precision to their work that was previously difficult to achieve. This collaboration is not about replacing human intelligence but augmenting it, leveraging the strengths of AI and ML to enhance human creativity and ingenuity.

This shift toward AI and ML in software development is not just a technological advancement; it's a cultural shift in the programming world. It encourages a more exploratory, innovative approach to software creation, where developers are empowered to push the boundaries of what is possible. As we delve deeper into this section, we will incorporate ML's influence on software development, from automating and optimizing tasks to revolutionizing debugging and testing methodologies. Integrating AI and ML is a journey toward a future where software development is more intelligent, efficient, and aligned with users' and developers' evolving needs and expectations.

Transforming Development with AI and ML

Integrating Artificial Intelligence (AI) and Machine Learning (ML) into software development profoundly transforms the field. This fusion is not just an enhancement of existing processes; it's a complete overhaul of how developers approach and handle many tasks. AI and ML are revolutionizing the coding landscape, driving efficiency and opening up new horizons for innovation.

One of the most impactful changes brought about by AI in software development is the automation and optimization of various tasks. AI technologies can handle traditionally manual and time-consuming functions, such as code generation and algorithm optimization. For example, tools like TensorFlow and PyTorch reshape how developers build and deploy machine learning models. These tools provide frameworks that enable developers to create sophisticated models more efficiently, accelerating the process from conceptual design to actual deployment. The influence of AI in coding goes beyond mere automation; it's about enhancing the efficiency and quality of the code produced, ensuring that applications are functional and optimized for peak performance.

Another significant area where AI and ML are making strides is debugging and testing. In traditional software development, debugging can be a tedious and time-consuming process. However, with ML algorithms, it's possible to predict potential flaws in the code, thereby reducing the time and effort required for debugging. Automated testing tools powered by AI bring an added layer of sophistication. They can adapt to changes in the codebase, conducting tests that are more comprehensive and accurate. This adaptability ensures that applications are robust at launch and maintain reliability as they evolve.

Predictive analytics is yet another domain where AI is making a substantial impact. By analyzing past user interactions, AI can predict future behavior, allowing developers to craft applications that are not only more personalized but also more engaging. This aspect of AI is particularly crucial in creating user experiences that resonate with the target audience. Predictive analytics helps developers understand user preferences and behaviors, enabling them to design features and functionalities that align closely with user expectations. This level of personalization is vital in today's competitive digital landscape, where engaging and retaining users is as important as attracting them.

Incorporating AI and ML into software development is an incremental change and a revolutionary shift. This transformation enables developers to automate and optimize tasks, enhance debugging and testing processes, and leverage predictive analytics to create more personalized user experiences. As we continue to explore the capabilities of AI and ML, their role in shaping the future of software development is becoming increasingly evident, heralding a new era of efficiency, innovation, and user-centric design.

Ethical Considerations and Challenges

When integrating Artificial Intelligence (AI) and Machine Learning (ML) into software development, navigating the complex terrain of ethical considerations and challenges is crucial. While immensely powerful, these technologies bring with them a set of issues that require careful consideration and responsible management.

A significant ethical challenge in AI is dealing with bias and fairness. AI systems are fundamentally shaped by the data on which they are trained. This data, reflective of real-world scenarios, often contains inherent biases. These biases can lead to unfair outcomes in AI-driven decisions when not addressed. A striking example of this can be seen in facial recognition technologies, where instances of racial discrimination have emerged, highlighting the critical need for fairness in algorithms. Ensuring that AI systems are fair and unbiased is not just a technical challenge; it's a moral imperative. It involves a deep understanding of the data used and the context in which these systems operate. Developers and companies must be vigilant in identifying and mitigating biases, ensuring that AI systems are equitable and just for all users.

Another critical ethical consideration revolves around the environmental impact of AI and ML, particularly the energy consumption associated with training large language models (LLMs). The computational power required for these models is substantial, leading to significant energy use and carbon emissions. Addressing this issue involves optimizing algorithms for energy efficiency, exploring alternative energy sources, and being mindful of the environmental costs associated with AI development.

Another ethical aspect pertains to transparency and accountability in AI systems. Some AI and ML models, especially those based on complex algorithms, are often likened to "black boxes" due to their opaque nature. Understanding how these systems arrive at certain decisions or predictions can be challenging. This lack of transparency raises concerns, particularly when AI-driven decisions significantly impact individuals' lives. Accountability becomes a question mark when it's unclear how or why an AI system made a particular decision. Addressing this concern requires a concerted effort to make AI systems more interpretable and their decision-making processes more transparent. This enhances the trustworthiness of AI systems and ensures that developers and organizations can be held accountable for the decisions made by their AI-driven applications.

Navigating these ethical considerations is integral to responsible AI and ML development. As we continue to harness the power of these technologies in software development, it's imperative to remain aware of these challenges. By actively working to ensure fairness, transparency, accountability, and environmental responsibility, we can leverage AI and ML to enhance the efficiency and capabilities of software development and do so in a manner that upholds ethical standards and promotes trust and equity.

AI and ML in Practice

In the dynamic world of software development, the practical applications of Artificial Intelligence (AI) and Machine Learning (ML) are theoretical concepts and fundamental, tangible tools that reshape how developers work. These technologies are not just about automating tasks; they're about augmenting and enhancing developers' capabilities in remarkable ways.

A prime example of AI's transformative impact in practice is GitHub Copilot, powered by OpenAI's Codex. GitHub Copilot has been nothing short of a game-changer for many developers. It's not just a tool that assists with coding; it's an intelligent companion that suggests whole lines or blocks of code. Imagine writing a piece of code with a virtual assistant alongside you, offering suggestions, and completing complex structures. This kind of AI-driven assistance exemplifies how technology can augment a developer's capabilities, making the coding process faster and more efficient. GitHub Copilot is a glimpse into a future where AI partners with developers, enhancing their creativity and productivity.

Another noteworthy development in this arena is the emergence of AI-driven development environments, such as Kite. Tools like Kite leverage ML to provide intelligent code completions. What sets these tools apart is their ability to understand the context of the written code, offering relevant and helpful suggestions. This capability significantly reduces the repetitive aspects of coding and anticipates the developer's needs, thereby streamlining the coding process. It's a subtle yet powerful way AI can enhance the coding experience, allowing developers to focus more on problem-solving and creative aspects rather than getting bogged down by routine tasks.

These examples of AI and ML in practice demonstrate a profound shift in the software development landscape. It's a shift from AI as a distant, complex technology to a close, invaluable ally in the coding process. As these technologies continue to evolve and integrate more deeply into development environments, they promise to make coding more efficient, intuitive, and enjoyable. The future of software development, augmented by AI and ML, is not just about writing code; it's about crafting solutions in collaboration with intelligent tools that understand and enhance the developer's workflow.

Future Trends: AI and ML Shaping Development

As we look toward the future, Artificial Intelligence (AI) and Machine Learning (ML) are not just altering software development tools but reshaping the foundations of how we approach software creation. The promise of AI and ML extends far beyond their current applications, heralding a new era of intelligent, efficient, and user-centric software development.

One of the most anticipated developments in this field is the emergence of AI-powered personalized development environments. Future AI-driven tools are expected to offer more customized experiences fine-tuned to individual coding styles and preferences. This personalization will lead to a more seamless and intuitive development process, where the tools adapt to the developer rather than vice versa. Imagine an environment that learns from your coding habits and preferences, evolving to suit your needs better and enhance your productivity. This level of personalization makes the development process more efficient and enjoyable, as developers work in an environment that truly understands and supports their unique workflow.

Another exciting trend is the potential for AI algorithms to provide real-time suggestions for code optimization and refactoring. This advancement would revolutionize how we write and maintain code, leading to more efficient and high-quality code bases. AI-driven real-time optimization means the code is continuously analyzed and improved, reducing the likelihood of errors and inefficiencies. This process saves time and ensures the codebase remains robust and scalable.

AI and ML are also set to transform quality assurance. ML models can significantly enhance quality assurance processes by predicting where bugs are most likely to occur and suggesting optimal testing strategies. This predictive approach to quality assurance means that potential issues can be identified and addressed before they arise, drastically reducing the time and resources typically spent on testing and debugging.

It's essential to recognize that AI and ML in software development are more than just advanced tools; they are catalysts for fundamental change. As these technologies continue to advance, they promise to enhance the developer experience profoundly. However, the true challenge lies in leveraging these technologies ethically and sustainably. It's crucial to ensure that AI and ML augment human capabilities rather than replace them, maintaining a balance where technology is a partner in the creative process of software development. The future of AI and ML in software development is bright and full of possibilities. Still, it is up to us to steer these technologies toward enhancing, empowering, and elevating the human aspect of software creation.

Virtual and Augmented Reality Development

In the fascinating realm of technology, Virtual Reality (VR) and Augmented Reality (AR) have emerged as more than just cutting-edge entertainment; they have become transformative tools across various industries. These technologies are redefining the boundaries between the digital and physical worlds, offering immersive experiences that revolutionize how we interact with technology and with each other.

Integrating VR and AR into developer experiences (DevEx) is particularly noteworthy. For developers, creating applications in these spaces involves unique challenges and opportunities that significantly influence their work and productivity. VR and AR have evolved considerably from their early days as niche mediums primarily used for gaming and entertainment. Today, they play pivotal roles in fields as diverse as education, healthcare, real estate, and retail. This evolution has necessitated the development of new tools, frameworks, and best practices tailored to the specific demands of VR and AR environments, further enhancing DevEx by providing developers with the resources needed to build more intuitive and immersive applications. VR immerses users entirely in a digital environment, allowing for previously impossible experiences, such as exploring virtual worlds or simulating complex tasks for training purposes. AR, on the other hand, overlays digital information in the real world, enhancing everyday experiences with interactive, context-rich information. Developers working in these areas must consider factors such as user interface design in 3D spaces, real-time data processing, and the seamless integration of virtual elements with the physical world, all of which require rethinking traditional development paradigms.

The power of VR and AR lies in their ability to blend the digital and physical realms in engaging and practical ways, directly impacting how developers approach problem-solving and innovation. This blending opens up many possibilities for learning, working, shopping, and even receiving medical care. In education, for instance, VR can transport students to historical sites or simulate scientific phenomena, providing immersive learning experiences that deepen understanding. In retail, AR apps allow customers to visualize products in their homes before purchasing, enhancing decision-making and customer satisfaction. For developers, the ability to create these experiences means accessing new tools and learning new skills, which ultimately enriches DevEx by pushing the boundaries of what is possible in software development.

The development of VR and AR technologies represents a significant step forward in interacting with digital content. For developers, these advancements mean continually adapting to new technologies and methods, ensuring they can meet the growing demands of creating immersive and interactive experiences. It's a move toward more interactive, immersive, and personalized experiences, breaking down the barriers between real and virtual. As these technologies evolve, they promise to transform our interactions with the world around us, offering new and exciting ways to experience, learn, and connect. This transformation also highlights the importance of a robust DevEx that supports developers in navigating the complexities of VR and AR development, ensuring they have the tools and knowledge to succeed in this rapidly evolving field.

Innovations in VR and AR Development

The realm of Virtual Reality (VR) and Augmented Reality (AR) development is ushering in a new era of innovations, creating experiences that are visually stunning and deeply immersive. These technologies are redefining what it means to interact with digital content, extending the boundaries of our physical world into the realms of virtual and augmented environments.

VR and AR have the unique ability to create engaging and lifelike experiences. Take virtual meetings in platforms like Oculus Rift, for instance. They offer an immersive experience beyond traditional video conferencing, making participants feel like they are in the same physical space. AR applications transform the retail shopping experience by allowing customers to visualize products in real-world settings. This application of AR technology is not just a novelty; it's a practical tool that helps customers make more informed purchasing decisions by seeing products in their intended environment.

The applications of VR and AR extend far beyond gaming and entertainment, crossing into various disciplines. For example, AR has found a significant role in education, enhancing learning experiences by bringing abstract concepts to life. This visual and interactive approach to learning helps students grasp complex ideas more easily. In the field of medicine, VR is playing a transformative role, particularly in complex surgical procedures. Surgeons use VR for 3D visualization, which assists them in planning and performing surgeries with greater precision. This application of VR in medicine is not just improving outcomes; it's revolutionizing how medical professionals train and prepare for procedures.

The evolution of development tools and platforms has been pivotal in making VR and AR more accessible to a broader range of developers. Platforms like Unity and Unreal Engine have been instrumental in this evolution. They support various programming languages and offer extensive libraries, enabling developers to create rich, interactive experiences. These tools are not just about providing the technical means to develop VR and AR applications; they are about empowering developers to explore the full potential of these technologies. With these platforms, creating VR and AR experiences is no longer confined to specialists; it's becoming a domain accessible to a wide range of creators, from independent developers to large-scale enterprises.

The innovations in VR and AR development are opening up new frontiers in how we interact with technology. From immersive user experiences to cross-disciplinary applications, these technologies are not just changing the landscape of entertainment and gaming but impacting education, medicine, retail, and more. As development tools evolve, making these technologies more accessible, we expect to see even more creative and innovative uses of VR and AR, profoundly impacting various aspects of our lives.

Challenges in VR and AR Development

In the fascinating world of virtual reality (VR) and augmented reality (AR) development, developers face significant challenges, and the innovation potential is vast. Understanding these challenges is crucial for anyone interested in the field, whether as a developer, a user, or a technology enthusiast.

One of the primary challenges in VR and AR development is hardware limitations. Despite rapid technological advancements, developers are often constrained by the need for powerful processors and high-quality displays. These hardware requirements can limit the accessibility and scalability of VR and AR applications. For instance, to achieve the immersive VR experience, a high level of graphical fidelity and smooth performance is required, which can only be delivered by high-end, often expensive, hardware. This impacts the development cost and limits the user base to those who can afford such hardware. Similarly, in AR, the reliance on advanced sensors and camera technologies to accurately overlay digital information onto the real world can pose a challenge, especially when aiming for widespread accessibility.

Another critical area of concern is user accessibility and comfort, particularly in VR. Ensuring a comfortable and enjoyable user experience is paramount for adopting VR technology. Issues such as motion sickness, eye strain, and user fatigue are real challenges that must be addressed. These problems arise from the disconnect between what the user's eyes see and what their body feels, especially in highly immersive environments. Developers are continually seeking ways to mitigate these issues, from improving the design of VR headsets to optimizing software for more natural movement and interaction, all aimed at making VR experiences more user-friendly and accessible.

The complexity involved in developing realistic and engaging VR/AR experiences is another significant challenge. Crafting these experiences is not just about advanced programming; it involves a deep understanding of 3D modeling, user interface design, and user experience principles. Developers need to create environments that are not only visually appealing but also intuitive and interactive. This requires a skill set that spans multiple disciplines, making VR and AR development a complex field. The challenge is to seamlessly integrate these different aspects to create experiences that are immersive, engaging, and, most importantly, enjoyable for the user.

While VR and AR technologies offer exciting possibilities for creating new and immersive experiences, the challenges of hardware limitations, user accessibility and comfort, and the complexity of development are significant. Addressing these challenges is crucial for the continued growth and adoption of VR and AR technologies. As developers and companies navigate these challenges, they push the boundaries of what's possible, paving the way for more advanced, user-friendly, and accessible VR and AR experiences.

Ethical and Sustainability Considerations

The fascinating journey into Virtual Reality (VR) and Augmented Reality (AR) brings a set of ethical and sustainability considerations that are paramount in today's tech-conscious society. As we delve into these technologies, we must be aware of their implications beyond their technical and entertainment value, especially concerning privacy and environmental impact.

One of the most pressing ethical concerns in VR and AR is privacy. By their very nature, these technologies can track and analyze user movements and interactions in a highly detailed manner. For instance, a VR headset can collect data on how a user moves or reacts in a virtual environment, while AR applications might gather information about real-world interactions. This level of data collection raises significant privacy concerns. Ensuring user privacy and data security in VR and AR applications is a technical and moral challenge. Developers and companies involved in these technologies must navigate these concerns thoughtfully, implementing robust data protection measures and maintaining transparency with users about what data is collected and how it is used. It's about creating a balance where the immersive potential of VR and AR can be enjoyed without compromising individual privacy.

Another crucial consideration is the environmental impact of VR and AR technologies. The production, consumption, and disposal of VR and AR hardware pose significant ecological challenges. These devices often require various materials and components, some of which have a considerable environmental footprint. Moreover, the question of disposing of or recycling these technologies at the end of their lifecycle adds another layer to the ecological challenge. As these technologies grow in popularity, the need for sustainable manufacturing and waste management practices becomes increasingly important. This includes considering the entire lifecycle of products, from design to disposal, and seeking ways to minimize the ecological impact. It also involves educating users and stakeholders about the environmental implications of these technologies and encouraging responsible usage and disposal practices.

As we embrace the advancements in VR and AR technologies, we must do so with a conscientious approach, considering the ethical and sustainability challenges they present. Addressing privacy concerns and the environmental impact of these technologies is not just about compliance or corporate responsibility; it's about shaping a future where technological innovation harmonizes with ethical practices and sustainable living. As developers, users, and enthusiasts, our role extends beyond mere consumption or creation; it includes being stewards of technology that respects individual privacy and sustains our environment.

Case Studies: Success Stories in VR and AR

Exploring the realms of Virtual Reality (VR) and Augmented Reality (AR) reveals a series of success stories highlighting these technologies' vast potential. These case studies demonstrate the innovative applications of VR and AR and provide a glimpse into how they are reshaping industries and enhancing user experiences.

VR is making significant strides in education, changing the traditional classroom experience. Applications like Google Expeditions are at the forefront of this transformation. They offer students an immersive learning environment that transcends the physical boundaries of a classroom. Imagine a history lesson where instead of reading about ancient civilizations, students can virtually explore them, walking through historical sites and experiencing the culture and environment of a bygone era. This level of immersion in educational content can enhance understanding and retention, making learning informative but also engaging and exciting. VR in education represents a shift from passive learning to an interactive, experiential form where students actively participate in their learning journey.

AR is also making waves, particularly in the retail sector, with applications transforming the shopping experience. A prime example is IKEA's AR app, which allows customers to visualize furniture in their homes before purchasing. This application of AR technology solves a common challenge in furniture shopping: the uncertainty of how a piece of furniture will look and fit in one's space. By enabling customers to see products in their intended environment, the app enhances and personalizes the shopping experience. This interactive and personalized experience is a significant leap from traditional retail shopping, offering customers a more informed and confident buying process.

These case studies in VR and AR are more than just examples of technological innovation; they are testaments to the transformative power of these technologies across different sectors. Whether enhancing how we learn or revolutionizing how we shop VR and AR are opening up new possibilities and redefining experiences. As these technologies evolve and find new applications, they promise to bring even more groundbreaking changes, impacting how we interact with the world and each other.

The Future of VR and AR Development

The landscape of Virtual Reality (VR) and Augmented Reality (AR) is rapidly evolving, moving toward more integrated and immersive experiences. This evolution is propelled by the advancements in Mixed Reality (MR), an exciting blend of VR and AR. MR is poised to create experiences that are more seamless and integrated, blurring the lines between the digital and physical worlds to an unprecedented degree. Imagine a world where digital and physical elements are so intricately intertwined that they create a new realm of experience that is more immersive and interactive than ever before. This convergence of VR and AR into MR is not just a technological advancement; it's a step toward creating a reality that transcends traditional boundaries, offering new ways to interact with our surroundings.

The potential applications of VR and AR are vast and varied, and their adoption across different sectors is poised to grow significantly. The implications are immense, from healthcare, where VR can be used for patient treatment and medical training, to real estate, where AR can aid property visualization. Each sector presents unique opportunities to leverage these technologies, whether it's for training, education, marketing, or entertainment. This widespread adoption across various industries is a testament to VR and AR technologies' versatility and transformative potential of VR and AR technologies.

As we look toward the future, a key focus in developing VR and AR will likely be user-centric design. This approach emphasizes creating experiences that are not only technologically advanced but also comfortable, accessible, and intuitive for users. The success of VR and AR technologies hinges on their ability to provide enriching and enjoyable experiences without causing discomfort or fatigue. Designing with the user in mind ensures a broader audience adopts and embraces these technologies.

VR and AR development represents a technological frontier, with opportunities to create immersive and interactive experiences like never before. As these technologies continue to evolve, their impact on various industries and aspects of life is expected to be profound. However, navigating the challenges—hardware limitations, user comfort, ethical considerations, or environmental sustainability—is crucial for their continued growth and acceptance. In this book section, we will delve deeper into these dimensions, exploring the future of VR and AR and their role in enhancing both the developer and user experience. This exploration is about understanding the technologies and appreciating their potential to transform how we perceive and interact with the world.

Blockchain and Decentralized Applications

The advent of blockchain technology and decentralized applications, commonly known as DApps, heralds a significant shift in the digital landscape. It introduces a new paradigm in how we interact with and perceive technology. This shift is not merely a technological advancement; it represents a fundamental change in the architecture and philosophy of digital applications.

At its core, Blockchain technology offers a new way of storing and managing data. Unlike traditional centralized systems where data is stored and controlled by a single entity, blockchain distributes data across a network of computers. This decentralized approach ensures that no single point maintains the data, enhancing security and reducing the risk of data manipulation or loss. It's a radical departure from the conventional centralized databases and serves as the foundation upon which DApps are built.

DApps are applications that run on this decentralized network, typically a blockchain. The decentralized nature of these applications means that no single authority controls them, starkly contrasting traditional applications. This decentralization brings many benefits, including increased transparency, security, and resistance to censorship. Transactions and interactions within DApps are recorded on the blockchain, ensuring they are transparent and immutable. This level of transparency is particularly impactful in scenarios where trust and accountability are paramount. Moreover, the security inherent in blockchain technology makes DApps resistant to common vulnerabilities that plague traditional centralized applications, such as hacking and data breaches.

From a Developer Experience (DevEx) perspective, blockchain and DApps introduce opportunities and challenges. On the one hand, developers can work with cutting-edge technology emphasizing transparency and security, which can be incredibly rewarding.

On the other hand, the steep learning curve and the complexity of developing decentralized networks can be daunting, especially for those accustomed to traditional centralized systems. To enhance DevEx in the blockchain space, it's crucial to provide robust development tools, clear documentation, and supportive communities that help developers navigate this new terrain.

Additionally, blockchain's emphasis on transparency and immutability can lead to a more collaborative and open development environment where contributions are more easily tracked and verified. This can foster a more inclusive and accountable development process, aligning with the broader goals of improving DevEx by creating environments where developers feel supported and their work is valued.

The emergence of blockchain technology and DApps is not just an evolution in software development; it's a rethinking of how digital applications function at their core. By leveraging the principles of decentralization, transparency, and security, blockchain and DApps offer a new and exciting landscape for digital interactions. This technology is poised to reshape various sectors, from finance to supply chain management, offering a more secure, transparent, and equitable digital experience. As developers continue to engage with these technologies, the focus on enhancing DevEx will be crucial to ensuring that the potential of blockchain and DApps can be fully realized, making them accessible and practical tools for a broader range of developers and users alike.

Core Features of Blockchain and DApps

In the contemporary digital landscape, blockchain technology and decentralized applications (DApps) stand out as revolutionary concepts. Each has core features that reshape how data and transactions are processed. These features significantly depart from traditional centralized systems, offering a new security, transparency, and efficiency paradigm.

At the heart of blockchain technology is the principle of decentralization. Unlike traditional centralized systems, where data is stored in a single location, blockchain distributes data across a network of computers. This data distribution eliminates single points of failure, greatly enhancing the security and resilience of the system. In a blockchain, no central repository could be a target for attacks, making it inherently more secure against hacking and data breaches. This decentralization is not just a technical feature; it represents a shift toward a more democratized approach to data management, where the control and ownership of data are spread across a network rather than being held by a single entity.

Another defining feature of blockchain is its transparency and immutability. Every transaction made on a blockchain is recorded on a public ledger that is transparent to all participants in the network. Once a transaction is recorded, it cannot be altered or deleted, ensuring the data's integrity. This feature is particularly crucial in financial systems and supply chain management applications, where trust and accountability are paramount. In finance, for instance, blockchain's transparency and immutability enable a level of security and trust essential for transactions. In supply chain management, these features allow for accurate tracking of products and materials, ensuring authenticity and compliance.

Smart contracts are another innovative feature of blockchain technology. These are self-executing contracts with the terms of the agreement directly written into lines of code. Smart contracts automate processes and transactions, significantly reducing the need for intermediaries. This automation streamlines operations, making them more efficient and less prone to human error. Smart contracts can be used in various applications, from automating insurance claims to facilitating real estate transactions. The beauty of smart contracts lies in their ability to execute transactions automatically once predetermined conditions are met, providing a level of efficiency and reliability that traditional contracts cannot offer.

The core features of blockchain and DApps—decentralization, transparency, immutability, and smart contracts—are not just technological innovations; they are reshaping the fundamentals of how data is managed and transactions are conducted. These features represent a shift toward more secure, transparent, and efficient systems, offering a glimpse into a future where technology enables higher trust and streamlined processes.

Challenges in Developing Blockchain and DApps

Developing Blockchain technology and Decentralized Applications (DApps) comes with unique challenges that are as complex as technology. These challenges are crucial for developers and enthusiasts to understand as they shape the landscape of how these technologies are adopted and evolved.

One of the most significant challenges in blockchain development is scalability, particularly evident in well-known blockchains like Ethereum. These systems often need help handling large volumes of transactions quickly and cost-effectively. As more users and applications come on board, the demand on the network increases, frequently leading to congestion and higher transaction fees. This scalability issue is a crucial hurdle, as the ability to process transactions swiftly and affordably is fundamental to blockchain technology's widespread adoption and utility.

Another challenge lies in the user experience associated with blockchain and DApps. The underlying complexity of blockchain technology often results in a steep learning curve for users. Many DApps need help to offer user-friendly interfaces, making it challenging for those without technical expertise to navigate and utilize these applications effectively. This gap in user experience is a significant barrier to broader adoption, as the true potential of any technology lies in its accessibility and ease of use for the general populace.

Moreover, blockchain and cryptocurrencies are still very much in flux. This evolving regulatory landscape poses a challenge for developers, as they must navigate a terrain that needs to be clarified and subject to change. Ensuring compliance with existing and future regulations is crucial, not just for the legality of the projects but also for gaining the trust of users and investors. The uncertainty in this domain can deter development and innovation, as developers must tread cautiously amidst changing regulations and potential legal implications.

While the development of blockchain and DApps presents exciting possibilities, the challenges of scalability, user experience, and regulatory uncertainty are significant. Addressing these challenges is essential for these technologies' growth and sustainable development. As developers and innovators navigate these hurdles, their efforts will determine the future of blockchain and DApps and shape the landscape of modern technology and digital interactions.

Ethical and Sustainability Aspects

Understanding the ethical and sustainability aspects of Blockchain technology and Decentralized Applications (DApps) is essential for exploring these technologies. As these technologies advance and become more integrated into our digital lives, it's crucial to acknowledge and address the challenges they present in terms of environmental impact and data privacy.

Blockchain technology's environmental impact is a significant ethical concern, particularly regarding energy consumption. Blockchain networks, especially those that use proof-of-work (PoW) consensus mechanisms, require substantial computational power. This power-intensive process often leads to high energy consumption, raising environmental concerns. For instance, the energy used in cryptocurrency mining processes like Bitcoin has been much debated. The ecological footprint of these activities is considerable. As blockchain technology grows in popularity and usage, the impact on energy consumption and, consequently, the environment becomes an increasingly pressing issue. There's a growing need for more sustainable practices within the blockchain space, whether by adopting more energy-efficient consensus mechanisms or other innovative solutions to mitigate this environmental impact.

Another critical aspect to consider is data privacy. While one of the key features of blockchain is transparency, this transparency can sometimes be at odds with user privacy and data protection. In a blockchain, transactions are recorded on a public ledger, which, by design, is accessible to everyone in the network. This level of openness, while ensuring transparency and trust in the system, also raises questions about the privacy of the data and the individuals involved in the transactions. Navigating the balance between openness and privacy is a delicate task. It requires thoughtful consideration of how data is recorded and accessed on the blockchain to protect user privacy without compromising the integrity and trust fundamental to the technology.

As we delve into blockchain and DApps, we must consider their ethical and sustainability challenges. The environmental impact of blockchain, particularly in terms of energy consumption, and the concerns around data privacy are critical issues that need addressing. As developers, users, and enthusiasts of these technologies, our responsibility extends beyond innovation and efficiency. It includes a commitment to ethical practices and sustainable solutions that ensure blockchain technology's long-term viability and positive impact.

Case Studies and Examples

Exploring the world of Blockchain and Decentralized Applications (DApps) through real-world case studies and examples offers a clearer understanding of their transformative potential. These examples illustrate the practical applications of blockchain technology and showcase how they're reshaping industries and consumer experiences.

Ethereum is a prime example of how blockchain technology can foster significant innovation in financial services. It has become the backbone of the decentralized finance (DeFi) movement, which aims to create more open and accessible financial systems. DeFi applications built on Ethereum challenge traditional financial models by offering alternatives to services like loans, savings, and insurance, all without the need for traditional financial intermediaries like banks. This shift toward DeFi represents a significant transformation in the financial sector, offering greater accessibility and potentially more democratic financial services. Ethereum's role in this movement highlights blockchain's capability to support and drive innovation in crucial sectors like finance.

Another area where blockchain technology is making a substantial impact is in supply chain management. Blockchain-based supply chain applications like VeChain are revolutionizing how goods are tracked and traced from production to consumption. In traditional supply chains, tracking the journey of a product can be a complex and opaque process, often leading to inefficiencies and a lack of trust. However, with blockchain, every step in the supply chain can be recorded transparently and immutably, improving traceability and enhancing consumer trust. For example, a blockchain-based system can provide consumers with verifiable information about the origins and journey of a product, from the raw materials used to its manufacturing and delivery. This level of transparency is beneficial for consumers increasingly concerned about the authenticity and sustainability of their purchases and for companies looking to establish trust and accountability in their supply chains.

These case studies—Ethereum in the world of DeFi and blockchain in supply chain management—exemplify blockchain technology's broad and impactful applications. They demonstrate that blockchain is not just a theoretical concept or limited to cryptocurrencies; it's a practical, versatile technology already transforming various industries. As blockchain technology continues to evolve, its potential to innovate and improve different sectors of the economy and aspects of our daily lives becomes increasingly evident.

Future Directions in Blockchain and DApps Development

As we venture further into Blockchain and Decentralized Applications (DApps), the future directions of these technologies reveal exciting and transformative possibilities. Each development shows a more straightforward path toward more efficient, integrated, and sustainable blockchain networks. These advancements are not just technical enhancements; they represent a revolutionary shift in approaching data security, transparency, and decentralization.

One of the most significant areas of development is the emergence of Layer 2 solutions, particularly with platforms like Ethereum. These solutions address critical challenges such as scalability and speed, which have been significant hurdles in the widespread adoption of blockchain technology. By implementing Layer 2 scaling solutions, Ethereum and similar platforms are working toward creating more efficient blockchain networks that can handle a larger volume of transactions at higher speeds. This advancement promises to make blockchain technology more practical and usable in various applications, from financial transactions to complex decentralized systems.

Another critical direction in the evolution of blockchain and DApps is the focus on cross-chain interoperability. The future of blockchain technology lies in its ability to allow different blockchain networks to interact and integrate seamlessly. This interoperability is crucial for the development of more versatile and functional DApps. It enables various blockchain platforms to communicate and share information, opening up possibilities for more complex and integrated applications. This level of interoperability will enhance the functionality of DApps and expand their potential use cases across different sectors.

Sustainability is also becoming a central focus in blockchain development. Innovations in consensus mechanisms, such as the shift toward proof-of-stake (PoS), are geared toward reducing the environmental impact of blockchain technology. Unlike proof-of-work (PoW) mechanisms, which require significant computational power and energy consumption, PoS offers a more energy-efficient alternative. This shift is crucial in addressing environmental concerns associated with blockchain technology and ensuring its long-term sustainability.

The future of blockchain and DApps is marked by efforts to enhance scalability, interoperability, and sustainability. These technologies represent a paradigm shift in digital security, transparency, and efficiency. As technology matures and integrates into various sectors, from finance to supply chain management, it is poised to create more efficient, transparent, and equitable systems. However, successfully addressing the challenges of scalability, user experience, and environmental impact will be critical for the long-term success and acceptance of blockchain technologies. This book section delves deeply into these emerging trends, exploring their implications for developer experience and their broader impact on technology.

The Role of Ethics and Sustainability in DevEx

This subsection underscores the importance of embedding robust data security measures and privacy protocols in development processes in an era of rampant data breaches and privacy concerns. It examines how companies like Apple have prioritized user privacy, setting a new standard for data security in the tech industry.

This introduction sets the stage for a thorough exploration of how ethics and sustainability are reshaping the landscape of developer experience. It emphasizes that the future of technology is not just about what we can do but also about what we should do.

Privacy and Data Security

In today's digital age, privacy and data security are critical pillars, defining the trust and integrity of every application and service. These concepts are beyond mere buzzwords; they form the backbone of user confidence and the ethical framework within which technology operates. This chapter explores how privacy and data security are integral to shaping the developer experience (DevEx).

The significance of privacy and data security in technology cannot be overstated. As we rely on digital solutions daily, how these technologies handle our personal information becomes a paramount concern. This chapter delves into the multifaceted role of privacy and data security in DevEx, examining how these aspects influence the technical aspects of development and the ethical and user-centric considerations that developers must navigate.

This chapter discusses more than just the mechanisms of protecting data or complying with privacy laws. It's about understanding the broader impact of these practices on user trust and the ethical responsibilities of developers. This exploration is crucial for anyone creating, deploying, and managing digital technologies. The aim is to provide insights into how developers can create functional and efficient applications and secure and trustworthy environments that respect user privacy and data integrity.

Privacy and data security are foundational elements in the development of digital technologies. Their importance transcends technical requirements, touching on trust, ethics, and user respect. This chapter aims to equip developers with the knowledge and perspective to navigate these crucial aspects effectively, ultimately enhancing the developer experience and fostering a more secure and ethical digital world.

Understanding the Landscape

The landscape of modern technology is evolving at a breathtaking pace, particularly in fields like Artificial Intelligence (AI), the Internet of Things (IoT), and cloud computing. This rapid technological advancement increases the complexity and volume of data, which presents opportunities and significant responsibilities for developers, especially regarding safeguarding user data.

As technology advances, developers find themselves at the forefront of a new era where data is not just a resource but a crucial responsibility. The sheer volume of data generated by modern technologies like AI and IoT is staggering, and its management and protection are paramount. This responsibility is not just about ensuring the integrity and security of the data but also about protecting the privacy and rights of individuals. In this fast-evolving digital age, developers must be more vigilant than ever in implementing robust data protection measures and maintaining a high standard of data ethics.

Alongside technological advancements, the regulatory landscape concerning data handling and privacy is also undergoing significant changes. Legislation such as the General Data Protection Regulation (GDPR) in the European Union and the California Consumer Privacy Act (CCPA) in California has reshaped how data is handled globally. These legal frameworks are designed to protect user data and ensure privacy, imposing strict guidelines and hefty penalties for non-compliance. Navigating these frameworks has become an essential skill for developers. They must understand and adhere to these regulations to ensure that the technologies they develop are innovative and compliant. This development aspect is particularly challenging given the dynamic nature of legal frameworks around data privacy, which often vary from region to region.

Understanding the current landscape of technology development involves grappling with the rapid pace of technological advancements and the complex regulatory environment. Developers must balance the drive for innovation with the imperative to safeguard user data and comply with evolving legal frameworks. This balance is crucial in building technology solutions that are effective and cutting-edge but also responsible and trustworthy in the eyes of users and regulators. As we delve deeper into this landscape, the role of developers extends beyond technical expertise to encompass a broader understanding of data ethics and legal compliance.

Best Practices in Privacy and Data Security

Upholding privacy and data security is paramount in modern technology development. Best practices in these areas are not just recommendations but essential components of responsible and sustainable development. Understanding and implementing these practices is crucial for developers at the forefront of creating our digital world.

One of the foundational approaches in this context is Privacy by Design. This philosophy dictates that data protection protocols should be integrated into the development process from the very beginning. It's not about treating privacy as an afterthought or a box-ticking exercise. Instead, it involves anticipating potential privacy risks and embedding privacy considerations into the DNA of every project. This approach requires a shift in mindset, where privacy becomes a core component of the design process, guiding decisions and shaping the final product.

Conducting regular security audits is another vital best practice. In the fast-evolving world of technology, threats and vulnerabilities continuously emerge. Periodic reviews and updates of security measures are, therefore, essential. These audits are not merely about compliance; they are proactive steps to identify and address potential vulnerabilities before they are exploited. Regular security assessments help maintain a robust defense against emerging threats, ensuring that systems and data remain secure over time.

Encryption and secure data storage are also cornerstones of data security. Implementing robust encryption protocols for data at rest and in transit ensures that data is protected from unauthorized access. This is particularly important in an era where data breaches are increasingly common and can have far-reaching consequences. Alongside encryption, choosing reliable and secure data storage solutions is equally crucial. It's about ensuring that the infrastructure used to store data is safe and resilient, capable of protecting data against various risks, including cyber-attacks, system failures, and physical damages.

Best privacy and data security practices, such as Privacy by Design, regular security audits, robust encryption, and data storage, are not optional extras but essential components of modern technology development. As developers and technologists, the responsibility lies in creating innovative and efficient solutions and ensuring that these solutions are secure, resilient, and respectful of user privacy. Adopting these best practices is critical to building trust and credibility in the digital products and services that shape our world.

Case Studies and Examples

In the intricate tapestry of privacy and data security, real-world case studies and examples provide invaluable insights into this domain's best practices and pitfalls. These instances illuminate the consequences of action or inaction and are potent lessons for developers and companies in the digital age.

Apple's approach to privacy is a notable example of how prioritizing user data protection can significantly enhance a brand's reputation and consumer trust. Apple's stringent privacy policies, particularly evident in its App Store, demonstrate a commitment to user privacy beyond mere compliance. This commitment concerns adhering to legal standards and embedding privacy as a core value in the company's ethos. Apple's approach sends a clear message that user privacy is not just a feature or a benefit but a fundamental right. This stance on privacy has earned Apple acclaim and trust from users and set a benchmark in the industry, encouraging other companies to follow suit.

On the other end of the spectrum is the Facebook-Cambridge Analytica scandal, a stark reminder of the repercussions of data misuse. This incident highlighted data protection and privacy vulnerabilities, showing how easily user data can be exploited for purposes beyond the intended use. The scandal underscored the need for stringent data protection measures and raised awareness among users and regulators about the importance of data privacy. It served as a wake-up call for the industry, highlighting the critical need for transparency and accountability in how user data is collected, used, and protected. The fallout from this incident has had far-reaching implications, leading to increased scrutiny of data practices and a push for more robust regulatory frameworks globally.

These case studies—Apple's emphasis on privacy and the Facebook-Cambridge Analytica scandal—represent two sides of the privacy and data security coin. They exemplify the impact policies and practices in this area can have on a company's reputation, user trust, and regulatory compliance. For developers and companies navigating the digital landscape, these examples offer valuable lessons in prioritizing user privacy and the potential consequences of failing to do so. In the evolving digital world, understanding and learning from these case studies is crucial in shaping approaches that are not only innovative but also ethical and user-centric.

Challenges and Continuous Evolution

Navigating the technology field, especially in privacy and data security, presents challenges that require a delicate balance and continuous evolution. These challenges are not static; they become complex as technology advances and cybersecurity threats evolve. Understanding and addressing these challenges is essential for developers to create practical and trustworthy digital experiences.

One of the primary challenges that developers face is balancing convenience and security. In creating user-friendly experiences, it's vital to ensure that robust security measures are not compromised. Users often seek ease of use and seamless interactions in digital applications, but this should not come at the expense of their data security and privacy. Striking this balance is critical to effective Developer Experience (DevEx). It involves designing systems that are not only intuitive and accessible but also secure and resilient. This balance is a tightrope walk, requiring a deep understanding of user behavior and security principles. Developers must innovate ways to integrate robust security protocols into applications without hindering usability, ensuring the end product is safe and user-friendly.

Another ongoing challenge is adapting to emerging cybersecurity threats. The cybersecurity landscape is constantly changing, with new threats emerging ever-increasingly. Developers must stay ahead of these trends, continuously updating their knowledge and skills to protect against these evolving threats. This means staying informed about the latest security technologies, understanding the tactics of cyber adversaries, and being proactive in implementing preventive measures. The responsibility of a developer in this context goes beyond just building applications; it includes being a guardian of data security, constantly vigilant and prepared to respond to new challenges.

Technology development continues to face the challenges of balancing convenience and security and adapting to emerging threats. These challenges require developers to be adaptable, knowledgeable, and vigilant. As technology evolves, so must the approaches to ensuring data security and privacy. Navigating these challenges is critical to building digital experiences that are effective and engaging but also secure and trustworthy. For developers, this continuous evolution is not just a professional requirement; it's a commitment to safeguarding the digital landscape for all users.

Ethical Considerations

In the intricate and ever-evolving world of technology development, ethical considerations regarding data use play a crucial role. This realm goes beyond legal compliance; it encompasses a moral obligation that every developer must acknowledge and uphold. Ethical data use is a cornerstone in building trust and maintaining the integrity of digital applications.

The ethical use of data involves being transparent about how data is collected and used. This transparency is not just a matter of providing information; it's about ensuring that users fully understand and consent to how their data is handled. Respecting user consent is a fundamental aspect of ethical data use. It's about giving users control over their data, allowing them to make informed decisions about what they share and how it's used. This approach builds trust and respect between users and technology providers, reinforcing that user data is not merely a commodity but a responsibility.

Developers must also recognize the broader impact of their decisions on privacy and data security. These decisions can significantly influence societal norms and expectations. In an age where digital technologies are deeply integrated into everyday life, the way these technologies handle user data can set precedents and shape public perceptions about privacy and data security. Developers, therefore, have a responsibility to consider the societal implications of their work. Their choices can foster a culture of privacy and security or contribute to a landscape where user data is undervalued and unprotected.

In this context, Developer Experience (DevEx) is crucial in supporting developers in making ethical decisions. By integrating tools, guidelines, and resources directly into the development environment, DevEx can help developers understand the moral implications of their choices in real time. For instance, providing automated checks for data privacy compliance or offering contextual tips on ethical coding practices can guide developers to align their work with ethical standards more effectively. Additionally, fostering a DevEx culture that emphasizes ethical considerations in code reviews and team discussions can reinforce the importance of these values across the development lifecycle.

Privacy and data security are not merely technical issues but foundational aspects that profoundly influence the developer experience (DevEx). They require a delicate balance of technical acumen, ethical consideration, and an understanding of the legal landscape. As technology development progresses, these elements will continue to shape the industry. They are pivotal in determining how users worldwide perceive, adopt, and trust technology.

By embedding ethical considerations into the fabric of DevEx, organizations can empower developers to create technically robust applications that are aligned with the highest standards of ethical responsibility. This approach ensures that the technology we build today contributes positively to society, fostering trust and long-term value for all users.

This subsection delved into the complex relationship between privacy, data security, and DevEx. We have underscored the importance of these factors in creating secure, trustworthy, and user-centric applications. Understanding and implementing ethical data practices is not just a professional requirement for developers; it is an essential part of their contribution to a more secure and ethical digital world.

Accessibility and Inclusivity

This section profoundly and thoughtfully explores the crucial roles of accessibility and inclusivity in software development. These concepts, far from mere afterthoughts or box-ticking exercises, are integral to shaping the ethics and sustainability of the developer experience (DevEx). This chapter explores the profound impact of these principles on creating technology that is functional, efficient, respectful, and accommodating of a diverse range of users.

Accessibility and inclusivity in software development ensure that digital products are usable and welcoming to everyone, regardless of their abilities or backgrounds. This encompasses a broad spectrum of considerations, from designing interfaces that are navigable by people with various disabilities to creating content that is sensitive and respectful of cultural differences. It's an approach that challenges developers to think beyond the traditional scope of functionality and efficiency, urging them to consider how their creations affect and include all potential users.

This section explores the various dimensions of accessibility and inclusivity in depth. We look at how these principles are essential from a moral, ethical, and practical business perspective. Inclusive and accessible software reaches a broader audience, fosters greater user satisfaction, and builds a stronger, more positive brand image. This exploration is not just about understanding the "why" behind accessibility and inclusivity; it's about delving into the "how"—the strategies, best practices, and considerations that make these principles an integral part of the DevEx.

This section of the book is designed to be enlightening and informative. It guides seasoned developers and newcomers through the vital role that accessibility and inclusivity play in crafting superior digital experiences. The aim is to instill a deeper understanding and appreciation of these principles, showcasing how they contribute to creating a more inclusive and equitable digital world.

The Essence of Accessibility and Inclusivity

In software development, accessibility and inclusivity are vital in creating applications and tools that cater to a broad spectrum of users. This section delves into the essence of these crucial concepts.

Accessibility in software development is about crafting applications and tools usable by people with various abilities and disabilities. It's a commitment to consider and address the needs of individuals with multiple impairments, including auditory, cognitive, neurological, physical, speech, and visual challenges. This approach goes beyond mere compliance with standards; it's about deeply understanding how people interact with technology and ensuring that these interactions are as barrier-free as possible. It involves designing software easily navigated and understood by all users, regardless of their physical or cognitive abilities. This aspect of development is not just about technical adaptation; it reflects empathy and understanding toward the diverse needs of users.

For internal Developer Experience (DevEx), this commitment to accessibility means choosing inclusive tools and practices that accommodate the diverse needs of the developers you work with. Ensuring that development environments, documentation, and resources are accessible to all team members fosters a culture of inclusivity within the development process. This empowers every developer to contribute effectively and feel valued within the team, regardless of background or abilities.

Extending beyond accessibility, inclusivity in software development ensures that applications are usable and welcoming to people from diverse backgrounds, cultures, and experiences. Inclusivity in software design means recognizing and valuing the vast spectrum of human diversity and reflecting on how software is created. It's about creating environments where differences are not just acknowledged but celebrated. Inclusivity involves understanding the cultural, geographical, and social nuances of users and integrating these considerations into the design and functionality of software. It's about building applications that resonate with a global audience, ensuring everyone feels represented and valued regardless of background.

Choosing inclusive tools and frameworks is essential for internal DevEx. This includes selecting platforms that support multiple languages, considering different communication styles, and accommodating varying levels of technical expertise within the team. By making these thoughtful choices, you ensure your development process is as inclusive as the software you aim to create.

Accessibility and inclusivity are more than just design principles; they are foundational aspects of creating software that respects and embraces the diversity of its users. These concepts are crucial in shaping functional, efficient, empathetic, and welcoming applications. As we delve into this topic, we aim to shed light on the importance of these principles in enhancing the developer experience and creating a more inclusive and accessible digital world.

The Importance of Development

Integrating accessibility and inclusivity right from the initial stages of software development is not just a good practice; it's a moral imperative and, in many cases, a legal necessity. This approach to development is essential in creating products that are genuinely beneficial and accessible to a diverse user base. As we explore this topic, it becomes clear how important these principles are in the world of technology.

Legal frameworks in various regions have started to recognize the criticality of accessibility in digital products. For instance, in the United States, the Americans with Disabilities Act (ADA) mandates specific standards for digital accessibility. These standards are not just guidelines; they are legal requirements that ensure software products are accessible to individuals with disabilities. The ADA's provisions underline the importance of making digital spaces as accessible as physical ones, acknowledging the increasing role of technology in everyday life. Adhering to such legal standards is not only about compliance; it's about committing to ethical responsibility in software development.

This commitment extends internally as well. When selecting tools and platforms for your development teams, it's crucial to consider accessibility and inclusivity. Ensuring that internal tools are accessible to all employees, including those with disabilities, reflects the same ethical responsibility and legal adherence that applies to consumer-facing products. This also fosters a more inclusive and supportive workplace environment, enhancing productivity and job satisfaction.

Furthermore, embracing the principles of accessibility and inclusivity extends far beyond legal compliance; it significantly impacts a product's market reach and user base. When software is designed with accessibility and inclusivity in mind, it becomes usable and appealing to a much wider audience. This inclusivity in design opens up the product to segments of the population that might otherwise be excluded due to various impairments or cultural differences. As a result, the product becomes more marketable and widely used and demonstrates a company's commitment to social responsibility and equity.

For internal development environments, choosing tools and practices that support accessibility and inclusivity ensures that all team members, regardless of their physical or mental abilities or background, can contribute effectively. This approach aligns with legal and moral obligations and enhances the developer experience (DevEx) by ensuring every employee can engage fully with the tools and processes in place.

Integrating accessibility and inclusivity in software development is crucial for moral and legal reasons. These principles are instrumental in widening a product's appeal and ensuring compliance with legal standards like the ADA. As developers and creators in the digital world, we ensure that our products are accessible and inclusive, reflecting a commitment to diversity and equality. This approach benefits the broader market and creates a more inclusive and supportive work environment for developers, reinforcing the importance of thoughtful, inclusive decision-making in every development aspect.

Challenges and Strategies

When implementing accessibility in software development, developers often encounter various challenges. These hurdles frequently stem from a lack of awareness or a deep understanding of users' diverse needs, especially those with various disabilities. Overcoming these challenges is crucial to creating inclusive and accessible digital products. This part of the chapter delves into these challenges and explores strategies to address them effectively.

One of the critical steps in overcoming the barriers to accessibility is education. Developers need to be aware of the different types of impairments that users may have, ranging from visual and auditory to cognitive and motor disabilities. Understanding these diverse needs is the first step toward building more accessible software. This education isn't just about knowing the types of disabilities; it's about developing empathy and a deeper appreciation for these users' challenges. Empathy plays a critical role in guiding developers to design and build software that is not only functional but also genuinely accessible and user-friendly.

Adopting certain best practices is another strategy to enhance accessibility. One of the most comprehensive resources is the Web Content Accessibility Guidelines (WCAG). Following these guidelines can help developers create digital content accessible to a wide range of people, including those with disabilities. WCAG provides a set of recommendations that are recognized internationally and cover a wide range of recommendations for making web content more accessible.

Additionally, various tools and technologies should be considered during the development process. These include screen readers, voice recognition software, and alternative input devices, which are essential for many users with disabilities. Integrating support for these tools into software products can significantly improve accessibility. It's about creating software that is not just usable for a majority but adaptable and accommodating for all users, regardless of their physical or cognitive abilities.

Addressing the challenges of implementing accessibility in software development requires education, empathy, and adopting best practices like Web Content Accessibility Guidelines (WCAG). Developers must consider various tools and technologies that enhance accessibility, ensuring their products are genuinely inclusive. This approach fulfills social responsibility and enriches the user experience, making technology more accessible and beneficial for everyone. As developers, embracing these strategies is critical to creating a digital world that is inclusive, equitable, and accessible to all.

Incorporating User Feedback

Incorporating user feedback is a pivotal step in developing software that is truly accessible and inclusive. This process goes beyond conventional testing and involves actively seeking input from a diverse range of users, especially those who have disabilities or come from varied cultural and social backgrounds. Understanding and valuing the perspectives of these users is key to creating genuinely inclusive software.

Gathering this feedback can be achieved through various means, but one of the most effective is conducting user testing sessions. These sessions are designed to include people with multiple disabilities and from different backgrounds. By engaging directly with these users, developers can gain insights into their challenges and needs when interacting with digital products. This direct feedback is invaluable in identifying areas where the software may fall short regarding accessibility and inclusivity. It provides a real-world perspective that can sometimes be overlooked in standard development processes.

Microsoft's Inclusive Design Toolkit serves as an exemplary resource in this regard. This toolkit offers developers guidance on understanding and implementing inclusivity in their projects. It's not just a set of guidelines; it's a comprehensive approach that encourages developers to think deeply about the diverse experiences of users. The toolkit helps frame inclusivity not as a challenge to overcome but as an opportunity to enhance and enrich the software development process. By utilizing such resources, developers can broaden their understanding of inclusivity and learn practical ways to integrate these principles into their work.

Incorporating user feedback, especially from people with disabilities and diverse backgrounds, is crucial in developing accessible and inclusive software. Tools and resources like Microsoft's Inclusive Design Toolkit provide valuable guidance. As developers, embracing this approach is not just about fulfilling a requirement; it's about committing to create software that is truly for everyone. This commitment to inclusivity enriches the user experience and contributes to building a more equitable and diverse digital world.

Ethical Considerations

The journey toward creating accessible and inclusive software goes beyond mere compliance with standards and regulations; it encompasses a profound ethical dimension. This moral aspect involves recognizing and respecting the fundamental right of all individuals to participate fully in the digital world. As we delve into this topic, we explore the profound implications of these considerations on software development.

At its core, the ethical commitment to accessibility and inclusivity in software development ensures that no one is left behind in our increasingly digital society. It's about acknowledging that neglecting these aspects can lead to digital exclusion, significantly impacting individuals' social and economic opportunities. In a world where digital access is often a prerequisite for many aspects of daily life, from education to employment, digital exclusion can have far-reaching consequences. It can exacerbate existing inequalities and hinder individuals from fully participating in society.

Therefore, the ethical responsibility lies in developing functional software for the majority but accessible and inclusive for all. This approach involves understanding the diverse needs of users, including those with disabilities and those from varied cultural and socioeconomic backgrounds. It's about creating digital products and services that are technically sound, empathetic, and considerate of the full spectrum of human diversity.

Embracing the ethical dimensions of accessibility and inclusivity in software development is crucial. It's a commitment to building a digital world that is equitable and accessible to everyone. This commitment goes beyond adhering to legal standards; it's about fostering a digital environment that supports diversity, promotes inclusion, and ensures that everyone, regardless of their abilities or background, has equal access to digital resources and opportunities. As developers and creators in the digital realm, upholding these ethical considerations is imperative, contributing to a more inclusive and equitable digital future for all.

Case Studies

The field of software development has witnessed significant advancements in making technology more accessible and inclusive, as seen through case studies like voice-assisted technologies. Amazon's Alexa and Apple's Siri are prime examples of how technology has evolved to aid a broader range of users, including those with visual impairments.

Voice-assisted technologies have revolutionized how users interact with digital devices, breaking down barriers for those who may have found traditional interfaces challenging. For users with visual impairments, these technologies provide an alternative way to access information and control devices, relying on voice commands instead of visual cues. This advancement represents a significant step toward inclusivity, allowing users who might have been excluded from the digital realm to engage with technology more fully.

Furthermore, the evolution of these technologies reflects a growing understanding and appreciation for diversity. Modern voice-assisted technologies have been developed to understand and respond to various accents and speech patterns. This improvement is a technical achievement and a commitment to inclusivity, ensuring these technologies are accessible to users from diverse linguistic and cultural backgrounds. The ability of voice-assisted technologies like Alexa and Siri to comprehend and interact with various speech patterns demonstrates a recognition of technology users' global and multicultural nature.

Case studies such as Amazon's Alexa and Apple's Siri illustrate the ongoing efforts in software development to enhance accessibility and inclusivity. These technologies are not just tools for convenience; they are manifestations of a broader move toward creating digital experiences that are accessible and welcoming to all users, regardless of their abilities or backgrounds. As technology continues to advance, these examples serve as benchmarks for what is possible in creating a more inclusive digital world.

Future Outlook

As we look toward the future, the technology landscape is rapidly evolving, bringing a heightened importance of accessibility and inclusivity. These principles are desirable attributes and essential components of an ethical Developer Experience (DevEx). As new technologies such as artificial intelligence (AI) and virtual/augmented reality (VR/AR) continue to emerge and integrate into our daily lives, they bring opportunities and challenges to ensure they are accessible and inclusive to all users.

Integrating AI in various applications offers tremendous potential for enhancing user experiences. However, it also poses unique challenges in ensuring that these AI-driven technologies are designed to be accessible to people with different abilities and backgrounds. Similarly, VR and AR technologies create immersive experiences that were once impossible. Yet, ensuring these experiences are accessible to users with various physical and sensory capabilities remains a critical challenge. These emerging technologies must be developed with a keen awareness of inclusivity, ensuring they cater to a diverse user base and not inadvertently exclude certain groups.

Accessibility and inclusivity are not just about meeting legal requirements; they are about building ethically sound and socially responsible technology products. By embracing these principles, technology products can reach a wider audience, thus becoming more successful and impactful in the market. This approach is not merely a business strategy; it's a commitment to creating technology that genuinely serves everyone. It's about acknowledging the diversity of users and striving to create digital experiences that are not just functional but also welcoming and respectful of this diversity.

As we explore the future outlook of technology development in this subsection, the emphasis on accessibility and inclusivity stands out as a crucial consideration. These principles are fundamental in shaping technology products that are legally compliant and ethically sound. They ensure that the digital world we are building is inclusive, equitable, and accessible, reflecting a technology landscape for everyone. As developers and creators in this dynamic field, embracing accessibility and inclusivity is paramount in creating delightful and efficient developer environments.

Environmental Impact and Energy Efficiency

There is a profound exploration into the increasingly critical role of environmental impact and energy efficiency in the developer experience (DevEx). As the world becomes more conscious of ecological concerns, software development is not immune to these challenges and responsibilities. This book section delves deeply into the significance of environmental considerations in modern software development. It examines how these vital aspects can seamlessly integrate into the DevEx framework.

The discussion about environmental impact and energy efficiency in software development is timely and essential. In an era of omnipresent technology, how software is designed, developed, and deployed significantly affects our environmental footprint. This section emphasizes the importance of these considerations, moving them from the periphery to the center of the development process. It's about acknowledging that the choices developers make, from their coding practices to the infrastructure they use, have real-world consequences on energy consumption and environmental sustainability.

Moreover, this section explores practical ways to effectively integrate environmental impact and energy efficiency into the DevEx framework. It's not just about understanding the importance of these issues but also about implementing tangible strategies and practices that can make software development more environmentally friendly. The focus is on equipping developers with the knowledge and tools to make more informed decisions that align with environmental sustainability.

The discussion on environmental impact and energy efficiency is crucial, reflecting the growing awareness and responsibility within the tech community toward ecological issues. It highlights the importance of these considerations in shaping the developer experience and the broader impact of technology on our planet. This exploration invites developers and tech professionals to rethink and reframe their approach to software development, intending to create efficient, effective, environmentally conscious, and sustainable technology.

The Growing Importance of Environmental Sustainability

In recent years, the technology industry has faced growing scrutiny over its environmental footprint, bringing to light the crucial issue of environmental sustainability. This concern has become incredibly prominent when considering the high energy consumption and carbon emissions associated with data centers, a fundamental component of the digital infrastructure. As a result, there is a burgeoning movement within the field of software development to adopt more sustainable practices.

The pursuit of environmental sustainability in software development is not just about reducing the direct energy consumption of software and hardware. It involves a holistic view of the development lifecycle, considering the broader environmental impacts at every stage, from design to deployment. This approach requires developers to think critically about the resources their software consumes and the waste it generates. It's about making conscious choices that minimize environmental harm, such as optimizing code for efficiency or choosing greener hosting options.

This growing emphasis on environmental sustainability reflects a broader shift in the tech industry toward responsibility and mindfulness about its role in global ecological issues. It's a recognition that the decisions made in software development have far-reaching consequences beyond the digital realm. Developers and tech professionals are increasingly responsible for creating innovative and efficient solutions and ensuring that these solutions are environmentally conscious. This commitment to sustainability is becoming an integral part of ethical software development, shaping how technology companies are viewed by consumers and contributing to a more sustainable future.

The growing importance of environmental sustainability in software development responds to the urgent need to mitigate the tech industry's ecological impact. It represents a shift toward more responsible and sustainable practices, where the environmental implications of software and hardware are considered and addressed throughout the development lifecycle. This approach is essential for creating compelling, innovative, environmentally conscious, sustainable technology.

Energy-Efficient Software Design

Energy efficiency has become a primary objective in software design, reflecting a significant shift in developers and the tech industry's priorities. Optimizing code for energy efficiency is now critical in applications and services, particularly those running continuously, like cloud-based and mobile apps.

The need for energy-efficient software design stems from a growing recognition of technology's environmental impacts. With digital services becoming increasingly ubiquitous, their cumulative energy consumption can be substantial. Thus, developers are responsible for ensuring their code is functionally efficient and energy-efficient. This involves a nuanced understanding of how different software design decisions affect energy consumption.

For instance, the choice of algorithms and data structures plays a significant role in determining the computational resources required by an application. Efficient algorithms and data structures can minimize the processing power needed, reducing the application's energy consumption. This consideration is especially crucial in the context of applications in constant use, as even minor inefficiencies can add up to significant energy usage over time.

Energy-efficient software design is no longer an afterthought but a fundamental aspect of modern software development. Developers must consider the energy implications of their design choices, striving to create software that minimizes environmental impact. This approach to development contributes to the sustainability of the tech industry and aligns with the broader global effort to reduce energy consumption and combat climate change. As we continue exploring software development, the emphasis on energy efficiency underscores developers' responsibility to create innovative and environmentally conscious technology.

Sustainable Development Practices

Sustainable development practices within the technology sector are evolving to encompass a holistic approach beyond coding. This broader perspective includes critical considerations about the materials and processes used in hardware manufacturing. Let's explore how leading companies like Apple and Google are setting examples in this domain.

These companies have significantly reduced their carbon footprint, aligning with the growing global emphasis on environmental responsibility. By investing in renewable energy sources and enhancing their recycling practices, they are demonstrating a commitment to reducing the environmental impact of their operations. Such initiatives are not merely corporate social responsibility endeavors; they represent a more profound recognition of the need to integrate sustainable practices into every aspect of technology production.

In software development, sustainability also extends to choices made regarding hosting services and data centers. Opting for more energy-efficient hosting services or data centers powered by renewable energy can significantly reduce the environmental impact of digital operations. These choices reflect an understanding that sustainability in technology is not just about the end product but also about the infrastructure that supports it. The choice of energy-efficient and environmentally friendly infrastructure is a crucial aspect of sustainable development practices in software.

Sustainable development practices in the tech industry are expanding to cover software, hardware, and infrastructure. Companies like Apple and Google are leading the way in this effort, demonstrating that investments in renewable energy and improved recycling practices can significantly reduce the environmental impact of technology. This chapter subsection delves into the importance of such sustainable practices, emphasizing that they are essential not only for the health of our planet but also for the long-term sustainability of the tech industry itself. As we look to the future, these practices are increasingly becoming benchmarks for the industry, influencing how companies approach the development and deployment of technology.

Balancing Performance with Sustainability

Performance versus sustainability presents a critical challenge in software development, especially today when efficiency and environmental responsibility are paramount. This issue is particularly pronounced in high-performance computing and real-time data processing applications, which are essential in artificial intelligence (AI) and big data analytics. These applications are typically energy-intensive, posing a significant dilemma for developers striving to achieve top-tier performance and sustainability.

High-performance computing and real-time data processing are the backbones of many advanced technologies. They enable complex calculations, large-scale data analyses, and real-time decision-making, which are crucial in areas like AI, where speed and accuracy are critical. However, the energy consumption associated with these processes can be substantial. This high energy demand conflicts with the growing need for sustainable practices in technology development.

With this challenge, developers must innovate and reconcile these seemingly conflicting goals. One approach is to optimize the efficiency of algorithms, ensuring they perform their tasks using the least computational resources necessary. Another strategy involves offloading specific tasks to less energy-intensive processes. This might mean delegating some tasks to cloud services or employing more energy-efficient hardware where feasible.

Balancing performance with sustainability requires a thoughtful approach to software design and development. It involves a deep understanding of the intricacies of both high-performance computing and sustainable practices. Developers must constantly seek innovative solutions, optimizing software performance while minimizing environmental impact. As this chapter unfolds, it becomes clear that this balance is not just a technical challenge but also an ethical imperative, underscoring the responsibility of developers in shaping a sustainable future for technology.

Case Studies and Examples

The quest for environmental sustainability in technology has led to several noteworthy case studies and examples showcasing how innovation and commitment can lead to remarkable outcomes. These examples illustrate the potential for significant energy savings and environmental benefits and serve as benchmarks for the tech industry.

A prime instance of this innovation is seen in Google's DeepMind project. By leveraging machine learning, DeepMind significantly reduced the energy used to cool their data centers by 40%. This achievement is a testament to the power of AI and machine learning in optimizing energy use in large-scale operations. Data centers, known for their high energy consumption, are crucial infrastructures in the digital world. DeepMind's success in reducing energy use demonstrates how intelligent technology can be employed to make substantial improvements in energy efficiency. This case study is not just about reducing energy consumption; it's an example of how cutting-edge technology can be harnessed to address critical environmental challenges.

Another significant example of pursuing sustainable technology practices is the Green Software Foundation. This initiative represents a collaborative effort to build a trusted ecosystem of people, standards, tooling, and best practices dedicated to green software. The foundation's mission is to foster a community where developers and organizations can unite to share knowledge and resources, all aimed at creating more environmentally friendly software. By establishing standards and best practices for green software, the foundation is paving the way for a more sustainable approach to software development. This initiative highlights the importance of community and collaboration in achieving environmental goals in the tech industry.

These case studies—Google's DeepMind and the Green Software Foundation—are more than just examples of successful projects; they inspire the entire tech industry. They demonstrate that it is possible to make significant strides toward more sustainable technology practices with innovation, dedication, and collaboration. As these examples show, the path to environmental sustainability in technology is not just feasible but also imperative, marking a crucial step in ensuring that the tech industry contributes positively to the global ecological landscape.

Future Directions

The trend toward environmentally sustainable development within the technology sector is expected to gain significant momentum in the coming years. This movement is not just a fleeting trend but a fundamental shift in how software development is approached. This chapter subsection delves into the future directions of this essential shift, encompassing a range of practices from green coding to energy-efficient hardware.

Green coding practices, which focus on writing software that is efficient in terms of computational resources, are becoming increasingly widespread. These practices are not just about optimizing code for performance but also about minimizing energy consumption. This approach is critical in a world where digital solutions are ubiquitous, and their environmental footprint cannot be ignored. Similarly, the adoption of energy-efficient hardware is becoming more prominent. This includes hardware designed to perform tasks with minimal energy use, contributing to reducing technology's carbon footprint.

Artificial Intelligence (AI) and machine learning also play pivotal roles in optimizing energy use. These technologies are harnessed to create systems that intelligently manage and reduce energy consumption in data centers and broader applications. This use of AI and machine learning exemplifies how cutting-edge technology can be a powerful ally in achieving environmental sustainability.

Furthermore, legislative and policy changes, such as carbon pricing, are expected to further incentivize sustainable software development. These changes could make it more economically viable for companies to invest in green technologies and practices, aligning financial incentives with environmental goals.

The importance of environmental impact and energy efficiency in software development is increasingly recognized as an integral component of the developer experience (DevEx). Addressing these environmental concerns is essential for the planet's sustainability and crucial to tech companies' economic viability and social responsibility. This chapter subsection underscores the need for a paradigm shift in the approach to software development, focusing more on environmental stewardship. It highlights the growing recognition that sustainable development practices are vital for the health of our environment and the long-term success and credibility of technology companies and the industry.

Key Takeaways

- Emerging trends and technologies, including low-code/no-code platforms, AI, VR/AR, and Blockchain, are redefining the role of developers in the tech industry.

- Integrating these technologies with a solid ethical foundation, focusing on privacy, data security, accessibility, inclusivity, and environmental sustainability, is crucial for a responsible and future-proof DevEx.

- A proactive and holistic approach to DevEx is needed, blending technological innovation with ethical and sustainable practices.

- The future of DevEx lies in creating environments where technology and humanity converge harmoniously and productively.

- Continuous learning and adaptation are required for navigating the evolving technological landscape and ethical imperatives.

- Embracing a dynamic and multifaceted approach to DevEx is critical for developers, team leaders, and organizations to contribute to responsible, inclusive, and sustainable technology development.

CHAPTER 12

Interviews and Expert Insights

This chapter provides a mosaic of conversations, narratives, and reflections from thought leaders who have significantly contributed to the evolving landscape of Developer Experience (DevEx). Each section is dedicated to an expert who shares their journey, challenges, insights, and visions for the future of DevEx. Their stories are personal and professional growth accounts and serve as beacons guiding the broader tech community toward creating more intuitive, inclusive, and engaging developer environments.

From the strategic to the empathetic, from an organization's internal workings to its external engagement with its products, this chapter offers a panoramic view of DevEx. It invites readers to explore, reflect, and, ultimately, contribute to the ongoing dialogue on how best to support and empower the developer community.

Taylor Barnett-Torabi

In the evolving technology landscape, the spotlight often shines on the intricacies of developer experience (DevEx), a vast and critical domain to the advancement of software development. In an enlightening discussion

© K. Rain Leander 2025
K. R. Leander, *Developer Experience Unleashed,*
https://doi.org/10.1007/979-8-8688-0242-3_12

with Rain Leander, Taylor Barnett-Torabi delves deep into the multifaceted world of DevEx, sharing insights from a career dedicated to bridging the gap between developers and the tools that empower them.

For Barnett-Torabi, developer experience encompasses the entirety of a developer's interaction with a tool or service, from the initial encounter to the nuanced processes of integration and utilization. This broad perspective includes the technical aspects, such as documentation and API usability, and the human elements—how sales emails, support interactions, and even billing can influence a developer's perception and use of a product. Barnett-Torabi's view is that a genuinely great DevEx extends beyond the code; it's about crafting a cohesive journey that respects the developer's time, intelligence, and needs.

A significant theme in Barnett-Torabi's narrative is the importance of feedback loops in enhancing DevEx. Drawing on experiences from launching key features at PlanetScale, Barnett-Torabi highlights how collecting, organizing, and acting on user feedback can lead to significant product improvements. Personally following up with users who had requested features showcases an exemplary commitment to closing the feedback loop, not just for product development but also to build trust and rapport within the developer community.

Barnett-Torabi stresses that effective developer advocacy involves more than just transmitting user feedback to the engineering teams; it requires a nuanced understanding of internal dynamics and the ability to influence decision-making processes. This interplay between advocating for users and navigating internal politics is pivotal in driving changes that resonate with the user base and improve the developer experience.

Barnett-Torabi reflects on the challenges and opportunities in creating a cohesive ecosystem of developer tools. The conversation touches on the necessity for tools to function in isolation and interoperate seamlessly, allowing developers to craft solutions that are greater than the sum of their parts. This vision for the future emphasizes the need for standards, like OpenAPI, that promote compatibility and ease of integration among disparate tools.

An underlying current in Barnett-Torabi's discussion is the value of interdisciplinary collaboration in enhancing DevEx. By engaging with various teams—from engineering and product management to marketing and support—developer advocates like Barnett-Torabi play a critical role in synthesizing diverse perspectives into a unified approach to improving DevEx. This collaborative spirit is essential for addressing complex challenges such as API design, security, and the balance between offering flexibility and maintaining a guided path for users.

Throughout the conversation, Barnett-Torabi shares personal anecdotes from their journey in tech, from the early days of participating in hackathons to the challenges of navigating product management and developer relations roles. These stories underscore the evolution of DevEx as a field and highlight Barnett-Torabi's contributions to shaping it. Through efforts like direct user engagement and the advocacy for feedback-driven development, Barnett-Torabi exemplifies the profound impact that thoughtful, user-centric approaches can have on the technology landscape.

Raymond Camden

Raymond Camden, a luminary in developer relations and web technologies, has dedicated his career to enhancing the Developer Experience (DevEx). His approach to DevEx is deeply rooted in empathy and a keen understanding of the developer's journey, from initial engagement to deep technology integration. Camden's perspective sheds light on the nuanced distinction between creating a functional feature and crafting an experience developers are eager to use. He illustrates this with a simple yet profound example: the transition from requiring measurements in meters to accommodating inputs in miles, reducing friction, and demonstrating attentiveness to user preferences.

Camden's journey in improving DevEx has been marked by proactive initiatives, particularly in documentation. Recognizing the gap in getting started guides, he took it upon himself to write quick-start guides for APIs, ensuring that developers could quickly embark on their first project. This effort, driven by his self-awareness and understanding of potential stumbling blocks in documentation, led to tangible successes. One notable achievement was a significant increase in sign-ups, a testament to the impact of thoughtful, accessible documentation on developer engagement.

Clear, concise documentation and a frictionless sign-up process are hallmarks of an exceptional DevEx for Camden. He reflects on the evolution of service access, noting a shift away from the once-commonplace requirement of a credit card for trial access. Today, APIs and services that allow immediate, barrier-free experimentation represent the gold standard in DevEx. Camden appreciates platforms that accommodate exploratory engagement, allowing developers to "kick the tires" without upfront commitment.

The landscape of developer relations and DevEx has undergone significant changes, with a move toward self-service and instant accessibility marking a departure from the days of manual setup and ISP-mediated website creation. Camden observes that today's tools and platforms, such as Postman and serverless technologies, facilitate a more streamlined experience, enabling him to focus on showcasing the value of APIs without needing to instruct on basic HTTP call mechanics.

From his rich experience across various roles and technologies, Camden underscores the importance of assuming a beginner's mindset. He advocates for documentation that avoids assumptions, prioritizes simplicity, and directly addresses the user's needs. The goal is to welcome developers into the product ecosystem as swiftly and smoothly as possible, fostering a community where feedback is encouraged and actively sought. Camden's experiences highlight the ongoing need for feedback mechanisms that empower users to report issues or suggest improvements quickly.

Camden's DevEx and developer relations insights underscore the field's continuous evolution. From the tangible impact of well-crafted documentation to the broader shifts toward self-service and instant accessibility, his contributions illuminate the path toward creating developer experiences that are not just functional but genuinely desirable. His approach, marked by empathy, simplicity, and a relentless pursuit of improvement, is a guiding light for those dedicated to enhancing the developer journey in an ever-changing technological landscape.

Chris DeMars

Chris DeMars, a seasoned advocate for accessibility in the developer experience (DevEx) realm, shares a compelling narrative that encapsulates the essence and challenges of ensuring seamless, fluid, and inclusive interactions across the digital ecosystem. His journey, underscored by a dedication to making technology accessible to all, offers a glimpse into the complexities and triumphs encountered.

DeMars defines DevEx as an experience that should be seamless, fluid, and accessible for developers, regardless of the medium—conversational, interactive, or digital. This inclusive perspective is not just a professional stance but reflects his deep commitment to accessibility, shaping his career and advocacy work.

One significant challenge DeMars faced was ensuring the continuous prioritization of essential, albeit less glamorous, aspects of DevEx, such as product feedback integration and documentation updates. His experience at Split, a feature management and experimentation platform, illustrates this challenge vividly. Through conversations with Kyle Welch, formerly of Eventbrite, DeMars learned about the difficulties Eventbrite faced in utilizing Split's features to their fullest potential. This feedback highlighted a gap in the user interface's intuitiveness, specifically regarding the functionality to "kill a split" or end an experiment.

Armed with this insight, DeMars approached his product and design teams at Split, advocating for improvements based on honest user feedback. His team's proactive response, already working on enhancements to address similar feedback, showcased the importance of open communication channels between developers, advocates, and product teams. This collaboration ensured a more intuitive and seamless experience for Split's users, reinforcing the value of feedback loops in shaping product development.

For DeMars, accessibility stands paramount in the hierarchy of DevEx priorities. His assertion that "accessibility is your ROI" underscores the fundamental idea that products inaccessible to any segment of users risk alienating potential adopters, driving them toward more inclusive alternatives. DeMars's advocacy for accessibility extends beyond compliance or legal obligation; it is about empathy, inclusivity, and the recognition that every user deserves an equitable experience.

DeMars's contributions to making the RxJS documentation accessible, in collaboration with Jen Luker and others, highlight his hands-on approach to fostering accessibility in the developer community. This project, among others, illustrates his belief in the power of collaborative efforts to drive significant improvements in how technology is developed and consumed.

Looking to the future, DeMars sees artificial intelligence (AI) as a burgeoning area within DevEx, with the potential to innovate and overreach. His cautious optimism about AI's role in developer tools reflects a broader concern for balancing technological advancement and human-centric values. DeMars jests about a "Skynet" scenario as a metaphorical line in the sand, emphasizing the need for ethical considerations and human oversight in integrating AI within developer ecosystems.

Throughout his career, DeMars has learned the importance of speaking up for what matters, even when it ruffles feathers. His experiences underscore the necessity of advocating for accessibility, simplifying technical jargon, and ensuring products are designed with all users in mind. His journey is a testament to one individual's impact on making the tech world more inclusive, one project at a time.

Wesley Faulkner

In the realm of technology, where evolution is constant, and the drive toward enhancing user and developer experiences never ceases, Wesley Faulkner emerges as a figure of insightful innovation and dedicated advocacy for Developer Experience (DevEx). His narrative, as shared in a conversation with Rain Leander, offers a deep dive into the complexities and challenges of improving DevEx within the tech industry. This article seeks to unfold Faulkner's journey, his approach to DevEx, and the insightful perspectives he brings to the table.

Faulkner's definition of Developer Experience is both specific and holistic. He emphasizes the importance of tools and interfaces that developers interact with while using a product. This includes everything from command-line interfaces and error messages to documentation and its accessibility, including whether it features embedded code samples or offers copy-paste options for direct implementation. For Faulkner, the essence of DevEx lies in minimizing friction and ensuring that developers can comprehend the available resources and implement them seamlessly.

However, Faulkner's approach extends beyond the specifics of tool interaction. He advocates for a general principle of reducing developer frustration at every stage of their journey. This encompasses their initial encounter with a platform or site and continues through every aspect of their interaction with the product. The goal is clear: to lower barriers, streamline processes, and, ultimately, enrich the developer's interaction with the technology.

Despite his clear vision and deep understanding of what constitutes an excellent developer experience, Faulkner admits to encountering significant headwinds in implementing his ideas. Often, these challenges stem not from a lack of knowledge or capability but from structural and cultural obstacles within organizations. Faulkner notes that leadership within developer relations, and by extension DevEx, sometimes harbors different focuses from those dedicated to improving the developer journey.

This misalignment, where developers are seen more as a means to an end rather than the primary focus, hinders the adoption and prioritization of initiatives to enhance DevEx.

Faulkner's experiences reveal a standard narrative in the tech industry: the pursuit of rapid iteration and profitability frequently overshadows the maintenance and improvement of existing features—a critical component of DevEx. This perspective not only elucidates the structural barriers to improving developer experiences but also highlights the broader industry challenges of valuing and integrating developer feedback into the product development lifecycle.

Despite these challenges, Faulkner remains optimistic about the potential for change within individual organizations and across the industry. His strategy for navigating and effecting change involves a two-pronged approach: ensuring alignment between personal values and those of potential employers and advocating for a broader industry-wide shift in recognizing the value of DevEx.

Faulkner emphasizes the importance of vetting potential employers for their commitment to DevEx principles, suggesting that aligning with a company that shares a similar valuation of developer feedback and experience is crucial for those seeking to make an impact in this space. Additionally, he advocates for a collective effort among industry leaders to standardize and promote best practices in DevEx, suggesting the formation of compendiums or manifestos that could serve as benchmarks for excellence in developer relations and experience.

Wesley Faulkner's journey and insights shed light on the multifaceted nature of Developer Experience and the myriad challenges that advocates like him face in pushing for its improvement. Our conversation underscores the importance of strategic, empathetic approaches to DevEx, the need for structural and cultural shifts within organizations, and the potential for collective action to elevate the priority of developer experience within the tech industry.

As the dialogue around DevEx evolves, Faulkner's perspectives offer valuable lessons and inspiration for current and future advocates. His commitment to creating more intuitive, inclusive, and engaging environments for developers stands as a testament to the potential for positive change in the tech landscape, paving the way for a future where developer experience is not just an afterthought but a central pillar of product development and organizational culture.

Alexander Graebe

Alexander Graebe, a recognized thought leader in developer platforms, web technologies, and web3, has significantly contributed to the tech community. His journey reflects a deep commitment to empowering developers worldwide through open-source initiatives, global conferences, and significant publications. Known for his success in launching and scaling products used by tens of thousands of developers, startups, and BigTech partners, Graebe's expertise in full-stack engineering and leadership in tech teams highlights his multifaceted role in shaping the future of technology.

Improving Developer Experience (DevEx) poses unique challenges, especially in articulating the business outcomes of DevEx initiatives to executives. Graebe emphasizes the importance of deliberately defining success measures and tracking progress toward goals. He advocates for using clear communication to demonstrate the impact of DevEx efforts, underlining that DevEx is an ongoing process, like improving UX for consumers, that evolves with product updates and shifts in developer expectations.

One of Graebe's notable success stories in DevEx improvement comes from his time at Flow, where developer tests were conducted to identify friction points in the developer journey. By focusing resources on the learning stage, significant enhancements were made to the documentation system, information architecture, and onboarding features, leading to a marked improvement in developer satisfaction and the "time-to-wow" factor.

Graebe believes that outstanding DevEx is characterized by products that empower developers, streamline product flows, offer a compelling try-before-you-buy experience, and support different learning preferences. These elements combine to create a DevEx that meets and exceeds developer expectations.

Looking ahead, Graebe envisions the evolution of DevEx to include a distinction between internal and external DevEx, with increased adoption of DevEx practices across various teams within organizations. He predicts AI will significantly facilitate the end-to-end developer journey, while spatial programming and immersive experiences will offer new dimensions for DevEx.

Emerging technologies such as GraphQL and AI are expected to significantly impact DevEx, with a shift toward more flexible API interfaces and dynamic documentation efforts. Graebe also highlights the trend of developers maintaining services end-to-end, increasing the scope of their responsibilities.

Graebe's diverse background, spanning engineering, DevRel, and product roles across open-source and web3 ecosystems, has shaped his holistic approach to DevEx. His experiences have taught him the importance of multi-disciplinary efforts and a clear vision for DevEx across teams. By creating vision and roadmap documents for DevEx and forming DevEx pods for specific projects, Graebe has successfully orchestrated alignment across teams, ensuring a cohesive and impactful DevEx strategy.

Among the valuable lessons Graebe has learned is that developers value great branding and always search for tools that enhance their capabilities. He emphasizes the need for DevEx efforts to be driven by clear goals and metrics, which has guided his evolving approach to DevEx throughout his career.

In projects requiring a strong focus on DevEx, Graebe has championed interdisciplinary collaboration, working closely with marketing, design, engineering, and product teams to create holistic developer experiences. His strategy of internally sharing a "State of Developer Experience" report has been instrumental in bridging the gap between different disciplines and aligning stakeholders toward common DevEx goals.

In specialized domains like Web3, Graebe underscores the importance of engaging community contributors and leveraging external solutions to address developers' needs effectively. His work exemplifies a commitment to improving DevEx by fostering an open and collaborative ecosystem, demonstrating best practices that resonate across the tech industry.

Amara Graham

Amara Graham stands at the forefront of transforming Developer Experience (DevEx) within the tech industry, championing initiatives that significantly enhance how developers engage with products. Her journey, marked by dedication and strategic focus, offers valuable insights into elevating DevEx from a concept to a core organizational ethos. As we delve into Graham's experiences and perspectives, her story unfolds as a testament to the pivotal role of DevEx in shaping the future of product development and management.

One of the biggest challenges Graham faced in improving DevEx was the vast and influential nature of DevEx itself, which permeates all aspects of the product delivery experience. She found that the key to overcoming this challenge was to focus on specific areas of improvement, resisting the temptation to let external definitions of DevEx dictate her organization's approach. This strategic focus enabled her to prioritize initiatives with the most promise for meaningful impact.

Graham shares a notable success story highlighting the transformation within Camunda's products organization. Previously described as "developer friendly," the organization embarked on cross-functional initiatives to enhance the developer experience. This collaborative effort not only underscored the importance of DevEx within the company but also set a new standard for how product teams across the organization could work together to achieve a common goal.

When asked what differentiates an outstanding DevEx from a mediocre one, Graham emphasizes the importance of intuitive experiences tailored to developer personas. An exceptional DevEx, according to Graham, is one where developers feel, "This just works." She notes that the experience can sometimes become too curated for a specific programming language or, conversely, too generic, underscoring the need for a balanced approach that meets developers where they are.

In the future, Graham envisions DevEx evolving into its distinct organizational function, bridging the gap between Engineering and Product Management. She anticipates that DevEx will become synonymous with dogfooding, improving adoption and onboarding efficiencies, and fostering cohesive experiences that boost developers' sentiment and product engagement. This forward-thinking approach positions DevEx as a central pillar in the strategic planning and execution of product development efforts.

Emerging technologies, particularly Artificial Intelligence (AI), will significantly impact DevEx in the coming years. Graham predicts that AI will serve as a powerful tool for gap analysis, identifying shortcomings in products, documentation, and onboarding processes. Drawing a parallel with how SEO improved content findability on the Internet, she expects AI to play a similar role in addressing product gaps and enhancing the developer experience.

Graham's unique background, having worked in large and small companies and roles spanning enterprise and community or Open Source Software (OSS), has profoundly influenced her approach to DevEx. Her experiences have led her to view the community in its broadest sense, acknowledging that developers at enterprise companies may also engage with community or free-tier options as part of their evaluation process. This inclusive perspective on community underscores the idea that DevEx should cater to everyone, not just unpaid or free-tier users.

Amara Graham's journey in improving DevEx underscores the importance of strategic focus, cross-functional collaboration, and a deep understanding of the developer community. Her vision for the future of DevEx, coupled with her insights into the role of emerging technologies, offers a blueprint for how organizations can elevate their developer experiences. As the tech industry continues to evolve, Graham's contributions to DevEx highlight the importance of placing developers' needs and experiences at the heart of product development and management strategies.

Caroline Lewko

Caroline Lewko, a seasoned veteran in developer relations and technology, delves into the intricate landscape of Developer Experience (DevEx), shedding light on the evolving nuances between internal and external DevEx. Her insights offer a compelling glimpse into the challenges and opportunities of defining and improving DevEx in today's tech-driven world.

Lewko articulates a nuanced understanding of DevEx, distinguishing between the needs and approaches of internal and external developer experiences. She suggests that while internal DevEx focuses on enhancing productivity and efficiency within an organization, external DevEx centers on creating a seamless and engaging experience for external developers interacting with a company's products or services. This distinction underscores the diverse facets of DevEx and the importance of tailoring strategies to meet different objectives.

One of the significant challenges Lewko highlights is the common oversight in documentation—a critical component of DevEx. She recounts instances where companies have underestimated the value of clear, accessible, and contextual documentation, opting instead for homegrown solutions or minimizing the importance of context and audience understanding. Lewko emphasizes that successful DevEx requires tools and practices that facilitate easy updates, collaboration, and deep knowledge of the developer's journey, urging companies to leverage existing tools to enhance documentation and developer engagement.

Lewko's approach to improving DevEx is deeply rooted in empathy and a commitment to understanding the developer's perspective. She advocates for comprehensive audits of the developer experience, employing friction tests to identify and address points of frustration or confusion. These audits serve as eye-openers for product teams, revealing the gap between a product's intended use and the actual developer experience. By showcasing real developer frustrations, Lewko and her team can make a compelling case for the necessity of continuous improvement in DevEx.

Furthermore, Lewko discusses the evolution of DevEx and its growing recognition as a critical factor in technology adoption and satisfaction. She observes a shift toward acknowledging the interconnectedness of documentation, product design, and developer tools, stressing that outstanding DevEx is not just about excellent documentation but also about creating an ecosystem that supports the developer at every step. This holistic view of DevEx is gaining traction, with more organizations recognizing the value of regular audits, diverse content formats, and cross-functional collaboration to cater to various developer needs and preferences.

Looking toward the future, Lewko envisions a landscape where the lines between internal and external DevEx may blur, advocating for a unified approach that values consistency, reliability, and supportability across all developer interactions. She calls for a shared vocabulary and strategies encompassing internal productivity and external engagement, suggesting that the distinctions between the two may become less pronounced as companies strive to create comprehensive, inclusive developer experiences.

Caroline Lewko's reflections on DevEx offer invaluable insights into the complexities and potentials of crafting experiences that genuinely resonate with developers. Her emphasis on empathy, context, and continuous improvement serves as a guiding principle for companies looking to elevate their DevEx, highlighting the importance of putting the developer at the heart of technological innovation and community building.

Rebecca Marshburn

Rebecca Marshburn, Head of Community at Common Room, offers an insightful perspective on the multifaceted concept of developer experience (DevEx), which resonates deeply within the tech industry. Marshburn brings a fresh, empathetic viewpoint to understanding and supporting developers' professional and personal journeys. Her approach to defining DevEx highlights the emotional and logical aspects that contribute to what she sees as the essence of a genuine experience in development.

Marshburn eloquently describes DevEx as the journey of solving puzzles, facing challenges, and creating solutions within the software development process. She paints a vivid picture of a developer navigating through various resources—from Stack Overflow inquiries to GitHub discussions—searching for answers and solutions. This journey, characterized by its highs and lows, underscores the day-to-day realities and the emotional rollercoaster developers undergo in their quest to build and innovate.

A critical aspect of Marshburn's discussion on DevEx revolves around involving developers early in the project cycle, even before the MVP (Minimum Viable Product) stage. She argues that this early involvement benefits the development process by preventing potential setbacks and ensures more humane and realistic project timelines. Marshburn highlights the disconnect that can occur when developers are not included in early project discussions, using an anecdote to illustrate how such exclusion can lead to misaligned expectations and increased pressure on development teams.

Marshburn further explores the impact of DevEx from both internal and external perspectives. Internally, she emphasizes the value of a development process that considers the well-being of developers, advocating for a balance between rapid delivery and maintaining a sustainable work environment. Externally, she discusses the importance of providing users with access to accurate documentation and responsive support systems. Marshburn states these elements are crucial in fostering a positive developer experience, even when faced with inevitable challenges like bugs or missing features.

In discussing what sets an outstanding developer experience apart, Marshburn distinguishes between the internal experience of developers working on a project and the external experience of users interacting with the final product. She underscores the importance of strategic involvement, where developers have a say in the project's direction and strategy, ensuring their insights and expertise inform the development process. Marshburn points to reliable knowledge, up-to-date documentation, and a responsive, transparent support system as critical factors in achieving an exceptional DevEx.

Marshburn presents a compelling case for a more empathetic and inclusive approach to software development through her discussion. By prioritizing the human elements of the development process, she advocates for practices that not only enhance the efficiency and quality of the end product but also contribute to a more positive and fulfilling experience for developers and users alike. Marshburn's insights into DevEx offer valuable guidance for fostering environments where innovation can thrive, balanced with a deep respect for the human aspect of technology creation.

Jeremy Meiss and Jessica West

The concept of Developer Experience (DevEx) has become a central focus for companies striving to foster environments where creativity and productivity thrive. Jeremy Meiss and Jessica West, two professionals deeply entrenched in the nuances of DevEx, offer a wealth of insights that illuminate the complexities and transformative potential of optimizing the developer journey.

DevEx, as Jeremy and Jessica define it, transcends mere interaction with a product or platform. It encompasses the entire spectrum of a developer's engagement, from the initial awareness and onboarding to the ongoing use and community involvement. Jessica views DevEx through a multifaceted lens, emphasizing the importance of first impressions, ease of navigation, and the pivotal "aha" moments that affirm a developer's decision to engage with technology. For Jeremy, DevEx is about removing every barrier that hinders a developer's productivity, ensuring that tools and services meet and exceed the expectations of those who rely on them daily.

One intriguing aspect of their conversation is the recognition of both external and internal facets of DevEx. While external experiences focus on how developers interact with a company's products from the outside, internal experiences delve into the efficiencies and obstacles developers encounter within an organization. This duality highlights the breadth of DevEx, suggesting that a holistic approach that addresses both internal mechanisms and external perceptions is essential for fostering an environment conducive to innovation and success.

The dialogue between Jeremy and Jessica sheds light on the dynamic nature of DevEx, acknowledging its evolution alongside industry advancements and individual career growth. Initially, developer experience might have been narrowly defined by the ease of debugging or the clarity of response codes. However, as the industry matured and the tools at developers' disposal expanded, so did the definition of DevEx.

It now includes considerations of community support, documentation quality, and the inclusivity of feedback mechanisms—elements that create a supportive ecosystem for developers.

A significant part of optimizing DevEx lies in the cultural and emotional aspects of a company's ethos. The willingness to listen to feedback, the openness to change, and the ability to make informed decisions based on a comprehensive understanding of developers' needs are critical components of a positive DevEx. Jessica and Jeremy emphasize the importance of a culture that values feedback and prioritizes the continuous improvement of tools and processes. With a foundational commitment to these principles, any attempt to enhance DevEx will likely stay within its potential.

Through their experiences, both Jeremy and Jessica have encountered challenges and successes that underscore the complexity of improving DevEx. From advocating for more inclusive and functional free plans to navigating the intricacies of internationalization and localization, their stories reveal the perseverance and strategic thinking required to effect meaningful change. These narratives highlight the tangible benefits of a well-considered DevEx strategy and remind us that progress often requires time, patience, and a deep-seated respect for the developer community.

The conversation between Jeremy Meiss and Jessica West offers a compelling exploration of Developer Experience from two seasoned professionals' perspectives. Their insights reveal that DevEx is not a static concept but a dynamic and evolving aspect of technology that demands a nuanced understanding of developers' needs, aspirations, and challenges. As the industry continues to develop, so will the approaches and strategies for enhancing DevEx, which are driven by a shared commitment to creating environments where developers can thrive.

Lorna Mitchell

With her extensive developer experience and documentation background, Lorna Mitchell brings a unique perspective to the challenges and triumphs of improving developer workflows. Her journey reflects a deep commitment to enhancing the tools and processes that developers rely on, underpinned by a philosophy emphasizing practicality, persistence, and empathy.

One of Mitchell's primary hurdles was ensuring the continuation of essential, albeit less glamorous, tasks amidst the whirlwind of new ideas and projects. In developer experience and relations alike, the key to success often lies in meticulously refining and maintaining existing tools and strategies rather than constantly pursuing novel initiatives. This approach requires a steadfast focus on the foundational elements of developer support, like documentation and tooling, which are crucial for a seamless developer journey.

Mitchell shares a particularly telling experience with a documentation migration project. Despite the allure of expanding the documentation with new sections, video lessons, or certification programs, Mitchell recognized the importance of completing the ongoing migration. Her resolution to prioritize this foundational work, despite its lack of immediate glamour, underscores the significance of foundational maintenance in developer experience. Her ability to drive this project forward, backed by top-level organizational support, highlights the critical role of internal advocacy and clear, confident leadership in achieving project goals.

Documentation, as Mitchell emphasizes, is transformative. It is the backbone of developer support, enabling users from various backgrounds to utilize products effectively. By improving the accessibility, reliability, and comprehensiveness of documentation, Mitchell enhanced the immediate user experience and fostered a culture of contribution and collaboration within the organization. This culture extended the impact of her work far beyond the scope of the initial project, creating a lasting legacy of improved developer support and engagement.

At the heart of Mitchell's philosophy is the concept of boundaries. Understanding a tool or platform's limits and intended use cases is crucial for delivering an outstanding developer experience. This clarity allows for the creation of technically robust solutions that are intuitively aligned with the developers' needs. Mitchell's focus on clearly defined problems and solutions, devoid of unnecessary complexities, is a testament to her pragmatic approach to developer experience.

Looking forward, Mitchell envisions a future where the principles of DevEx follow a trajectory similar to DevOps, characterized by a growing consensus on best practices, frameworks, and shared language. This evolution will enable a more cohesive and practical approach to enhancing the developer experience, rooted in a collective understanding of what works and why.

Mitchell's passion for documentation and developer experience is driven by her recognition of their potential as multipliers. By empowering developers with the tools and knowledge they need, she contributes to a broader ecosystem of innovation and creativity. Her commitment to writing, sharing, and improving documentation is not just about solving problems once but about enabling others to build solutions she could never achieve alone. This multiplier effect, where each contribution amplifies the capabilities of countless others, lies at the heart of Mitchell's enthusiasm for her work.

In a world where the minutiae of developer support can often be overlooked, Lorna Mitchell stands as a beacon of what can be achieved through dedication, empathy, and a steadfast focus on the essentials. Her journey offers valuable lessons for anyone looking to make a meaningful impact on the developer experience, highlighting the transformative power of well-crafted documentation and the importance of nurturing a culture of collaboration and continuous improvement.

Dani Sarfati

Dani Sarfati, a seasoned professional with a rich IT, infrastructure, and DevOps background, shares his journey and insights into Developer Experience (DevEx). His narrative provides a fascinating glimpse into the challenges and successes encountered while striving to enhance DevEx within various organizational contexts.

Sarfati's definition of DevEx focuses on the development cycle's efficiency—specifically, the coding phase and the surrounding tooling—leading to deploying code into a development environment. He emphasizes the distinction between this cycle and the on-call responsibilities that some developers face, suggesting that DevEx, in his view, centers more on the pre-production aspects of development.

One of Sarfati's most notable experiences came from his first role on a development team as a Site Reliability Engineer (SRE). He encountered the significant challenge of transitioning a Java-based project to Docker to streamline environment setup times. This initiative aimed to reduce the hour-long setup times for development environments, which is a considerable bottleneck in the development process. Despite the potential benefits, Sarfati observed resistance due to the business's focus on delivering customer-facing features, highlighting a familiar tension between improving internal developer workflows and meeting external product development deadlines.

Sarfati recounts a specific instance where a team member pursued the Docker transition, hoping to improve DevEx. However, after several months of effort and facing the reality of the project's constraints, the individual left the organization searching for opportunities that aligned more closely with their aspirations. This story reflects the often challenging nature of implementing significant changes within established development environments and how such efforts can impact team morale and individual career paths.

Despite these challenges, Sarfati shares a success story from a different role, where he significantly reduced the deployment time from half a day to approximately 20 minutes. By leveraging his unique position—having transferred from an infrastructure team to a development team—he was able to bridge the gap between the two domains and facilitate a more efficient deployment process. This achievement improved the internal DevEx and demonstrated the value of cross-functional collaboration and understanding.

Sarfati's experiences underline several critical themes in DevEx: the importance of tooling and automation in facilitating efficient development workflows, the challenges of balancing internal improvements with external deliverables, and the potential for significant impact through cross-functional collaboration. His journey highlights the complex landscape of DevEx, where successes are celebrated amid ongoing challenges, and the pursuit of better developer experiences continues to evolve.

Erin Staples

Erin Staples shares a captivating narrative that underscores the essence of Developer Experience (DevEx) with a blend of personal anecdotes, professional insights, and a spirited outlook toward fostering environments where developers can thrive. Throughout her journey, Staples delineates the nuances of DevEx through the lens of her varied experiences, painting a picture of what it means to navigate, contribute to, and reshape the tech landscape.

Staples begins by reflecting on her appreciation for direct communication, a trait she admires and found abundant during her decade in the Netherlands. This preference for straightforwardness extends into her professional interactions, where she champions transparency and eschews political maneuvering. Her narrative reveals a commitment to being genuine, even in the face of challenges, such as when her forthrightness on social media led to discussions about the "spiciness" of her tweets. Staples' experiences underscore the importance of maintaining one's voice and authenticity, especially when it intersects with professional advocacy and the role of a developer advocate.

Staples' journey is marked by moments of tension between her strong personality and the corporate dynamics that sometimes favor conformity over individuality. She recounts instances where her directness and strength were at odds with corporate expectations, highlighting a broader issue many face in the tech industry: the delicate balance between fitting into a predefined mold and pushing the boundaries to foster innovation and change. Her encounters serve as poignant reminders of the challenges of navigating corporate environments, particularly for those who, like Staples, are willing to maintain their vibrancy for politics.

At the heart of Staples' narrative is a deep-seated belief in the transformative power of developer experience. She advocates for a DevEx that accommodates and celebrates curiosity, experimentation, and the diverse ways people engage with technology. Staples discusses the importance of feedback mechanisms and the role of community contributions in shaping a more inclusive and responsive tech ecosystem. Her approach to DevEx is holistic, considering the technical aspects and the cultural and interpersonal dynamics that influence how technology is developed, deployed, and experienced.

Throughout her conversation, Staples does not shy away from discussing her obstacles, from the struggle to find her place in various tech domains to the ongoing battle against industry norms that often stifle innovation and individuality. Yet, her outlook remains hopeful and forward-looking. She envisions a future where the tech industry recognizes the value of diverse perspectives and skill sets and actively seeks to integrate them into developer experience.

Staples' story is a call to action for the tech industry to embrace the multifaceted nature of developer experience. It reminds us that DevEx is not just about tools and technologies but about creating spaces where curiosity is nurtured, and everyone feels empowered to contribute their unique insights and ideas. Through her experiences, challenges, and reflections, Staples offers valuable lessons on the importance of authenticity, direct communication, and the transformative potential of a well-considered approach to developer experience.

Mary Thengvall

Mary Thengvall, a prominent figure in the developer relations and developer experience (DevEx) fields, offers a nuanced perspective on the evolving landscape of developer experience. Her insights are shaped by years of experience navigating the complexities of building communities and fostering environments where developers can thrive. Thengvall's approach to defining DevEx is multifaceted, recognizing the balance between enhancing the user experience within a product and cultivating a holistic experience that encompasses interactions with the product, company, and broader community.

Thengvall identifies a significant dichotomy in the discourse around DevEx: one school of thought focuses on optimizing the in-product experience to ensure developers can utilize tools and features without external assistance, aiming for a seamless transition from novice to proficient users. The other perspective emphasizes creating an engaging, comprehensive experience that endears developers to a brand or community, encouraging long-term loyalty and participation.

This division, Thengvall notes, does not imply that these approaches are mutually exclusive. Instead, she argues for a synergistic view where improving the in-product experience and fostering community engagement are critical components of a successful DevEx strategy. This holistic approach aligns with Thengvall's broader philosophy that, while distinct, developer relations and experience share common goals and can benefit from an integrated strategy.

One of the recurring themes in Thengvall's work is the importance of empathy in shaping DevEx. Empathy for users—understanding their needs, challenges, and preferences—is crucial for designing experiences that resonate with developers. This empathetic approach extends beyond the product to include forums, documentation, contributions, and other aspects of the developer ecosystem.

Thengvall also touches on the emerging distinction between internal and external DevEx. Internal DevEx focuses on enhancing productivity and satisfaction among a company's engineering team, often to improve retention and efficiency. In contrast, external DevEx aims to create positive experiences for developers outside the company who interact with its products or services. While these areas have traditionally been viewed through separate lenses, Thengvall suggests a growing recognition of their interconnectedness and the benefits of a unified approach to DevEx.

Reflecting on the future of DevEx, Thengvall anticipates that emerging technologies, particularly AI, will play a significant role in enabling more rapid iteration and improvement of developer tools and environments. AI could offer prototypes and suggestions that accelerate the refinement of user interfaces and product features, facilitating a more dynamic and responsive approach to addressing developer needs.

Throughout her career, Thengvall has consistently advocated for a comprehensive, empathetic, and data-driven approach to DevEx. Her experiences and reflections underscore the ongoing evolution of the field, highlighting the potential for innovative technologies to enhance the way developers interact with products and communities. As the landscape of DevEx continues to shift, Thengvall's insights provide valuable guidance for those seeking to create genuinely impactful and enjoyable developer experiences.

Key Takeaways

- Empathy and Inclusivity: Understanding and addressing developers' diverse needs and challenges are fundamental to enhancing DevEx.

- Strategic Focus and Collaboration: Targeted initiatives and cross-functional teamwork are essential for meaningful improvements in DevEx.

- The Role of Emerging Technologies: Technologies such as AI have the potential to significantly impact DevEx, offering new ways to address developers' needs.

- Documentation and Accessibility: Clear, accessible documentation and a focus on inclusivity are critical components of a superior DevEx.

- Internal vs. External DevEx: Recognizing the interconnectedness of internal developer efficiency and external developer engagement is critical to a holistic DevEx strategy.

- Continuous Evolution: DevEx is an ever-evolving field requiring ongoing reflection, adaptation, and innovation.

CHAPTER 13

Conclusion

As we draw the curtains on our exploration of Developer Experience (DevEx), it's crucial to acknowledge that our journey is far from over. This concluding chapter is not merely a summary of what we've learned but a beacon guiding us toward the uncharted territories of continuous improvement in DevEx.

The Ongoing Journey of Enhancing DevEx

In the dynamic and ever-changing world of technology, the concept of Developer Experience (DevEx) remains a crucial yet evolving aspect of the software industry. As we dive deeper into this journey, it's essential to understand that what defines excellence in DevEx today might set the standard for tomorrow. This fluid nature of DevEx signifies that enhancing it is not a one-time effort but a continuous journey of growth, adaptation, and improvement.

Understanding the Evolution of Technology and Developer Needs

The first step in this ongoing journey is recognizing the ever-evolving landscape of technology. New technologies, methodologies, and trends emerge rapidly, each bringing challenges and opportunities for developers. Keeping up with these changes is beneficial and essential for

K. R. Leander, *Developer Experience Unleashed*,
https://doi.org/10.1007/979-8-8688-0242-3_13

providing a DevEx that resonates with the current and future needs of the developer community. This constant evolution demands a proactive approach to learning and adaptation, ensuring that the support and tools available to developers are relevant and ahead of the curve.

Embracing the Feedback Loop

Central to enhancing DevEx is the feedback loop concept. Engaging with the developer community to gather feedback is critical in understanding their needs, frustrations, and desires. This feedback serves as a compass, guiding the adjustments and improvements needed in tools, documentation, and support structures. Analyzing and acting on this feedback ensures that the development environment remains conducive to productivity, innovation, and satisfaction. The feedback loop is not a one-time process but a continuous cycle of listening, understanding, and implementing, fostering a culture of constant improvement.

Fostering a Supportive Developer Community

Another cornerstone of ongoing DevEx enhancement is cultivating a vibrant and supportive developer community. Such communities are support networks and incubators for innovation, offering a platform for sharing insights, ideas, and experiences. These communities provide a real-world testing ground for new features and improvements, allowing immediate and authentic feedback. Additionally, they serve as a source of motivation and inspiration, showcasing the potential impacts of excellent DevEx on individual projects and the wider industry. Fostering these communities emphasizes the value placed on developers' contributions and experiences, reinforcing the commitment to meeting and exceeding their expectations.

The journey of enhancing the Developer Experience is a testament to the commitment to excellence in the software industry. It underscores the importance of staying informed, engaging with feedback, and fostering community as integral components of this ongoing process. By embracing these principles, we can ensure that the developer experience continues to evolve in tandem with the technological landscape, meeting and anticipating the needs of developers around the globe. This journey is not without its challenges, but with a compassionate, informed, and proactive approach, it promises to yield significant benefits for developers and the industry.

The Potential Impact of Outstanding DevEx on the Software Industry and Beyond

As we contemplate the broader implications of Developer Experience (DevEx), it becomes clear that its reach extends far beyond the immediate confines of individual developers or singular projects. Outstanding DevEx can catalyze widespread innovation and growth within the software industry and across the entire spectrum of modern life.

Catalyzing Innovation Through Inclusivity

One of the most profound impacts of exceptional DevEx is its ability to democratize technology. By designing developer tools and platforms that are intuitive and accessible, we effectively lower the barrier to entry for a diverse array of individuals. This inclusivity enriches the technology sector with a multitude of perspectives, fostering a breeding ground for innovation and creative problem-solving. The diversity of thought and experience from a broader pool of contributors leads to more robust, innovative solutions that can address a more comprehensive range of challenges.

Accelerating Software Development

Another significant benefit of outstanding DevEx is the dramatic increase in the speed and efficiency of software development. When developers are equipped with the right tools and resources, projects that took months can now be completed in weeks or even days. This acceleration enhances productivity and enables faster time-to-market for new technologies. This efficiency is invaluable in today's fast-paced world, where being first can be a decisive competitive advantage. It allows companies to stay ahead in the race for innovation, offering new solutions and capturing market opportunities quicker than ever before.

Transforming Industries and Enhancing Lives

The ripple effects of improved DevEx are felt across almost every sector. As software becomes increasingly integral to our daily lives, the quality of developer experiences directly influences the quality of software solutions in industries as varied as healthcare, finance, education, and entertainment. Better developer tools and environments lead to better software, which can significantly enhance the quality of life, streamline complex processes, and open up new avenues for entertainment and education. In essence, by focusing on improving DevEx, we contribute to a cycle of continuous improvement that benefits society as a whole.

Embracing the Journey Ahead

While this book may signify a milestone in your understanding of DevEx, remember that the journey does not end here. The technology landscape is in perpetual motion, constantly evolving and presenting new challenges and opportunities. As such, pursuing enhanced DevEx is an ongoing adventure that demands constant learning, adaptation, and an unwavering commitment to excellence. By embracing this journey and striving for continuous improvement, you are advancing your knowledge and skills and contributing to a future where technology is more innovative, inclusive, and capable of changing the world for the better. Let this book be a conclusion and a launchpad into the exciting, ever-evolving world of Developer Experience.

Change of Direction

As we navigate the multifaceted world of Developer Experience (DevEx), it's pivotal to acknowledge that the path ahead may sometimes be a challenge. In the journey to cultivate an environment that fosters innovation and efficiency, we may encounter unforeseen challenges and changes in direction. With a spirit of resilience and adaptability, let's explore these challenges and arm ourselves with strategies to navigate them effectively.

The landscape of DevEx is as dynamic as the technology it seeks to enhance. Leadership or strategic vision changes within an organization can herald significant adjustments in the prioritization and support for DevEx initiatives. These changes manifest as reduced budgets, shifts in organizational priorities, or even a lack of understanding and support for the critical role of DevEx. Each scenario presents its obstacles, from discontinuing essential tools and platforms to alterations in team structures or communication channels. Moreover, shifts in technology focus, cultural dynamics, increased pressures on time-to-market, and new compliance or regulatory demands can further complicate the landscape.

In facing these challenges, the key lies in our ability to remain flexible and proactive. We can navigate these turbulent waters by prioritizing critical aspects of DevEx, advocating for its value, seeking alternatives to discontinued tools, and maintaining open lines of communication. Adapting our strategies to align with new priorities and technological directions while preserving a culture that values developer needs and experiences is crucial.

This section highlights the potential hurdles and offers a beacon of hope. It underscores the importance of advocacy, resilience, and the continuous pursuit of excellence in DevEx. Despite the uncertainties and challenges that may arise, our commitment to enhancing the developer experience must remain unwavering. By preparing for these eventualities and adopting a flexible approach, we can ensure that DevEx continues to thrive, driving innovation and efficiency across the software industry and beyond.

Let's approach these challenges not as insurmountable barriers but as opportunities to demonstrate our adaptability and dedication to the principles of outstanding DevEx. Doing so contributes to a more resilient, innovative, and inclusive technological future.

Reduced Budget for DevEx Initiatives

In the ever-fluctuating world of technology and organizational priorities, a challenge often arises when a reduced budget is allocated for Developer Experience (DevEx) initiatives. This financial constraint can significantly impact the pace of improvement and innovation within DevEx, potentially slowing down enhancements or necessitating the rollback of existing functionalities. However, even within the confines of a tightened budget, there are strategies to ensure that DevEx remains a priority and continues to evolve.

Maximizing Impact with Limited Resources

The key to navigating reduced budgets is maximizing the impact of available resources. This involves a strategic reassessment of ongoing and planned DevEx initiatives to identify those that offer the most significant benefit to the developer community with the least financial outlay. It's about doing more with less, prioritizing projects that improve efficiency, reduce developer friction, or provide the most requested enhancements by the community.

Prioritizing Critical Aspects of DevEx

With a reduced budget, prioritizing the most critical aspects of DevEx becomes essential. This prioritization involves carefully analyzing the developer journey and identifying the most crucial touchpoints for developer satisfaction and productivity. Focus on maintaining and enhancing these key areas to ensure that, despite financial constraints, developers still have a positive and productive experience. This might mean prioritizing improving core tools and platforms, streamlining documentation, or ensuring that support channels remain responsive and helpful.

Advocating for DevEx Value

In times of budget cuts, it becomes even more crucial to advocate for the value of DevEx within the organization. This advocacy involves demonstrating how investments in DevEx contribute to the organization's broader goals, such as increasing developer productivity, attracting top talent, or reducing time-to-market for new products and features. By clearly articulating the return on investment (ROI) of DevEx initiatives, you can make a compelling case for maintaining or even increasing funding in the long term.

Seeking Alternative Solutions

Finally, when faced with reduced budgets, exploring alternative solutions that can achieve similar DevEx outcomes at a lower cost is vital. This might involve leveraging open-source tools, collaborating with other organizations on joint DevEx initiatives, or exploring more cost-effective service providers. It also means being creative and innovative, finding new ways to enhance the developer experience without significant financial investment.

Dealing with reduced budgets for DevEx initiatives is undoubtedly challenging but manageable. By maximizing the impact of limited resources, prioritizing the most critical DevEx aspects, advocating for the value of DevEx, and seeking alternative solutions, you can continue to make meaningful improvements to the developer experience. Remember, the goal is to maintain a trajectory of continuous improvement, ensuring that developers have the tools, support, and environment they need to succeed, even in the face of financial constraints.

Shift in Organizational Priorities

In the ever-dynamic world of software development, a shift in organizational priorities can sometimes feel like navigating a ship through stormy seas. This challenge becomes particularly pronounced when such shifts seem to deprioritize Developer Experience (DevEx), an area we've come to understand as pivotal to innovation, efficiency, and overall project success. Let's explore this challenge and strategies for navigating these waters, ensuring that DevEx remains a central tenet of our organizational ethos.

Understanding the Shift

Changes in leadership or strategic direction are common in organizations striving to adapt to market trends, financial pressures, or new visions. However, these changes can inadvertently sideline DevEx initiatives, leading to halted projects or redirecting resources from areas critical for developer efficiency and satisfaction. This shift can stem from various factors, including new leadership unfamiliar with the nuances of DevEx or a reevaluation of company goals that prioritize other areas of perceived immediate impact.

Navigating the Shift

The key to navigating a shift in organizational priorities lies in flexibility, advocacy, and strategic realignment. Here's how you can approach this challenge:

Staying Adaptable: Flexibility in the face of change is valuable. It's essential to assess the new priorities and find ways to adapt your DevEx initiatives to align with them. This might mean pivoting your focus or demonstrating how enhancing DevEx can contribute to the organization's revised goals.

Realigning Strategies: Take the opportunity to review and realign your DevEx strategies with the new organizational priorities. This might involve redefining project goals, timelines, and metrics to ensure they resonate with the company's revised direction. It's an opportunity to reassess what's most critical and ensure your efforts contribute to broader company objectives.

Embedding DevEx in New Goals: Find innovative ways to embed the principles of excellent DevEx into the fabric of the new organizational priorities. This could involve demonstrating how improved developer tools and environments can accelerate achieving these new goals, enhance product quality, or reduce time-to-market.

Advocating for DevEx: Perhaps the most crucial step is to continue advocating for the importance of DevEx. This involves communicating the tangible benefits of investing in developer experience, such as increased productivity, higher quality output, and more robust innovation. Use data and case studies to make a compelling case for why DevEx should remain a priority, even amidst shifting organizational goals.

A shift in organizational priorities doesn't have to spell doom for DevEx initiatives. Instead, it presents an opportunity to demonstrate the adaptability, resilience, and intrinsic value of prioritizing a stellar developer experience. By staying adaptable, realigning strategies, embedding DevEx in new organizational goals, and continuing to advocate for its importance, you can ensure that DevEx remains at the heart of your organization's quest for excellence, irrespective of the changing winds of corporate direction. Remember, the ultimate goal is to foster an environment where developers can thrive, innovate, and contribute to the organization's success, regardless of the prevailing strategic priorities.

Lack of Understanding or Support for DevEx

In the intricate tapestry of organizational dynamics, a common thread that sometimes unravels is a lack of understanding or support for Developer Experience (DevEx). This challenge often emerges with shifts in leadership or strategic focus, leading to scenarios where the pivotal role of DevEx in driving innovation, productivity, and overall project success is not fully recognized. Let's unpack this challenge and explore strategies for weaving DevEx back into the fabric of organizational priorities.

Recognizing the Challenge

The crux of the issue lies in a gap between the perceived and actual value of DevEx. New leadership or stakeholders may not immediately see how investing in DevEx aligns with broader business goals, such as reducing time-to-market, enhancing product quality, or fostering innovation. This disconnect can stem from a variety of factors, including a focus on short-term gains over long-term benefits, a lack of exposure to the direct impact of DevEx on developer productivity and morale, or simply differing priorities.

Advocating for DevEx

The path to bridging this understanding gap starts with advocacy. Advocacy involves articulating the value of DevEx in a language that resonates with stakeholders and leadership. Here's how you can approach this:

Demonstrate Impact: Use data and case studies to highlight how improvements in DevEx lead to tangible outcomes, such as increased efficiency, reduced bug rates, and faster time-to-market. Real-world examples of enhanced DevEx directly contributing to project success stories can be particularly compelling.

Align with Business Objectives: Frame DevEx initiatives within overarching business goals. For instance, if the organization is focused on innovation, illustrate how a superior DevEx fosters a more creative and experimental development culture. If the priority is speed, show how streamlined workflows and better tools reduce development cycles.

Educate and Engage: Sometimes, a lack of support stems from a lack of understanding. Educational sessions, workshops, or even informal discussions about the principles of DevEx and its benefits can enlighten stakeholders on its importance. Engaging them in the DevEx process, perhaps through direct involvement in feedback loops or trial runs of new tools, can turn skeptics into advocates.

Build Bridges: Find allies within the organization who understand and have experienced the benefits of focusing on DevEx. These allies can come from various departments—product management, quality assurance, and customer support. Together, you can form a chorus of voices that champion the cause of DevEx from multiple perspectives.

Cultivating Support

Cultivating support for DevEx is an ongoing process. It involves an initial buy-in and maintaining a dialogue about DevEx's role and impact. This means regularly updating stakeholders on the progress of DevEx initiatives, celebrating successes, and learning from setbacks. It also means being receptive to feedback from leadership and finding ways to continuously align DevEx initiatives with the evolving goals and priorities of the organization.

A lack of understanding or support for DevEx within an organization can pose significant challenges, but it also offers advocacy and education opportunities. By demonstrating the tangible benefits of DevEx, aligning it with business objectives, and engaging stakeholders in the process, you can help bridge the gap and ensure that DevEx remains a central pillar of your organization's strategy. Remember, embedding DevEx in the organizational fabric is a marathon, not a sprint. It requires patience, persistence, and a deep belief in the value of creating an environment where developers can do their best work.

Discontinuation of DevEx Tools and Platforms

Navigating the discontinuation of essential DevEx tools and platforms presents a unique challenge, akin to losing a trusted compass during an expedition. This situation can arise from various factors, such as changes in organizational strategy, budget cuts, or shifts in technology focus. The impact of losing these tools and platforms can be significant, potentially disrupting workflows, lowering productivity, and diminishing the quality of the developer experience. However, with a thoughtful approach and strategic planning, mitigating these effects and finding a path forward is possible.

Understanding the Impact

The discontinuation of tools and platforms that developers rely on can be disheartening. These tools are often integral to daily workflows, enabling developers to code, test, and deploy more efficiently. Their sudden absence can create gaps in the DevEx ecosystem, leading to frustration and a potential decrease in productivity as developers scramble to find alternatives or adapt to new systems.

Exploring Alternatives

The first step in addressing this challenge is to explore alternatives that offer similar or improved functionalities. This exploration involves researching the market for existing tools and platforms that can seamlessly integrate into your current workflow. The goal is to identify solutions that replace the discontinued tools and potentially enhance DevEx by introducing new features or more intuitive interfaces. It's also an opportunity to consult with the developer community within and outside your organization to gather recommendations and insights on effective alternatives.

Advocating for Essential Tools

When the discontinuation of tools and platforms is under consideration but has yet to be finalized, advocating for their importance becomes critical. This advocacy involves presenting a compelling case to decision-makers about the value of these tools to the development process. Highlighting tangible benefits, such as improved productivity, higher code quality, and reduced time-to-market, can underscore their essential role in the DevEx. Additionally, demonstrating the potential costs and disruptions associated with discontinuing these tools can further strengthen your argument.

Adapting to Change

In situations where the discontinuation of tools and platforms is inevitable, adapting to change is critical. This adaptation involves the technical transition to new tools and supporting developers through the change. Providing training, resources, and ample time to adjust can ease the transition, helping to maintain productivity and morale. Establishing feedback channels is also essential, allowing developers to voice their concerns and experiences with the new tools. This feedback can be invaluable in making further adjustments and ensuring that the new solutions meet the needs of your development team.

The discontinuation of DevEx tools and platforms is undoubtedly challenging, but it also presents an opportunity for growth and improvement. You can navigate this change by exploring alternatives, advocating for essential tools, and supporting your team through the transition. Remember, the goal is to maintain or enhance the developer experience, ensuring your team has the tools they need to succeed. Flexibility, proactive planning, and open communication are your allies in this journey, helping to turn a potential setback into a stepping stone for a better DevEx.

Change in DevEx Team Structure

In the dynamic world of technology and software development, the structure of teams can often be as fluid as the projects they work on. Leadership or strategic direction changes can lead to significant alterations in team configurations, including those responsible for Developer Experience (DevEx). While sometimes necessary for growth and adaptation, such changes can bring uncertainty and challenges in maintaining the momentum and focus on DevEx initiatives. Let's explore how to navigate these changes while ensuring the core objectives of enhancing developer experience remain a priority.

Understanding the Impact of Team Restructuring

The restructuring of a DevEx team can manifest in several ways. For example, the team might be disbanded, its members dispersed into other teams, or it could be merged with another team with a different focus. Each scenario presents its own set of challenges. The dispersion of DevEx responsibilities can dilute focus and slow down initiatives while merging teams, which might lead to a clash of priorities or cultures. The key challenge here is maintaining a cohesive strategy for DevEx amidst these changes.

Maintaining DevEx Focus During Transition

The transition period following a change in team structure is critical. It's essential to ensure that the importance of DevEx is not just preserved but emphasized. Here are some strategies to consider:

Communicate Clearly and Frequently: Open lines of communication are essential. Ensure that everyone involved understands the reasons behind the restructuring and the expected outcomes. Clear communication can mitigate uncertainty and foster a sense of stability among team members.

Reaffirm DevEx Goals: Revisit and reaffirm the goals and objectives of your DevEx initiatives. This might also be an opportune time to reassess and realign these goals with the new team structure and organizational priorities. Ensuring these goals are understood and shared across the newly formed team is crucial for continued focus and momentum.

Leverage New Synergies: While restructuring can present challenges, it can also offer new opportunities for synergy. Integrating different skills, perspectives, and experiences can enrich the DevEx initiatives. Look for ways to harness these new dynamics to enhance collaboration and innovation within the team.

Advocate for DevEx Representation: Ensure that there are dedicated advocates for DevEx within the new team structure. These individuals can be champions for DevEx principles, ensuring they remain a central focus in project planning and execution. Their role can be crucial in bridging gaps and building a shared understanding of the importance of DevEx across different teams.

Monitor and Adapt: Keep a close eye on the impact of the team restructuring on DevEx initiatives. Be prepared to adapt strategies to address new challenges or leverage unexpected opportunities. Continuous monitoring allows for timely interventions to keep DevEx initiatives on track.

Changes in the DevEx team structure can be disorienting, but they don't have to derail the progress of enhancing the developer experience. By focusing on clear communication, reaffirming goals, leveraging new synergies, advocating for DevEx within the new structure, and staying adaptable, it's possible to navigate these changes effectively. Remember, the ultimate goal is creating an environment where developers can thrive and do their best. With thoughtful planning and a commitment to the principles of DevEx, even significant team restructuring can be turned into an opportunity for growth and improvement.

Altered Communication Channels

In the intricate ecosystem of an organization, communication channels are the lifelines that ensure ideas, feedback, and information flow seamlessly across teams and departments. These channels are especially critical in the context of Developer Experience (DevEx), where the continuous exchange of insights and feedback between developers and DevEx teams can significantly influence the effectiveness of development environments and tools. However, when new leadership steps in, one of the changes that often occurs is the alteration of these vital communication channels. This shift can disrupt the established rhythm of feedback and dialogue, potentially impacting DevEx initiatives. Let's explore how to navigate these changes, ensuring that the voice of the developer community continues to be heard and acted upon.

Understanding the Impact

Altered communication channels can lead to a disconnect between the DevEx team and the developer community it serves. This disconnection can result in missed feedback, delayed responses to issues, and a general sense of detachment among developers. Moreover, it can hinder the collaborative effort required to improve development tools and environments continuously. Recognizing the potential risks associated with these changes is the first step in addressing them.

Establishing New Lines of Communication

The key to mitigating the impact of altered communication channels lies in quickly establishing new lines of communication. This process involves

Identifying New Channels: Depending on the direction of the organizational changes, new communication channels might include revamped internal messaging systems, meetings, or digital collaboration platforms. Identifying these channels early and making them accessible to developers is crucial.

Promoting Transparency: Clear and transparent communication about the changes in communication channels can help ease the transition for developers. It's essential to explain why changes are happening, the new channels, and how they can be accessed.

Encouraging Engagement: With new channels, encouraging active engagement is vital. This might involve initiating conversations, soliciting feedback on the new system, and demonstrating that developer input is valued and considered in decision-making processes.

Ensuring Feedback Is Heard

Merely establishing new communication channels is not enough; it's equally important to ensure that these channels effectively capture and address developer feedback.

Feedback Mechanisms: Implement mechanisms for collecting and analyzing feedback received through the new channels. This could involve regular surveys, feedback sessions, or tools allowing anonymous input.

Actionable Insights: Ensure the collected feedback is translated into actionable insights. This means not just listening but actively responding to the concerns and suggestions of the developer community, thereby reinforcing the value of their input.

Continuous Evaluation: Regularly assess the effectiveness of the new communication channels. Are they meeting the needs of both the DevEx team and the developer community? Continuous evaluation will help identify areas for improvement and ensure that the channels remain robust and responsive.

Changes in communication channels can pose challenges to maintaining a solid and effective DevEx environment. Still, they also offer an opportunity to reevaluate and possibly enhance how dialogue and feedback are managed within an organization. By quickly establishing and promoting new channels, ensuring that developer feedback is effectively captured and acted upon, and continuously evaluating the effectiveness of these channels, organizations can maintain and even strengthen the vital link between DevEx teams and the developer community they support. In navigating these changes with empathy, transparency, and a commitment to engagement, we can ensure that the foundation of solid communication upon which excellent DevEx is built remains unshaken.

Shift in Technology Focus

Shifts in focus are not just standard; they're expected. These shifts can range from adopting new programming languages and frameworks to embracing entirely new architectural paradigms like microservices or serverless computing. For teams dedicated to Developer Experience (DevEx), such shifts represent a significant challenge: ensuring that the tools, processes, and environments they curate remain relevant and supportive of these new directions. Let's explore how to navigate a shift in technology focus, ensuring that DevEx remains a pillar of support for developers during these transitions.

Understanding the Nature of the Shift

The first step in addressing a shift in technology focus is to understand its scope and implications. Is the shift a response to emerging industry trends, a strategic decision to capture new markets, or a necessity dictated by technical debt? Understanding the motivations behind the shift can provide valuable insights into how DevEx needs to adapt. It's also essential to gauge the new skills, tools, and processes developers will need to navigate this change successfully.

Adapting DevEx Strategies

Once the nature and implications of the technology shift are understood, the next step is to adapt DevEx strategies to align with this new direction. This adaptation involves several vital actions:

Updating Tools and Environments: Assess the current suite of tools and environments to determine what needs to be updated, replaced, or introduced to support the new technology focus. This might involve evaluating new IDEs, version control systems, or deployment tools that better align with the adopted technologies.

Skill Development and Training: A shift in technology focus often requires developers to learn new languages, frameworks, or paradigms. Organizing training sessions, workshops, or providing access to online courses can help smooth this transition, ensuring developers feel supported and empowered to acquire new skills.

Revising Documentation and Support Structures: Ensure documentation, knowledge bases, and support structures are updated to reflect the new technology focus. Clear, accessible documentation is crucial for developers to quickly get up to speed with new technologies and best practices.

Facilitating a Smooth Transition

The transition to a new technology focus can be disruptive, but there are ways to minimize this disruption and encourage a smoother change:

Pilot Programs: Before rolling out changes organization-wide, consider implementing pilot programs or beta groups. These can provide valuable feedback on the effectiveness of the new tools and processes, allowing for adjustments before a full-scale rollout.

Feedback Loops: Maintain open communication channels with the developer community throughout the transition. Feedback loops can help identify pain points, gauge the effectiveness of the new DevEx initiatives, and adjust real-time strategies based on developer input.

Celebrating Milestones: Recognizing and celebrating milestones during the transition can help maintain morale and reinforce the value of the new technology focus. Acknowledging the achievements of teams and individuals who have successfully adapted to the new focus can motivate others.

A shift in technology focus is a significant event that can redefine the landscape in which DevEx operates. By understanding the nature of the shift, adapting DevEx strategies accordingly, and facilitating a smooth transition for developers, DevEx teams can ensure that they continue to provide the support and resources that developers need to thrive. Embracing these changes with a proactive, informed approach can turn the challenge of a technology shift into an opportunity for growth, innovation, and enhanced developer satisfaction.

Cultural Shifts

In the dynamic world of technology, the culture within an organization is not just a backdrop; it's the stage upon which all action unfolds. Cultural shifts, particularly those influenced by top-level changes, can profoundly affect every aspect of an organization, including its Developer Experience

(DevEx). Such shifts might range from changes in communication styles and decision-making processes to alterations in the values and priorities that drive the organization. Let's delve into understanding these shifts and exploring strategies to ensure that the culture continues to support and enhance DevEx.

Recognizing the Significance of Cultural Shifts

Cultural shifts within an organization can subtly start affecting the developer's environment and morale. It might change how open and collaborative the workspace feels or how much innovation is encouraged and rewarded. For DevEx, a supportive culture is crucial; it allows developers to experiment, learn, and grow. Recognizing the early signs of these shifts is critical to adapting and maintaining a positive DevEx amid change.

Nurturing a Supportive Culture

In times of cultural shift, actively working to cultivate a culture that values and supports developer needs is essential. Here's how you can approach this:

Promote Open Communication: Encourage an environment where developers feel comfortable sharing their ideas, challenges, and feedback. Open lines of communication can help identify areas where the DevEx can be improved and where the cultural shifts are impacting.

Foster Collaboration: Collaboration is at the heart of innovation. Encourage practices that promote teamwork, such as pair programming, code reviews, or shared learning sessions. These practices improve the quality of work and help create a sense of community and shared purpose.

Celebrate Innovation and Failure: A culture that celebrates innovation encourages taking risks. It's equally important to have an environment where failure is seen as a step toward learning and growth. This approach fosters a resilient and innovative developer community willing to push the boundaries of what's possible.

Advocate for Developer Well-being: Ensure that the organizational culture prioritizes the well-being of its developers. This includes recognizing the importance of work–life balance, providing opportunities for professional growth, and creating a supportive workplace environment. A culture that cares for its developers nurtures outstanding DevEx.

Adapting to New Cultural Norms

As new cultural norms begin to take shape, adapting your DevEx strategies to align with these norms is crucial. This might involve

Aligning DevEx Initiatives with New Values: If the cultural shift involves a new set of organizational values, revisit your DevEx initiatives to ensure they reflect them. For example, if the shift emphasizes sustainability, consider how DevEx can contribute to more sustainable development practices.

Engaging with Leadership: Engage with new leadership to understand their vision for the organization's culture and how DevEx fits into this vision. Demonstrating how a strong DevEx aligns with and supports the desired cultural shift can help secure their support and advocacy.

Listening and Adapting: Pay close attention to the feedback from the developer community during times of cultural shift. Their insights can provide valuable guidance on how to adapt DevEx initiatives to fit the evolving culture better.

Cultural shifts in an organization present both challenges and opportunities for DevEx. By recognizing the impact of these shifts, nurturing a supportive culture, and adapting DevEx strategies to align with new cultural norms, it's possible to maintain and enhance the developer experience. Remember, the strength of an organization's culture lies in its people. By focusing on open communication, collaboration, innovation, and well-being, you can help shape a culture that supports DevEx and empowers developers to achieve their best.

Increased Time-to-Market Pressures

In the fast-paced world of software development, time-to-market can be a critical factor in determining a product's success or failure. New leadership might bring a renewed focus on accelerating delivery times, often placing increased pressure on development teams to deliver faster. While this can drive efficiency and focus, it also risks compromising the quality of the developer experience (DevEx) and, by extension, the quality of the software being developed. Navigating these pressures requires a nuanced approach that balances speed with quality, ensuring the rush to deliver does not undermine the foundations of excellent DevEx.

Understanding the Pressures

The push for faster time-to-market usually comes from the need to stay competitive, respond to customer demands more swiftly, or capitalize on new market opportunities. While these are valid business imperatives, they can lead to a culture of rushed development processes, where the emphasis on speed overshadows the need for thorough testing, thoughtful design, and developer well-being.

Balancing Speed with Quality

The challenge is finding a balance that allows for rapid delivery without sacrificing the pillars of good DevEx. Here's how this can be approached:

Efficient Processes: Streamlining development processes can reduce time-to-market without compromising quality. This involves identifying and eliminating bottlenecks in the development pipeline, adopting agile methodologies for more adaptive planning and delivery, and automating repetitive tasks where possible.

Quality Assurance Integration: Integrating quality assurance (QA) throughout the development process, rather than as a final step, can help catch and resolve issues earlier. This approach, often called shift-left testing, ensures that quality is continuously focused, not just a final hurdle.

Developer Support Systems: Maintaining robust support systems for developers is crucial, especially under tight deadlines. This includes providing access to the right tools, ensuring adequate training and resources, and fostering an environment where developers feel supported.

Feedback Loops: Encouraging open and continuous feedback from developers about the impact of increased pressures can help identify when the balance is tipping too far toward speed at the expense of quality or developer well-being. This feedback is invaluable for adjusting strategies and processes in real time.

Advocating for a Balanced Approach

Advocating for a balanced approach to time-to-market pressures involves communicating the long-term value of maintaining high standards of DevEx and software quality. This includes

Demonstrating the Impact: Providing evidence of how rushed development can lead to increased bugs, technical debt, and burnout among developers can be a powerful way to advocate for a more balanced approach.

Highlighting Success Stories: Sharing examples where a balanced approach has led to successful outcomes can help make the case for quality over speed. Highlight how maintaining high DevEx standards has contributed to projects' overall success.

Engaging Leadership: Engaging with new leadership to discuss the importance of balancing time-to-market pressures with the need to maintain a positive DevEx is crucial. This dialogue can help ensure that leadership understands the value of DevEx in achieving long-term success.

Increased time-to-market pressures are a reality of the modern software development landscape. However, it's possible to meet these pressures by streamlining processes, integrating quality assurance, supporting developers, and advocating for a balanced approach without compromising the developer experience. Ultimately, the goal is to ensure that in the drive for speed, the quality of both the development process and the software itself remains high, laying the groundwork for sustained success in an ever-competitive market.

Compliance and Regulatory Changes

In an era where software development is not just about building features but also about ensuring compliance with an ever-growing tapestry of regulations, new compliance requirements, or regulatory changes can significantly impact Developer Experience (DevEx). These changes might stem from data protection laws, industry-specific regulations, or international standards an organization must adhere to. While necessary for safeguarding privacy, security, and quality, compliance and regulatory changes can pose a considerable challenge for DevEx, especially when introduced rapidly or without adequate preparation. Let's navigate this complex terrain, understanding how to adapt DevEx strategies to comply with these changes while minimizing their impact on developer workflows and productivity.

Understanding the Scope of Changes

The first step in navigating compliance and regulatory changes is to understand their scope and the specific requirements they impose fully. This involves collaboration between legal, compliance, and development teams to interpret the regulations accurately and identify the areas of your DevEx that will be affected. Whether it's data handling practices, software security measures, or the documentation process, clearly understanding these requirements is crucial for formulating an adequate response.

Adapting DevEx Strategies

Once the requirements are precise, the next step is to adjust your DevEx strategies to meet these new compliance standards. This adaptation can take several forms:

Integrating Compliance into the Development Process: Incorporate compliance checks and balances throughout the development lifecycle, from planning to deployment. This could involve automated testing for compliance-related issues, regular audits, or incorporating compliance criteria into the definition of done for development tasks.

Training and Awareness: Ensure all developers know the new compliance requirements and understand their roles in maintaining compliance. This might involve targeted training sessions, updates to onboarding processes, or regular communications highlighting compliance best practices.

Tooling and Automation: Leverage tools and automation to ease the compliance burden on developers. This could include automated code analysis tools that check for compliance issues, encryption tools for data protection, or documentation generators that help meet regulatory requirements for record-keeping.

Minimizing Impact on Developer Experience

While adapting to compliance and regulatory changes is essential, minimizing their impact on the developer experience is also important. This involves

Streamlining Compliance Tasks: Look for ways to make compliance tasks as frictionless as possible. This might include integrating compliance checks into existing tools and workflows or automating repetitive compliance-related tasks to free up developers to focus on their core work.

Maintaining Open Communication: Keep lines of communication open between the development team and compliance officers. Developers should feel supported in addressing compliance questions and concerns, and there should be a transparent process for resolving compliance-related issues that arise during development.

Balancing Compliance and Creativity: Ensure compliance requirements do not stifle innovation. Encourage a culture where compliance and creativity are complementary rather than conflicting objectives and where developers feel empowered to find innovative solutions that meet compliance standards and product goals.

Compliance and regulatory changes present a unique challenge to DevEx, requiring a balance between meeting legal and regulatory obligations and maintaining a positive and productive developer experience. Organizations can navigate these challenges by understanding the scope of these changes, adapting DevEx strategies accordingly, and working to minimize their impact on developer workflows. Remember, the goal is not just to comply with regulations but to do so in a way that supports and enhances the work of your development team, ensuring that compliance becomes a seamless part of the development process rather than an obstacle to innovation.

In each scenario, the key is to remain flexible, proactive, and committed to advocating for the best possible DevEx. Remember, challenges and setbacks are part of any journey, and the field of DevEx is no exception. By preparing for these potential negatives and having strategies to address them, you can continue to impact the ever-evolving landscape of developer experience positively.

The Journey Continues

As we draw this exploration of Developer Experience (DevEx) to a close, it's clear that the journey toward enhancing DevEx is perpetual, marked by continuous adaptation, learning, and improvement. Throughout this chapter, we've delved into the multifaceted nature of DevEx, recognizing it as an evolving field that requires constant vigilance, innovation, and a deep understanding of the developer's needs and challenges. The landscape of technology and software development is ever-changing, and with it, the parameters of what constitutes an excellent DevEx shift.

The impact of outstanding DevEx extends far beyond the immediate confines of developer workstations or code repositories. It has the potential to catalyze innovation, drive efficiency, and significantly influence the broader industry landscape, lowering barriers to entry and fostering a more inclusive, diverse technological community. This inclusivity enriches the pool of ideas and solutions and propels the industry toward more innovative horizons, impacting virtually every aspect of modern life.

However, the path of enhancing DevEx is not without its obstacles.

Leadership changes, shifts in organizational priorities, budget constraints, and evolving technology landscapes pose significant challenges. Each requires a proactive, flexible approach to ensure that the essence of DevEx—creating a supportive, efficient, and enjoyable environment for developers—is not lost amidst these shifts. Strategies such as advocating for DevEx, adapting to new technological focuses, and maintaining a culture that values open communication and collaboration are crucial in navigating these changes.

As we conclude, it's important to remember that the journey of enhancing DevEx is just beginning. It's a journey that requires a commitment to continuous learning, an openness to change, and a dedication to understanding and addressing the evolving needs of developers. By embracing these challenges as opportunities for growth, we can continue contributing to a future where technology development is not just about what we create but how we create it—efficiently, inclusively, and with a deep respect for the developer experience.

Key Takeaways

- Enhancing DevEx is a continuous journey requiring adaptability and a commitment to improvement.

- Outstanding DevEx can significantly impact the software industry, driving innovation, lowering barriers to entry, and increasing development efficiency.

- Navigating changes in leadership, organizational priorities, and technology landscapes is crucial for focusing on DevEx.

- Strategies for adapting to these changes include advocating for DevEx, leveraging feedback, and fostering a culture that supports open communication and collaboration.

- The journey of enhancing DevEx is an opportunity to contribute to a more innovative, inclusive, and efficient technological future.

APPENDIX A

Resources and Further Reading

As the software development landscape continually evolves, so does the wealth of knowledge and resources available to those navigating it. The list presented in this appendix is dynamic, reflecting the ever-changing nature of technology and methodologies in the field. While not exhaustive, these resources serve as a solid starting point for delving into the multifaceted world of Developer Experience (DevEx).

On these pages, you will find a curated selection of books, online courses, articles, and other materials that have been influential and informative in the realm of DevEx. They offer insights into best practices, emerging trends, and foundational concepts crucial for anyone looking to enhance their understanding and skills in creating delightful and efficient developer environments.

Remember, this list is just a beginning. The journey of learning and improvement in software development is ongoing, and staying informed and adaptable is critical. We encourage readers to continually seek out new sources of knowledge, engage with the community, and share their discoveries. You will likely find your favorites to add to this ever-growing knowledge repository as you progress.

Happy learning!

© K. Rain Leander 2025
K. R. Leander, *Developer Experience Unleashed*,
https://doi.org/10.1007/979-8-8688-0242-3

Introduction to Developer Experience

The Developer's Guide to Content Creation by Stephanie Morillo—This is for understanding the value of content in the developer experience.

Online Course: "Introduction to Software Development"—Provides a foundational understanding of software development relevant to understanding DevEx.

The Essence of Developer Experience

Continuous Delivery: Reliable Software Releases through Build, Test, and Deployment Automation by Jez Humble and David Farley—A seminal work on DevOps practices.

Don't Make Me Think by Steve Krug—Though focused on UX, it offers valuable insights applicable to DevEx.

Crafting Exceptional Documentation

Every Page is Page One by Mark Baker—Excellent for understanding modern approaches to technical documentation.

Online Course: "Technical Writing"—Courses on platforms like Coursera or LinkedIn Learning offer practical skills in technical writing.

Streamlining Developer Tooling

Effective DevOps by Jennifer Davis and Ryn Daniels—Explores tooling in the context of DevOps culture.

Version Control with Git by Jon Loeliger and Matthew McCullough—A comprehensive guide to using Git.

Designing Developer-Centric APIs

API Design Patterns by JJ Geewax—For understanding API design principles and patterns.

GraphQL: Up and Running by Eve Porcello and Alex Banks—Offers a deep dive into designing GraphQL APIs.

Providing Stellar Developer Support

Building Successful Online Communities: Evidence-Based Social Design by Robert E. Kraut and Paul Resnick—Useful for understanding community dynamics.

Webinar Series: "Developer Relations and Community Building"— Offers insights from industry experts.

Ensuring Performance and Reliability

Site Reliability Engineering: How Google Runs Production Systems by Niall Richard Murphy, Betsy Beyer, Chris Jones, and Jennifer Petoff—A "must read" for understanding performance at scale.

The Art of Monitoring by James Turnbull—Covers monitoring and observability in-depth.

Measuring Developer Experience

Lean Analytics: Use Data to Build a Better Startup Faster by Alistair Croll and Benjamin Yoskovitz—Provides a framework for measuring and analyzing performance.

Measuring User Experience by William Albert and Thomas Tullis— Teaches valuable methods for user research applicable to DevEx.

Real-world DevEx Improvement Strategies

Accelerate The Science of Lean Software and DevOps: Building and Scaling High Performing Technology Organizations by Nicole Forsgren, Jez Humble, and Gene Kim—Offers strategies for improving tech organization performance.

The Phoenix Project: A Novel about IT, DevOps, and Helping Your Business Win by Gene Kim, Kevin Behr, and George Spafford—A novel that provides insights into IT and software development processes.

Developer Experience Case Studies

The Cathedral & the Bazaar by Eric S. Raymond—Explores lessons from open-source software projects.

The Future of Developer Experience

Augmented: Life in the Smart Lane by Brett King—For insights into emerging technologies like AI and AR/VR.

Designing for Sustainability: A Guide to Building Greener Digital Products and Services by Tim Frick—Covers the sustainability aspect of tech development.

APPENDIX B

Tools and Technologies

As we venture into the dynamic realm of developer experience (DevEx), we must acknowledge the ever-evolving landscape of tools and technologies that play a pivotal role in shaping it. This appendix presents a curated list of tools and technologies carefully chosen to enhance and streamline various aspects of DevEx, from documentation to performance optimization.

It's important to note that this list is by no means exhaustive. The tech world is constantly in flux, with new tools emerging, existing ones being updated, and others becoming obsolete. As such, the recommendations provided here are a snapshot of the current state of the art in developer tools and technologies. We encourage readers to stay attuned to the latest developments in the field and consider this list a starting point for exploring the vast array of options available.

The technologies and tools listed in this appendix are intended to provide practical guidance and serve as a resource for enhancing the developer experience in various domains. They have been selected based on their popularity, functionality, and the value they add to different stages of the development process. However, every project and team has unique needs, and what works best in one context may be better in another. Therefore, we recommend assessing each tool's suitability based on specific project requirements, team preferences, and the overall development environment.

© K. Rain Leander 2025
K. R. Leander, *Developer Experience Unleashed*,
https://doi.org/10.1007/979-8-8688-0242-3

As you delve into this list, we invite you to approach it with an open mind, a willingness to experiment, and a readiness to adapt to the changing tides of technology. The ultimate goal is to craft a developer environment that is efficient, productive, and delightful to work in.

Based on the structure and content outlined for this book, here are some recommended tools and technologies for each relevant chapter.

Crafting Exceptional Documentation

Documentation Platforms: Docusaurus, ReadTheDocs, Confluence
API Documentation Tools: SwaggerUI, Redoc, Postman
Collaborative Writing Tools: Google Docs, Notion, Microsoft Office 365
Version Control for Documentation: Git, GitHub, Bitbucket

Streamlining Developer Tooling

Text Editors and IDEs: Visual Studio Code, JetBrains IntelliJ IDEA, Sublime Text
Version Control Systems: Git
Build Tools: Jenkins, GitHub Actions, CircleCI
Testing Frameworks: JUnit (Java), PyTest (Python), Jest (JavaScript)
Debugging Tools: GDB, Chrome DevTools, Visual Studio Debugger
Continuous Integration/Continuous Deployment: GitHub Actions, GitLab CI, Azure DevOps

Designing Developer-Centric APIs

API Design Tools: Swagger Editor, Stoplight, Postman
API Gateways: Kong, Apigee, AWS API Gateway
GraphQL Tools: Apollo Server, GraphQL Yoga, Relay
gRPC Tools: Protobuf, gRPC-Web, BloomRPC

Providing Stellar Developer Support

Communication Platforms: Slack, Microsoft Teams, Discord

Knowledge Base Software: Zendesk, Freshdesk, Help Scout

Community Platforms: Stack Overflow for Teams, GitHub Discussions, Discourse

Feedback Tools: Typeform, SurveyMonkey, UserVoice

Ensuring Performance and Reliability

Monitoring Tools: Datadog, Prometheus, New Relic

Logging Tools: ELK Stack (Elasticsearch, Logstash, Kibana), Splunk, Graylog

Incident Management: PagerDuty, OpsGenie, VictorOps

Performance Testing: JMeter, LoadRunner, Gatling

Chaos Engineering: Chaos Monkey, Gremlin, Litmus

Measuring Developer Experience

Analytics Tools: Google Analytics, Mixpanel, Amplitude

User Testing Tools: UserTesting, Lookback.io, Hotjar

Feedback and Survey Tools: Qualtrics, Google Forms, SurveyMonkey

Real-world DevEx Improvement Strategies

Project Management Tools: JIRA, Asana, Trello

Roadmapping Software: Aha!, ProductPlan, Roadmunk

Collaboration Tools: Miro, Figma, Lucidchart

The Future of Developer Experience

Low-code Platforms: OutSystems, Mendix, Microsoft PowerApps
AI & ML Development Tools: TensorFlow, PyTorch, Jupyter Notebooks
VR/AR Development: Unity, Unreal Engine, Vuforia
Blockchain Development: Ethereum, Hyperledger, Truffle Suite

Developer Experience in Specialized Domains

Game Development: Unity, Unreal Engine, Godot
Data Science and Machine Learning: Anaconda, RStudio, Apache Spark
IoT Development: Arduino, Raspberry Pi, AWS IoT
Cybersecurity Tools: Wireshark, Metasploit, Nessus

DevEx Templates and Checklists for Evaluation and Improvement

This part of the book is a practical toolkit for evaluating and improving the developer experience (DevEx) in various software development environments.

In this appendix, you will find a range of templates and checklists. These have been meticulously curated to provide a structured approach to assessing and enhancing DevEx. Each tool has been developed with adaptability, continuous evaluation, and customization.

Understanding the diverse nature of software development projects, we ensured that every template and checklist could be adapted to different project sizes and types. Whether you are part of a small startup or a large enterprise, these resources are relevant and applicable to your environment.

Software development is an ever-evolving field, as is the concept of DevEx. Therefore, our resources emphasize the importance of ongoing evaluation and iterative improvements. This approach is about identifying strengths and weaknesses and continuously monitoring and adapting to changes in the development environment.

We also recognize that each project has its unique requirements and challenges. Consequently, while these templates and checklists serve as comprehensive starting points, they are designed to be customized to meet the specific needs of your project and team. This ability to tailor the resources ensures that your evaluations and improvements align with your project goals and developer needs.

As you explore this appendix, consider these resources as a foundation for building a more efficient, enjoyable, and productive developer environment. The ultimate aim is to foster a culture where improving the developer experience is a continual process and a key priority.

We hope you find these tools valuable in your journey to elevate the Developer Experience in your projects.

Here's a compilation of DevEx templates and checklists for this book. These are designed to aid in evaluating and improving various aspects of developer experience (DevEx).

Developer Experience Evaluation Template
General Assessment

- Definition and understanding of DevEx in the context of the project
- Alignment of DevEx with overall software development goals

Component Assessment

- Documentation quality and accessibility
- Tooling effectiveness and efficiency
- API design clarity and usability
- Developer support availability and responsiveness
- Performance and reliability benchmarks

DevEx Improvement Checklist

Documentation

- Clear, concise, and up-to-date content
- Accessible and inclusive language
- Efficient organization and easy navigation

Tooling

- Relevance and effectiveness of selected tools
- Integration and workflow optimization
- Customization and extension capabilities

API Design

- Consistency and predictability

- Security and performance considerations

- Effective versioning and deprecation strategies

Developer Support

- Responsive and diverse communication channels

- Availability of self-service resources

- Efficient feedback incorporation system

Performance and Reliability

- Robust monitoring and observability tools

- Effective incident management protocols

- Comprehensive security and compliance measures

DevEx Metrics and KPIs Tracking Template
Adoption Metrics

- Tool and documentation usage statistics

- API adoption and usage rates

Performance Indicators

- Time to resolve issues and bugs
- System downtime and performance metrics

Developer Satisfaction

- Survey and interview feedback
- Community engagement and participation levels

DevEx Roadmap Planning Template
Identifying Improvement Areas

- Current pain points and challenges
- Opportunities for innovation and enhancement

Setting Goals and Milestones

- Short-term and long-term objectives
- Prioritization of initiatives

Implementation and Tracking

- Steps for changes and new implementations
- Mechanism for tracking progress and impact

Developer Support Workflow Checklist
Initial Contact and Triage

- Efficient ticketing system setup
- Precise categorization and prioritization of issues

Resolution and Follow-Up

- Timely and effective resolution strategies
- Post-resolution follow-up and feedback collection

Performance and Reliability Audit Checklist
System Monitoring

- Comprehensive monitoring coverage
- Effective alerting systems

Optimization and Testing

- Regular performance optimization
- Thorough load and stress testing protocols

Resilience Planning

- Redundancy and failover strategies
- Chaos engineering and fault tolerance tests

Developer Community Engagement Template

Community Building

- Platforms and channels for community interaction
- Engagement strategies and content planning

Feedback and Collaboration

- Mechanisms for collecting community feedback
- Collaborative projects and initiatives

APPENDIX D

Frequently Asked Questions (FAQs)

FAQs are not typically regarded as a modern technical communication or documentation practice. Instead of organizing information in a "bucket of items" approach, as often seen in FAQs, it is generally more effective to structure content for better findability and usability or incorporate it clearly into the primary documentation.

Let's delve into the everyday curiosities, uncertainties, and pivotal questions you might have about the expansive world of Developer Experience (DevEx). As you've journeyed through this book, you've encountered a wealth of information covering everything from the nuances of API design to the broader strokes of DevEx strategy. It's natural to have questions, and we're here to address them.

However, while this section aims to address key points, consider this as a transitional phase toward structuring documentation that is inherently more organized and user-centric. Instead of relying on FAQs, we advocate for integrating these answers directly within relevant sections, ensuring the information is contextually placed and easier to find. This approach aligns with modern best practices in technical communication, promoting a more intuitive and streamlined user experience.

Picture this section as a conversational nook, a place where we sit down together, perhaps with a cup of coffee, to untangle the threads of DevEx. This isn't just a Q&A; it's a dialogue that extends the rich discussions from each chapter. We've compiled these questions from common queries that bubble up in the field and reflections on the material we've presented. They're the questions that keep developers, team leaders, and innovators up at night, pondering the best ways to create, enhance, and measure the developer experience.

We start with the basics, addressing DevEx and why it's an indispensable part of modern software development. This is crucial for setting the stage, especially if you're new to the concept or looking for a firmer grasp of its fundamentals. From there, we explore more intricate aspects, like the evolution of software development methodologies and their impact on DevEx, the art of crafting documentation that speaks to the developer, and the selection of tools that don't just do the job but enhance the creative process.

Understanding the nuances of API design is another journey, one that's critical in today's interconnected software landscape. We delve into questions that help you navigate this terrain, focusing on best practices, versioning, and the ever-important security aspect. Then there's the human side of DevEx—developer support. Here, we tackle how to create platforms and resources that empower developers, fostering an environment of efficiency and innovation.

Performance and reliability are non-negotiable in software development, so we've included questions to guide you through optimizing these aspects. Similarly, measuring the success of your DevEx initiatives is a complex but necessary endeavor, and we provide insights into identifying and analyzing key performance indicators.

As we venture into real-world strategies and case studies, the questions become more scenario-based, reflecting challenges and successes in diverse environments—from startups to large organizations. The future of

DevEx is an exciting frontier, brimming with emerging technologies and ethical considerations. Our questions here prompt you to consider how these advancements will shape the development landscape.

Going forward, we encourage the integration of these insights directly within the relevant documentation sections, creating a more cohesive and user-friendly resource.

Introduction to Developer Experience

What is Developer Experience (DevEx), and why is it increasingly important in software development?

Developer Experience (DevEx) refers to developers' overall experience and effectiveness while working with specific tools, technologies, environments, and processes. It encompasses everything from the ease of setting up a development environment to the clarity of documentation, efficiency of the tools, and responsiveness of support networks. DevEx is about creating an environment where developers can be most productive and enjoy their work.

The increasing importance of DevEx in software development stems from a few key trends. First, as software development becomes more complex and integral to every aspect of our lives, the need for efficient and enjoyable development processes becomes more critical. Good DevEx can lead to more innovative, high-quality software, as developers are less bogged down by cumbersome processes and more engaged in their work.

Furthermore, organizations offering superior DevEx can attract and retain top developers in the competitive tech talent landscape. A developer's experience can directly influence their effectiveness and, consequently, the success of their projects. A positive DevEx can also enhance community involvement and contribution in an open-source and collaborative development era, which is vital for many projects.

How does improving DevEx benefit both individual developers and organizations?

Improving DevEx has a ripple effect that benefits not just individual developers but entire organizations. For developers, a superior DevEx means reduced friction and frustrations in their daily work. It leads to an environment where they can focus more on creative problem-solving than tedious, repetitive tasks or navigating poorly designed systems. This improvement in work quality can lead to greater job satisfaction, lower burnout rates, and a stronger sense of accomplishment.

For organizations, the benefits are multifold. Enhanced DevEx can increase productivity, as developers can work more efficiently and effectively. It also fosters innovation; developers who are not mired in cumbersome processes have more mental bandwidth to think creatively and push boundaries. Furthermore, a good DevEx attracts and retains talented developers in a competitive market. Happy developers are more likely to produce better work, be more engaged, and stay with the company longer, reducing turnover costs.

Lastly, an organization with a good DevEx reputation in the broader ecosystem can build a stronger community around its products and services. This community engagement can lead to more robust and rapid development, user feedback, and a better product or service.

What are the core objectives of this book about enhancing DevEx?

The core objectives of this book are to equip readers with the knowledge, strategies, and actionable insights needed to enhance the developer experience within their organizations or projects significantly. It aims to

- Provide a comprehensive understanding of what constitutes a good DevEx and why it's vital in modern software development

- Offer practical guidance on evaluating and improving various aspects of DevEx, such as documentation, tooling, API design, and developer support

- Share insights and best practices from industry leaders and successful case studies, translating these learnings into applicable strategies

- Foster a mindset that prioritizes the continuous improvement of DevEx as an integral part of the software development culture

- Empower readers to implement changes that enhance DevEx and advocate for these improvements within their teams and organizations

This book is a roadmap for transforming how we approach software development, focusing on creating an environment where developers can thrive and innovate.

The Essence of Developer Experience

How has the evolution from Waterfall to Agile and DevOps impacted DevEx?

The transition from Waterfall to Agile and further to DevOps represents a paradigm shift in software development methodologies, significantly impacting Developer Experience (DevEx). In the Waterfall model, the process was linear and sequential, often leading to a siloed approach where developers had limited scope for flexibility or iteration. This usually resulted in a rigid and sometimes frustrating DevEx, where late-stage changes were costly or impossible.

With the advent of Agile methodologies, there was a shift toward more iterative and collaborative development. Agile focuses on flexibility, continuous feedback, and cross-functional teamwork, greatly enhancing DevEx by allowing developers to see and respond to real-time changes. This iterative approach improved the adaptability of development teams and made the development process more transparent and engaging for developers.

DevOps took this further by integrating development and operations, emphasizing automation, continuous integration, and continuous deployment. This has streamlined many tedious and manual tasks, significantly improving DevEx. Automating processes in DevOps reduces the time spent on repetitive tasks, allowing developers to focus more on creative problem-solving. Additionally, the continuous nature of DevOps provides developers with immediate feedback on their work, enhancing the sense of accomplishment and engagement.

In what ways does DevEx intersect with and differ from User Experience (UX)?

DevEx and UX, while distinct, share some common grounds. Both focus on creating positive experiences for the developers building the product (DevEx) or the end user (UX). The intersection lies in that a good DevEx can often lead to a better UX. When developers have a smooth, efficient, and enjoyable experience building software, it frequently translates into higher quality, more user-friendly products.

However, the focus areas of DevEx and UX differ significantly. UX concentrates on the end-user's interaction with the product, aiming to make it intuitive, enjoyable, and effective. In contrast, DevEx focuses on the tools, processes, and environments that developers building the software engage with. While UX is concerned with the final product's look, feel, and navigability, DevEx is about the efficiency of codebases, clarity of documentation, robustness of tools, and effectiveness of development processes.

What are the critical components of DevEx that every developer should be aware of?

Critical components of a good DevEx include

- Efficient Tools and Technologies: This includes everything from IDEs to version control systems to build and deployment tools. Efficient tools are reliable, integrate well with other systems, and streamline development.

- Clear and Comprehensive Documentation: Good documentation is invaluable for developers. It should be clear, concise, up-to-date, and include examples.

- Responsive Support and Ecosystem: Access to a supportive community and responsive support channels can significantly enhance DevEx, providing avenues for resolving issues and sharing knowledge.

- Streamlined Processes and Workflows: Processes that reduce friction, like simplified code reviews, efficient bug-tracking systems, and transparent deployment workflows, contribute to a positive DevEx.

- Learning and Growth Opportunities: Continuous learning is a big part of DevEx. Developers appreciate opportunities for professional growth through training, workshops, or challenging projects.

How can organizations balance traditional development practices with the need for better DevEx?

Balancing traditional development practices with the need for better DevEx involves a strategic approach where organizations can gradually integrate modern methodologies and tools without disrupting existing workflows. This can be done by

- Incremental Adoption: Instead of overhauling systems overnight, organizations can adopt new practices and tools incrementally. For example, initially integrate agile practices within a waterfall framework before transitioning completely.

- Training and Skill Development: Educating teams about the benefits and usage of new methodologies and tools can smooth the transition and improve developer acceptance.

- Pilot Projects: Trying new practices in small, controlled environments before a full-scale roll-out can help understand their impact on DevEx and iron out any issues.

- Feedback Mechanisms: Encouraging developers to provide feedback on new tools and processes can help make necessary adjustments and ensure that changes positively impact DevEx.

The goal is to create a symbiotic relationship between traditional practices and new approaches, leveraging both strengths to enhance the overall Developer Experience.

Crafting Exceptional Documentation

What types of documentation are most vital for positive DevEx?

Several types of documentation are crucial for a positive Developer Experience (DevEx). Firstly, **API References** are indispensable as they provide the necessary details for developers to effectively understand and interact with APIs. They should be precise and comprehensive, covering all functionalities, parameters, and return types.

Tutorials and Guides offer step-by-step instructions and are essential for helping new users get started. They should be easy to follow, offering practical examples to demonstrate everyday use cases.

Conceptual Documentation provides a higher-level view of the technology, explaining the "why" and not just the "how." This includes architecture overviews, design rationales, and scenario-based explanations.

End-to-end Examples or **Case Studies** demonstrate how various software parts work together in real-world scenarios. They are precious for understanding the software's practical application.

Lastly, **Troubleshooting Guides and FAQs** address common issues and questions. This part of the documentation helps reduce frustration by offering quick solutions to developers' typical problems.

How can documentation be crafted to be inclusive and accessible to all developers?

To make documentation inclusive and accessible, start by using clear and straightforward language. Avoid jargon and technical terms that might not be universally understood. When such terms are necessary, provide definitions or links to explanations.

417

Ensure that your documentation is well-structured and easy to navigate. Use headers, tables of contents, and indexes effectively. Consider your audience's diverse backgrounds—not everyone might have the same expertise or technical background.

Accessibility also means catering to developers with disabilities. This includes providing alt text for images, ensuring screen reader compatibility, and offering documentation in multiple formats, like text, video, and audio.

Cultural inclusivity is also vital. Be mindful of using examples and language that do not unconsciously alienate segments of your audience. Where possible, provide documentation in multiple languages.

In what ways can outdated or unclear documentation negatively impact DevEx?

Outdated or unclear documentation can significantly hinder a developer's workflow. While it might save time as developers try to use deprecated features or follow obsolete practices, it can also lead to frustration and a lack of trust in the documentation and, by extension, the product itself.

Unclear documentation, on the other hand, can be just as problematic. If the documentation is not straightforward, developers may misinterpret functionalities, leading to improper implementation and potential bugs. It can also increase the learning curve unnecessarily, making the technology seem more complex than it is.

In both cases, developers might resort to external resources like forums or community discussions. While these can be helpful, relying solely on them can lead to inconsistent practices and information fragmentation.

What are some best practices for maintaining and updating documentation efficiently?

Maintaining and updating documentation efficiently requires a systematic approach. First, treat documentation as an integral part of your product development rather than an afterthought. It should be updated along with the software it describes.

Implement a process for regular reviews and updates of the documentation. This could be tied to your software release cycle. Encourage contributions from various team members, including developers, testers, and support staff, to ensure comprehensive coverage of all aspects.

Use documentation tools and platforms that allow for easy collaboration and version control. This makes it easier to track changes, review contributions, and ensure consistency across all documentation.

Finally, gather feedback from users and incorporate it into your documentation. User feedback is invaluable in identifying unclear, incomplete, or outdated areas. This could be done through surveys, feedback buttons on documentation pages, or monitoring community forums.

Streamlining Developer Tooling

What criteria should be considered when selecting tools to enhance DevEx?

When selecting tools to enhance Developer Experience (DevEx), several criteria must be considered to ensure the tools align well with the developers' needs and the project's goals.

Compatibility and Integration: The tools should seamlessly integrate with the existing ecosystem, including other tools, platforms, and systems. This reduces friction and enhances productivity.

Usability and Learning Curve: Tools should be intuitive and easy to use. A steep learning curve can be a significant barrier. User-friendly interfaces and good documentation can make a big difference.

Performance and Reliability: Tools should be fast and reliable. Performance issues or frequent crashes can disrupt development and lead to frustration.

Scalability: The tool should be able to scale with the project. It should handle increased workloads or grow as the project expands.

Support and Community: A robust support system and an active community can significantly enhance DevEx. This ensures that help is available when needed, and a vibrant community can provide valuable resources, plugins, and advice.

Customizability: The ability to customize the tool to suit specific needs or preferences is crucial. This includes support for plugins, extensions, or scripting capabilities.

How can developers effectively customize and extend their tools using plugins and scripting?

Customizing and extending tools can significantly enhance DevEx, making everyday tasks more efficient and aligned with individual or project-specific needs.

Many tools support plugins that extend their functionality. Developers should explore official and community-created plugins that can add specific features or streamline processes. When selecting plugins, consider compatibility, support, and community reviews.

Scripting allows for the automation of repetitive tasks or the integration of multiple tools. Developers can write scripts to automate routine operations, which saves time and reduces the chance of human error. Many tools offer scripting APIs, which should be leveraged to create custom workflows.

When customizing tools, it's essential to document these customizations. This documentation can be helpful when onboarding new team members or troubleshooting issues.

What role does tool integration play in streamlining the development workflow?

Tool integration is critical in streamlining the development workflow. Integrated tools work together seamlessly, allowing data and processes to flow from one tool to another without manual intervention. This reduces the time spent on mundane tasks like data entry, switching between different platforms, or converting data formats.

For example, integrating a version control system with a continuous integration/continuous deployment (CI/CD) pipeline automates the process of testing and deploying code. This not only saves time but also reduces the risk of human error.

Effective integration also provides a more holistic view of the development process, making it easier to track progress, identify bottlenecks, and ensure consistency across different stages of development.

How can cross-platform development considerations impact the choice of development tools?

Selecting tools that support multiple platforms is crucial in a cross-platform development environment. This could mean choosing inherently cross-platform tools that function seamlessly on different operating systems.

- Support the generation of cross-platform code, ensuring that the codebase can be deployed across various platforms without significant modifications.

The choice of tools in a cross-platform scenario also impacts testing and deployment. Tools should support or integrate with cross-platform testing frameworks to ensure the application performs consistently across all targeted platforms.

Additionally, cross-platform development often involves considering different user interfaces and platform experiences. Tools that offer UI/UX design support for multiple platforms can be precious.

The choice of tools in cross-platform development should facilitate creating, testing, and deploying applications across different platforms, maintaining consistency and efficiency.

Designing Developer-Centric APIs

What fundamental principles should guide the design of developer-centric APIs?

Designing developer-centric APIs revolves around principles that prioritize ease of use, clarity, and reliability for the developer.

Consistency: A consistent API design makes it easier for developers to understand and use the API. This includes consistent naming conventions, request/response formats, and behavior across API parts.

Simplicity and Intuitiveness: The API should be as simple as possible. Complex functionalities should be abstracted to provide a clear and intuitive interface. Developers should be able to start using the API with minimal learning curve.

Flexibility: The API should be flexible enough to handle different use cases and scenarios. This includes providing various endpoints and parameters to cater to different needs.

Performance and Efficiency: APIs should be designed to ensure quick responses and efficient data handling. This is crucial as slow or inefficient APIs can significantly hamper development.

Security: Security is paramount. APIs should be designed to protect sensitive data and ensure safe transactions, incorporating authentication, authorization, and data validation.

How do API styles like REST, GraphQL, and gRPC cater to varied DevEx needs?

Each API style offers unique features that cater to different Developer Experience (DevEx) needs:

REST (Representational State Transfer): REST is known for its simplicity and statelessness. It uses standard HTTP methods and is based on resource-oriented architecture, making it intuitive and easy for web development. REST suits applications requiring standard CRUD (create, read, update, delete) operations.

GraphQL: GraphQL lets developers query precisely what they need, reducing over-fetching or under-fetching data. It's beneficial for complex systems with interrelated data and applications where data requirements constantly change.

gRPC (Google Remote Procedure Calls): gRPC is ideal for high-performance, low-latency applications, like microservices. It uses protocol buffers and HTTP/2, providing efficient, robust, and language-agnostic data exchange. gRPC is beneficial in environments where speed and scalability are crucial.

What strategies can be employed for effective API versioning and deprecation?

Effective API versioning and deprecation strategies are essential to avoid disrupting the developer's work.

Semantic Versioning: Employing semantic versioning helps indicate the nature of API changes. For instance, significant version changes could mean breaking changes, while minor and patch versions signify backward-compatible improvements and bug fixes.

Clear Communication: Communicate changes, deprecations, and version updates once implemented. Ensure a clear upgrade path and a transition period to allow developers ample time to adapt their applications.

Deprecation Policies: Establish a standard deprecation policy. This should include a reasonable timeline for developers to migrate from deprecated versions and support for older versions for a given period.

Versioning in the API Design: Incorporate versioning into the API design from the start. This can be done through URL paths, headers, or other mechanisms allowing developers to specify the version they interact with.

How does good API documentation contribute to a positive DevEx?

Good API documentation is crucial for a positive DevEx as it is often the first point of interaction for developers with the API.

Comprehensiveness: Documentation should cover all aspects of the API, including endpoints, parameters, data formats, error codes, and examples. It should leave no room for guesswork.

Clarity and Organization: The information should be presented concisely and well organized. Logically structuring the documentation and providing a searchable format can significantly enhance its usability.

Real-world Examples: Including real-world use cases and examples makes the documentation practical and relatable. It helps developers understand how the API can be used in their scenarios.

Interactive Elements: Providing interactive elements like API explorers or sandboxes within the documentation allows developers to test and experiment with the API directly, significantly improving understanding and adoption.

Good API documentation empowers developers by providing them with all the necessary information in an accessible and practical manner, leading to a smoother development process and better results.

Providing Stellar Developer Support

What are the most effective channels for developer support?

Effective developer support channels are easily accessible and responsive and offer clear and helpful solutions. The most effective ones include

Dedicated Support Portals: These are one-stop shops for support resources, including links to documentation, FAQs, and contact forms. They help centralize support and provide a comprehensive resource base.

Forums and Community Platforms: Platforms like Stack Overflow or GitHub issues allow for community-driven support. Developers can ask questions, share solutions, and learn from peers' experiences here.

Social Media and Instant Messaging: These channels offer a more informal and immediate way to seek help and can be effective for quick queries or building a rapport with the developer community.

Email and Ticketing Systems: For more detailed or specific issues, email and ticketing systems provide a direct line to support teams, allowing for more personalized assistance.

Each channel caters to different needs and preferences, and a combination usually works best to cover all bases.

How can self-service resources empower developers and enhance DevEx?

Self-service resources empower developers by giving them the tools to solve problems independently, reducing wait times and fostering a sense of accomplishment. Essential self-service resources include

Comprehensive Documentation: Well-organized and detailed documentation is developers' first line of self-help. It should cover various topics, from setup and configuration to advanced use cases.

Interactive Tutorials and Learning Tools: These help developers learn independently and get hands-on experience with the software or tools.

Troubleshooting Guides and FAQs: These resources help quickly address common problems and questions without waiting for support.

By providing these resources, developers can find answers and solutions quickly, reducing downtime and keeping their focus on productive tasks.

What approaches work best for incorporating developer feedback into product development?

Incorporating developer feedback into product development is crucial for continuous improvement. Practical approaches include

Regular Surveys and Feedback Forms: These can be used to gather structured feedback on various aspects of the product or support.

User Testing and Beta Programs: Inviting developers to test new features or versions and provide feedback can yield valuable insights into real-world usage and issues.

Monitoring Forums and Community Platforms: These places are often where developers discuss problems and workarounds, providing a wealth of feedback.

Feedback Loops in Support Channels: When developers reach out for support, they can gather feedback about their challenges and needs.

Collecting and acting on this feedback is essential, showing developers that their input is valued and leads to tangible improvements.

What role do communities play in fostering a supportive environment for developers?

Communities play a pivotal role in creating a supportive environment for developers. They act as a platform for peer support, knowledge sharing, and networking. In a thriving community

Peer Support: Developers can ask questions and share expertise, which is especially beneficial for complex or niche issues.

Knowledge Sharing: Communities often become knowledge repositories, with members contributing tutorials, code snippets, and best practices.

Networking and Collaboration: They provide opportunities for developers to connect, which can lead to collaborations, job opportunities, and more.

Moral Support: Sometimes, knowing that others face similar challenges can be comforting. Communities can offer moral support and camaraderie.

Communities amplify individual developers' collective knowledge and experience, creating an environment conducive to learning, collaboration, and mutual support.

Ensuring Performance and Reliability

What are the fundamental techniques for ensuring software performance and reliability?

Ensuring software performance and reliability involves a multifaceted approach:

Efficient Code Practices: Writing efficient, clean, and manageable code is the foundation. This consists of optimizing algorithms, minimizing resource usage, and following coding best practices.

Thorough Testing: Rigorous testing, including unit testing, integration testing, and performance testing, helps identify and rectify issues before deployment.

Scalability Planning: Designing software with scalability in mind ensures it can handle increased load without degradation in performance.

Redundancy and Failover Mechanisms: Implementing redundancy in critical components of the system and designing failover mechanisms enhances reliability, ensuring system functionality in case of component failures.

Regular Updates and Maintenance: Continuously monitor, update, and maintain the software to address new challenges, security vulnerabilities, and performance bottlenecks.

How do monitoring and observability contribute to better DevEx?

Monitoring and observability are crucial for maintaining the health of a software system and contribute significantly to Developer Experience (DevEx) by

Proactive Issue Detection: Monitoring tools can detect issues in real time, allowing developers to address problems before they impact users.
Performance Insights: Observability tools provide insights into how the system performs under various conditions, helping developers optimize the system for better performance.
Informed Decision-Making: With comprehensive monitoring and observability, developers can make informed decisions about system changes, updates, and optimizations.
Reduced Downtime: By quickly identifying and resolving issues, monitoring, and observability contribute to reduced system downtime, enhancing the overall reliability of the software.

What is the role of chaos engineering in enhancing software resilience?

Chaos engineering is a technique where engineers intentionally introduce disturbances into a system to test its resilience and ability to maintain functionality. Its role includes

Identifying Weaknesses: By deliberately causing failures, chaos engineering helps identify weaknesses in the system that might not be evident during normal operations.
Improving Fault Tolerance: It forces the system to deal with various failure scenarios, improving its fault tolerance and ability to handle real-world issues.

Building Confidence: Successfully withstanding chaos experiments builds confidence in the system's reliability and the team's ability to handle unexpected problems.

Encouraging Proactive Development: Practicing chaos engineering encourages a proactive approach to software development, focusing on building robust and resilient systems.

How can developers balance the need for performance optimization with rapid development cycles?

Balancing performance optimization with rapid development cycles can be challenging, but several strategies can help:

Incremental Optimization: Instead of extensive optimization at once, developers can focus on incremental improvements over time, aligning with the development cycles.

Prioritization of Performance Issues: Not all performance issues are equal. Prioritizing critical problems that significantly impact user experience can help manage resources effectively.

Automated Performance Testing: Incorporating automated performance testing into the development pipeline helps identify performance issues early and often.

Leveraging Performance Monitoring Tools: Using monitoring tools to track performance continuously allows for quick identification and resolution of issues without significant delays in development.

Fostering a Performance-aware Culture: Encouraging a culture where performance is a consideration at every stage of development ensures that it is not an afterthought but an integral part of the development process.

Ensuring performance and reliability while maintaining rapid development cycles requires a balanced approach, where performance considerations are integrated into the development process without impeding speed and agility.

Measuring Developer Experience

What metrics are most effective for assessing DevEx?

Assessing Developer Experience (DevEx) effectively requires a blend of metrics to capture various aspects of a developer's interaction with tools and processes.

Time-to-First-Hello-World (TTFHW): This measures how quickly a new developer can set up and run a simple program. It's an indicator of the ease of initial setup and tooling.

Bug Fix Time: The average time it takes to resolve issues can indicate the effectiveness of the development environment and support.

Deployment Frequency: How often code is deployed can signal the efficiency of the development pipeline.

Tool Adoption and Usage Rates: These metrics show how much and effectively developers use the provided tools.

Developer Satisfaction Surveys: Regular surveys can gauge subjective aspects of DevEx, such as satisfaction with tools, documentation, and support.

How can qualitative research methods like interviews and usability testing improve DevEx?

Qualitative research methods offer in-depth insights into the subjective experiences of developers, which are crucial for improving DevEx.

Interviews: Conducting interviews with developers provides rich, nuanced feedback. Developers can articulate their experiences, challenges, and suggestions in detail, offering a deeper understanding of their needs and pain points. Interviews are instrumental during the early stages of the development lifecycle when gathering initial feedback and understanding user needs is critical. They can also be applied after significant updates to assess the impact of user satisfaction.

Usability Testing: Observing developers as they interact with tools and processes can reveal usability issues that need to be evident through other means. This can inform improvements in tool design, documentation, and workflows. Usability testing is most effective during the design and prototyping phases and before major releases to address any potential issues before broader deployment.

These methods complement quantitative metrics by providing context and understanding behind the numbers, leading to more informed decisions on enhancing DevEx.

In what ways can analytics and usage data provide insights into DevEx improvements?

Analytics and usage data are invaluable for gaining objective insights into how developers interact with tools and processes.

Tool Engagement Metrics: Tracking which features are used most and most minor can indicate what's working well and what might be unnecessary or need improvement.

Error and Exception Reports: An automated collection of errors and exceptions can pinpoint common challenges developers face, highlighting areas for improvement.

Performance Metrics: Load times, response times, and system downtimes can directly impact DevEx and need constant monitoring.

Workflow Analysis: Analyzing the flow of tasks and processes can identify bottlenecks or inefficiencies in the development workflow.

What strategies can be employed to improve DevEx based on gathered data iteratively?

A systematic approach is required to improve DevEx iteratively based on gathered data.

Data-Driven Decision-Making: Use the collected metrics and qualitative feedback to decide what aspects of DevEx need improvement.

Continuous Feedback Loop: Establish a constant feedback loop where developers can regularly provide insights and feedback on the changes made.

Incremental Changes: Instead of overhauling everything immediately, make small, gradual changes. This allows for assessing the impact of each change and making adjustments as needed.

Measure Impact of Changes: After implementing changes, measure their impact using the same metrics. This will show whether the change had the desired effect on DevEx.

Encourage a Culture of Continuous Improvement: Foster a culture where continuous improvement of tools, processes, and practices is a shared goal among all team members.

Improving DevEx is an ongoing process that requires a blend of quantitative and qualitative insights and a willingness to make iterative changes based on data-driven insights.

Real-world DevEx Improvement Strategies

How can organizations create a practical DevEx improvement roadmap?

Creating a practical DevEx improvement roadmap involves several key steps:

Assessment: Begin with a thorough evaluation of your organization's current state of DevEx. This consists of understanding the tools, processes, and practices currently in place and how they impact the developers.

Setting Clear Objectives: Define what you want to achieve with the DevEx improvements. Objectives should be specific, measurable, achievable, relevant, and time-bound (SMART).

Involvement of Stakeholders: Include developers, team leads, and other relevant stakeholders in the roadmap creation process. Their input is invaluable as they are the ones directly affected by these improvements.

Prioritization: Based on the assessment and objectives, prioritize the areas that need improvement. Consider factors like impact, feasibility, and resources required.

Actionable Steps: Break down each priority area into actionable steps. This could involve adopting new tools, revising processes, or providing training and resources.

Timeline and Milestones: Establish a realistic timeline for implementing these steps, with clear milestones to track progress.

What are some common pitfalls to avoid when implementing DevEx initiatives?

Some common pitfalls to avoid when implementing DevEx initiatives include

Overlooking Feedback: Ignoring or not collecting feedback from developers who are the end-users of these initiatives can lead to ineffective solutions.

Resisting Change: Resistance to change, especially from management or senior team members, can hinder the adoption of new practices or tools.

One-Size-Fits-All Approach: Not recognizing the unique needs of different teams or projects can result in solutions that don't fit all scenarios.

Underestimating Resources: Underestimating the time, budget, or resources needed for implementation can lead to incomplete or delayed initiatives.

Lack of Communication: Failing to communicate the purpose, benefits, and progress of DevEx initiatives can lead to a lack of buy-in or understanding among team members.

How can feedback loops be established to ensure continuous DevEx enhancement?

Establishing effective feedback loops for continuous DevEx enhancement involves

Regular Surveys and Feedback Channels: Implement regular surveys and open channels for feedback. This could be through tools like online forms, meetings, or informal chats.

Iterative Approach: Use an iterative approach to implement changes. After each change, gather feedback to see if it meets the developers' needs and expectations.

Data-Driven Adjustments: Use data from tools and systems to make informed adjustments. This includes usage statistics, performance metrics, and error rates.

Responsive Action: Show that the feedback is valued by taking action on it. Acknowledging and responding to suggestions is crucial, even if not all recommendations are implemented.

What role does organizational culture play in fostering DevEx improvement?

Corporate culture plays a significant role in promoting DevEx improvement. A culture that values continuous learning, open communication, and innovation creates an environment conducive to DevEx improvements.

Encouraging Experimentation: A culture that encourages trying new things without fear of failure allows for exploring new tools and practices that could improve DevEx.

Collaboration and Sharing: Cultures that promote collaboration and knowledge sharing can accelerate the adoption of best practices across the organization.

Valuing Developer Input: An organizational culture that genuinely respects and acts on developer input fosters a sense of ownership and engagement, which is critical for successful DevEx initiatives.

Continuous Improvement: Cultures prioritizing continuous improvement create an environment where DevEx can be continuously evaluated and enhanced.

A practical DevEx improvement roadmap, avoiding common pitfalls, establishing effective feedback loops, and fostering a supportive organizational culture is vital to successfully improving DevEx in a real-world setting.

Developer Experience Case Studies

What are some common challenges faced by large organizations in improving DevEx?

Improving Developer Experience (DevEx) in large organizations often encounters specific challenges:

Legacy Systems and Processes: Many large organizations have legacy and entrenched processes. Updating these can be complex, time-consuming, and met with resistance.

Scale and Complexity: The sheer size and complexity of projects in big organizations can make uniform DevEx improvements difficult. What works for one team may not work for another.

Change Management: Implementing change in large organizations requires navigating through layers of management and bureaucracy, which can slow down the process.

Communication Gaps: With many developers and teams, ensuring effective communication and alignment on DevEx initiatives can be challenging.

How have startups used innovative DevEx strategies to gain a competitive edge?

With their agility and flexibility, startups have leveraged innovative DevEx strategies effectively:

Embracing the Latest Technologies: Startups often adopt the latest tools and technologies, which can be more efficient, user-friendly, and better suited to modern development practices.

Fostering a Culture of Innovation: Startups typically have a culture that encourages experimentation and rapid adaptation, which can lead to the discovery of more effective DevEx strategies.

Customized Solutions: Startups are more likely to develop customized tools and processes tailored to their specific needs, enhancing the effectiveness of their DevEx.

Close-knit Teams: Smaller teams in startups facilitate closer collaboration and quicker feedback loops, enabling faster improvements in DevEx.

How can DevEx principles be adapted for specialized domains like IoT or AI?

Adapting DevEx principles for technical domains like IoT (Internet of Things) or AI (Artificial Intelligence) involves understanding the unique requirements and challenges of these fields:

Domain-Specific Tools and Processes: Tools and processes must cater to the specific requirements of IoT and AI development, like data processing capabilities for AI or integration capabilities for IoT.

Educational Resources: Given the specialized nature of these fields, providing ample learning resources and documentation becomes even more crucial to help developers understand and effectively work with these technologies.

Performance and Scalability: Considering AI's data-intensive nature and IoT's distributed nature, performance optimization and scalability must be critical DevEx focus.

Security and Privacy: With the sensitive nature of data in AI and IoT, DevEx must incorporate robust security and privacy considerations in tools and processes.

What lessons can be learned from the case studies about balancing stakeholder needs with DevEx?

Balancing stakeholder needs with DevEx improvements is crucial, and the case studies highlight several lessons:

Alignment with Business Goals: DevEx improvements should align with the business goals and objectives. Demonstrating how better DevEx contributes to faster delivery and better product quality can align stakeholders' interests.

Incremental Changes: Gradual improvements rather than significant, disruptive changes are more likely to be accepted and supported by stakeholders.

Effective Communication: The benefits of DevEx improvements in return on investment, productivity, and quality can help gain stakeholder buy-in.

User-Centric Approach: Keeping the focus on the end-user, whether the developer in the case of DevEx or the final customer, ensures that the improvements are meaningful and impactful.

Understanding the unique challenges and opportunities in different environments and strategically aligning DevEx efforts with organizational goals and stakeholder needs is vital to successful DevEx improvement initiatives.

The Future of Developer Experience

How are emerging technologies like AI and blockchain reshaping DevEx?

Emerging technologies are significantly reshaping Developer Experience (DevEx) in several ways:

Artificial Intelligence (AI): AI is transforming DevEx by automating routine tasks, such as code generation and testing, thus allowing developers to focus on more complex and creative aspects of programming. AI-powered tools can also provide personalized assistance to developers, enhancing their productivity and learning.

Blockchain: Blockchain technology introduces new paradigms in secure and decentralized application development. It's changing DevEx by requiring developers to learn and adapt to concepts like smart contracts and distributed ledgers. This shift demands new tools and approaches in development, testing, and deployment.

AI and blockchain are pushing the boundaries of traditional development practices, necessitating a change in how developers interact with technology and tools and underscoring the need for continuous learning and adaptation.

What role will ethics and sustainability play in DevEx's future?

Ethics and sustainability are becoming increasingly important in the realm of DevEx. As technology becomes more integral to everyday life, the ethical implications of software development are magnified.

Ethical Considerations: Developers are more aware of the moral impact of their work. Tools and processes that help identify and mitigate ethical risks (like bias in AI algorithms) will become crucial for DevEx.

Sustainability: With growing concerns about climate change, sustainable development practices are gaining importance. This includes creating energy-efficient code, using green data centers, and considering the environmental impact of computing resources.

In the future, DevEx will likely encompass tools and practices that assist developers in navigating these ethical and sustainability considerations effectively.

How can DevEx be leveraged to attract and retain top talent?

A positive DevEx can be a significant factor in attracting and retaining top talent in the technology sector. Developers look for environments where they can work efficiently and creatively.

State-of-the-Art Tools and Processes: Offering the latest and most effective tools and processes can strongly attract developers who want to work in cutting-edge environments.

Continuous Learning and Growth: Opportunities for learning and professional growth are crucial to keeping developers engaged and motivated. Environments that support ongoing learning and exploration of new technologies are very appealing.

Work–Life Balance and Flexibility: Aspects of DevEx that support a healthy work–life balance, like efficient workflows that reduce overtime and flexible tooling that supports remote work, can also attract top talent.

How is DevEx expected to evolve in the context of rapid technological advancements?

As technology advances rapidly, DevEx is expected to evolve in several ways:

Integration of More Advanced Tools: Tools will become more sophisticated, integrating advanced technologies like machine learning, predictive analytics, and real-time collaboration features.

Increased Focus on User Experience for Developers: As the developer's role becomes more crucial, there will be an increased focus on making their experience as seamless and enjoyable as possible.

Adaptability and Flexibility: DevEx tools and processes must be highly adaptable and flexible to keep pace with rapidly changing technologies and development practices.

Emphasis on Collaboration and Remote Work: With the rise of remote work and global teams, DevEx will increasingly facilitate effective collaboration across distances and time zones.

The future of DevEx is intricately linked with the evolution of technology, and a focus on ethics, sustainability, and the overall well-being and productivity of developers will be essential.

Interviews and Expert Insights

What are industry leaders' most unexpected insights or perspectives regarding DevEx?

From interviews with industry leaders, several incredible insights emerge regarding Developer Experience (DevEx):

DevEx as a Driver of Organizational Culture: Leaders often highlight how focusing on DevEx can lead to broader cultural shifts, promoting values like collaboration, innovation, and continuous learning.

DevEx's Impact on Customer Experience: Surprisingly, many leaders draw a direct line between DevEx and customer experience (CX). They note that when developers have a positive experience, this often translates into higher-quality products, which improves CX.

Cost-effectiveness of DevEx Investments: Another insight is that investing in DevEx, while initially perceived as costly, can be cost-effective in the long run. Improvements in DevEx can lead to faster development cycles, reduced downtime, and higher developer retention rates.

DevEx as a Reflection of Company Values: Some leaders view DevEx as reflecting a company's values and priorities. They believe that a company that invests in DevEx is committed to quality, innovation, and employee satisfaction.

How do experts envision the role of DevEx in interdisciplinary collaboration and innovation?

Experts see DevEx playing a crucial role in multidisciplinary collaboration and innovation:

Fostering a Collaborative Environment: A positive DevEx can break down silos between different departments. When developers have tools that facilitate collaboration and communication, working with professionals from other disciplines is easier.

Spurring Innovation: Good DevEx often gives developers the time and mental space to innovate. When inefficient processes or tools do not bog them down, they can think more creatively and contribute ideas beyond their traditional scope.

Enabling Rapid Prototyping: With a streamlined DevEx, interdisciplinary teams can quickly build and test prototypes, accelerating innovation.

What are the key takeaways from developers' experiences concerning DevEx at different stages of their careers?

Developers at various stages of their careers offer varied perspectives on DevEx:

For Early-Career Developers: They often highly value clear documentation and accessible learning resources. A positive DevEx for them means having the tools and information needed to learn and increase.

Mid-Career Developers: These developers typically emphasize the importance of efficient workflows and processes. They appreciate DevEx, which helps them maximize their productivity without unnecessary bureaucratic hurdles.

Senior Developers and Tech Leads: They often focus on the scalability and reliability of tools and processes. For them, a good DevEx also means mentoring others effectively, which requires collaborative tools and environments.

These insights and perspectives underline the multifaceted nature of DevEx and its far-reaching impact beyond just the technical realm, influencing organizational culture, interdisciplinary collaboration, innovation, and developers' professional growth at all stages of their careers.

Index

A

Accessibility and inclusivity
  case studies, 326
  challenges/strategies, 322, 323
  crafting applications, 319
  development, 321, 322
  ethical considerations, 325
  incorporating user
    feedback, 324
  integrating AI, 327
  superior digital experiences, 319
ADA, *see* Americans with
    Disabilities Act (ADA)
Adoption/retention rates
  developer satisfaction/
    feedback, 189, 191
  error rates/bug reports,
    187, 188
  first successful task
    completion, 186
  KPIs, 184, 185
Agile methodologies, 6–7, 258,
    385, 414
AI, *see* Artificial Intelligence (AI)
AI and Machine Learning (ML)
  ethical considerations/
    challenges, 289, 290

practical applications, 290
shaping development,
    292, 293
software development's
    strategic, 287
transforms development, 287
Amazon, 25, 29
Amazon's Alexa, 326
Amazon Web Services (AWS), 206
Americans with Disabilities Act
    (ADA), 321
Apache Hadoop, 243, 244, 246,
    249, 251
Apache JMeter, 72, 174
API, *see* Application Programming
    Interface (API)
API Blueprint, 125
API design
  API governance, 128–130
  deprecation, 118, 119
  description format, 125
  design patterns
    GraphQL APIs, 110–112
    gRPC APIs, 113, 115
    REST APIs, 108–110
  discovery, 120, 124, 126, 127
  documentation, 120–124, 131
  OpenAPI, 124

© K. Rain Leander 2025
K. R. Leander, *Developer Experience Unleashed*,
https://doi.org/10.1007/979-8-8688-0242-3